CALL and complexity

Short papers from EUROCALL 2019

Edited by Fanny Meunier, Julie Van de Vyver,
Linda Bradley & Sylvie Thouësny

research-publishing.net

Published by Research-publishing.net, a not-for-profit association
Contact: info@research-publishing.net

© 2019 by Editors (collective work)
© 2019 by Authors (individual work)

CALL and complexity – short papers from EUROCALL 2019
Edited by Fanny Meunier, Julie Van de Vyver, Linda Bradley, and Sylvie Thouësny

Publication date: December 2019

Rights: the whole volume is published under the Attribution-NonCommercial-NoDerivatives International (CC BY-NC-ND) licence; **individual articles may have a different licence**. Under the CC BY-NC-ND licence, the volume is freely available online (https://doi.org/10.14705/rpnet.2019.38.9782490057542) for anybody to read, download, copy, and redistribute provided that the author(s), editorial team, and publisher are properly cited. Commercial use and derivative works are, however, not permitted.

Disclaimer: Research-publishing.net does not take any responsibility for the content of the pages written by the authors of this book. The authors have recognised that the work described was not published before, or that it was not under consideration for publication elsewhere. While the information in this book is believed to be true and accurate on the date of its going to press, neither the editorial team nor the publisher can accept any legal responsibility for any errors or omissions. The publisher makes no warranty, expressed or implied, with respect to the material contained herein. While Research-publishing.net is committed to publishing works of integrity, the words are the authors' alone.

Trademark notice: product or corporate names may be trademarks or registered trademarks, and are used only for identification and explanation without intent to infringe.

Copyrighted material: every effort has been made by the editorial team to trace copyright holders and to obtain their permission for the use of copyrighted material in this book. In the event of errors or omissions, please notify the publisher of any corrections that will need to be incorporated in future editions of this book.

Typeset by Research-publishing.net
Cover theme by © 2019 Frédéric Verolleman
Cover layout by © 2019 Raphaël Savina (raphael@savina.net)

Fonts used are licensed under a SIL Open Font License

ISBN13: 978-2-490057-54-2 (Ebook, PDF, colour)
ISBN13: 978-2-490057-55-9 (Ebook, EPUB, colour)
ISBN13: 978-2-490057-53-5 (Paperback - Print on demand, black and white)
Print on demand technology is a high-quality, innovative and ecological printing method; with which the book is never 'out of stock' or 'out of print'.

British Library Cataloguing-in-Publication Data.
A cataloguing record for this book is available from the British Library.

Legal deposit, France: Bibliothèque Nationale de France - Dépôt légal: décembre 2019.

■ UCLouvain

Table of contents

x   Peer-review committee

xiii   Preface
Fanny Meunier and Julie Van de Vyver

1   Virtual reality from the perspective of Saudi faculty
Hana Alhudaithy

7   The role of educational technologists in the provision of language courses in higher education: a case study
Christopher Allen and David Richardson

13   Piloting Netflix for intra-formal language learning
Antonie Alm

19   A comparison of learner characteristics, beliefs, and usage of ASR-CALL systems
Gemma Artieda and Bindi Clements

26   The use of digital media in the Russian language classroom: an empirical study conducted in Austria, South Tyrol, and Germany
Sonja Bacher

33   Using LARA for language learning: a pilot study for Icelandic
Branislav Bédi, Cathy Chua, Hanieh Habibi, Ruth Martinez-Lopez, and Manny Rayner

39   "Let's date!" A 360-degree video application to support foreign language learning
Anke Berns, Iván Ruiz-Rube, José Miguel Mota, Juan Manuel Dodero, Edson Castro, Oona Ryynanen, and Lissy Werner

45   Annotated scientific text visualizer: design, development, and deployment
John Blake

Table of contents

51   First contact with language corpora: perspectives from students
Alex Boulton

57   Mobile literacy among Syrian refugee women teachers
Linda Bradley, Rima Bahous, and Ali Albasha

63   Negotiating for meaning in interaction: differences between virtual exchanges and regular online activities
Laia Canals

69   Shouting in space: promoting oral reading fluency with Spaceteam ESL
Walcir Cardoso, David Waddington, Enos Kiforo, and Anne-Marie Sénécal

75   Data-driven learning in ESP university settings in Romania: multiple corpus consultation approaches for academic writing support
Mădălina Chitez and Loredana Bercuci

82   Integrating a virtual reality application to simulate situated learning experiences in a foreign language course
Maria Christoforou, Eftychia Xerou, and Salomi Papadima-Sophocleous

88   Learners as teachers? An evaluation of peer interaction and correction in a German Language MOOC
Elisabeth Clifford, Christine Pleines, Hilary Thomas, and Susanne Winchester

94   Video assessment module: self, peer, and teacher post-performance assessment for learning
Matthew Cotter and Don Hinkelman

100   Learning to design a mobile hunt on Actionbound: a complex task?
Carole Delforge, Julie Van de Vyver, and Alice Meurice

107   A pilot study of Alexa for autonomous second language learning
Gilbert Dizon and Daniel Tang

113   A case study of a learner's use of an online translator as a cognitive tool in a SCMC context
Morgane Domanchin

118	The effects of an online learning management system on students' academic socialization: a qualitative study on a Chinese graduate course *Liu Dong, Li Cheng, Shixin Dong, and Guanzhen Wu*
124	Affordances for cultural adjustment of international students learning Chinese as a second language in a mobile-assisted learning environment *Shixin Dong, Li Cheng, Liu Dong, and Guanzhen Wu*
130	Critical cultural awareness and learning through digital environments *James D. Dunn*
137	Learner attitudes towards data-driven learning: investigating the effect of teaching contexts *Luciana Forti*
144	ColloCaid: a tool to help academic English writers find the words they need *Ana Frankenberg-Garcia, Geraint Rees, Robert Lew, Jonathan Roberts, Nirwan Sharma, and Peter Butcher*
151	Re-orienting CALL through the lens of complexity theory *Robert Godwin-Jones*
157	ReDesigning intercultural exchanges through the use of augmented reality *Stella Hadjistassou, Maria Iosifina Avgousti, and Petros Louca*
163	Virtual exchange supporting language and intercultural development: students' perceptions *Eric Hagley and Matthew Cotter*
169	Leveraging collaborative work for game-based language learning *Dirk Hansen, Carlee Arnett, and Ferran Suñer*
174	Integrating Xreading into class time using post-reading tasks *Peter Harrold*
180	MOOCs as environments for learning spoken academic vocabulary *Clinton Hendry and June Ruivivar*

Table of contents

186 Effects of HVPT on perception and production of English fricatives by Japanese learners of English
Atsushi Iino

193 Creating collaborative digital stories to promote community awareness
Bradley Irwin

199 Students' perceptions about the use of digital badges in an online English terminology course: a three-year study
Jun Iwata, Shudong Wang, and John Clayton

206 Complexity and tool selection for purposeful communication in telecollaborative encounters
Kristi Jauregi Ondarra

212 Student perceptions of group writing processes and feedback
Kym Jolley

218 Assessment of interculturality in online interactions: methodological considerations
Ana Kanareva-Dimitrovska

223 Student perceptions of virtual reality use in a speaking activity
Samar Kassim, Neil Witkin, and Adam Stone

229 Pedagogical frameworks and principles for mobile (language) learning to support related teacher education
Ton Koenraad

236 Quality for online language courses – a coaching program for teachers
Kirsi Korkealehto

241 Towards sustainable language learning in higher education – engagement through multimodal approaches
Kirsi Korkealehto and Vera Leier

247 'So close, yet so different' – reflections on the multicultural course of Slavic languages
Anna Kyppö

252 MALL tools tried and tested
Bruce Lander, Valentina Morgana, Jaime Selwood, Tim Knight, Robert Gettings, Mari Yamauchi, Julie Van de Vyver, and Carole Delforge

257 Connecting extensive reading to TOEIC performance
Paul A. Lyddon and Brandon Kramer

263 Understanding the complexities associated with conceptualising pedagogical scenarios for online multimodal interaction between two languages and cultures
Oneil N. Madden and Anne-Laure Foucher

270 Second language learning in knowledge forums: an analysis of L2 acquisition of students participating in the knowledge building international project
Marni Manegre and Mar Gutiérrez-Colón

275 Brazil and Colombia virtual exchange project: the Brazilian view
Claudia Beatriz Martins and Maristela Werner

280 Assemblage theory: coping with complexity in technology enhanced language learning
Blair Matthews

285 Learners' emotional response to a complex video-creation task
Alice Meurice, Véronique Henin, and Marie Van Reet

291 Learner-adaptive partial and synchronized captions for L2 listening skill development
Maryam Sadat Mirzaei and Kourosh Meshgi

297 Collaborative learning through story envisioning in virtual reality
Maryam Sadat Mirzaei, Qiang Zhang, Kourosh Meshgi, and Toyoaki Nishida

304 The use of Quizlet to enhance vocabulary in the English language classroom
Salvador Montaner-Villalba

310 Designing tasks for developing complex language skills and cognitive competence in the distance learning of Slovak as a foreign language
Michaela Mošaťová and Jana Vyškrabková

Table of contents

314 An iCALL approach to morphophonemic training for Irish using speech technology
Neasa Ní Chiaráin and Ailbhe Ní Chasaide

321 Children's perspectives on the use of robotics for second language learning in the early years of primary education: a pilot study
Susan Nic Réamoinn and Ann Devitt

327 Improving the English skills of native Japanese using artificial intelligence in a blended learning program
Hiroyuki Obari and Stephen Lambacher

334 Time to evaluate: the students' perspective of an online MA in CALL programme
Salomi Papadima-Sophocleous and Christina Nicole Giannikas

340 Tablets in second language learning: learners' and teachers' perceptions
Amira Shouma and Walcir Cardoso

345 How EFL learners react to a learning framework integrating learning records on multiple systems
Hiroya Tanaka, Akio Ohnishi, Ken Urano, Shinya Ozawa, and Daisuke Nakanishi

350 Not a language course (!): teaching global leadership skills through a foreign language in a flipped, blended, and ubiquitous learning environment
Nobue Tanaka-Ellis and Sachiyo Sekiguchi

356 SimpleApprenant: a platform to improve French L2 learners' knowledge of multiword expressions
Amalia Todirascu and Marion Cargill

362 CALL replication studies: getting to grips with complexity
Cornelia Tschichold

367 Complexity and potential of synchronous computer mediated corrective feedback: a study from Sri Lanka
W. A. Piyumi Udeshinee, Ola Knutsson, and Sirkku Männikkö-Barbutiu

373 Defining teachers' readiness for online language teaching: toward a unified framework
Koen Van Gorp, Luca Giupponi, Emily Heidrich Uebel, Ahmet Dursun, and Nicholas Swinehart

379 Fostering cultural competence awareness by engaging in intercultural dialogue – a telecollaboration partnership
María Villalobos-Buehner

385 Towards the design of iCALL tools for beginner mandarin chinese learners in Ireland
Hongfei Wang and Neasa Ní Chiaráin

391 Computer-mediated communication in Chinese as a second language learning: needs analysis of adolescent learners of Chinese at beginner level in Ireland
Mengdi Wang, Ciaran Bauer, and Ann Devitt

397 Joining the blocks together – an NLP pipeline for CALL development
Monica Ward

402 Digital stories: improving the process using smartphone technology
Jeremy White

407 Asynchronous online peer judgments of intelligibility: simple task, complex factors
Suzanne M. Yonesaka

413 Author index

■ UCLouvain

Peer-review committee

- Carlee Arnett; *University of California, Davis, California, United States*
- Gemma Artieda; *Wall Street English, Barcelona, Spain*
- Maria Iosifina Avgousti; *University of Cyprus, Nicosia, Cyprus*
- Sonja Bacher; *Innsbruck University, Innsbruck, Austria*
- Branislav Bédi; *The Árni Magnússon Institute for Icelandic Studies, Reykjavík, Iceland*
- Loredana Bercuci; *West University of Timișoara, Timișoara, Romania*
- Jan Berggren; *Linnaeus University, KSGYF, Kalmar, Sweden*
- Anke Berns; *University of Cadiz, Cádiz, Spain*
- John Blake; *University of Aizu, Aizu-wakamatsu, Japan*
- Laia Canals; *Universitat Oberta de Catalunya, Barcelona, Spain*
- Walcir Cardoso; *Concordia University, Montreal, Canada*
- Mădălina Chitez; *West University of Timișoara, Timișoara, Romania*
- Maria Christoforou; *Cyprus University of Technology, Limassol, Cyprus*
- Bindi Clements; *Wall Street English, Barcelona, Spain*
- Matthew Cotter; *Hokusei Gakuen University Junior College, Sapporo, Japan*
- Ann Devitt; *Trinity College Dublin, Dublin, Ireland*
- Gilbert Dizon; *Himeji Dokkyo University, Himeji, Japan*
- James Dunn; *Tokai University, Hiratsuka, Japan*
- Luciana Forti; *University for Foreigners of Perugia, Perugia, Italy*
- Christina Nicole Giannikas; *Cyprus University of Technology, Limassol, Cyprus*
- Luca Giupponi; *Michigan State University, East Lansing, United States*
- Robert Godwin-Jones; *Virginia Commonwealth University, Richmond, Virginia, United States*
- Mar Gutiérrez-Colón; *Universitat Rovira i Virgili, Tarragona, Spain*
- Stella Hadjistassou; *University of Cyprus, Nicosia, Cyprus*
- Eric Hagley; *Muroran Institute of Technology, Muroran, Japan*
- Emily Heidrich Uebel; *Michigan State University, East Lansing, Michigan, United States*
- Clinton Hendry; *Concordia University, Montreal, Canada*
- Don Hinkelman; *Sapporo Gakuin University, Ebetsu, Japan*
- Bradley Irwin; *Nihon University College of International Relations, Mishima, Japan*

Peer-review committee

- Makoto Ishii; *Keio University, Tokyo, Japan*
- Jun Iwata; *Shimane University, Shimane, Japan*
- Kristi Jauregi Ondarra; *Utrecht University, Utrecht, The Netherlands*
- Ana Kanareva-Dimitrovska; *Aarhus University, Aarhus, Denmark*
- Ola Knutsson; *Stockholm University, Stockholm, Sweden*
- Ton Koenraad; *TELLConsult, Vleuten, Netherlands*
- Kirsi Korkealehto; *Häme University of Applied Sciences, Hämeenlinna, Finland*
- Brandon Kramer; *Osaka Jogakuin University and Junior College, Osaka, Japan*
- Shuichi Kurabayashi; *Cygames, Inc., Tokyo, Japan*
- Anna Kyppö; *University of Jyväskylä, Jyväskylä, Finland*
- Stephen Lambacher; *Aoyama Gakuin University, Tokyo, Japan*
- Bruce Lander; *Matsuyama University, Matsuyama, Japan*
- Vera Leier; *University of Canterbury, Christchurch, New Zealand*
- Paul Lyddon; *University of Shizuoka, Shizuoka, Japan*
- Oneil Madden; *University Clermont Auvergne, Clermont-Ferrand, France*
- Marni Manegre; *Universitat Rovira i Virgili, Tarragona, Spain*
- Ruth Martinez-Lopez; *Seville University, Seville, Spain*
- Claudia Beatriz Martins; *Federal University of Technology – Paraná, Curitiba, Brazil*
- Blair Matthews; *University of St Andrews, St Andrews, Scotland*
- Kourosh Meshgi; *Kyoto University, Kyoto, Japan*
- Maryam Sadat Mirzaei; *RIKEN AIP/Kyoto University, Kyoto, Japan*
- Salvador Montaner-Villalba; *Universidad Nacional de Educación a Distancia, Madrid, Spain*
- José Miguel Mota; *University of Cádiz, Cádiz, Spain*
- Neasa Ní Chiaráin; *Trinity College Dublin, Dublin, Ireland*
- Susan Nic Réamoinn; *Trinity College Dublin, Dublin, Ireland*
- Hiroyuki Obari; *Aoyama Gakuin University, Tokyo, Japan*
- Salomi Papadima-Sophocleous; *Cyprus University of Technology, Limassol, Cyprus*
- Christine Pleines; *The Open University, Milton Keynes, United Kingdom*
- Manny Rayner; *University of Geneva, Geneva, Switzerland*
- Geraint Rees; *University of Surrey, Guildford, United Kingdom*
- June Ruivivar; *Concordia University, Montreal, Canada*
- Anne-Marie Sénécal; *Concordia University, Montreal, Canada*
- Amira Shouma; *Concordia University, Montreal, Canada*
- Nobue Tanaka-Ellis; *Tokai University, Kanagawa, Japan*
- Hilary Thomas; *The Open University, Milton Keynes, United Kingdom*

Peer-review committee

- Cornelia Tschichold; *Swansea University, Swansea, Wales*
- W. A. Piyumi Udeshinee; *Stockholm University, Stockholm, Sweden*
- Koen Van Gorp; *Michigan State University, East Lansing, Michigan, United States*
- María Villalobos-Buehner; *Rider University, Lawrenceville, New Jersey, United States*
- Olga Vinogradova; *National Research University Higher School of Economics, Moscow, Russia*
- Hongfei Wang; *Trinity College Dublin, Dublin, Ireland*
- Monica Ward; *Dublin City University, Dublin, Ireland*
- Eftychia Xerou; *Cyprus University of Technology, Limassol, Cyprus*
- Iwao Yamashita; *Juntendo University, Mishima, Japan*
- Suzanne Yonesaka; *Hokkai-Gakuen University, Sapporo, Japan*
- Chang Zhang; *Trinity College Dublin, Dublin, Ireland*

Preface

Fanny Meunier[1] and Julie Van de Vyver[2]

The theme selected for the 2019 EuroCALL conference held in Louvain-la-Neuve was 'CALL and complexity'. We decided to opt for a positive vision of complexity. As languages are known to be intrinsically and linguistically complex, as are the many determinants of learning (additional) languages, we wanted to view complexity as a challenge to be embraced collectively. The 2019 conference allowed us to pay tribute to providers of Computer Assisted Language Learning (CALL) solutions and to recognize the complexity of their task, to acknowledge the notion of complexity to ensure the provision of ad hoc CALL solutions, and to draw both learners' and teachers' attention to complexity issues so that they can make the most of their learning/teaching experience.

The 27th EuroCALL conference was hosted by UCLouvain in Louvain-la-Neuve (Belgium), in collaboration with KU Leuven, from the 28th to the 31st of August 2019. The local organizing team, with the help of the EuroCALL executive committee and the scientific committee, worked hard to offer the participants a well-filled conference program which included no fewer than:

- 189 paper presentations;
- 4 symposia;
- 10 workshops; and
- 46 posters.

All of these activities were divided into the following sub-themes in CALL: social inclusion, computer mediated communication and telecollaboration, corpora and language learning, digital bi- and multi-literacies, digital game-based language

---

1. Université Catholique de Louvain, Louvain-la-Neuve, Belgium; fanny.meunier@uclouvain.be; https://orcid.org/0000-0003-2186-2163
2. Université Catholique de Louvain, Louvain-la-Neuve, Belgium; julie.vandevyver@uclouvain.be; https://orcid.org/0000-0001-8820-8380

How to cite this article: Meunier, F., & Van de Vyver, J. (2019). Preface. In F. Meunier, J. Van de Vyver, L. Bradley & S. Thouësny (Eds), *CALL and complexity – short papers from EUROCALL 2019* (pp. xiii-xv). Research-publishing.net. https://doi.org/10.14705/rpnet.2019.38.976

learning, intelligent CALL, mobile assisted language learning, natural language processing applications, open educational resources and practices, research trends, second language acquisition principles, task complexity, teacher education and professional development, the complexity, accuracy, and fluency framework, and virtual reality and gamification.

We were lucky to have three wonderful keynote presentations!

The first one, by Andrea Révész (University College London, UK), addressed 'Task complexity and technology-mediated language learning: issues and possibilities'. Andrea explained that despite the substantial theoretical and empirical work on cognitive task complexity in task-based language teaching, the bulk of research on task complexity has so far been conducted in face-to-face settings. Less is known about the effects of task complexity on L2 use and development in technology-mediated environments. In her talk, she explored how the cognitive complexity of technology-mediated tasks may influence L2 production and learning. She also offered suggestions on how task complexity research may be extended in technology-mediated contexts to inform task-based language teaching theory and practice.

The second one, by Detmar Meurers (University of Tübingen, Germany), focused more specifically on 'Analyzing linguistic complexity'. As pointed by Detmar, linguistic complexity can be analyzed at all levels of the linguistic system, language use, and human processing. Such analyses can provide empirically rich perspectives on second language development, especially given large-scale data available through CALL systems. After illustrating that with EFCAMDAT[3] data by 174,000 learners of the Englishtown system, Detmar explored how we can turn from such post-hoc observations of development to CALL interventions aimed at fostering complexity development through adaptive input.

The last keynote, by Jan Elen (KU Leuven, Belgium), was titled 'Dealing with complex learning: opportunities offered by technology'. Jan showed us that although complex learning goals are at the core of education, achieving such goals is difficult. Technology may help in two respects. First, as the result of technology of education, Instructional Design (ID) models may offer a framework to structure effective education for complex learning. Second, as technology for education and within the context of an ID model, technological tools can be used to support

---

3. EF-Cambridge Open Language Database (https://corpus.mml.cam.ac.uk/efcamdat2/public_html/)

students' learning activities. His talk also offered numerous concrete illustrations of all these opportunities.

More information about the keynote speeches, as well as the full program, may be found on the conference website: http://www.eurocall2019.be

We would like to extend our warmest thanks to all participants, presenters, keynotes, special interest groups, and program committee members who made EuroCALL 2019 such a great success.

We would also like to thank the authors of the papers and the many reviewers who offered their time and expertise to ensure the high quality of the submissions included in the present volume. Finally, we express our deepest gratitude to Sylvie Thouësny and Linda Bradley for their hard work and dedication to EuroCALL and its publications.

We hope you will enjoy reading this volume as it offers a rich glimpse into the numerous debates that took place during EuroCALL 2019. We look forward to continuing those debates and discussions with you at the next EuroCALL conferences!

Virtual reality from the perspective of Saudi faculty

Hana Alhudaithy[1]

Abstract. Nowadays, we live in an ever-evolving technological world. There is thus a growing need to explore the use of modern technology in education in general, and in higher education in particular. The present paper investigates the use and effectiveness of Virtual Reality (VR) in higher education from the perspective of Saudi faculty at the College of Languages and Translation, King Khalid University (KKU). A mixed-method research design was applied. A questionnaire and focus group interviews were used to collect quantitative and qualitative data. Results indicated a limited use of VR among faculty due to lack of facilities, insufficient support (particularly for junior faculty), and lack of female technicians for the female-only campus and cultural aspects (e.g. female privacy). It is important to consider the need for high-speed internet and enhanced facilities for both students and faculty alike.

Keywords: virtual reality, faculty, perspective.

1. Introduction

Recently, it has been evident that a number of developing countries, including the Kingdom of Saudi Arabia (KSA) are implementing big changes to higher education. The key objective of these changes is to enhance educational standards and economic development and stability. The KSA government's attempts to accomplish this objective have been relatively successful. Educational technology advancements and information technology investment in Saudi universities are a major and positive result of the national development that aims to ensure quality education and communication. Sarkar (2012) explains that improving the educational system is a key aim of educational technology. By employing

---

1. University of the West of England, Bristol, United Kingdom; hana2.alhudaithy@live.uwe.ac.uk; King Khalid University, Abha, Saudi Arabia; hrashed@kku.edu.sa; https://orcid.org/0000-0002-4560-0363

How to cite this article: Alhudaithy, H. (2019). Virtual reality from the perspective of Saudi faculty. In F. Meunier, J. Van de Vyver, L. Bradley & S. Thouësny (Eds), *CALL and complexity – short papers from EUROCALL 2019* (pp. 1-6). Research-publishing.net. https://doi.org/10.14705/rpnet.2019.38.977

more effective and efficient technology, the quality of education can be enhanced (Alfarani, 2016).

The present paper aims to explore the use of VR in higher education institutions and its effectiveness from Saudi faculty's viewpoints. According to Getso and Bakon (2017), VR means a digital environment (world) where students can engage in and interact with each other and with other objects and it supports multiple learning styles such as ImmerseMe, Expeditions, Mondly, FluentU, and Cardboard.

2. The use of learning technology in Saudi Arabia

Over the last decade, higher education in KSA has witnessed major developments and the Saudi government has spent vast amounts of time and money for improving the educational sector (Alamri, 2011).

According to Al-Asmari and Rabb Khan (2014), there is a lack of information about the use of educational technology in KSA and other Middle-Eastern countries, where the official usage of web-based technologies is significantly slower than the Western countries. Nonetheless, Alfarani (2016) refers to a number of reports showing an increase in the use of tablets, smartphones, and mobile devices in higher education classes in KSA. Moreover, Daggett (2014) stresses that the application of technology in education is still a new concept, thus governments and authorities do not have a great deal of experience in this field.

3. Method

The current paper aims to investigate the use and effectiveness of VR in higher education from the perspective of Saudi faculty at the College of Languages and Translation, KKU. To achieve this objective, a mixed-method approach (qualitative and quantitative) was employed. A case study is adopted to explore a specific target population (academic members) in a specified place (KKU in KSA). It is the best method since it helps generate a rich insight into the topic.

3.1. Tools

The questionnaire (a quantitative questionnaire and an open-ended qualitative questionnaire) and focus groups were utilized to collect the required data.

3.2. Data collection

Arabic is the national language of KSA, thus the tools were presented in English with an Arabic translation to avoid misunderstanding. The questionnaire comprised 12 items distributed to two domains: perceptions of VR (eight items) and challenges in taking up VR (four items), see supplementary materials.

As for social science research and educational studies, focus groups are deemed a highly beneficial tool of exploring opinions, perspectives and experiences of participants (Cohen, Manion, & Morrison, 2007). In the present paper, focus groups were used to create interpersonal relations among the participants to generate rich information that supports or undermines the implementation of VR. Participants were distributed to three focus groups, each of which consisted of five females. Thematic analysis was used to analyse the data collected from the focus groups by reading the data and defining the emerging themes using a word-based technique, inspection techniques, and coding.

In May 2018, the questionnaire was distributed online in English and Arabic to male and female faculties (see Table 1). It remained open for four months to allow most faculties to participate.

Table 1. Sample and questionnaire items

Participants			Questionnaire	
Gender	Male	female	Domain	Item
	68	59		
Focus group	15 females		Perceptions of VR	8
			Challenges in taking up VR	4
Total	127		Total	12

4. Discussion

The results indicate that (96%) of participants use one or more type of VR technology in teaching. In addition, (75%) of participants agree that VR technologies are easy to be employed in the teaching and learning process. There were no significant gender differences evident in the questionnaire responses regarding the use of VR in education. However, the findings of qualitative analysis indicate that fewer facilities and services are available on female campuses. For this reason, subsequent focus groups concentrated on females to identify the causes behind the results of this research and other studies in KSA relating to the implementation of VR.

Similar opinions reported by both genders may be a result of being governed by university regulations which are exclusively created from a male perspective. In this context, women have a limited power and do not participate actively in the decision-making process. Alfarani's (2016) findings support this result indicating that females were more often afraid to make decisions due to fear of losing their job if they did not agree with the prevailing opinions. Women therefore commonly repeated the majority opinion and stuck to the university's general resolutions in order to safeguard their own jobs. This was very much the case until April 2016, when the Crown Prince Muhammed Bin Salman announced the new Saudi Vision 2030, in which women would be afforded more rights, and would be made into stronger and more influential society members.

Furthermore, information obtained from the focus group indicated that the lack of information and communications technology knowledge that junior faculties possess could be a major factor hindering the use of VR in their classrooms. Arabic language as well was considered to be one of the barriers in using VR and this also confirmed by Albalooshi, Mohamed, and Al-Jaroodi (2011).

Therefore, students and faculty should attend training courses to assist them with such technology. When student and faculty can understand the great potential of VR and are able to use it effectively, then their knowledge will be improved and they can use this powerful tool in their classrooms.

Besides holding training and ensuring resources, it is important to raise students' as well as faculties' awareness about the importance of employing VR in education. One participant indicated that VR should be promoted and students should be informed about its potential to assist in specific subject areas. The functions most appropriate for each topic of study should be pointed out, particularly for foreign languages education. If used properly, VR may aid in enhancing the performance of students as well as faculty.

5. Conclusions

To sum up, Saudi faculties agree that employing VR could have a pivotal position in teaching and learning, especially for foreign languages education. However, there are several problems associated with VR. Nonetheless, the participants appear to have hope and enthusiasm when it comes to using modern technology, particularly VR, which can enhance foreign language education and improve students' motivation.

There appears to be an optimistic future for the use of VR in higher education, however it is crucial to address any relevant drawbacks such as the potential costs. Future studies may explore the use of modern technology and its advantages for faculty and students. They may also explore the benefits and drawbacks of using a variety of technologies in different contexts and cultures.

6. Acknowledgments

I offer my sincerest thanks to my supervisors; Nigel Newbutt and Liz Falconer. I would not have accomplished and completed this paper without the exceptional support that I have received from them. Studying my PhD has been very expensive, and I offer my sincerest thanks to KKU Doctoral Fellowship for supporting the larger project financially, since this essentially allowed the present paper to flourish.

7. Supplementary materials

https://research-publishing.box.com/s/27d2ver2o1nd4k5ps0vkocnl3j3gg6k6

References

Al-Asmari, A. M., & Rabb Khan, M. S. (2014). E-learning in Saudi Arabia: past, present and future. *Near and Middle Eastern Journal of Research in Education,2014*(1). https://doi.org/10.5339/nmejre.2014.2

Alamri, M. (2011). Higher Education in Saudi Arabia. *Journal of Higher Education Theory and Practice, 11*, 88-91.

Albalooshi, N., Mohamed, N., & Al-Jaroodi, J. (2011). The challenges of Arabic language use on the internet. *Internet Technology and Secured Transactions 2011 International Conference Proceedings* (pp. 378-382). IEEE.

Alfarani, L. A. (2016). *Exploring the influences on faculty members' adoption of mobile learning at King Abdulaziz University, Saudi Arabia*. PhD Thesis. The university of Leeds.

Cohen, L., Manion, L., & Morrison, K. (2007). Research methods in education (6th ed.) Routledge.

Daggett, B. (Ed.). (2014). Addressing current and future challenges in education. International Center for Leadership in Education. *22nd Annual Model Schools Conference, June, 2014.*

Getso, M. M. A., & Bakon, K. A. (2017). Virtual reality in education: the future of learning. *International Journal of Information System and Engineering, 5*(2), 30-39. https://doi.org/10.24924/ijise/2017.04/v5.iss2/30.39

Sarkar, S. (2012). The role of information and communication technology (ICT) in higher education for the 21st century. *The Science Probe, 1*, 30-40.

The role of educational technologists in the provision of language courses in higher education: a case study

Christopher Allen[1] and David Richardson[2]

Abstract. In recent years, schools, municipalities, and universities have made increasing use of educational technologists (edtechs) to support teaching staff in the delivery of technology-based courses in face-to-face, blended, or purely online formats. This paper is a case study focusing on the types of training and support provision provided by three edtechs within the arts and humanities faculty of a large provincial university in southern Sweden. The edtechs also identify a number of obstacles in the way of developing Information and Communication Technology (ICT) and computer assisted language learning expertise among teaching staff.

Keywords: edtech, ICT, language teaching, professional training.

1. Introduction

The wholesale introduction of digital technology into higher education over the past 25 years has brought with it an increasing need for both technological and pedagogical support for academic staff tasked with the implementation of the technology in the courses they teach. Edtechs and learning designers are examples of new professional categories which have emerged in the wake of these developments. In the case of digitally advanced countries like Sweden, many university faculties have employed edtechs who work to provide faculty support and encourage collaborative working practices in ICT as well as acting in some cases as instructional course designers with institutional Virtual Learning Environments (VLEs). More rarely, edtechs may also be engaged in researching and surveying emerging trends in the educational uses of technology.

---

1. Linnaeus University, Kalmar, Sweden; christopher.allen@lnu.se
2. Linnaeus University, Kalmar, Sweden; david.richardson@lnu.se

How to cite this article: Allen, C., & Richardson, D. (2019). The role of educational technologists in the provision of language courses in higher education: a case study. In F. Meunier, J. Van de Vyver, L. Bradley & S. Thouësny (Eds), *CALL and complexity – short papers from EUROCALL 2019* (pp. 7-12). Research-publishing.net. https://doi.org/10.14705/rpnet.2019.38.978

Following the introduction of VLEs in the 1990's, the impact of VLEs in higher education has received extensive attention in the literature (e.g. Britain & Liber, 1999; Weller, 2007a). Nevertheless, there has been a dearth of research into the important work being done by edtechs supporting VLE use in the institutions and subject areas they serve. However, institutional VLE use has been the subject of criticism (Weller, 2007b; Leslie, 2007). This short paper presents a preliminary case study of the role played by edtechs in the provision of blended and online courses in a language department at a Swedish university.

2. The study

This paper presents a case study based on semi-structured interviews (see supplementary materials) with three edtechs currently working within a university's arts and humanities faculty in Sweden. In addition to modern languages, the edtechs provide support to members of staff in the subject areas of design, music, media and communication, art, cultural studies, and journalism.

The interviews were carried out separately with each edtech during the Spring 2019 term (see supplementary materials for a list of questions), focusing on their supporting roles for academic staff within the university's department of language. In Questions 6a-6d, respondents had to rate importance on a scale of one (*not important*) to seven (*very important*). The department makes extensive use of *Moodle* as a VLE; the ICT infrastructure available to teaching staff is advantageous, with facilities for screencasting (*Kaltura CaptureSpace*) and a streaming server enabling the full integration of video material with the VLE. The cloud-based video conferencing tool *Zoom* is also supported and fully integrated into the *Moodle* learning platform.

The respective backgrounds of the edtechs are listed below in Table 1, with fictitious names used to protect their anonymity throughout.

Table 1. Respective backgrounds and experience of the edtechs

Edtech	Background and experience
Rebecca	10 years experience in ICT supporting role; background as a computer technician and Information Technology (IT) systems support
Anna	official job title of edtech since 2013 but overall 10 years experience with ICT
Paul	24 years experience in IT/ICT pedagogical support; 10 years with the official job title of edtech developer

Interview video material in the form of *Zoom* recordings was subsequently uploaded to the university's secure *Box* digital storage facility; the material was otherwise not transcribed or edited in any form.

3. Discussion

3.1. General

There appeared to be a uniformity in the support provision regardless of subject specialisms, with one or two notable exceptions which will be outlined below. Overwhelmingly, provision of support and interaction with teaching staff centred around *Moodle*, the institutional VLE adopted by the university and the closely integrated tools of *Zoom* for video conferencing and *Kaltura CaptureSpace*.

3.2. Highlighting important aspects of the work of the institutional edtech

Paul highlighted his role in building relations and developing an ongoing climate of cooperation marked by continuity rather than seeing himself as some sort of one off 'helpdesk' (see Table 2). Another important aspect was his availability to language teachers seeking ICT support. Paul also stressed the practical aspects of his job as an edtech in encouraging teachers to make use of and experiment with ICT tools and resources in their teaching. Anna described her role in terms of dealing with more acute support problems. Paul focused on the need to keep himself up-to-date via social networks and forums, while Anna highlighted the importance of keeping in phase with internal documentation and university ICT policy. Rebecca stressed the importance of the final product outcome, in creating a good digital environment, retaining students on both blended and online courses, and ensuring satisfactory levels throughput (the proportion of students enrolled that complete the course).

Table 2. Highlighting areas of importance

Support area	Rating 7=very important; 1=not important		
	Anna	Rebecca	Paul
Providing technical support for language teachers	7	7	7
Providing pedagogical support for language teachers	7	6	7

Establishing collaborative learning practices within language teaching staff instructional design (i.e. designing courses and course templates) using Moodle and VLE implementational policy	6	7	6
Researching emerging trends in ICT for the language teaching sector and keeping language teaching staff updated with technical developments in the field	5	7	7

3.3. Main types of support offered

Of the areas listed in Question 5 (see supplementary materials), the provision of one-to-one consultative support was seen as the most important and effective. From Paul's experience, this form of support was the most effective in ensuring that teachers were able to get started with an initial course room in *Moodle*; group training courses with more than ten teachers were not seen as an effective delivery mode. The highlighting of early adopters as enthusiasts was also seen as important; Paul stressed the importance of teacher enthusiasts inspiring other teachers more effectively than edtechs. Online support was not an area with positive experiences for Paul and 'brownbag' lunchtime courses and sessions were not seen as being effective with teachers needing time for relaxation.

3.4. Edtechs and specific support for language teachers

As mentioned previously, the edtechs did not see a great difference between the support they provided to language teachers and other faculty members. The department has however run a language lab for a number of years, although support provision for this facility was no longer a significant part of the edtech's job description. Two edtechs did however single out ICT tools and resources for synchronous interactivity (such as using *Zoom*) in language proficiency training for communicative dialogues and information gap activities. The edtechs were asked whether they lacked any specific subject area knowledge (i.e. relating to language teaching and applied linguistics etc.) in terms of the support they are able to offer the department's teaching staff.

While none of the edtechs had any formal university background in language/ language teaching, any perceived lack of knowledge relating to language was not seen as being important in their provision of ICT support. Significantly, however, Anna brought up the need to understand better the types of ICT usage among language teachers in schools, given the importance of language teacher training within the department/faculty. In many cases these resources differ from the tools used by the university; for example the *Google Classroom* suite is commonly used by teachers in the Swedish state system as a VLE/learning management system as opposed to *Moodle*.

3.5. Obstacles

The main problem in raising ICT expertise among academic staff identified by respondents was the lack of priority given to ICT and digital skills by university management. Paul stressed the lack of importance given to digital skills when language staff are employed and the over-emphasis on more traditional academic merits, such as publication lists of research articles. Departmental heads need to be more aware of these demands and offer greater rewards for the acquisition of digital skills in career path development. Anna mentioned for example the award of digital badges for specific skills acquisition.

4. Conclusions

The edtechs are clearly committed to the provision of support regarding institutional use of the Moodle VLE and its integration with *Zoom* and *CaptureSpace*. The VLE, *Zoom* and *CaptureSpace* package is seen as the embodiment of the personal learning environment for teaching staff. The place of the institutional VLE in the faculty's support for ICT in language teaching seems assured at least for the time being; this situation seems to fly in the face of some commentators such as Weller (2007b), who somewhat prematurely foresaw the death of the institutionalised VLE. This situation obviously reflects administrative decisions taken within the institution but it would seem that the edtechs interviewed do not favour Leslie's (2007) alternative solution of 'loosely coupled teaching', where teachers use their own external tools and resources outside the institutional VLE. The identification of a lack of priority – on the part of management in higher education – given to the acquisition of teaching staff ICT expertise is a very important one; raising the status of ICT skills among other more academic merits would potentially have a positive aspect on blended and online course provision.

5. Acknowledgements

We would like to thank the Department of Languages, Linnaeus University, for financial support in attending the EuroCALL 2019 conference in Belgium.

6. Supplementary materials

https://research-publishing.box.com/s/jyfadmghckxs79zqbqmh4w4yghb824k5

References

Britain, S., & Liber, O. (1999). *A framework for the pedagogical evaluation of virtual learning environments*   https://web.archive.org/web/20140709094115/http://www.jisc.ac.uk/media/documents/programmes/jtap/jtap-041.pdf

Leslie, S. (2007, October 27). *Your favourite 'loosely coupled teaching' example*. https://scottleslie.ca/edtechpost/wordpress/2007/10/29/best-loosely-coupled-teaching-examples/

Weller, M. (2007a). *Virtual learning environments: using, choosing and developing your VLE*. Routledge.

Weller, M. (2007b). *The VLE/LMS is dead.* The Ed Techie. https://nogoodreason.typepad.co.uk/no_good_reason/2007/11/the-vlelms-is-d.html

Piloting Netflix for intra-formal language learning

Antonie Alm[1]

Abstract. The expansion of the *Netflix* TV-network around the globe has made foreign language films and TV-series accessible for formal and informal language learning experiences. As students in educational settings are starting to engage in informal second language (L2) *Netflix* viewing, it is time that new pedagogical approaches support learners to optimise the resource for successful language learning. This pilot study reports on a project conducted with 12 intermediate level German students who watched self-selected German TV-series. For three weeks, students described and commented on each other's viewing experiences in their weekly blogs. In a final report, participants reflected on their affective and cognitive engagement with the series. Findings of this study indicate that previous informal exposure to *Netflix* series positively impacted on the participants' willingness to engage in extensive out-of-class listening. The learning experience in the formal context positively affected subsequent informal L2-series watching.

Keywords: Netflix, German, intra-formal language learning.

1. Introduction

Foreign language movies have long been a popular resource in language education. The emergence of *Netflix*, available in over 190 countries and in 26 languages, however, has made foreign films more accessible. Second language (L2) students who enjoy TV-series in their native language might also feel inclined to look up similar programmes in other languages. It is this potential predisposition to engage in L2 entertainment that opens a new foundation for alternative language learning approaches. This paper explores the idea of using *Netflix* as a resource for extensive listening in an intermediate level language class and proposes the concept of intra-formal language learning as a pedagogical framework.

---

1. University of Otago, Dunedin, New Zealand; antonie.alm@otago.ac.nz

How to cite this article: Alm, A. (2019). Piloting Netflix for intra-formal language learning. In F. Meunier, J. Van de Vyver, L. Bradley & S. Thouësny (Eds), *CALL and complexity – short papers from EUROCALL 2019* (pp. 13-18). Research-publishing.net. https://doi.org/10.14705/rpnet.2019.38.979

1.1. Netflix

Accessible around the globe, on demand, and on mobile devices, *Netflix* has taken the television experience to a new level (Jenner, 2018). Popular TV-series are released as entire seasons, tempting viewers to engage in addictive binge-watching. The powerful appeal of some of the series makes them not only an easily accessible but also highly motivating resource for language learning. Further, the language features provided by *Netflix* can support language learners at all levels.

Viewers are able to watch a foreign language film or series in its original version, dubbed, with subtitles in their native (L1) or target (L2) language. The options are multiple. One can even choose to watch a film in one's L1 with L2 subtitles. Vanderplank (2016) has for a long time and more recently, again discussed the benefits of captions for language learning. Initially conceived for the hard of hearing, they present a beneficial learning tool for language learners. The variety of choices available on *Netflix* multiplies learner options, as also shown by Dizon (2018) who used *Netflix* for English language students in Japan.

The language learning community outside academia has also been quick to point out the learning potential of *Netflix*: language learning blogs such as *FluentU* have written about How to Navigate Netflix for Learning Languages[2], *Lindsay does Languages* published The ultimate guide to Netflix for language learning[3], and *The Guardian* reports on How Netflix could transform the way we learn languages[4]. In addition, some web browsers have developed extensions to add functionality to *Netflix* subtitles (e.g. *Language Learning with Netflix*[5], *Mate translate*, or *LingvoTV*).

The convenient access to the language resource, its inbuilt and extended learning tools, as well as the ability to download many programmes to mobile devices make *Netflix* an appealing tool for language learning in either the formal or informal learning context.

1.2. Intra-formal language learning

The terms *formal*, *non-formal* and *informal* have been used to describe the nature of learning (other-initiated or self-initiated), and where it is taking place (in an

---

2. https://www.fluentu.com/blog/netflix-languages/
3. https://www.lindsaydoeslanguages.com/the-ultimate-guide-to-netflix-for-language-learning/
4. https://www.theguardian.com/education/2019/mar/02/netflix-languages-education
5. https://languagelearningwithnetflix.com/

accredited or non-accredited educational or private setting). The boundaries between these categories have become fluid over recent years as formal educational contexts often include out-of-class experiences, and as informal (prior) knowledge is increasingly recognised in formal contexts (e.g. badge system). It is, however, useful to maintain conventional definitions to discuss the conditions of different learning experiences and the impact they have on each other. I further use the term *intra-formal* to describe the interdependent nature of informal (self-initiated and out-of-class) and formal (classroom-bound) learning experiences. Intra-formal language learning draws on prior informal L2 exposure and world knowledge (students use *Netflix* in their L1, have L1 viewing habits), raises the learners' metacognitive awareness (through discussion and self-reflection), and prepares them for more significant subsequent informal L2 engagement (Figure 1).

Figure 1. Intra-formal language learning

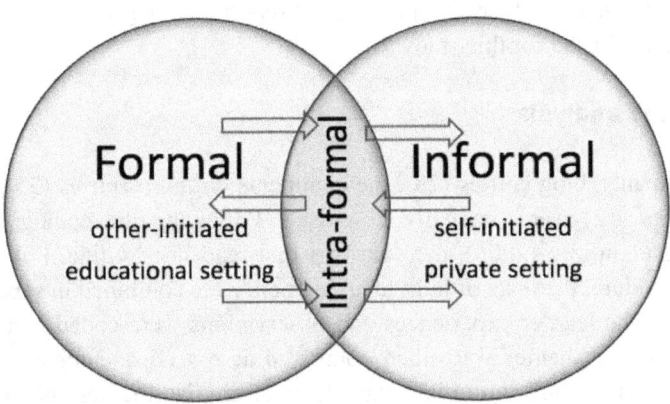

This paper reports on a pilot study on the use of *Netflix* for language learning. It investigates the metacognitive strategy development of a group of intermediate language learners, influenced by both formal and informal elements, by the task design, and the personal prior experiences and preferences. The wider study seeks to explain from the perspective of formal learning, under which conditions learners engage in self-study, as well as from the perspective of informal learning, and the behaviour learners display based on prior (informal) experiences and their personal preferences for extensive listening (TV-series watching). This short paper focuses on the learning strategies participants developed based on their out-of-class learning experiences.

2. Method

2.1. Participants and task description

The study involved 12 intermediate level German language students (B2) who watched self-selected German TV-series in their own time. The participants were introduced to German TV-series on *Netflix* and on other video streaming services. In addition, strategies for one-way listening were discussed in class. For three weeks, students watched their individual series and wrote about their viewing experiences in their weekly blogs. Participants were guided to write in their first blog entry about their first impressions of their chosen series, in their second post where and when they watched the series and in their third post how they 'viewed' and 'listened to' the series, reflecting on their learning strategies. Their final report was structured in three parts, covering (1) the content of their series, (2) adopted listening strategies, and (3) their learning experience. Participants were able to read and comment on each other's blogs and final reports. They granted permission for their work to be used for this study.

2.2. Data analysis

The participants' blog entries (28), the comments on these entries (35), and their final reports (12) were manually processed. Following the coding criteria of Ellis and Barkhuizen (2005), the data was first read line-by-line. For this open-coding procedure, the texts of individual learners were combined in separate word documents. The learner experiences and observations were coded and organised into themes. The themes were then compared across all documents and a new document was created, grouping extracts with similar themes into categories. The following strategies emerged: selection and planning strategies, and listening strategies, which were divided into the following categories: subtitle use, use of background information, listening for global understanding, replay, looking up words and directed attention. The collective use of these strategies is presented in the next section.

3. Discussion

Participants chose a range of different TV-series, from *Netflix* and other video streaming services (*ARD Mediathek, MySpass, YouTube*): *Babylon Berlin* (6), *Charité* (2), *Die Heiland* (1), *Meuchelbeck* (1), *Hilfe Hochzeit* (1), *Jim Knopf* (1).

The selections reflect personal interests and preferences, also providing different learning conditions for individual participants (e.g. no subtitles on *MySpass*). Their approaches consequently varied from person to person. The strategies listed below represents a collection of strategies representative for a minimum of three participants. Phrased as recommendations, they reflect the insights participants gained during the activity:

- *Selection*: find a series that is interesting, at the right level, and fits in with daily activities (length of episode). This creates realistic goals from the outset.

- *Preparation*: read episode guide – recommended by most participants ("I don't know why I haven't done this before").

- *Develop regular routines*: the ability to make viewing a habit was seen as a major factor for both enjoyment and language development.

- *Time management*: related to routine, the need to put enough time aside to read the episode guide, to watch the programme, and to replay scenes with difficult vocabulary or complicated storylines. Choose times when rested, to improve focus.

- *Getting into it*: listening for the gist, instead of listening for individual words which slow down the viewing process. Don't make this a vocabulary learning exercise only. Focusing on body language, movement of lips, setting to support understanding. Some find it important to watch whole episodes (not sections) for a sense of achievement which in turn fosters commitment.

- *Replay*: the magic word to improve understanding. Replay whole episodes, scenes or only specific words, and write them down to remember. The inbuilt replay function in *Netflix* and many other providers makes this an easy option.

- *Vocabulary app*: some participants liked the idea of using an app to review the vocabulary they had learned.

4. Conclusions

The ability to choose their own series, guided by personal interest and preference for content and format, increased the willingness of the participants to fully engage in this project. Prompted to reflect on their strategy use, they shared and discussed their viewing and learning experiences in their individual blogs. The development of planning and listening strategies in collaboration with their classmates equipped participants with a range of useful strategies for future viewings beyond the classroom.

References

Dizon, G. (2018). Netflix and L2 learning: a case study. *The EuroCALL Review, 26*(2), 30-40. https://doi.org/10.4995/eurocall.2018.9080

Ellis, R., & Barkhuizen, G. P. (2005). Analysing learner language. Oxford University Press.

Jenner, M. (2018). *Netflix and the re-invention of television*. Springer. https://doi.org/10.1007/978-3-319-94316-9

Vanderplank, R. (2016). *Captioned media in foreign language learning and teaching: subtitles for the deaf and hard-of-hearing as tools for language learning*. Springer. https://doi.org/10.1057/978-1-137-50045-8

A comparison of learner characteristics, beliefs, and usage of ASR-CALL systems

Gemma Artieda[1] and Bindi Clements[2]

Abstract. Wall Street English[3] has built online activities that allow students to record phrases and receive word-level Automatic Speech Recognition (ASR) driven pronunciation feedback. Students in language centres in China, Vietnam, Saudi Arabia, and Italy (N=2,867) used ASR-Computer Assisted Language Learning (CALL) activities, and some (N=482) completed a questionnaire. A high number of students reported that ASR-CALL activities helped them to improve their pronunciation. However, the study found remarkable differences in usage of product features across countries, with students from Vietnam and China using more retries than Saudi Arabia, and students from Italy using the fewest retries. Students from China, Vietnam, and Saudi Arabia more frequently listened to model audios than students from Italy. A series of Kruskal-Wallis tests revealed significant group differences between dominant L1 and students' beliefs and perceptions using ASR, and between age groups and students' beliefs and perceptions using ASR. This study points to the importance of considering regional differences, and suggests that learner engagement may depend not only on the effectiveness of the technology, but also on learner beliefs and perceptions.

Keywords: ASR, speech recognition, pronunciation, pronunciation feedback, learner beliefs and perceptions.

1. Introduction

ASR-CALL activities offer considerable opportunities for individualised practice and personalised feedback on pronunciation (Levis, 2007), and recent studies

---

1. Wall Street English, Barcelona, Spain; gemma.artieda@wallstreetenglish.com; https://orcid.org/0000-0001-8807-8571
2. Wall Street English, Barcelona, Spain; bindi.clements@wallstreetenglish.com; https://orcid.org/0000-0002-4901-4070
3. Wall Street English is an international school of English for adults.

How to cite this article: Artieda, G., & Clements, B. (2019). A comparison of learner characteristics, beliefs, and usage of ASR-CALL systems. In F. Meunier, J. Van de Vyver, L. Bradley & S. Thouësny (Eds), *CALL and complexity – short papers from EUROCALL 2019* (pp. 19-25). Research-publishing.net. https://doi.org/10.14705/rpnet.2019.38.980

demonstrate that ASR-CALL activities can have a measurable impact on learning (inter alia, Golonka et al., 2014).

Perceptions regarding the difficulty of achieving English pronunciation skills may be linked to L1/nationality (cf. Cenoz & Lecumberri, 1999; Simon & Taverniers, 2011), and while there are commonalities, beliefs regarding effective learning strategies have been found to differ according to learner L1/nationality (Nowacka, 2012). Such beliefs may lead to pre-conceptions relating to the effectiveness of ASR-CALL activities, which may affect student engagement. This study explores adult students' engagement with ASR-CALL activities and aims to address the following research questions.

- Do students think pronunciation activities with ASR help them improve their pronunciation?

- Do students in four countries (China, Vietnam, Italy, and Saudi Arabia) make different use of ASR-CALL activity features?

- Are there differences between L1s and age groups in students' beliefs and perceptions on learning pronunciation using ASR?

2. Method

2.1. Context and participants

Wall Street English uses proprietary learning content to deliver a blended-learning course, offering a combination of multimedia self-study lessons and face-to-face teacher-led classes. It incorporated ASR word-level pronunciation feedback into three multimedia activity types: (1) repeat and practise, (2) read and record, and (3) conversation.

Students were exposed to these ASR activities as part of their course over six weeks. Researchers had access to anonymised back-end data at the end. Participants ($N=2,867$) completed ASR-powered course activities, and 482 of these responded to an optional, anonymous online questionnaire. There was an unequal age range distribution in questionnaire participants in terms of the most common age groups: 19-40 in China, 16-40 in Vietnam, 16-30 in Saudi Arabia, and 23-60 in Italy (Table 1).

Table 1.   Participants

	China		Vietnam		Saudi Arabia		Italy		Total
	N	%	N	%	N	%	N	%	N
Studied activities with ASR	1,153	40%	1,192	42%	171	6%	351	12%	2,867
Took the questionnaire	153	32%	173	36%	85	18%	71	15%	482

2.2.   Instruments

Learners completed the activities as part of their normal studies. They were familiar with them, only ASR feedback was new. Questionnaire items (see Table 2 and Table 3) were based on previous research. A six-step Likert scale (from 1=not at all to 6=fully agree) was used.

3.   Results and discussion

Ninety-five percent of students believed that pronunciation activities with ASR helped improve their pronunciation. Vietnamese students were the most enthusiastic (98.8%), closely followed by students in Italy (98.5%), then in Saudi Arabia (95.2%), and, finally, students in China (91.5%).

Concerning the usage of ASR activity features, students in all territories used a much lower number of attempts than they were allowed. Students in China, Saudi Arabia, and Italy only used one attempt ($Mdn=1$) and those in Vietnam used two ($Mdn=2$), whereas they were allowed three attempts in Activities 1 and 2, and four in 3. For listening to model audio recordings, students in China and Vietnam reported using this feature the most (82%), less so for students in Saudi Arabia (57%) and in Italy (41%). Finally, students in Vietnam reported listening to own utterance recordings the most (80%), less so for students in China (66%) and in Saudi Arabia (61%), and remarkably lower usage was reported by students in Italy (57%).

Finally, we investigated potential between-group differences in age groups and L1s in students' beliefs and perceptions about L2 pronunciation items. The analyses for age revealed statistically significant differences between age groups and all items but one (Item 4 – see Table 2). Differences were favourable to the youngest age group (16-22), suggesting that older learners may have less overall confidence in their ability to acquire pronunciation skills (Marinova-Todd, Marshall, & Snow, 2000).

Table 2. Kruskal-Wallis test results for beliefs and perceptions about L2 pronunciation and age ranges

#	Items	N	M(SD)	Mean Rank	df	χ^2	p	Effect Size d
1	I believe that I will eventually be able to speak English very well.	482			2	49	.000*	0.66
	16-22	167	5.26(.83)	268.45				
	23-30	153	4.97(1.21)	243.62				
	31-60+	162	4.75(1.18)	211.72				
2	I can use technology to help me improve my pronunciation.	482			2	14.4	.001*	0.32
	16-22	167	5.22(.93)	272.34				
	23-30	153	4.73(1.23)	219.60				
	31-60+	162	4.80(1.27)	230.39				
3	I feel at ease when I have to speak English.	482			2	19.3	.000*	0.03
	16-22	167	4.37(1.27)	278.53				
	23-30	153	3.83(1.42)	227.26				
	31-60+	162	3.74(1.39)	216.77				
4	I feel insecure about my pronunciation.	482			2	.9	.624	
	16-22	167	3.67(1.55)	248.46				
	23-30	153	3.60(1.57)	242.02				
	31-60+	162	3.53(1.39)	233.83				
5	It is important for me to speak English with an excellent English pronunciation.	482			2	.21	.000*	0.12
	16-22	167	5.64(.90)	269.93				
	23-30	153	5.43(1.02)	241.87				
	31-60+	162	5.24(1.05)	211.85				
6	I am happy with my pronunciation as long as people can understand me.	482			2	8.4	.015*	0.23
	16-22	167	3.76(1.60)	259.58				
	23-30	153	3.21(1.78)	216.05				
	31-60+	162	3.59(1.55)	246.90				

* $p<0.05$, $d_{cohen}=0.2$ (small), 0.5 (medium), 0.8 (large)

Results for L1 analyses are displayed in Table 3. The analyses yielded statistically significant differences between L1s and all beliefs and perceptions about L2 pronunciation statements, in line with some findings reported in Nowacka (2012).

The effect sizes were noticeably larger than for age groups, which may help to explain some differences found in feature usage. For example, students from Italy, who reported the lowest instances of listening to both the sample and their own recorded audios, also demonstrated lowest self-belief in ability to be able to speak English very well, and placed lowest importance on being able to speak with excellent pronunciation.

Table 3. Kruskal-Wallis test results for beliefs and perceptions about L2 pronunciation with L1s

#	Items	N	M(SD)	Mean Rank	df	χ^2	p	Effect Size d
1	I believe that I will eventually be able to speak English very well.	482			3	29.5	.000*	0.48
	Chinese	153	4.83(1.37)	234.89				
	Vietnamese	173	5.20(.85)	259.07				
	Arabic	85	5.29(.89)	276.22				
	Italian	71	4.52(.99)	171.37				
2	I can use technology to help me improve my pronunciation.	482			3	19.1	.000*	0.37
	Chinese	153	4.58(1.42)	211.92				
	Vietnamese	173	5.19(.92)	266.75				
	Arabic	85	5.12(1.05)	264.54				
	Italian	71	4.77(1.07)	216.13				
3	I feel at ease when I have to speak English.	482			3	37.9	.000*	0.56
	Chinese	153	3.70(1.52)	217.84				
	Vietnamese	173	4.47(1.21)	289.59				
	Arabic	85	3.92(1.39)	231.39				
	Italian	71	3.49(1.09)	187.42				
4	I feel insecure about my pronunciation.	482			3	13.9	.003*	0.30
	Chinese	153	3.47(1.67)	228.31				
	Vietnamese	173	3.93(1.35)	270.12				
	Arabic	85	3.22(1.66)	208.49				
	Italian	71	3.60(1.35)	239.70				

5	It is important for me to speak English with an excellent English pronunciation.	482			3	113.1	.000*	1.09
	Chinese	153	5.35(1.13)	236.86				
	Vietnamese	173	5.71(.68)	269.73				
	Arabic	85	5.88(.42)	294.76				
	Italian	71	4.45(1.16)	118.96				
6	I am happy with my pronunciation as long as people can understand me.	482			3	77.1	.000*	0.85
	Chinese	153	2.62(1.63)	168.05				
	Vietnamese	173	3.76(1.52)	251.76				
	Arabic	85	4.43(1.51)	315.31				
	Italian	71	4.09(1.19)	286.42				

* $p<0.05$, $d_{cohen}=0.2$ (small), 0.5 (medium), 0.8 (large)

4. Conclusions

Learners were overwhelmingly positive towards ASR-CALL's potential in helping improve their pronunciation. However, differences in feature usage were observed between students of different L1s/nationalities, which may be related to differences in learner beliefs.

5. Acknowledgements

We would like to thank students and staff in the participating Wall Street English centres.

References

Cenoz, J., & Lecumberri, M. (1999). The acquisition of English pronunciation: learners' views. *International Journal of Applied Linguistics, 9*(1), 3-15. https://doi.org/10.1111/j.1473-4192.1999.tb00157.x

Golonka, E., Bowles, A., Frank, V., Richardson D., & Freynik, S. (2014). Technologies for foreign language learning: a review of technology types and their effectiveness. *Computer Assisted Language Learning, 27*(1), 70-105. https://doi.org/10.1080/09588221.2012.700315

Levis, J. (2007). Computer technology in teaching and researching pronunciation. *Annual Review of Applied Linguistics, 27,* 184-202. https://doi.org/10.1017/s0267190508070098

Marinova-Todd, S. H., Marshall, D. B., & Snow, C. E. (2000). Three misconceptions about age and L2 learning. *TESOL Quarterly, 34*(1), 9-34. https://doi.org/10.2307/3588095

Nowacka, M. (2012). Questionnaire-based pronunciation studies: Italian, Spanish and Polish students' views on their English pronunciation. *Research in Language, 10*(1), 43-61. https://doi.org/10.2478/v10015-011-0048-3

Simon, E., & Taverniers, M. (2011). Advanced EFL learners' beliefs about language learning and teaching: a comparison between grammar, pronunciation, and vocabulary. *English Studies, 92*(8), 896-922. https://doi.org/10.1080/0013838x.2011.604578

The use of digital media in the Russian language classroom: an empirical study conducted in Austria, South Tyrol, and Germany

Sonja Bacher[1]

Abstract. This work-in-progress study focuses on the implementation of digital media into the Russian language classroom at secondary schools in the German-speaking countries of Austria, Germany, and the trilingual region South Tyrol. The data were collected in a mixed-methods procedure: quantitative data from online-questionnaires and qualitative data from face-to-face, semi-structured interviews with teachers and learners of Russian. The data from the online-surveys were analysed with descriptive statistics and that of the interviews with qualitative content analysis. The results from the online-surveys illustrate the kinds of digital devices that are employed, the frequency of their use, and the purposes digital media are intended to fulfil in the Russian language classroom. Another finding concerns the teachers' digital literacy, suggesting that only half of the Russian teachers can create online language learning tasks. The paper closes with implications for pre- and in-service teacher education and future research.

Keywords: digital media, Russian language classroom, digital literacy, teacher training.

1. Introduction

Although new communication technologies are omnipresent in everyday life, and school syllabi together with educational standards require foreign language teachers to integrate digital media into their teaching (BMB, 2018; KMK, 2012), such technologies and media have not yet been consistently employed in the

---

1. Innsbruck University, Innsbruck, Austria; sonja.bacher@uibk.ac.at

How to cite this article: Bacher, S. (2019). The use of digital media in the Russian language classroom: an empirical study conducted in Austria, South Tyrol, and Germany. In F. Meunier, J. Van de Vyver, L. Bradley & S. Thouësny (Eds), *CALL and complexity – short papers from EUROCALL 2019* (pp. 26-32). Research-publishing.net. https://doi.org/10.14705/rpnet.2019.38.981

foreign language classroom (Biebighäuser, Zibelius, & Schmidt, 2012; Bos et al., 2016; Feierabend, Plankenhorn, & Rathgeb, 2017). In this respect, Roche (2008) stresses the fact that the question is not *whether or not* digital media should be used but rather *how* they should be implemented to provide added-value to the language learning process.

The current study aims at investigating the types of digital media, their frequency of application, and the specific purposes they are used for in the Russian language classroom. Furthermore, this study examines whether and in how far Russian teachers are satisfied with the teacher education they received in the field of digital media, as well as the digital literacy of teachers and adolescent learners of Russian. The fact that there are little empirical data available in this area concerning Russian taught at schools outside of Russia by non-L1 and L1 Russian teachers highlights the importance of this baseline study. The findings have implications for pre- as well as in-service teacher training and for further research.

2. Methods

The data were collected by triangulating quantitative and qualitative research methods (*between-method*) (Caspari, Klippel, Legutke, & Schramm, 2016). The concurrent mixed-methods design is meant to enhance the reliability and validity of the data (Kelle, 2014; Maxwell, 2004). In order to research the current implementation of digital media into the Russian language classroom, online-questionnaires containing multiple choice, Likert, and rating scale questions were employed. To gain more insights, semi-structured interviews with secondary school teachers and adolescent learners of Russian were conducted. The online-survey data were analysed with descriptive statistics (Raab-Steiner & Benesch, 2012) and the interview transcripts with qualitative content analysis (Mayring, 2015).

2.1. Online-questionnaires

The online-surveys were accessible for several months, during which time 158 teachers and 411 learners of Russian participated; of those, 65.2% of the teachers and 76.4% of the pupils finished the questionnaire. Reasons may lie with the length of the online-questionnaires or Internet connection problems (cf. Gräf, 2010). The teacher-questionnaire included 31 and the learner-questionnaire 19 questions. Only fully completed questionnaires were analysed. As regards the country of residence, 55 teachers came from Austria, 41 from Germany, and six from South Tyrol, while 142 pupils came from Austria, 119 from South Tyrol, and 47 from Germany. The comparably low number of participants from Germany was caused by the lengthy process of obtaining permission from the authorities to conduct a study with pupils. In total, seven participants did not indicate their country of residence.

2.2. Semi-structured interviews

The interviews complement the data from the online-questionnaires. Within four months, seven teacher and five learner interviews were held. Teachers and pupils were asked to relate their personal viewpoints and experiences concerning the use of digital media in class. The interviews were audio-recorded, transcribed, and analysed with qualitative content analysis (Mayring, 2015).

3. Discussion of results

In the online-surveys, teachers and pupils were asked to indicate the frequency of use of certain digital devices in Russian classes. Figure 1 shows the teacher responses, Figure 2 the pupil responses. More than half of the teachers and pupils stated that there are no interactive whiteboards at their schools. Even if whiteboards are available, they appear to be infrequently used. Interview data suggest that this is due to a lack of training of how to employ interactive whiteboards. The computer and smartphone can be said to play some role in the Russian language classroom with 20.39% of the teachers but only 3.82% of the pupils indicating that they always use computers in class. This discrepancy might be explained by the fact that teachers use computers for presentation or organisational purposes (see Figure 3). In the interviews, teachers commonly stated that there is only one computer in each classroom. Better technical equipment and targeted training would most probably facilitate the implementation of digital media.

Figure 3 shows for what purposes Russian teachers use digital media in class. Teachers could give multiple answers. More than 80% of them integrate digital media to foster audiovisual reception or for motivational purposes. In the online-survey, two thirds of the pupils indicated that the implementation of digital media motivates them to some extent. Interview data suggest that this is partly due to the authentic language use and cultural information conveyed through digital media. More than 50% of the teachers employ digital media to facilitate intercultural learning. When it comes to developing pupils' writing skills or critical media literacy, digital media seem to play a minor role. Further research could establish the reasons why this is the case. School syllabi refer to the development of critical media literacy as one of the major learning objectives of the 21st century (BMB, 2018; KMK, 2012).

Figure 1.   Frequency of use of digital devices

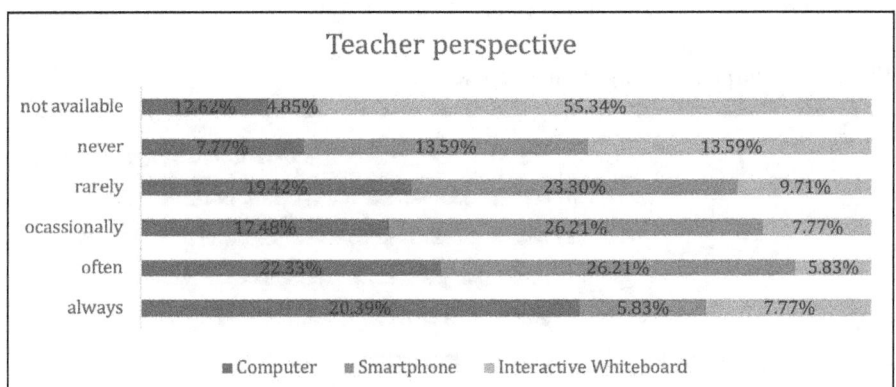

Figure 2.   Frequency of use of digital devices

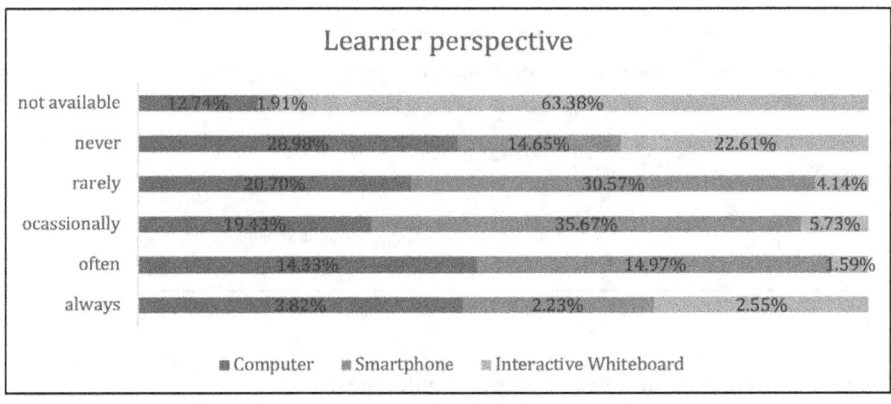

Finally, teachers and pupils were asked to assess their digital literacy on the basis of can-do-statements that had been grouped into three major categories, namely *technical and user skills, critical understanding,* and *participation and production* (Celot, 2015; Vuorikari, Punie, Carretero, & Van den Brande, 2016). One such statement in the teacher-questionnaire refers to the teachers' ability of designing online-tasks. Only half of the teachers feel that they are somewhat able to do so (see Figure 4). An interconnection between the teachers' age, whose mean was 41.7 years, and university curricula then in force can be assumed. In the online-survey, 69% of the teachers indicated that courses focusing on the integration of digital media into the language classroom were not part of their pre-service teacher education. Interview and online-survey data also suggest a lack of professional development courses in this field.

Figure 3. Purposes of digital media use

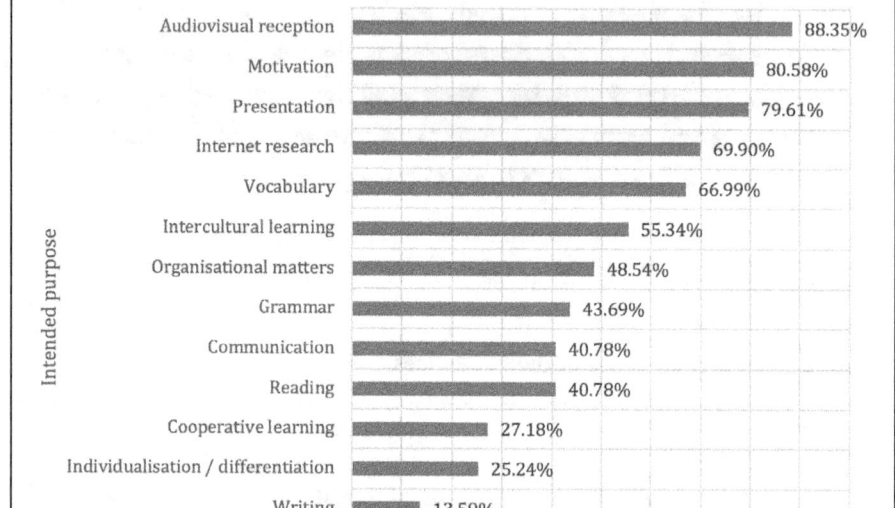

Figure 4. Teachers' ability of designing online-tasks

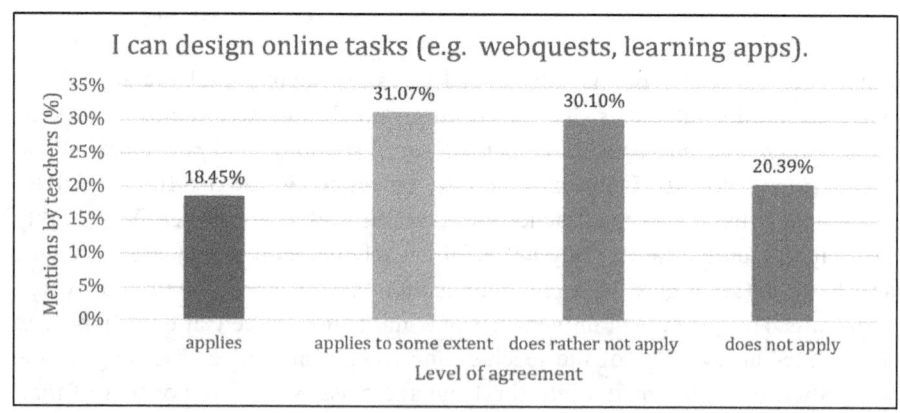

4. Conclusion

The most frequently reported merits of using digital media in the Russian language classroom were the increase in learner motivation, authentic language use, a real-world focus, and intercultural learning opportunities. With regard to authenticity and intercultural learning, school syllabi stipulate the integration of digital media (BMB, 2018; KMK, 2012). In the online-surveys and interviews, teachers indicated a lack of specific digital devices or training of how to use these. The implementation of digital media could be facilitated by better digital learning equipment and constant technical support (cf. Bos et al., 2016). Courses focusing on using digital media in the foreign language classroom should form an integral part of pre- and in-service teacher training programmes. Especially in rural areas, a wider choice of professional development courses in this field is needed. Further research might clarify the reasons why specific learning objectives (e.g. media critique) appear to be neglected.

5. Acknowledgements

I would like to thank my supervisors at Innsbruck University.

References

Biebighäuser, K., Zibelius, M., & Schmidt, T. (Eds). (2012). *Aufgaben 2.0: Konzepte, Materialien und Methoden für das Fremdsprachenlehren und -lernen mit digitalen Medien.* Narr.

BMB. (2018). *AHS-Lehrplan für die modulare Oberstufe: lebende Fremdsprache (Erste, Zweite).* Bundesministerium Bildung, Wissenschaft und Forschung. https://bildung.bmbwf.gv.at/schulen/unterricht/lp/lp_ahs.html

Bos, W., Lorenz, R., Endberg, M., Eickelmann, B., Kammerl, R., & Welling, S. (Eds). (2016). *Schule digital – der Länderindikator 2016: Kompetenzen von Lehrpersonen der Sekundarstufe I im Umgang mit digitalen Medien im Bundesländervergleich.* Waxmann.

Caspari, D., Klippel, F., Legutke, M., & Schramm, K. (2016). *Forschungsmethoden in der Fremdsprachendidaktik: ein Handbuch.* Narr. https://doi.org/10.14220/odaf.2016.32.2.128

Celot, P. (2015). *Assessing media literacy levels and the european commission pilot initiative.* https://eavi.eu/wp-content/uploads/2017/08/assessing.pdf

Feierabend, S., Plankenhorn, T., & Rathgeb, T. (2017). *JIM-Studie – Jugend, Information, (Multi)Media: Basisuntersuchung zum Medienumgang 12 bis 19-jähriger in Deutschland.* Medienpädagogischer Forschungsverbund Südwest.

Gräf, L. (2010). *Online-Befragung: eine praktische Einführung für Anfänger.* LIT.

Kelle, U. (2014). Mixed methods. In N. Baur & J. Blasius (Eds), *Handbuch der empirischen Sozialforschung* (pp. 153-166). Springer VS. https://doi.org/10.1007/978-3-531-18939-0_8

KMK. (2012). *Fachlehrplan Sekundarschule Russisch.* Kultusministerium Sachsen-Anhalt. https://www.bildung-lsa.de/pool/RRL_Lehrplaene/Endfassungen/lp_sks_russ.pdf

Maxwell, J. A. (2004). Using qualitative methods for causal explanations. *Field Methods, 16*(3), 243-264. https://doi.org/10.1177%2F1525822X04266831

Mayring, P. (2015). *Qualitative Inhaltsanalyse: Grundlagen und Techniken.* Beltz.

Raab-Steiner, E., & Benesch, M. (2012). *Der Fragebogen: von der Forschungsidee zur SPSS-Auswertung.* Facultas.

Roche, J. (2008). *Mediendidaktik Fremdsprachen.* Hueber.

Vuorikari, R., Punie, Y., Carretero, S., & Van den Brande, L. (2016). *DigComp 2.0: the digital competence framework for citizens.* Council of Europe Publishing.

Using LARA for language learning: a pilot study for Icelandic

Branislav Bédi[1], Cathy Chua[2], Hanieh Habibi[3], Ruth Martinez-Lopez[4], and Manny Rayner[5]

Abstract. This paper presents a brief overview of LARA (Learning And Reading Assistant), an open source online tool that has been under development since summer 2018. LARA currently[6] contains a corpus of about 25 texts in ten languages and a crowdsourcing model used to expand the corpus. The central goal is to provide support for improving second language (L2) reading comprehension. The focus here is on the development of Icelandic content and its use during pilot testing amongst adult L2 learners of Icelandic. Preliminary feedback from users, while mostly positive, contained suggestions on how the tool might be improved.

Keywords: crowdsourcing, L2 learning, open source, pilot testing, reading.

1. Introduction

LARA is a free online tool which makes it easy to transform plain texts into a hyperlinked multimedia form designed to support non-native readers: it thus connects content providers, such as teachers, with readers/learners. When accessing LARA content, the user sees a split-screen with the text on one side and various options on the other. The unique feature of the interface is the personalised concordance created for each reader-user. That is, based on the reader's own history, words in the target language will be displayed in the contexts in which they previously appeared. Other functionalities include dictionary translations,

---

1. The Árni Magnússon Institute for Icelandic Studies, Reykjavík, Iceland; branislav.bedi@arnastofnun.is
2. Independent scholar, Geneva, Switzerland; cathyc@pioneerbooks.com.au
3. FTI/TIM University of Geneva, Geneva, Switzerland; hanieh.habibi@unige.ch
4. Seville University, Seville, Spain; ruthmart@gmail.com
5. University of Geneva, Geneva, Switzerland; emmanuel.rayner@unige.ch
6. Mid-July 2019

How to cite this article: Bédi, B., Chua, C., Habibi, H., Martinez-Lopez, R., & Rayner, M. (2019). Using LARA for language learning: a pilot study for Icelandic. In F. Meunier, J. Van de Vyver, L. Bradley & S. Thouësny (Eds), *CALL and complexity – short papers from EUROCALL 2019* (pp. 33-38). Research-publishing.net. https://doi.org/10.14705/rpnet.2019.38.982

voice recordings of words and passages, links to online grammar resources, and vocabulary lists ordered both alphabetically and by frequency of occurrence in the text. All of these can be accessed by pointing and clicking. Figure 1 illustrates our initial Icelandic resource, *Tína fer í frí* (Skriver, 1981), a children's book containing about 2,700 words. LARA's content repository currently contains 25 texts in ten languages, for a total of about 140,000 words. A detailed overview of LARA can be found in Akhlaghi et al. (2019).

Figure 1. LARA functionality for Icelandic text in a split-screen view. Featured are: translation tags, grammar information, audio icons, contextual word reference in the corpus

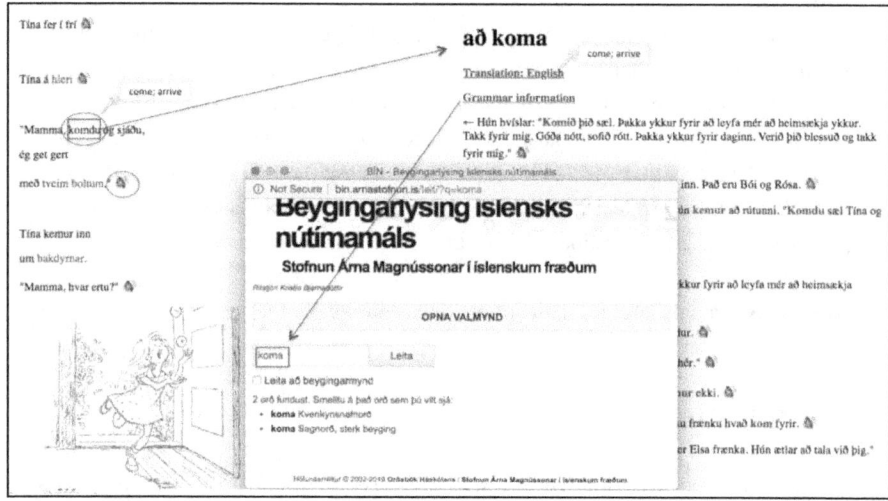

LARA's pedagogical model is built on Palincsar and Brown's (1984) interactive teaching to promote independent learning from reading comprehension, Oxford's (1990) reading strategy, and on the early example of Johns's (2002) Data-Driven Learning (DDL). Based on these sources, we consider L2 learning by reading comprehension can be facilitated by: (1) providing learners with texts that are suitable to their level, (2) making the content compatible with the reader's knowledge, and (3) supporting active strategies which readers may employ to enhance understanding and retention, and to facilitate comprehension (Palincsar & Brown, 1984, p. 118). DDL has from the start built on the affordances of text retrieval software in L2 education. In particular, it provides a framework for supporting scaffolding and learner autonomy (Boulton & Tyne, 2013; Corino & Onesti, 2019).

The use of corpora in L2 education is still relatively rare. Some of the best-known online corpus analysis tools with open access are the NoSketchEngine (Rychlý, 2007), SkELL (Baisa & Suchomel, 2014), AntConc (Anthony, 2019), and some others that are included in LexTutor (Cobb, 2019). The commonality of these tools is that they contain crowdsourced corpora consisting of online texts in various languages, provide information about the frequency of words, and support language learning by giving access to numerous occurrences of words, phrases, idioms, and other language expressions in context.

Organisationally, LARA is a part of the open source CALLector project[7], which in turn is closely linked to the enetCollect[8] COST network. Ethical issues are central to both LARA and CALLector. The users, be they teachers/content developers or learners/content users, are in control of their data, and the platform/tools are designed to be self-sufficient through best practices of crowdsourced free models. In terms of software engineering, the key medium-term goals are to make the content development process simple and user-friendly, with only basic computer skills required, and embed the platform in a dedicated social network which connects content developers and content users. Although initial LARA content is already being trialled by classroom teachers in Iceland and elsewhere, these goals have still only been partially achieved. In particular, the social network level is not yet available; the tools still need to be downloaded and installed on a local machine; and for some languages, currently including Icelandic, the process of annotating the text still requires laborious manual tagging of surface words by head-word (while automatic tagging is supported for many other languages). Work on all these issues is progressing. A first version of a LARA web portal is currently being tested, which will obviate the need to install software. Taggers for other languages, in particular, an open source Icelandic tagger, are being integrated, and we expect the social network to go live towards the end of 2019.

2. Pilot testing of LARA for learning Icelandic

The pilot test was organised around an anonymous questionnaire in March 2019. There were 47 voluntary participants consisting of learners enrolled in the Icelandic Practical Diploma Course at the University of Iceland: 21 female, 23 male, one 'other', two 'prefer not to say'; and 39 beginners, eight intermediate, coming from 17 countries. After a short introduction to the tool, they spent 60 minutes using it by reading the Icelandic text on their laptops while using headphones for listening.

7. https://www.unige.ch/callector/
8. http://enetcollect.eurac.edu

The instructor only assisted with technical issues. The learners were requested to use the tool on their own to achieve optimal first-time user experience results. Then they were given 20 minutes to respond to the questionnaire which included 31 questions about learners' background and perceived usefulness with Likert-scale answers (Davis, 1989), and open-ended questions about the assessment of digital tools (Nesbitt, 2013). The answers about the users' general experience and learning effect are summarised in Table 1. Most of the learners either agreed or strongly agreed with positive statements about LARA. Compared with the traditional way of reading a book, most users said that the tool's functionalities increased their efficiency in reading with understanding, learning vocabulary, and (to some extent) learning grammar. Nearly all students said that the integrated audio helped to learn more about pronunciation.

Results from open-ended questions suggest that over 90% of the learners liked the application. Problems experienced included: poor internet connection, missing or inaccurate word translations, and lack of support for mobile devices. Currently Chrome is the only browser permitting full functionality. About 70% suggested improvements, e.g. including instructions before the task, on-screen instructions to help navigate, options for both female and male voices, adding a bookmark, and options for changing font/background colour. About the same proportion of learners liked the design. About 81% of the learners said that the application met their needs; 11% suggested improvements like adding more explanations about grammar, sentence structure, vocabulary, and phrases. Eight percent said it did not meet their needs.

Table 1. Learners' perceptions regarding usefulness

No.	Question	Strongly agree	Agree	Neutral	Disagree	Strongly disagree
1.	The reading task would be difficult to perform without this application.	19%	49%	19%	11%	2%
2.	Using this application gives me greater control over my reading task.	38%	49%	9%	4%	-
3.	Using this application improves my understanding of the Icelandic text.	49%	47%	4%	-	-
4.	The application addresses my learning-related needs in this course.	40%	55%	2%	2%	-
5.	Using this application saves me time.	34%	55%	11%	-	-
6.	This application enables me to accomplish reading tasks more quickly.	34%	51%	15%	-	-

7.	This application supports critical aspects of my learning.	23%	53%	17%	6%	-
8.	Using this application allows me to accomplish more reading tasks than would otherwise be possible.	36%	51%	11%	2%	-
9.	Using this application reduces the time I spend on unproductive activities.	26%	38%	26%	11%	-
10.	Using this application enhances my effectiveness in reading.	32%	60%	6%	2%	-
11.	Compared to using books, using this application improves the quality of reading Icelandic texts.	45%	40%	11%	2%	2%
12.	Using this application increases my learning productivity.	28%	53%	19%	-	-
13.	Using this application makes it easier for me to read Icelandic texts.	38%	55%	4%	2%	-
14	Using this application makes it easier for me to learn vocabulary.	40%	47%	13%	-	-
15.	Using this application makes it easier for me to learn grammar.	28%	38%	26%	9%	-
16.	Using this application makes it easier for me to learn pronunciation.	49%	43%	4%	4%	-
17.	Overall, I find this application useful in my Icelandic course.	55%	38%	4%	-	2%

* Note: percentages may not add up to 100 due to rounding.

3. Conclusions and future work

Based on the above results, the tool appeals to learners: it assists them in the development of reading and associated skills including vocabulary, grammar, listening comprehension, and pronunciation. Learners find the current functionalities, i.e. dictionary translations, voice recordings of words and passages, links to online grammar resources, and vocabulary lists ordered both alphabetically and by frequency of occurrence in the text, practical and useful.

In the future, the crowdsourcing approach will enable content providers to add more texts in Icelandic, as is the case for other languages. The personalised concordance facility that allows learners to answer questions about vocabulary by reading concordance lines (Hunston, 2002) will become part and parcel of the learning process. The pilot test also included several suggestions from learners on how to improve the tool. Some important improvements have already been implemented and others are in the pipeline.

4. Acknowledgements

This article is based upon work from COST Action enetCollect (CA16105) supported by COST (European Cooperation in Science and Technology). Work at the University of Geneva was funded by the Swiss National Science Foundation under grant IZCOZ0_177065.

References

Akhlaghi, E., Bédi, B., Butterweck, M., Chua, C., Gerlach, J., Habibi, H., Ikeda, J., Rayner, M., Sestigiani, S., & Zuckermann, G. (2019). Overview of LARA: a learning and reading assistant. In *Proceedings SLaTE* 2019, Graz, Austria. https://doi.org/10.21437/slate.2019-19

Anthony, L. (2019). AntConc (Version 3.5.8) [Computer Software]. Waseda University. https://www.laurenceanthony.net/software

Baisa, V., & Suchomel, V. (2014). SkELL – web interface for English language learning. In *Eighth Workshop on Recent Advances in Slavonic Natural Language Processing* (pp. 63-70). Tribun EU. https://nlp.fi.muni.cz/raslan/2014/12.pdf

Boulton, A., & Tyne, H. (2013). Corpus linguistics and data-driven learning: a critical overview. In *Bulletin VALS-ASLA 97*, 97-118. https://core.ac.uk/download/pdf/20661944.pdf

Cobb, T. (2019). *Complete leixical tutor v.8.3* [computer program]. https://www.lextutor.ca

Corino, E., & Onesti, C. (2019). Data-driven learning: a scaffolding methodology for CLIL and LSP teaching and learning. In *Frontiers of Education, 4*(7), 1-12. https://doi.org/10.3389/feduc.2019.00007

Davis, F. D. (1989). Percieved usefulness, perceived ease of use, and user acceptance of information technology. In *MIS Quarterly, 13*(3), 319-340. https://doi.org/10.2307/249008

Hunston, S. (2002). *Corpora in applied linguistics*. Oxford University Press.

Johns, T. (2002). Data-driven learning: the perpetual challenge. In *Teaching and Learning by Doing Corpus Analysis* (pp. 105-117). Brill Rodopi. https://doi.org/10.1163/9789004334236_010

Nesbitt, D. (2013). Student evaluation of CALL tools during the design process. *Computer Assistad Language Learning, 26*(4), 371-387. https://doi.org/10.1080/09588221.2012.680471

Oxford, R. L. (1990). *Language learning strategies: what every teacher should know*. Heinle & Heinle.

Palincsar, A. S., & Brown, A. L. (1984). Reciprocal teaching of comprehension-fostering and comprehension-monitoring activities. *Cognition and Instruction, 1*(2), 117-175. https://doi.org/10.1207/s1532690xci0102_1

Rychlý, P. (2007). Manatee/Bonito – a modular corpus manager. In *1st Workshop on Recent Advances in Slavonic Natural Language Processing* (pp. 65-70). Masaryk University. https://nlp.fi.muni.cz/trac/noske

Skriver, E. (1981). *Tína fer í frí*. Námsgagnastofnun. Prenthúsið.

■ UCLouvain

"Let's date!" A 360-degree video application to support foreign language learning

Anke Berns[1], Iván Ruiz-Rube[2], José Miguel Mota[3], Juan Manuel Dodero[4], Edson Castro[5], Oona Ryynanen[6], and Lissy Werner[7]

Abstract. New technologies are changing the way of learning foreign languages. However, one of the main challenges for software developers and mobile assisted language learning designers remains the creation of learning environments for students' language immersion in and outside the classroom. This paper describes the design and evaluation of a VR-based mobile app called *Let's date!*. The app enables Common European Framework of Reference for languages (CEFR) A1 level German language learners to interact with an immersive environment and to practise several language skills. The results have proven that the use of 360° videos based on realistic situations and combined with a conversational agent is suitable to reinforce students' foreign language competencies.

Keywords: virtual reality, conversational agent, immersion, language learning.

1. Introduction

Nowadays, Virtual Reality (VR) technology has become more accessible to end-users. A look at the literature and commercial repositories, such as Apple App Store or Google Play Store, highlights that although there is an increasing interest in developing this type of apps for learning foreign languages, very few of them

---

1. University of Cádiz, Cádiz, Spain; anke.berns@uca.es; https://orcid.org/0000-0003-3129-7209
2. University of Cádiz, Cádiz, Spain; ivan.ruiz@uca.es; https://orcid.org/0000-0002-9012-700X
3. University of Cádiz, Cádiz, Spain; josemiguel.mota@uca.es; https://orcid.org/0000-0002-4980-0549
4. University of Cádiz, Cádiz, Spain; juanma.dodero@uca.es; https://orcid.org/0000-0002-4105-5679
5. University of Cádiz, Cádiz, Spain; edson.sv@gmail.com
6. University of Cádiz, Cádiz, Spain; oona.ryynanen@alum.uca.es
7. University of Cádiz, Cádiz, Spain; lissy.wernerwerner@alum.uca.es

How to cite this article: Berns, A., Ruiz-Rube, I., Mota, J. M., Dodero, J. M., Castro, E., Ryynanen, O., & Werner, L. (2019). "Let's date!" A 360-degree video application to support foreign language learning. In F. Meunier, J. Van de Vyver, L. Bradley & S. Thouësny (Eds), *CALL and complexity – short papers from EUROCALL 2019* (pp. 39-44). Research-publishing.net. https://doi.org/10.14705/rpnet.2019.38.983

explore the real potential of VR (Berns, Mota, Ruiz-Rube, & Dodero, 2018; García et al., 2019). One of the main advantages of VR technology is that it allows the creation of immersive, realistic environments in which the user can directly engage with the VR environment and its content. In this sense, VR is not only attractive for those who follow a second-language acquisition approach (Berns & Palomo-Duarte, 2015) but also for those who use a constructivist teaching approach (Huang, Rauch, & Liaw, 2010). In this context, the current paper intends to explore the possibilities of VR techniques to create realistic learning scenarios based on both approaches, providing students with opportunities for language immersion as well as interaction in the target language.

2. Method

2.1. Experimental setting and case study

An Android mobile app, *Let's date!,* was developed for this study. The app emulates a dating agency in which learners have to interact via voice messages with a virtual agency assistant. The app consists of a set of 360° video snippets that are delivered according to a conversation flow between the student and the virtual agency assistant (see Figure 1). The study was carried out in a CEFR A1 level German foreign language course at the University of Cádiz (Spain). A total number of 24 students participated in the experience. All the language items covered by the app were based on the course syllabus and parameters from the CEFR. Moreover, the software was developed by taking into account the target students' language knowledge and language skills.

Figure 1.   Student interacting with the VR environment and the agency assistant

The app enables students to immerse themselves in a realistic, life-like environment. It includes a conversational agent (chatbot) that simulates a human

conversation, handling at the same time the communication between the student and the agency assistant. Additionally this agent is responsible for recognising and understanding the students' voice message while interacting with the app and its content.

During the VR experience, students were first asked about their individual characteristics (character, physical appearance, interests, age, place of living, etc.). Next, they had to indicate their expectations regarding the characteristics of their ideal boy- or girlfriends. Questions are posed at the end of each video snippet so that the learner must answer them by first registering and then sending a voice message which is stored by the system. According to the answer given by the learner (comprehensible and coherent answer) either a new video snippet is delivered or the previous one is delivered once again (in case the answer was not comprehensible or incoherent). This way, students can revise and eventually correct the given answer. The general procedure is illustrated in Berns et al. (2018, p. 778). In addition, the app collects all the answers given by each learner, allowing the teacher to do future learning analytics. Furthermore, the input voice messages are used to enrich the corpus of answers hence taking into account linguistic variations (Berns et al., 2018).

2.2. App development

The mobile app was authored by using the VEDILS tool, an extended version of MIT App Inventor. This platform allows non-professional users to create VR scenario applications enriched with analytic capabilities (Mota et al., 2018). In addition, the DialogFlow platform was used to build the conversational agent (Reyes et al., 2019).

DialogFlow is a tool that enables developers to create both specific chatbots as well as extensions (called actions) for the Google Assistant, which is built-in and available on Android mobile devices. In order to improve the user experience, the agent was fed with numerous training phrases (see Figure 2). This was done through the administration page of DialogFlow.

The machine-learning component generated with DialogFlow was later integrated into the VEDILS mobile app. This component ingests the user voice input, transforms it into a text message, and extracts the required data. To this end, Google Text-To-Speech and Speech-To-Text cloud services were also integrated. The structured data obtained from the user's speech enable the app to choose the corresponding path of the decision flow.

Figure 2. Screenshot of the DialogFlow tool showing the training phrases for the user intention for expressing their preferences

2.3. Students' feedback on the learner experience

To gather students' feedback on the learning experience and their attitudes towards VR-based learning environments, they were asked to fill in a technology acceptance model questionnaire at the end of the learning experience (Berns et al., 2018). The questionnaire was based on the model proposed by Liu et al. (2010) and used by us to measure the perceived ease of use and usefulness, students' behavioural intention to use the app, and their attitude towards it, as well as the perceived playfulness.

Additionally, a five-point Likert-rating scale (from completely disagree to completely agree) was used for the analysis (Berns et al., 2018). Seventy-five percent of the participants confirmed that they became rapidly familiar with the app because of its ease of use. In terms of usefulness, most students rated the app as a handy tool for learning foreign languages, its potential for learning vocabulary, its usefulness for improving comprehension skills, and its possibilities for improving oral expression. Besides, all students agreed on the benefits that the app provides for working on pronunciation. It is noteworthy that all participants showed a very positive attitude towards using VR-based learning apps like the one used for the current study. Additionally, all of them recommend other students to use VR-based apps to support their language learning process. Lastly, three out of four students felt fully immersed in the virtual environment and enjoyed the learning experience very much. However, 25% of the students experienced some trouble during the experiment and use of the app, which was mostly due to problems related to the network connectivity. In these cases, learners had to restart the app from the very beginning.

3. Conclusions and future work

The case study presented in this paper shows the possibilities and potential of VR apps for improving the learning of foreign languages. This kind of novel experience enables students to strengthen their language competencies through immersive and realistic situations. The students' evaluation of their learning experience based on the use of a 360° video application called *Let's date!* highlights not only the potential of VR-based apps for facilitating language immersion and thus language acquisition (Gadelha, 2018), but also to focus on specific skills such as speaking and pronunciation, which are often difficult to address using more conventional learning tools (learning platforms, social network sites, etc).

The current study and the feedback received also suggest that the use of chatbots, which allowed students to experience real-world interaction and conversation in the target language, was paramount for their positive evaluation of *Let's date!* However, further studies with a longer duration and larger and more diversified sample sizes (experimental and control groups) are needed in order to generalise the results obtained in this quasi-experimental study. Finally, we will leverage the expertise acquired with the development and evaluation of the current app to develop new learning apps focusing on other situations and foreign languages.

4. Acknowledgements

This work was developed as part of the VISAIGLE project (TIN2017-85797-R), which is funded by the Spanish National Research Agency.

References

Berns, A., Mota, J. M., Ruiz-Rube, I., & Dodero, J. M. (2018). Exploring the potential of a 360 ° video application for foreign language learning. In F. J. García-Peñalvo (Ed.), *TEEM' 18. Proceedings of the Sixth International Conference on Technological Ecosystems for Enhancing Multiculturality* (pp. 776-780). ACM. https://doi.org/10.1145/3284179.3284309

Berns, A., & Palomo-Duarte, M. (2015). Supporting foreign-language learning through a gamified app. In R. Hernández & P. Rankin (Eds), *Higher education and second language learning. Supporting selfdirected learning in new technological and educational contexts* (pp. 65-82). Peter Lang. https://doi.org/10.3726/978-3-0353-0685-9/18

Gadelha, R. (2018). Revolutionizing education: the promise of virtual reality. *Childhood Education, 94*(1), 40-43. https://doi.org/10.1080/00094056.2018.1420362

García, S., Laesker, D., Caprio, D., Kauer, R., Nguyen, J., & Andujar, M. (2019). An immersive virtual reality experience for learning Spanish. In P. Zaphiris & A. Ioannou (Eds), *Learning and collaboration technologies. Ubiquitous and virtual environments for learning and collaboration. HCII 2019. Lecture Notes in Computer Science* (vol. 11591, pp. 151-161). Springer. https://doi.org/10.1007/978-3-030-21817-1_12

Huang, H.-M., Rauch, U., & Liaw, S.-S. (2010). Investigating learners' attitudes toward virtual reality learning environments: based on a constructivist approach. *Computers & Education, 55*(3), 1171-1182. https://doi.org/10.1016/j.compedu.2010.05.014

Liu, I.-F., Chang-Cheng, M., Sun, Y. S., Wible, D., & Kuo, C.-H. (2010). Extending the TAM model to explore the factors that affect intention to use an online learning community. *Computers & Education, 54*(2), 600-610. https://doi.org/10.1016/j.compedu.2009.09.009

Mota, J. M., Ruiz-Rube, I., Dodero, J. M., Person, T., & Arnedillo-Sánchez, I. (2018). Learning analytics in mobile applications based on multimodal interaction. In S. Caballé & J. Conesa (Eds), *Software data engineering for network elearning environments. Lecture notes on data engineering and communications technologies* (vol. 11, pp. 67-92). Springer. https://doi.org/10.1007/978-3-319-68318-8_4

Reyes, R., Garza, D., Garrido, L., De la Cueva, V., & Ramirez, J. (2019). Methodology for the Implementation of virtual assistants for education using Google Dialogflow. In L. Martínez-Villaseñor, I. Batyrshin & A. Marín-Hernández (Eds), *18th Mexican International Conference on Artificial Intelligence* (pp. 440-451). Springer. https://doi.org/10.1007/978-3-030-33749-0_35

Annotated scientific text visualizer: design, development, and deployment

John Blake[1]

Abstract. Prototypes of an annotated scientific text visualizer were designed, developed, and deployed. This pedagogic tool is designed to help undergraduates draft short research articles that conform to the generic expectations of their discourse community. This online tool enables users to discover and explore the language features present in short research articles. Users can select to visualize research articles in the field of computer science. The articles are categorized into four types. Users select to hide or reveal particular language features and their associated explanations in text, audio, or video formats. This enables them to create their own learning paths with this interactive tool. Students can use the visualizer to individualize their own learning interactively at their own pace on materials that are relevant to them.

Keywords: scientific writing, visualization, language features, individualized learning, discovery learning.

1. Introduction

This paper details the design, development, and deployment of a rapid prototype and an alpha release prototype of an annotated scientific text visualizer. This interactive pedagogic tool aims to help novice writers with English as an additional language by visualizing prototypical language features and providing multimedia explanations on demand. The inspiration for this tool stems from the noticing hypothesis (Schmidt, 2010), which claims that learners must first notice language features before learning them. Noticing is achieved through a discovery learning approach (Huang, 2008), enhanced using intelligent computer

---

1. University of Aizu, Aizu-wakamatsu, Japan; jblake@u-aizu.ac.jp; https://orcid.org/0000-0002-3150-4995

How to cite this article: Blake, J. (2019). Annotated scientific text visualizer: design, development, and deployment. In F. Meunier, J. Van de Vyver, L. Bradley & S. Thouësny (Eds), *CALL and complexity – short papers from EUROCALL 2019* (pp. 45-50). Research-publishing.net. https://doi.org/10.14705/rpnet.2019.38.984

assisted language learning (Amaral & Meurers, 2011). This is the first interactive visualization tool for novice writers of computer science research articles.

The purpose of this phase in the project was twofold. The first aim was to create a simple prototype to act as a visual aid that can be used in conjunction with the required specifications to show how the fully-fledged prototype should work. The second aim was to identify stakeholder expectations and improve our understanding of user needs to ensure that the scientific text visualizer not only meets but exceeds user expectations.

The following section provides the background details to the development of the scientific text visualizer. Section 3 describes the design specifications. Section 4 details the development of the rapid prototype, annotated articles, multimodal materials, and the alpha release. Section 5 concludes with the alpha release and lists future work.

2. Background

Both undergraduate and postgraduate students in the school of computer science at the University of Aizu in Northern Japan are required to submit short research articles in order to fulfill graduation requirements. This is a particularly onerous challenge for Japanese students who may have had little exposure to formal written English and less exposure to scientific writing. Ideally, students can dedicate a significant amount of time to read research articles in their field of research, and acquire the tacit knowledge required to write their own research paper. However, given the severe time constraints that many students face, this is not a viable option. A key problem for teachers of the associated technical writing courses is providing suitable examples and advice for all students. For example, within the field of computer science, some students may write more theoretical papers that rely on mathematical proofs while other students may develop and evaluate software, making it difficult for teachers to use examples that are relevant to all students.

Japanese students with little proficiency in English could make extensive use of Google Translate which since its switch to Google Neural Machine Translation now produces text that is more comprehensible than texts that those students could produce. This combined with the use of Grammarly or similar generic error detectors can produce somewhat comprehensible texts. This harnessing of technology however has no pedagogic purpose, and so the focus of this online tool is to help writers learn more about the target genre by providing explanations on demand in the mode and medium that users prefer. This individualized automated support is both technically feasible and eminently scalable.

Individualized learning can solve the problem of differing needs and differing wants of students sharing the same class. Students can select example research articles which are most relevant to the type of research they are engaged in. They can then select the language features that they want to better understand. As this tool is online, writers can access it at will on any web-enabled device. This is particularly pertinent as many writers draft the final version of their graduation thesis over the New Year holiday period.

3. Design

A software requirements specification was created detailing use cases and requirements from the perspectives of students, teachers, and researchers. Research in computer science may be classified into four categories, namely empirical, experimental, practical, and theoretical. Once users select the type of research article, and the specific article itself, they can individualize their learning by showing or hiding various language features on demand. The features incorporated are listed in Table 1. For each feature, explanations are provided in different modes (text, audio, and video) and mediums (Japanese and English).

Table 1. Language features to be visualized on demand using toggle buttons

#	Category	Details
1	organization	sections and moves
2	functions	description, explanation, exemplification, justification, reference to visuals
3	connections	coherence, cohesion (e.g. anaphoric and cataphoric pronouns)
4	linking	conjunctions, adverbs (transitions), and prepositions
5	tense	tense and aspect (e.g. present perfect progressive)
6	voice	passive, active (and ergative)
7	modality	hedging, boosting, and approximation
8	abstraction	packaging processes as nouns
9	information structure	end weight, focus, and flow (see Blake, 2015 for more details)
10	word type	first 1,000 words, second 2,000 words, academic word list

4. Development

Development can be divided into prototype creation (Prototype I and Prototype II) and materials creation (annotated articles and multimodal explanations). These are discussed in turn below.

4.1. Prototype I: Axure RP

A simple working prototype was made using Axure RP. A dropdown menu enables users to select research articles that are displayed in the center of the viewport. A row of ten toggle function buttons at the top allow users to hide/reveal language features. An exploratory panel appears above the research article when a function is selected. The exploratory panel contains an embedded video, a textual description, and a dropdown menu of other explanatory modes and mediums for the first function.

4.2. Materials creation

The initial dataset of 12 texts comprises abridged research articles written by undergraduates that were submitted as graduation theses, capstone projects, or final projects. Based on user feedback, texts over four pages were abridged. Where possible, raw text parsing is used, but when the state-of-the-art accuracy is insufficient, annotation tags are needed. For each function that requires annotation, html-like tags are used so that rule-based parsing can be used to visualize those particular language features. Users expect online learning resources to be interactive, highly visual and multimodal (Hafner, Chik, & Jones, 2015). Therefore, where possible, explanations are provided in text, image, audio, and file formats. Explanatory slideshows were created. Explanations were recorded in both English and Japanese to avoid the 'L2 halting effect' (Amaral & Meurers, 2011). The slideshows and audio files were merged to create videos.

4.3. Prototype II

The fully-fledged code version of the annotated text visualizer, Prototype II, allows users to select four types of computer science articles (practical, theoretical, empirical, and experimental) from a preloaded database of annotated articles. Users select the language features to be visualized on demand using toggle buttons to hide and reveal visualizations. When a toggle button is selected, the relevant features in the research article displayed in the viewport are highlighted and an explanatory panel appears. The explanatory panel is divided into two parts: embedded video area and links to additional video, audio, or text explanations. Explanations are currently available in English or Japanese, but other languages may be added.

5. Discussion and conclusion

This pedagogic tool gives users the power to explore the form and function with visual, audio, and video explanations. Through exploring the visualizations and interacting with multimedia explanations, user awareness of generic expectations can be raised. This prototype tool is scalable and can be extended to deal with other scientific domains and different genres of writing.

The next phase of this three-year project is to extend the depth and breadth of the language features that can be visualized. The next version of the scientific text visualizer will be developed by a team of students using the Python Django web framework and Vue.js as the students have taken elective courses on these technologies. In contrast to the early prototypes, the next version will adopt a mobile-first approach.

6. Acknowledgments

This research was supported by a Japan Society for the Promotion of Science (JSPS) *Kakenhi* Grant-in-aid for Scientific Research entitled 'Feature visualizer and detector for scientific texts', Grant Number 19K00850. I would also like to thank Maxim Mozgovoy for his technical expertise.

References

Amaral, L., & Meurers, D. (2011). On using intelligent computer-assisted language learning in real-life foreign language teaching and learning. *ReCALL, 23*(1), 4-24. https://doi.org/10.1017/s0958344010000261

Blake, J. (2015). Incorporating information structure in the EAP curriculum. *Conference proceedings of 2nd International Symposium on Innovative Teaching and Research in ESP.* UEC, Tokyo. http://www.shilab.bunka.uec.ac.jp/esp2015/proceedings/Blake_ESP2015.pdf

Hafner, C. A., Chik, A., & Jones, R. H. (2015). Digital literacies and language learning. *Language Learning & Technology, 19*(3), 1-7.

Huang, L.-S. (2008). Using guided, corpus-aided discovery to generate active learning. *English Teaching Forum, 46*(4), 20-27.

Schmidt, R. (2010). Attention, awareness, and individual differences in language learning. In W. M. Chan, S. Chi, K. N. Cin, J. Istanto, M. Nagami, J. W. Sew, T. Suthiwan & I. Walker (Eds), *Proceedings of CLaSIC 2010, Singapore, December 2-4* (pp. 721-737). National University of Singapore, Center for Language Studies.

■ UCLouvain

First contact with language corpora: perspectives from students

Alex Boulton[1]

Abstract. Corpora are not the preserve of corpus linguists. In education, learners and teachers can analyse almost any collection of text for linguistic or non-linguistic purposes where regular reading is not efficient or feasible. This paper describes students' first contact with corpora in a distance master's degree where they are required to build a corpus on a topic of their choice and complete a short research report. Following a brief outline of the course, we turn to a description of 122 papers submitted over the last 5 years, with particular attention on the Personal Feedback sections of each among both high- and low-achievers. The opening sentences typically reveal bewilderment on initial encounter with corpus linguistics, which contrasts with growing mastery or sudden enlightenment. Further analysis of the 30k-word corpus suggests that a corpus approach may not be immediately easy, but most users can derive benefits with a little perseverance even in adverse conditions.

Keywords: corpus linguistics, student feedback, ESP, data-driven learning.

1. Introduction

Corpus linguistics has shown multiple uses in language education, especially perhaps in describing language use for improved materials and resources, from dictionaries and grammar books to word lists and manuals. Language is a tremendously complex object, and learning is a correspondingly complex process, such that neither reference books nor intuition can ever contain all the answers to all the questions one might have. For highly focused questions or needs, specific corpora are required, sometimes tailored to the individual level (e.g. Charles, 2012). Fortunately, as numerous studies have shown, it is not necessary to be a

---

1. ATILF (CNRS & Université de Lorraine), Nancy, France; alex.boulton@atilf.fr; https://orcid.org/0000-0001-6306-8158

How to cite this article: Boulton, A. (2019). First contact with language corpora: perspectives from students. In F. Meunier, J. Van de Vyver, L. Bradley & S. Thouësny (Eds), *CALL and complexity – short papers from EUROCALL 2019* (pp. 51-56). Research-publishing.net. https://doi.org/10.14705/rpnet.2019.38.985

corpus linguist to benefit from the approach. If corpus use is relatively well known in Data-Driven Learning (DDL) (Johns, 1990) and teacher education (e.g. Leńko-Szymańska, 2017), in fact corpus tools and techniques can apply to almost any field that works with large quantities of text (Adolphs, 2006, p. 11). This paper describes a course where the students are free to choose any topic and the questions they want to ask, compile a corpus, and write up their research in a paper. While not being DDL per se, it draws on similar principles of authenticity, autonomy, constructivism, and discovery-based learning. The course projects are first described in relation to the students' fields of interest, then their personal feedback is explored to gain an insight into the process of appropriation of corpus tools for their own purposes.

2. Method

The course is part of a master's degree in English in a distance teaching programme in France, and has been running in different guises since 2002 (see Boulton, 2011). The students are mainly interested in English literature and cultural studies ('civilisation') rather than linguistics, and corpora were seen as a way to involve these different interests. Currently, the students are required to define a topic and the questions they want to ask, compile a corpus of at least 20k words for analysis using AntConc, and write up their research in a template paper following the usual IMRAD[2] format (10-15 pages), thus also preparing them for academic writing. A discovery approach is adopted whereby the students play with the texts and software to understand corpora in their own way rather than imposing lengthy instructions which have been found to be counterproductive in earlier iterations. The course has been fairly stable over the last five years (2013-2018), during which time 122 papers have been submitted (discounting resubmissions and blank papers), totalling 455k tokens.

3. Results

3.1. Overview

The topics were divided into the four main disciplines of English in France, allowing for multiple themes: 22% had an overt linguistic focus and 16% a pedagogical one,

---

2. IMRAD stands for the 'Introduction, Methods, Results, and Discussion' organisational structure.

while 30% looked at literature and 57% were concerned with cultural studies (see sample titles below). This highlights clearly that corpus linguistics is not just a linguistic affair – language analysis can be a way in many different topics reflecting the students' interests. This is important since single-use tools are likely to be abandoned quickly, while multi-purpose tools used repeatedly for different aims are more likely to be adopted (cf. Boulton, 2011).

Literature:

- Romeo and Juliet screen adaptations since 1950's

- The importance of invented words in the Harry Potter books

Cultural studies:

- Competition between Manchester City and Manchester United

- Societal notions in the same-sex marriage debate in the United States of America

3.2. Personal feedback

The template included a Personal Feedback section where the students were encouraged to reflect on their experience of corpus linguistics (Figure 1). These sections represent 30.5k tokens (M=249.6, SD=91.9, range=37/518); there was a modest correlation between length and mark (r=.35).

Figure 1. Personal feedback instructions

This is the *only* section where you should use self-reference (*I* or *me*, etc.). Tell the reader how your project developed, what difficulties you encountered and how you dealt with them, what you think you learned from this, your perception of corpus linguistics and its applications and how your feelings may have evolved as your work proceeded, whether you think you might use some of the tools or techniques in other areas of study in the future, and so on. It might help to think of this section as tips and advice for other students who read your work in the future. • This section will probably be about ½ **to 1 page** long.

Regular reading immediately shows that the opening sentences typically highlight a certain trepidation, as seen in the following sample from the first year of the course:

- "…<u>at first</u> I could not understand what a language could deal with a computer analysis."

- "I was <u>at first</u> quite overwhelmed with the idea of entering research in this field…"

- "I was literally scared when I <u>first</u> read what was expected for this course."

However, these all show initial impressions which change gradually over time, or suddenly in an epiphany from a particular query. From the same students:

- "However, little by little… I got involved in the game… it made me captivated and marvelled at the fact of how information technologies can help modern linguistics in the analysis of the language… The first results after the analysis motivated me a lot as I could see myself the fruits of my work and I could understand the functioning of English in real life… This course was a very useful discovery for me."

- "…but the understanding of the field and of the possibilities it offers only really dawned on me when I started to discover AntConc for myself… I was very impressed with all its functions and the way it can in an instant sort out data which would take hours of work if it were done manually. After working on this project for some time my anxiety about Corpus Linguistics disappeared. I realized I was enjoying working on this study more and more and even got curious. I would actually really enjoy another assignment in Corpus Linguistics to 'play' a bit more with AntConc as well as explore other tools."

- "In the end, little by little, I think I found a bit of light!"

Other negative words occur quite frequently, including 11x *scar** (for *scared*, *scary*, etc.), 5x *fear**, 3x *fright**, 7x *overwhelm** and 5x *daunt**. On the other hand, there were 93 occurrences of *interest** – never preceded immediately by *not*; and although there is also one example of *uninteresting*, the File View shows this is preceded by *at first* and followed by *but then*. Indeed, a cluster analysis shows that *first* occurs 130 times in 80 papers, *at first* has 40 occurrences, and *the first time* 16. Other positive reactions include 65x *useful**, 38x *enjoy**, 14x *curio**, and even 5x *fun*. The most frequent 6-grams both include *time*: *I spent a lot of time* and *it took me some time to* (4x each), and the *time(-)consuming* (15x) nature of corpus work is clearly an issue, at least in early stages when the students start to discover the software. The most significant adjective collocate (4L, 4R) of *AntConc* is *difficult* (6x, MI=3.9), though three include *not*; similarly, *easy* (4x, MI=3.4) was also used negatively in two occurrences; in between we have *useful* (8x, MI=3.7). A Keyword comparison of the top and bottom quartiles in terms of marks shows feedback from the most successful learners include positive items such as *curious* (f=9, LL=10.3), *clearer* (f=6, LL=6.9) and *benefit* (f=5, LL=5.7) among the top 20, while the least successful include *negative* (f=5, LL=8.3) and *complex* (f=4, LL=6.6).

4. Discussion and conclusion

This paper has attempted to show that corpus linguistics can be used for numerous purposes when dealing with text, and not just 'linguistics' or language learning. Many tools that have only a single use are likely to end up in a dusty drawer, while those that serve multiple functions are more likely to be taken out and used regularly. As such, communication between language teachers and other subject specialists is likely to be highly beneficial. In the present case, and with considerable autonomy, the students were able to build their own small corpora and analyse them in terms of their interests in literature and cultural studies in particular, all the while being exposed to considerable quantities of language in the genre that interested them. This suggests that corpus linguistics is indeed accessible even to students whose mindset is very much geared towards regular reading and qualitative interpretation of continuous text.

The objective in this course is to give the students a say in pursuing their own interests with only the basic methodology and tools imposed. Analysis of this small corpus requires the teacher to tackle the type of task required of the students and to walk in their shoes for a while. With a 30k word corpus, even free, simple corpus tools can help tremendously to gain a more objective picture from word lists (with or without a stoplist or lemmatisation), collocates, clusters, plot (for distribution) and of course concordances and file view to see the items in context. While we are not necessarily interested here in the 'aboutness' (Scott & Tribble, 2006) of the Personal Feedback section of the students' work, such tools show that initial negative reactions are outweighed by more positive views after hands-on experimentation in the majority of cases.

The course will hopefully be improved in two ways in the future. First, simply by being attentive to the views expressed in the Personal Feedback and adapting the course accordingly. Second, the intention is to make this small corpus available to students as practice material in introductory activities in the next iteration, where they may also benefit from being able to listen to each other.

References

Adolphs, S. (2006). *Introducing electronic text analysis: a practical guide for language and literary studies*. Routledge. https://doi.org/10.4324/9780203087701

Boulton, A. (2011). Bringing corpora to the masses: free and easy tools for language learning. In N. Kübler (Ed.), *Corpora, language, teaching, and resources: from theory to practice* (pp. 69-96). Peter Lang.

Charles, M. (2012). Proper vocabulary and juicy collocations: EAP students evaluate do-it-yourself corpus-building. *English for Specific Purposes, 31*(2), 93-102. https://doi.org/10.1016/j.esp.2011.12.003

Johns, T. (1990). From printout to handout: grammar and vocabulary teaching in the context of data-driven learning. *CALL Austria, 10*, 14-34.

Leńko-Szymańska, A. (2017). Training teachers in data-driven learning: tackling the challenge. *Language Learning & Technology, 21*(3), 217-241. http://llt.msu.edu/issues/october2017/lenko-szymanska.pdf

Scott, M., & Tribble, C. (2006). *Textual patterns: key words and corpus analysis in language education*. Amsterdam: John Benjamins. http://doi.org/10.1075/scl.22

Mobile literacy among Syrian refugee women teachers

Linda Bradley[1], Rima Bahous[2], and Ali Albasha[3]

Abstract. This research project investigates mobile literacy of Syrian refugee women teachers settled in Lebanon and Sweden. Our research provides input into Syrian refugee women teachers' professional aspirations and their connection to informal mobile learning. In both countries, training programs are used for these newly arrived teachers, enabling them to move forward in their careers, where digital and mobile learning play an important part. The purpose is to investigate how Syrian refugee women teachers are blending their teaching profession and vocational training with mobile literacy and digital technology. A qualitative method approach was applied, interviewing 20 refugee women in Lebanon and Sweden, all teachers from Syria. The outcomes show that the teachers are developing their vocational abilities in getting more career-oriented training in their areas of education by means of enhancing their language skills through mobile technology.

Keywords: mobile learning, MALL, professional learning, refugee, mobile apps, teacher training.

1. Introduction

The increasing migration from the Middle East has left remarkable consequences on a range of areas, such as infrastructure, demography, and education. The complexity of the situation for Syrians migrating to neighboring countries as well as further away has no less also affected the teaching and learning area of the large number of Syrian women teachers, who are struggling to participate in the labor market in the host countries. One important aspect of staying updated with

---

1. University of Gothenburg, Gothenburg, Sweden; linda.bradley@gu.se; https://orcid.org/0000-0002-7978-4113
2. Lebanese American University, Beirut, Lebanon; rbahous@lau.edu.lb; https://orcid.org/0000-0001-6987-4003
3. University of Gothenburg, Gothenburg, Sweden; alialbasha222@gmail.com

How to cite this article: Bradley, L., Bahous, R., & Albasha, A. (2019). Mobile literacy among Syrian refugee women teachers. In F. Meunier, J. Van de Vyver, L. Bradley & S. Thouësny (Eds), *CALL and complexity – short papers from EUROCALL 2019* (pp. 57-62). Research-publishing.net. https://doi.org/10.14705/rpnet.2019.38.986

the profession is to learn the language of the new country, where digital skills and mobile literacy are important tools (Bartram, Bradley, & Al-Sabbagh, 2018; Bradley, Berbyuk Lindström, & Sofkova Hashemi, 2017; Kaufmann, 2018).

Krause (2014) suggested that being a refugee can redefine and deconstruct community patterns. Displacement can actually provide women refugees with opportunities to assume new roles. It gives these refugee women the potential to improve their well-being and self-confidence (Jabbar & Zaza, 2016). However, the situation around refugees maintaining a career is still complex (Grzymala-Kazlowska & Phillimore, 2018). There are a number of obstacles in terms of structural barriers for being eligible for employment but also learning to communicate in the new context. In a study of women refugees in Australia, Watkins, Husna, and Richters (2012) describe language difficulties as the primary issue affecting the refugees' well-being. The transitional role of first being a teacher in the home country to being a learner in a new country and finally proceeding with professional life in the new country is indeed challenging.

The main purpose of the research is to investigate the mobile literacy of Syrian refugee women teachers participating in a vocational training program in Lebanon and Sweden. We address two research questions.

(1) What Mobile Assisted Language Learning (MALL) tools do Arabic speaking women refugee teachers use?

(2) How is mobile technology used as a tool to become included in a new society?

2. Theoretical framework

Mobile language learning enables learner-centered and ubiquitous learning characterized by interrupted, sporadic activities whenever there is an opportunity for it (Burston, 2015; Kukulska-Hulme, 2007). Mobile technologies support informal mobile language learning (Hager & Halliday, 2006). In other words, learning is taking place where it was not planned or intended as learning activities, which is what happens in everyday life in activities not traditionally designed as learning events. In line with autonomous learning, such self-regulation implies that learners are "active participants in their own learning process" (Zimmerman, 1989, p. 329).

The concept of Mobile Human Computer Interaction (MHCI) (Martiz & Recker, 2019) is considering the relationship between people, mobile computer systems, and their application on a daily basis. Martiz and Recker (2019) developed a framework to examine mobile phone appropriation based on MHCI, defining appropriation as "exploring, adapting, and adopting new uses for features in a technology, going beyond its intended regular use" (p. 16).

3. Methods

A qualitative method approach was applied with interviews and an analysis of MALL apps. Through teacher training centers for newly arrived migrants, all in all 20 Syrian refugee women teachers gave their consent to participate in interviews, ten teachers in each respective country. Face-to-face interviews were conducted in the respondents' mother tongue, Arabic, and subsequently translated to English for analysis with the research team. All interviews were audio-recorded and transcribed verbatim. The research team used Google Drive as a shared space and Skype for collaboration between Gothenburg and Beirut. Studying the professional situation of refugee women teachers in these two particular countries displays the situation in two countries which have both accepted a large number of Syrian refugees during the past few years, however, geographically, being far apart.

4. Analysis and results

Our results show that the respondents are quite active in terms of incorporating online tools in formal and informal learning to obtain their goal of proceeding with their professions as teachers in the new country. They all had a smartphone that was used actively; primarily social media for staying connected with friends and family but also for watching videos, surfing the web, and translating.

In terms of MALL, all respondents apart from one had used the phone to learn a new language. The respondents suggested 19 different MALL resources and apps distributed over 37 responses (see Table 1): MALL apps (22%), translation services (54%), video (16%), such as YouTube and TED talks, and other (8%). This is in line with Rosell-Aguilar (2017), suggesting that social media apps, dictionary apps, and translation apps are used for language learning together with MALL apps. The respondents were willing to use MALL apps for language learning, although our studies show that there were obstacles in terms of usability (Al-Sabbagh, Bradley, & Bartram, 2019) and limitations in these apps in terms of both language learning, pedagogy, user experience, and technology (Bartram et al., 2018).

Table 1. Resources and apps mentioned in the 37 responses by the respondents

Categorization of resources and apps	Resources and apps mentioned	Number of responses
Apps for language learning	Duolinguo, Memorize, Sayhej, Harvard University app for learning English, Språkplay, Melody, The American English Application, English with Disbeta	8
Apps used for but not created for language learning	Youtube, TED talks	6
Dictionaries and translation apps	Google translate, Lexin, Translator, Translate application, Dictionary	20
Surfing the internet	Swedish web, Swedish text, Google search for new teaching strategies and activities	3
Total		37

Moreover, the results displayed a group of self-directed learners in the new country, which was quite a transition from the teaching role in their home country. This transformation requires efforts to proceed, where an app serves as a tool to engage in formal as well as informal learning. As a consequence of migrating, teachers needed to orientate themselves in terms of practical issues where language learning skills play an important role to be included in the new society and for their career. In the process of continuing their careers in a new environment, the respondents were exploring and adopting uses of technology beyond the intended use (Martiz & Recker, 2019).

5. Conclusion

The overall results show that all Syrian refugee women teachers have used digital technology in terms of mobile applications in their own teaching and learning process. In addition, all of them have utilized different digital tools in their teaching sessions and are in the process of developing strategies for being autonomous learners in their vocational training. Most of them have shown that the training programs they have joined in Sweden or Lebanon are beneficial in strengthening and developing their teaching and learning skills as well as their language learning competency. All but one have used different language learning resources to make their aptitudes much more compatible. Mobile learning offered continuous professional development and additional training by using mobile applications that enhance the teaching and learning process and the use of MALL allowed these women to widen their scope and feel more confident using languages other than Arabic.

References

Al-Sabbagh, K., Bradley, L., & Bartram, L. (2019). Usability testing of mobile language learning applications for Arabic speaking migrants. *Journal of the European Confederation of Language Centres in Higher Education, 9*(1), 71-95. https://doi.org/10.1515/cercles-2019-0004

Bartram, L., Bradley, L., & Al-Sabbagh, K. (2018). Mobile learning with Arabic speakers in Sweden. In Proceedings of the Gulf Comparative Education Symposium (GCES) in Ras Al Khaimah, UAE, 5 – 11 April, 2018, 97-110. http://gces.ae/publications/

Bradley, L., Berbyuk Lindström, N., & Sofkova Hashemi, S. (2017). Integration and language learning of newly arrived migrants using mobile technology. *Journal of Interactive Media in Education, 2017*(1), Art. 3, 1-9. https://doi.org/10.5334/jime.434

Burston, J. (2015). Twenty years of MALL project implementation: a meta-analysis of learning outcomes. *ReCALL, 27*(1), 4-20. https://doi.org/10.1017/s0958344014000159

Grzymala-Kazlowska, A., & Phillimore, J. (2018). Introduction: rethinking integration. New perspectives on adaptation and settlement in the era of super-diversity. *Journal of Ethnic and Migration Studies, 44*(2), 179-196. https://doi.org/10.1080/1369183x.2017.1341706

Hager, P., & Halliday, J. (2006). *Recovering informal learning: wisdom, judgment and community. Lifelong Learning Book Series* (vol. 7). Springer.

Jabbar, S., & Zaza, H. (2016). Evaluating a vocational training programme for women refugees at the Zaatari camp in Jordan: women empowerment: a journey and not an output. *International Journal of Adolescence and Youth, 21*(3), 304-319. https://doi.org/10.1080/02673843.2015.1077716

Kaufmann, K. (2018). Navigating a new life: Syrian refugees and their smartphones in Vienna. Information. *Communication & Society, 21*(6), 882-898. https://doi.org/10.1080/1369118x.2018.1437205

Krause, U. (2014). Analysis of empowerment of refugee women in camps and settlements. *Journal of Internal Displacement, 4*, 29-52.

Kukulska-Hulme, A. (2007). Mobile usability in educational contexts: what have we learnt? *The International Review of Research in Open and Distributed Learning, 8*(2). https://doi.org/10.19173/irrodl.v8i2.356

Martiz, G., & Recker, M. (2019). Mobile phone use for English language learning in a Dominican Republic university classroom: a qualitative inquiry. *Computer-Based Learning in Context, 1*(1), 14-27.

Rosell-Aguilar, F. (2017). State of the app: a taxonomy and framework for evaluating language learning mobile applications. *CALICO Journal, 34*(2), 243-258. https://doi.org/10.1558/cj.27623

Watkins, P., Husna, R., & Richters, J. (2012). 'I'm telling you ... the language barrier is the most, the biggest challenge': barriers to education among Karen refugee women in Australia. *Australian Journal of Education, 56*(2): 126-141. https://doi.org/10.1177/000494411205600203

Zimmerman, B. (1989). A social-cognitive view of academic self-regulation. *Journal of Educational Psychology, 81*(3), 329-339. https://doi.org/10.1037/0022-0663.81.3.329

Negotiating for meaning in interaction: differences between virtual exchanges and regular online activities

Laia Canals[1]

Abstract. The present research explores the interactional nature of oral tasks carried out in two types of learner dyads in terms of their likelihood to foster negotiation for meaning during Language Related Episodes (LREs). Quantitative data analyses reveal how learners in same L1 dyads, Spanish English as a Foreign Language (EFL) learners, and in different L1 dyads, Canadian learners of Spanish and Spanish learners of English participating in a virtual exchange, modify their speech using negotiations and clarifications to make it comprehensible to their interlocutors. Eighteen different L1 dyads of university learners doing a virtual exchange (Canada-Spain) and eighteen dyads of Spanish-speakers learning English at the Spanish university carried out three oral communicative tasks online following the same procedures. Data were transcribed, LREs were identified, quantified for each dyad, and analyzed to determine their characteristics in terms of types of triggers, modified output, and type of feedback provided. Initial findings point to substantial differences in meaning negotiation occurring during LREs in each group. Different-L1 dyads exhibit more clarifications, meaning negotiation, and provide more feedback, which leads to higher amounts of comprehensible and modified output than learners in same L1 dyads.

Keywords: language related episodes, SCMC, oral interaction, meaning negotiation.

1. Introduction

Studies on Synchronous Computer-Mediated Communication (SCMC) have used the interactionist paradigm to prove the role that negotiation of meaning in learner-to-learner interaction activities play in L2 development (Loewen & Isbell, 2017). Meaning negotiation episodes allow for comprehensible input,

---

1. Universitat Oberta de Catalunya (UOC), Barcelona, Spain; ecanalsf@uoc.edu; https://orcid.org/0000-0002-9605-012X

How to cite this article: Canals, L. (2019). Negotiating for meaning in interaction: differences between virtual exchanges and regular online activities. In F. Meunier, J. Van de Vyver, L. Bradley & S. Thouësny (Eds), *CALL and complexity – short papers from EUROCALL 2019* (pp. 63-68). Research-publishing.net. https://doi.org/10.14705/rpnet.2019.38.987

corrective feedback, and modified output to occur, which direct learners' attention to form and are beneficial for L2 development. In addition, research on SCMC has increasingly focused on the importance of voice-based SCMC modalities to develop oral communication skills in interactive tasks conducted via videoconferencing as part of Virtual Exchanges (VE). This study determines the ability of oral collaborative interactive tasks carried out as part of VE to promote negotiation of meaning in learner-to-learner interactions between different L1 dyads (Canadian learners and Spanish learners' dyads) and compares that with interactions between same-L1 dyads (Spanish EFL learners carrying out the tasks in English).

The aim of the present research is to examine learner-to-learner interactions in order to characterize the LREs they produce. LRE sequences consist of focus-on-form episodes in meaning-focused interactive tasks triggered by a communication breakdown which involves meaning negotiation (Swain & Lapkin, 1995), including feedback and modified output.

The present research sets out to answer the following research questions.

- What are the characteristics of the LREs produced in each group (different L1 versus same L1 dyads) in terms of type of triggers (lexical, phonetic, and morphosyntactic)?

- Which LREs lead to more meaning negotiation, modified output, and feedback?

- What type of feedback is provided, and which type leads to more modified output and gets more noticed?

2. Participants and procedures

Seventy-two language learners at two universities, one in Canada and one in Spain, were divided into two groups. The first 36 participants took part in a virtual exchange where learners were paired up with a proficient speaker of the target language they were learning and carried out three oral communicative tasks using a videoconferencing tool. The other 36 participants, Spanish-speakers learning English at the Spanish university, carried out the same oral communicative tasks in English and online following the same procedures. The tasks consisted of three two-way open-ended communicative tasks which involved information exchange, decision-making, and comparison and analysis of information. The sessions were recorded and yielded 108 oral tasks (70 hours). Seven hundred and ninety-three LREs were identified, transcribed, and coded according to their length, dyad type, trigger type, amount and type of feedback, modified output, meaning negotiation, and resolution.

3. Results

Table 1 below displays that 36 dyads produced 793 LREs. Lexical triggers fostered more LREs regardless of the dyad type (53% and 64%), followed by global-misunderstanding triggers in the case of the same-L1 group (34%) and morphosyntactic ones (20%) in the case of the different-L1 group. However, out of the 54 interactive tasks carried out between same L1 dyads, 37 failed to produce any LREs. If we compare the amount of LREs produced overall, we observe that only 4% (N=32) are produced by learners in same L1 dyads. Within the same L1 group, we can observe how some triggers produced very few LREs: one phonetic trigger and four morphosyntactic ones. This made the comparison between dyads extremely challenging and hindered its generalizability. Therefore, this paper will only focus on the characteristics of dyads within the different L1 group.

Table 1. Trigger types in same L1 versus different L1 dyads

	Same L1 dyads		Different L1 dyads	
LRE triggers	N	%	N	%
Lexical	18	56	484	64
Phonetic	1	3	87	11
Morphosyntactic	4	12	155	20
Global	11	34	79	10
Total	32	4% of the total LREs	761	96% of the total LREs
Total LREs	793			

Table 2 displays the LREs which fostered more feedback, modified output, meaning negotiation, and resolutions. We observe that morphosyntactic triggers produced feedback at the highest rate (.64), followed by phonetic ones (.39). The LREs which have a phonetic trigger exhibited the highest rates of modified output (.83), followed closely by morphosyntactic (.75) ones and global (.70) ones. Regarding meaning negotiation, it was global misunderstandings which exhibit the highest rates (.65). Finally, we find high resolution rates for most LREs: phonetic (.95), morphosyntactic (.94) and lexical ones (.89).

Table 2. Instances of negotiation, modified output, feedback, and resolutions in different L1 dyads

	Lexical		Phonetic		Morphosyntactic		Global		Overall	
	Mean	SD	Mean	SD	Mean	SD	Mean	SD	Mean	SD
Feedback	0.18	0.39	0.39	0.49	0.64	0.48	0.04	0.21	0.30	0.46
Modified Output	0.69	0.46	0.83	0.38	0.75	0.44	0.70	0.47	0.72	0.45
Negotiation	0.27	0.45	0.20	0.40	0.20	0.40	0.65	0.49	0.26	0.44
Resolutions	0.89	0.31	0.95	0.21	0.94	0.23	0.83	0.39	0.91	0.29

When examining the types of feedback produced, in Table 3 we can observe that the great majority of the feedback learners provided to their partners were in the form of explicit corrections (N=192). Explicit corrections were also the ones which were more noticed (N=186) along with elicitations, which were noticed in more than half the time. Recasts, however, in two out of three cases got mostly ignored or not understood. Whenever they got noticed, elicitations lead to modified output at higher rates (75%) than any other feedback type. Recasts lead to modified output on two out of five occasions and explicit corrections, although they got more noticed, only lead to modified output in 24% of occasions.

Table 3. Feedback type, feedback effectiveness and modified output in different L1 dyads

	Recast	Corrections	Elicitation
	N	N	N
Ignored/unnoticed	9	6	3
Meaning understood	5	186	4
Meaning not understood	1	0	0
Total	15 (7%)	192 (90%)	7 (3%)
Lead to modified output	2 (40%)	45 (24%)	3 (75%)

4. Discussion and conclusions

The first finding underscores the fact that interactions between different L1 dyads taking part in a VE foster more meaning negotiation than interactions between same L1 dyads carrying out similar tasks, which is consistent with other findings (Bueno-Alastuey, 2013). Although earlier studies indicated that different LRE triggers showed similar numbers of instances of negotiation and feedback (Kenning, 2010), the current paper has observed a clear tendency for global triggers to produce more meaning negotiation and phonetic ones to lead to more modified output. This is consistent with findings by Lyster (2001) and with Bueno Alastuey (2011) who also found more modified output following phonetic triggers. On the other hand, morphosyntactic triggers led to more feedback, in the shape of explicit corrections which get more noticed, also observed by Ellis, Loewen, and Erlam (2006).

This study contributes to the growing body of research underscoring the benefits of learner-to-learner interaction in voice-based SCMC for L2 development. The ability to direct learners' attention to linguistic elements (focus-on-form) in meaning-related tasks, pivotal for the development of the target language, can be observed in the LREs allowing for comprehensible input, corrective feedback, and modified output to occur.

5. Acknowledgments

I would like to express my gratitude to Cristina Ráfales and her students at Dalhousie University and my students at Universitat Oberta de Catalunya for agreeing to participate in this research.

References

Bueno Alastuey, M. C. (2011). Perceived benefits and drawbacks of synchronous voice-based computer-mediated communication in the foreign language classroom. *Computer Assisted Language Learning, 24*(5), 419-432. https://doi.org/10.1080/09588221.2011.574639

Bueno-Alastuey, M. C. (2013). Interactional feedback in synchronous voice-based computer mediated communication: Effect of dyad. *System, 41*(3), 543-559. https://doi.org/10.1016/j.system.2013.05.005

Ellis, R., Loewen, S., & Erlam, R. (2006). Implicit and explicit corrective feedback and the acquisition of L2 grammar. *Studies in Second Language Acquisition, 28*(2), 339-368. https://doi.org/10.1017/s0272263106060141

Kenning, M. (2010). Collaborative scaffolding in online task-based voice interactions between advanced learners. *ReCALL, 22*(2), 135-151. https://doi.org/10.1017/s0958344010000042

Loewen, S., & Isbell, D. R. (2017). Pronunciation in face-to-face and audio-only synchronous computer-mediated learner interactions. *Studies in Second Language Acquisition, 39*(2), 225-256. https://doi.org/10.1017/s0272263116000449

Lyster, R. (2001). Negotiation of form, recasts, and explicit correction in relation to error types and learner repair in immersion classrooms. *Language Learning, 48*(2), 183-218. https://doi.org/10.1111/1467-9922.00039

Swain, M., & Lapkin, S. (1995). Problems in output and the cognitive processes they generate: a step towards second language learning. *Applied linguistics*, *16*(3), 371-391. https://doi.org/10.1093/applin/16.3.371

■ UCLouvain

Shouting in space: promoting oral reading fluency with Spaceteam ESL

Walcir Cardoso[1], David Waddington[2], Enos Kiforo[3], and Anne-Marie Sénécal[4]

Abstract. This study examined whether the pedagogical use of Spaceteam ESL (English as a Second Language), a digital *shouting* game, could contribute to the development of Oral Reading Fluency (ORF) among 71 English students in secondary schools in Mombasa, Kenya. Following a mixed-methods approach for data collection and analysis, we pre- and post-tested the participants on their ability to read aloud efficiently (*speed*) and accurately (*accuracy*) in three tasks: (1) phrases extracted from the game; (2) phrases not related to the game; and (3) an anecdote. Our findings indicate that participants who played Spaceteam ESL improved their ORF on all measures of *speed*, but no significant differences were observed in terms of *accuracy*. Overall, these findings corroborate our hypothesis that some of the affordances of Spaceteam ESL (e.g. speed reading) would contribute to the development of some aspects of ORF.

Keywords: Spaceteam ESL, digital game, oral reading fluency.

1. Introduction

For the development of reading fluency, Nation (2009) recommends that learners engage in proficiency-appropriate 'speed reading' activities, feel motivated to read, read intensively, and engage in activities involving other skills (e.g. speaking). However, because of the constraints that afflict the second language (L2) classroom (e.g. lack of time, focus on the teaching of new language features), these

---

1. Concordia University, CSLP, Montreal, Canada; walcir.cardoso@concordia.ca; https://orcid.org/0000-0001-6376-185X
2. Concordia University, CSLP, Montreal, Canada; david.waddington@concordia.ca; https://orcid.org/0000-0001-7091-7824
3. Aga Khan Academy, CSLP, Montreal, Canada; enos.kiforo@agakhanacademies.org; https://orcid.org/0000-0002-5337-8926
4. Concordia University, CSLP, Montreal, Canada; am.senecal@icloud.com; https://orcid.org/0000-0001-8725-0413

How to cite this article: Cardoso, W., Waddington, D., Kiforo, E., & Sénécal, A.-M. (2019). Shouting in space: promoting oral reading fluency with Spaceteam ESL. In F. Meunier, J. Van de Vyver, L. Bradley & S. Thouësny (Eds), *CALL and complexity – short papers from EUROCALL 2019* (pp. 69-74). Research-publishing.net. https://doi.org/10.14705/rpnet.2019.38.988

recommendations are difficult to pursue. One way of mitigating these limitations is via out-of-class learning. Digital games such as Spaceteam ESL have the potential to address these constraints and, at the same time, promote all of Nation's (2009) recommendations.

Spaceteam ESL (Waddington & Cardoso, 2017) is a free multiplayer and team-building digital *shouting* game for mobile devices in which players pilot a spaceship by controlling a panel with knobs and dials listed with English words (organized by levels, based on word frequency and pronunciation complexity). To keep the spaceship afloat, players must complete tasks by giving (speaking) and receiving (listening) *time-sensitive* orders that require the manipulation of the knobs and dials on their screen (e.g. 'activate funny chicken', requiring team members to press the 'funny chicken' button). If successful, each team continues to the next level of increasingly difficult gameplay (see Grimshaw & Cardoso, 2018, or visit spaceteamesl.ca for details). Figure 1 illustrates the game's interface involving two players.

Figure 1. Spaceteam ESL: two players

One of the interesting affordances of Spaceteam ESL is that it addresses Nation's (2009) four recommendations to promote reading fluency. In addition, it encourages the practice of one type of reading fluency, assumed to contribute to text comprehension: ORF, or one's ability to read aloud connected text *quickly* and *accurately* (Rasplica & Cummings, 2013), without a concerted cognitive effort. We hypothesized that Spaceteam ESL could contribute to the development of this type of oral fluency and, accordingly, asked the following question: can Spaceteam ESL contribute to the development of ORF in terms of *speed* and *accuracy*?

This study is part of a larger project financed by the Social Sciences and Humanities Research Council of Canada, which aims to improve teaching and learning through educational technology in sub-Saharan Africa.

2. Method

To investigate participants' improvement in oral/read-aloud fluency in terms of *speed* and *accuracy*, a mixed-methods approach to data collection and analysis was adopted consisting of both quantitative (using a pre-/post-test design to examine participants' ORF development in terms of speed and accuracy) and qualitative data (focus group).

Adolescent intermediate-level English learners (N=71) from three public schools in Mombasa (Kenya) were recruited to play Spaceteam ESL for a period of three weeks (three weekly sessions, each lasting approximately 45 minutes), as part of after-class extracurricular activities. Participants were pre-tested (audio recorded) on their ability to efficiently and accurately read aloud the following three tasks: ten phrases extracted from the game (n=38 morphemes, including free and bound forms), ten equivalent phrases not related to the game (n=112), and one 128-word anecdote (n=157). While *speed* was calculated in seconds using Audacity, *accuracy* was measured via a computation of the correct words read aloud in each task. At the end of the experiment, learners were post-tested using the same instruments (modified to avoid testing effects) and participated in focus group discussions that aimed to probe their perceptions of the experience.

3. Results

Using paired-samples t-tests, the participants' performances in read-aloud speed and accuracy before (pre-test) and after playing Spaceteam ESL (post-test) were analyzed for three tasks: ten phrases extracted from the game, ten equivalent phrases not related to the game, and one anecdote. The results are summarized in Table 1 below.

In terms of *speed*, participants read aloud Task 1 at a faster speed after playing Spaceteam ESL ($M=17.14$, $SD=3.52$) as opposed to before playing the game

($M=19.46$, $SD=3.66$). This difference, 2.32, BCa *95%* CI [1.55, 3.08], was significant, $t(70)=6.03$, $p<.001$, and represented an effect of $d=0.65$.

Relatively similar results were observed for Task 2, wherein participants read the target phrases at a faster speed after playing Spaceteam ESL ($M=40.17$, $SD=10.21$) than on the pre-test ($M=44.03$, $SD=9.18$). This difference, 3.85, BCa *95%* CI [2.51, 5.20], was once again significant, $t(70)=5.73$, $p<.001$, and represented an effect of $d=0.40$.

Finally, for Task 3, participants also read the 157-word passage at a faster speed after playing Spaceteam ESL ($M=54.92$, $SD=11.06$) than what was observed on the pre-test ($M=60.96$, $SD=11.34$). This difference, 6.05, BCa *95%* CI [4.25, 7.85], was significant, $t(70)=6.69$, $p<.001$, and represented an effect of $d=0.54$. Overall, these results indicate that participants improved their speed in all tasks after the treatment period.

Table 1. Comparison of speed and accuracy rates by task

Task		Speed (in seconds)				$p<$	Accuracy (morpheme)				$p=$
		Pre-test		Post-test			Pre-test		Post-test		
	N	M	SD	M	SD		M	SD	M	SD	
1	71	19.46	3.66	17.14	3.52	.001	36.31/38	1.72	36.62/38	1.65	.101
2	71	44.03	9.18	40.17	10.21	.001	106.54/112	5.38	106.27/112	6.41	.525
3	71	60.96	11.34	54.92	11.06	.001	153.34/157	3.86	155.55/157	4.30	.670

These findings are corroborated by the participants' statements during the focus group discussions, in which they reported that playing Spaceteam ESL helped improve their oral fluency: "it makes your brain to be faster, it makes you speak faster, it makes you read more fast than usual" and "[it helped me] getting quick in English and reading".

Regarding *accuracy*, paired-samples t-tests showed no significant differences from pre- to post-test in any of the tasks: $t(70)=-1.66$, $p=.101$ for Task 1; $t(70)=0.64$, $p=.525$ for Task 2; and $t(70)=-0.43$, $p=.670$ for Task 3. These results suggest that the proposed game-based pedagogy had no effect on improving the participants' ORF performance in terms of accuracy.

A thematic analysis of the qualitative data did not yield any obvious statements reflecting the game's potential to improve accuracy, thus validating the statistical results.

4. Discussion and conclusion

The goal of this study was to examine the effects of Spaceteam ESL on the development of ORF in terms of *speed* and *accuracy* – two measures of oral fluency (Rasplica & Cummings, 2013). Our findings suggest that while speed was significantly affected by gameplay, accuracy was not.

As hypothesized, the improvements observed in *speed* can be attributed to one of the affordances of Spaceteam ESL, a game that capitalizes on efficiency (fast speaking, reading, and listening) for successful gameplay. Interestingly, efficiency is the dominant feature in Nation's (2009) recommendations for fluency development. According to the author, to achieve fluency, L2 students should be involved in activities such as speed reading practice, repeated reading, paired reading, and scanning; they should also read a lot and feel motivated to read. We believe that Spaceteam ESL accomplishes all of these goals, *mutatis mutandis*.

The non-significant results involving accuracy can be explained by our (based on Nation's 2009) assumption that for fluency development, students should engage with "material that is very familiar and contains no unknown language features" (p. 8). Because students already knew the intricacies of the grapheme-to-phoneme rules of English orthography (a condition to participate in the study), their level of reading accuracy was already highly developed. This is confirmed by the high values observed on the pre-test in all accuracy tasks (e.g. 36.1/38 for Task 1 and 106.54/112 for Task 2), indicating a ceiling effect.

Despite these encouraging results, there are many limitations that need to be acknowledged and, accordingly, addressed in further investigations. The most serious one is the lack of a control group to be used as a benchmark to reliably measure the effects of gameplay on ORF development. Another limitation relates to the short duration of the experiment.

5. Acknowledgments

Asante sana to the Kenyan collaborators and their schools for their invaluable support: Lina Anyango (Changamwe), Rose Iminza (Aga Khan), Dickson Karanja (Sacred Heart), and Rosemary Waga (Aga Khan). This project was financed by the Social Sciences and Humanities Research Council of Canada.

References

Grimshaw, J., & Cardoso, W. (2018). Activate space rats! Fluency development in a mobile game-assisted environment. *Language Learning and Technology, 22*(3), 159-175. https://www.lltjournal.org/item/3086

Nation, I. (2009). *Teaching ESL/EFL reading and writing*. Routledge.

Rasplica, C., & Cummings, K. (2013). Oral reading fluency. https://council-for-learning-disabilities.org/what-is-oral-reading-fluency-verbal-reading-proficiency

Waddington, D., & Cardoso, W. (2017). Spaceteam ESL [software]. http://spaceteamesl.ca

Data-driven learning in ESP university settings in Romania: multiple corpus consultation approaches for academic writing support

Mădălina Chitez[1] and Loredana Bercuci[2]

Abstract. Corpora are valuable technology-supported learning resources to be used by autonomous language learners or during teacher-guided lessons. This study explores the potential of corpus consultation approaches for the improvement of English for Specific Purposes (ESP) students' academic writing skills. We investigated the effects of three types of Data-Driven Learning (DDL) activities in a sample group of 29 first-year and second-year students majoring in Geography for Tourism at a Romanian university, consisting of writing tasks supported by: a Learner Corpus (LC), a Native-Speaker Corpus (NSC), and a Web-based Corpus (WBC). The research methodology involves the combination of quantitative and qualitative data, extracted from pre- and post-intervention corpus analyses, with the results of a learner-satisfaction questionnaire. The findings indicate a significant differentiation in the complexity of the lexico-grammatical features used by learners in consequent intervention stages and a better integration of L2-related academic writing strategies into their written productions. The study yields first conclusions on the integration of computer-processed language databases in DDL strategies for ESP learners in the Romanian university context.

Keywords: academic writing, corpus consultation, learner corpus, expert corpus, Romanian academic writing, DDL, English for specific purposes, Romanian learner corpus.

---

1. West University of Timișoara, Timișoara, Romania; madalina.chitez@e-uvt.ro
2. West University of Timișoara, Timișoara, Romania; loredana.bercuci@e-uvt.ro

How to cite this article: Chitez, M., & Bercuci, L. (2019). Data-driven learning in ESP university settings in Romania: multiple corpus consultation approaches for academic writing support. In F. Meunier, J. Van de Vyver, L. Bradley & S. Thouësny (Eds), *CALL and complexity – short papers from EUROCALL 2019* (pp. 75-81). Research-publishing.net. https://doi.org/10.14705/rpnet.2019.38.989

© 2019 Mădălina Chitez and Loredana Bercuci (CC BY) 75

1. Introduction

Courses in ESP at the undergraduate level in Romania often have the aim of preparing students for their future profession, with the focus being on lexis and less frequently on writing. Typical ESP activities train students for a variety of real-life situations but often do not include academic communication and writing. Moreover, undergraduate students themselves are less motivated to become skilled in academic writing, perceiving it as difficult and unimportant for their careers. In reality, however, many Romanian undergraduate students pursue a master's degree, sometimes in English, and have trouble managing Anglo-American academic writing genre norms. The aim of this paper is to investigate whether certain DDL strategies (Boulton, 2017; Gilquin & Granger, 2010), such as multiple corpus consultation, can be used to teach lexis and academic writing concurrently.

2. Method

The present study investigates the outcome of a pedagogical experiment in which course participants used three types of corpus-based DDL activities to (1) identify challenges related to common lexis use, discipline-specific jargon, and academic writing norms, and (2) find suitable solutions for their own academic writing difficulties. The experiment was conducted at a Romanian university, as part of an ESP course, at a geography department. The participants were 19 first-year (Common European Framework of Reference for languages – CEFR – level B1) and ten second-year (CEFR level B2) undergraduate students specializing in Geography for Tourism. The L1 of all participants is Romanian.

Each student was first asked to produce a short research essay on a set topic. The essays were compiled into a learner corpus, TourLRN. In the first session thereafter, the students were asked to compare, using LancsBox (Brezina, Timperley, & McEnery, 2018), the most frequent words used in their texts to the LOCNESS corpus, an English NSC. They identified the following words as subject to overuse: *the, of, that, you, people*. The students were then asked to rephrase parts of their essays, as much as possible, to use the identified words less.

In the second session, the students were introduced to the British National Corpus (BNC) and asked to select two problematic words of phrases in their texts written in the first session. Each student used the BNC to discover collocations containing the selected words, which were largely non-specialized terms. The students were asked to include the collocations in their texts (Figure 1).

Figure 1. Methodology of corpus consultation intervention

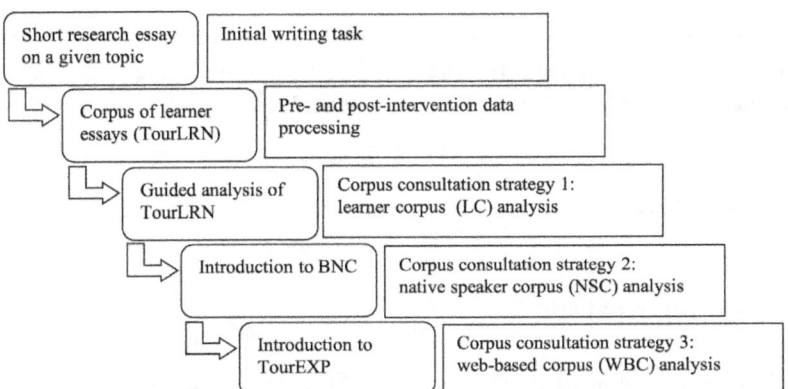

In the third session, the students used LancsBox (Brezina et al., 2018) to analyse an expert corpus, TourEXP, compiled by the researchers' team for the present study. The students were invited to identify discipline-specific terms and ngrams/collocates, as well as discipline-specific genre markers. They were asked to include at least three terms and four genre markers in their texts. The students were also introduced to the Whelk function in LancsBox and were encouraged to become familiar with the context of use for their chosen terms/phrases.

In all three sessions, students submitted un-revised versions of their texts and the teacher only pointed out group mistakes or linguistic inaccuracy patterns (e.g. overuse of *the*).

3. Data

3.1. Self-compiled corpora

For this study, we compiled two corpora: TourEXP and TourLRN. TourEXP is a web-based expert corpus made up of 155,521 tokens and was used solely for the purpose of in-class corpus consultation by the students. TourLRN is a learner corpus consisting of three sub-corpora: Batch 1 (pre-intervention texts, 8,176 tokens), Batch 2 (post-intervention texts, after the first corpus consultation session, 7,105 tokens), and Batch 3 (post-intervention texts, after the second corpus consultation session, 8,371 tokens). We performed a contrastive corpus analysis of the three versions of our students' texts.

3.2. Online questionnaire

At the end of the intervention study, the students were asked to fill in an online questionnaire in Romanian to gauge their perception of the utility of DDL techniques used in class. The questionnaire had 22 respondents.

4. Analysis

4.1. Corpus analysis

Not all students submitted all three versions of the essays. For the sake of accuracy, we compared the essays in three stages, namely Analysis 1 (A1): Batch 1 to Batch 2 (18x2 essays), Analysis 2 (A2): Batch 2 to Batch 3 (18x2 essays), and Analysis 3 (A3): Batch 2 to Batch 3 (23x2 essays).

4.1.1. Basic frequencies

As the teacher's personal observation was that the texts improved, in their last version, we looked at the fluctuation of highly frequent tokens in the students' ESP academic writing at different intervention stages (Figure 2).

Figure 2. Fluctuation of most frequent tokens form one corpus consultation stage to another

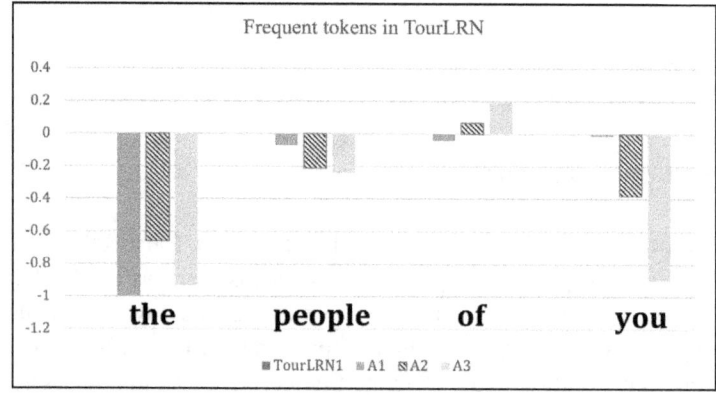

We noticed a decrease in the use of the definite article *the* (-1%) after the first corpus consultation exercise, then a slight increase (+ 0.34%) followed by a decrease in

Batch 3. A similar overall decrease pattern is noticed for *people* and *you*. On the other hand, students tended to use the preposition *of* more often than in their initial texts (TourLRN1) after being exposed to corpus data.

4.1.2. Ngram oscillation

We were also interested to see whether the discipline-specific lexical-grammatical constructions, i.e. collocations, were influenced by the use of corpora. Indeed, several typical collocations specific of the tourism sector were introduced in Batch 2 (*the tourism industry*) or Batch 3 (*in the tourism sector, travel insurance covers*). At the same time, several register makers oscillated toward formality: a decrease in the use of *a lot of* (by 0.05%), and disappearance, in Batch 3, of *a lot of people*, *a lot of things*. Several academic writing formulaic sequences also seemed to change the pattern of use from one text batch to another: *on the other hand* increased (by 0.2%) whereas *in conclusion* decreased (by 0.06%). However, the use of comparative transitions appeared to be challenging since appropriate rhetorical use was only observed in Batch 3 in a very limited number of texts.

Since the corpus size was rather small and created as a teaching exercise, we were content that most of our observations (correct use of *the*, diversification of the tourism terminology, or revision of informal style) were confirmed by absolute numbers. Percentages are used as indicators of use patterns.

4.2. Questionnaire analysis

Figure 3. Questionnaire results – usefulness of corpora for academic writing

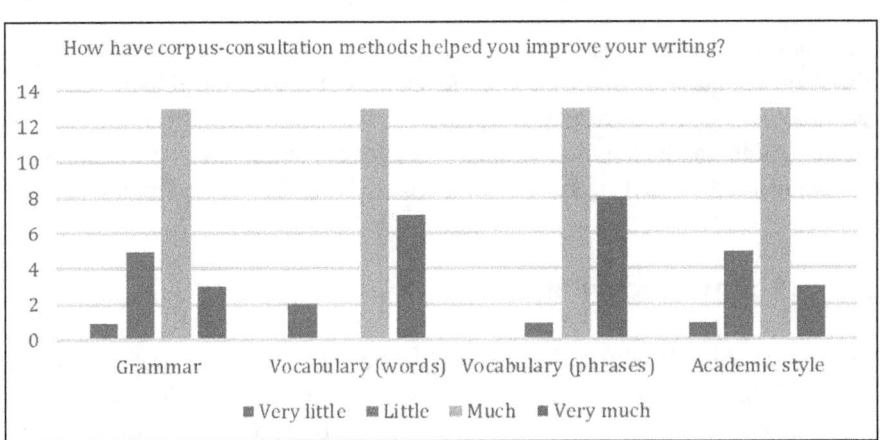

The questionnaire included questions such as: 'do you know what a corpus is?', 'which of the following types of corpora did you find most useful?', and 'how have the corpus-consultation methods helped you improve your writing?' (see Figure 3 above).

The results of the questionnaire were encouraging: all in all, all students admitted to have received information about the use of corpora for the first time during the evaluated course, they also considered the various methods of corpus consultation useful and they unanimously expressed their desire to learn more about corpora.

5. Discussion and conclusions

Although quite experimental in design, the study was able to pinpoint areas of academic writing which can be supported by corpus linguistics in ESP courses. First, typical L1-L2 grammatical interference tendencies, such as overuse of the definite article *the* (also confirmed by Chitez, 2014) can be corrected by corpus consultation guided exercises, which involve comparison of students' own writing with expert writing. The tendency toward informality in ESP academic writing, observed in TourLRN, can also be corrected during corpus consultation training. ESP phraseology is imported and diversified as well at the end of all three corpus consultation stages. As for register appropriateness, we noticed an improvement at the ngram level, as typical academic writing markers were not only more frequently used but also better integrated in text. Due to the small size of the corpus, some of the fluctuations mentioned above are difficult to assess. However, modifying written assignments with the help of corpora was perceived as a positive experience by all the students in the intervention.

Our study shows that corpus consultation methods may be an effective way of stimulating inductive language (i.e. texts have been changed and improved according to observed corpus phenomena) and genre norm learning in ESP courses. Additionally, the motivational value for the students is confirmed by the questionnaire, thus offering encouraging prospects for further investigations.

6. Acknowledgments

The present paper is part of a larger study investigating the use of DDL in ESP, a part of which was presented at the British and American Studies International Conference, 29th Edition in Timisoara. The study is conducted in the framework of the project ROGER (https://roger.projects.uvt.ro/), in progress at the West University of Timisoara, Romania, and funded by the Swiss National Science Foundation (program PROMYS).

References

Boulton A. (2017). Data-driven learning and language pedagogy. In S. Thorne & S. May (Eds), *Language, education and technology. Encyclopedia of language and education* (3rd ed.). Springer.
Brezina, V., Timperley, M., & McEnery, T. (2018). #LancsBox v. 4.x [software]. http://corpora.lancs.ac.uk/lancsbox
Chitez, M. (2014). *Learner corpus profiles: the case of Romanian learner English*. Peter Lang.
Gilquin, G., & Granger, S. (2010). How can data-driven learning be used in language teaching? In A. O'Keeffe & M. McCarthy (Eds), *The Routledge handbook of corpus linguistics* (pp. 359-370). Routledge. https://doi.org/10.4324/9780203856949.ch26

Integrating a virtual reality application to simulate situated learning experiences in a foreign language course

Maria Christoforou[1], Eftychia Xerou[2], and Salomi Papadima-Sophocleous[3]

Abstract. Immersion through Virtual Reality (VR) gives the subjective impression that the learner has a realistic experience (Dede, 2009). The pedagogical potential of VR provides the means of enabling constructivist places of contextualised learning. This paper aims to examine the potential the VR application *Mondly* may have to maximise interactivity and aid learners in proactively experiencing empirical conversations that emulate authentic contexts. The research took place in an undergraduate course Italian I (A1, Common European Framework of Reference for languages), offered by the Cyprus University of Technology. The present study adopts a quasi-experimental design to evaluate the impact of *Mondly* on Italian learning. Digital material is incorporated into the lesson to promote contextualised learning. An experimental group is subjected to learning through *Mondly* whereas a control group is subjected to conventional lectures utilising the same material as the experimental group.

Keywords: immersion, virtual reality, Mondly, contextualised situated constructivist learning.

---

1. Cyprus University of Technology, Limassol, Cyprus; maria.christoforou@cut.ac.cy; https://orcid.org/0000-0001-7598-6159
2. Cyprus University of Technology, Limassol, Cyprus; eftychia.xerou@cut.ac.cy
3. Cyprus University of Technology, Limassol, Cyprus; salomi.papadima@cut.ac.cy; https://orcid.org/0000-0003-4444-4482

How to cite this article: Christoforou, M., Xerou, E., & Papadima-Sophocleous, S. (2019). Integrating a virtual reality application to simulate situated learning experiences in a foreign language course. In F. Meunier, J. Van de Vyver, L. Bradley & S. Thouësny (Eds), *CALL and complexity – short papers from EUROCALL 2019* (pp. 82-87). Research-publishing.net. https://doi.org/10.14705/rpnet.2019.38.990

1. Introduction

New and more sophisticated technologies have permeated education in the past two decades, gradually remodelling teaching and learning (Garrote, 2018). Schwienhorst (2002) has highlighted the change in the area of computer-assisted language learning, which draws upon the Internet as a system that provides multiple communication tools to ensure authentic contexts in the target language and its speakers.

The exponential growth of wireless communication and multimedia environments have employed the use of VR in order to promote authentic and immersive learning environments. As a result, we are now witnessing a new paradigm shift in learning, from teacher-centred to learner-centred, since learners are no longer passive recipients of information, but they actively participate in the learning process which promotes real-world-like audiovisual simulations and scenarios (Chung, 2012). Immersion in a digital environment and the experiential, learner-centred approach of virtual environments draws upon the theory of situated learning. Dede (2009) supports that situated learning in immersive interfaces can aid learners join authentic communities with real-world settings and virtual entities as well as experiencing real-world scenarios.

The social character of learning was first proposed by Lave and Wenger (1991). They supported the idea that learning is a social process during which learners co-construct knowledge within an authentic environment. Learning is a process of enculturation so activities should be framed within a social context in order to be meaningful and authentic for learners. In fact, immersive technologies provide opportunities for situated learning since the reality of the authentic context is enhanced without minimising the validity of what needs to be learned.

Concerning foreign language learning, simulating authentic contexts in a traditional classroom setting can be a difficult task for the teacher. Teacher-fronted activities do little to enhance the negotiation of meaning and discourse in the target language (Houston, 2006). Hence, this paper aims to challenge the teaching of a foreign language, promoting intercultural communicative competence with the presence of the target language context. It presents an example of virtual learning environment, through the VR application *Mondly*, in a foreign language (Italian) class in order to put learners in a situated learning environment as a way of increasing authenticity in their learning context through realistic scenarios. *Mondly* is a foreign language learning app which focuses on a more contextualised approach to teaching a foreign language.

2. Method

2.1. Participants

Eighteen university students between 17-25 years old participated in the study. The 18 participants were seven males and 11 females. Participants, coming from six different cities during the study, were studying in a public university in southern Europe. The participants came from six different fields of study and the majority, 15 out of 18, were in the senior year of their studies.

2.2. Mondly application

Mondly is a language learning application which is compatible with Samsung Gear VR (Figure 1). Users may select one of the various contexts available and interact with a pedagogical agent who helps and asks questions to guide the conversation into a specific context. Users may respond by selecting one of the two or three possible answers presented on chatbots and express the answers orally. When users find the correct answer, a green check appears over the transcription of what was said, otherwise another answer should be given. The application integrates speech recognition and it is available in 33 languages, with levels ranging from beginner to advanced.

Figure 1. Samsung Gear VR powered by Oculus: the VR headset used in the study

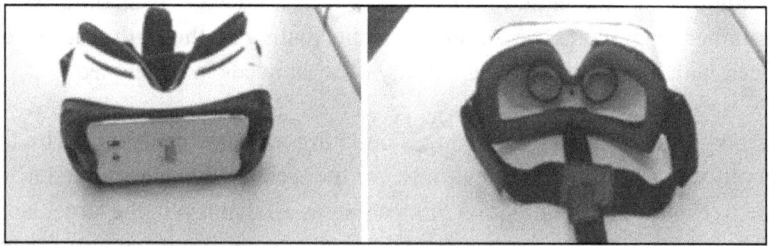

2.3. Research design and data collection

The present study adopts a quasi-experimental design to evaluate the impact of *Mondly* on Italian learning. The research data were collected in three days, in a total of six 45-min sessions of the lesson Italian I. Pre- and post-tests were conducted for the purposes of the research. The pre- and post-tests were the same in order to evaluate students' pre-knowledge and they were comprised of three different sections. In the first section, students completed six open questions of demographic data (name, age, department of study, interests, etc.). In the second section, students completed seven close questions and one open question regarding past experiences with VR software and hardware. In the third section, students had the opportunity to complete 14 multiple-choice questions based on the emerging situation they faced during the data collection through VR. For every one of the 14 multiple-choice questions, marks were given: zero for the wrong answer, one for the almost right answer, and two for the right answer. Students were divided into two groups: one experimental and one control group. In the experimental group, students worked individually on their pre-tests for 15 minutes, they experimented with the VR application for 15 minutes (in a total of three different days), and worked on their post-tests for 15 minutes, after their experience with the VR application and gear.

The students' experimentation with the VR application was divided in two different phases. During the first phase, the orientation phase, the students had the opportunity to test the equipment and their working state in the *Mondly* application. During the second phase, students experienced *Mondly*, and emerged into contextualised learning through the context of ordering at a restaurant, exchanging opinions about the food, drinking with the waitress, and meeting other guests of the restaurant. All of the research activities mentioned above were individually conducted, without any intervention from the instructor. In the control group, the students worked individually on their pre-tests and they were taught through a more traditional communicative method of teaching, including role play, in a 45-minute lesson session. They responded to questions and exercises involving the creation of dialogues and at the final stage, students worked individually on their post-tests.

3. Results and discussion

The present study adopted a quasi-experimental design to evaluate the impact of *Mondly* in an Italian class to promote contextualised learning. An experimental group was subjected to learning through *Mondly*, whereas a control group was subjected to conventional lectures utilising the same material as the experimental group. Both groups worked in the restaurant context.

An independent *t*-test was conducted to compare the performance of the control and the experimental group.

Table 1. Comparing the two groups' test means

Performance	Group	x	SD	T	p
Pre-test	Control	32.71	2.49	1.88	0.79
	Experimental	29.50	3.97		
Post-test	Control	32.42	3.10	2.39	0.030
	Experimental	28.90	2.92		

As we can see in Table 1, regarding the pre-test, the control group scored higher in comparison with the experimental group; the difference was not large enough to be statistically significant ($t=1.88$, $p=0.79$). Regarding the post-test group, as we can see, students in the control group scored higher than the students in the experimental group; the difference was statistically significant ($t=2.39$, $p=0.30$). The small student sample in both groups constitutes a limitation since a bigger sample of students is necessary to participate in the two groups in order to test whether the *Mondly* application helped simulate an authentic context. Furthermore, the in-class conduct of VR implementation displayed some impediments, such as student noise and the necessity to recharge the smart phone very frequently. The latter impediments hindered the normal flow of the lesson as well as speech recognition.

4. Conclusion

This paper described the implementation of the VR application *Mondly* for an Italian undergraduate course. Although the results showed that *Mondly* did not provide contextualised learning, it is suggested that a larger sample size would ensure better understanding and clearer and more accurate results. *Mondly* can also be used in other foreign language courses in order to gain a more complete perspective of the application. Finally, more contexts, i.e. being on a train or using a taxi, can be integrated as activities, since in our study we solely chose the restaurant setting. All the implications mentioned above ask for more extensive research in analysing the contextualised use of VR.

References

Chung, L. Y. (2012). Incorporating 3D-virtual reality into language learning. *International Journal of Digital Content Technology and its Applications, 6*(6), 249-255.

Dede, C. (2009). Immersive interfaces for engagement and learning. Science, *323*(5910), 66-69. https://doi.org/10.1126/science.1167311

Garrote, M. (2018). Instant-messaging for improving literacy and communication skills in FLT: students' evaluation. *The EuroCALL Review, 26*(2), 19-29. https://doi.org/10.4995/eurocall.2018.10373

Houston, T. (2006). Communication strategies in the foreign language classroom. *Applied Language Learning, 16*(2), 65-82.

Lave, J., & Wenger, E. (1991). *Situated learning: legitimate peripheral participation*. Cambridge University Press.

Schwienhorst, K. (2002). Why virtual, why environments? Implementing virtual reality concepts in computer-assisted language learning. *Simulation & Gaming, 33*(2), 196-209.

■ UCLouvain

Learners as teachers? An evaluation of peer interaction and correction in a German Language MOOC

Elisabeth Clifford[1], Christine Pleines[2], Hilary Thomas[3], and Susanne Winchester[4]

Abstract. The benefits of peer interaction, support, and feedback in Massive Open Online Courses (MOOCs) for Languages (LMOOCs) are well documented, but there has been little research on peer correction in MOOCs. Classroom-based research suggests that peer corrective feedback has significant potential for language development, but it also identifies a number of conditions for the feedback to be effective, notably a 'positive classroom atmosphere'; this may be hard to achieve on a MOOC, with its diverse cohort and large number of participants. Our mixed-method study reveals participants' conflicting expectations of learning from their peers on the one hand and actively contributing to their peers' learning on the other. Most participants believe they are not competent to provide helpful corrective feedback, and some think that the expectation to correct creates unwanted pressure and hinders communication. This paper encourages MOOC educators to address the challenge of creating a culture of learning through meaningful interaction whilst also finding ways of exploiting the opportunities offered by constructive peer correction.

Keywords: LMOOC, peer interaction, peer corrective feedback, error correction.

1. Introduction

Many MOOCs provide open discussion forums for commenting and interacting with educators and peers. The forums in LMOOCs additionally offer participants

---

1. The Open University, Milton Keynes, United Kingdom; e.clifford@open.ac.uk
2. The Open University, Milton Keynes, United Kingdom; christine.pleines@open.ac.uk
3. The Open University, Milton Keynes, United Kingdom; h.a.thomas@open.ac.uk
4. The Open University, Milton Keynes, United Kingdom; s.winchester@open.ac.uk

How to cite this article: Clifford. E., Pleines, C., Thomas, H., & Winchester, S. (2019). Learners as teachers? An evaluation of peer interaction and correction in a German Language MOOC. In F. Meunier, J. Van de Vyver, L. Bradley & S. Thouësny (Eds), *CALL and complexity – short papers from EUROCALL 2019* (pp. 88-93). Research-publishing.net. https://doi.org/10.14705/rpnet.2019.38.991

the opportunity to implement what they have learned, that is to write in the target language. Tasks are designed to push participants to use their linguistic resources in meaningful communication, and any errors they make can open opportunities for language development – provided learners are made aware of these. This could be achieved through promoting peer corrective feedback, thereby enhancing learner engagement in courses which typically have limited educator resources.

Previous studies have established that peer interaction in discussion forums of LMOOCs has a largely positive effect (Martín-Monje, Bárcena, & Ventura, 2013; Sokolik, 2014). In this study we looked more closely at factors contributing to the effectiveness of peer interaction and, specifically, corrective feedback. Classroom-based research has shown peer corrective feedback to have significant potential for language development (Philp, 2016; Sato & Ballinger, 2016; Sato & Lyster, 2012) and has identified learners' proficiency level, their social relations, and their willingness to collaborate as factors which affect the quality and quantity of feedback.

2. Method

The study was based on a post-beginner level MOOC for 'German at work' produced by the Open University and delivered via FutureLearn. The course included text-based and audio-visual resources, quizzes, speaking tasks, and structured writing, as well as open discussions, which are the focus of our study.

In order to explore how learners engaged with the course and how they learned from their peers, we analysed four types of data:

- user analytics (4,063 learners);

- learner contributions to in-course discussion forums (1,487 contributors);

- pre-course survey data (1,088 respondents); and

- verbal and written data from online focus groups (34 participants).

This paper focuses on learners' attitudes to 'peer corrective feedback', a term that refers to participants' replies to posts in the discussion forums, which contain any form of correction in response to an error.

3. Data analysis and discussion

3.1. Peer interaction and peer correction in discussion forums

In order to establish types of peer interaction and correction in our courses, we studied learner contributions in the week with the highest interactivity (Week 1 of 'German at work Post-beginners' 1). **User analytics** showed that of the 4,063 active participants worldwide, 1,487 contributed to the discussion forums resulting in a total of 6,241 postings by learners. A close reading of these **learner contributions to in-course discussion forums** revealed that most postings did not elicit direct responses, but where learner-learner interactions did occur they included general social interactions (greetings and introductions), technical support, 'moral' peer support (e.g. encouragement to overcome challenges), and explanations of linguistic or cultural aspects. The postings also included 172 instances of peer correction, which were distributed as follows (Table 1).

Table 1. Peer corrections

Area of correction	Number of individual corrections
Vocabulary/phrases	81 (47.1%)
Grammar	45 (26.2%)
Spelling/punctuation	40 (23%)
Cultural aspects	6 (3.5%)

Peer corrective feedback included explicit correction, recasts, questioning, and translation, and was often integrated into a meaningful response, as in the following example:

"Ich bin an accountant".

"Ach so. Du bist einen Steuerberater. Sehr schön".

The corrections were provided by a small number of engaged learners (2.3% of forum contributors) including at least four first language speakers. Seventy-five percent of corrective feedback was provided entirely in the target language. Most of the corrective feedback was positively acknowledged by the recipient through thank you messages or likes, and some participants demonstrated uptake by editing the original message or in a subsequent posting. Often recipients saw the need to explain themselves ("This was my first attempt"), and there was a small number of requests for confirmation by other participants or educators. Although all corrections were potentially helpful, occasionally they introduced new errors as in the example above where the appropriate word "Steuerberater" is provided but the article "einen" is incorrect.

3.2. Attitudes to peer correction

The **pre-course survey data** indicated a significant discrepancy between participants' goal of learning from the expertise of others (49.5%) and their goal of sharing their own expertise (15.5%). We found a similar discrepancy when asking focus group participants about their attitudes to peer correction. Whilst many expressed at least partially positive attitudes to receiving corrective feedback by peers, attitudes to correcting others were predominantly negative. Out of the 34 **focus group** participants, 30 gave their opinion on being corrected by peers and 28 gave their opinion on correcting others. Their views are summarised in Figure 1.

Figure 1.   Attitudes to peer correction

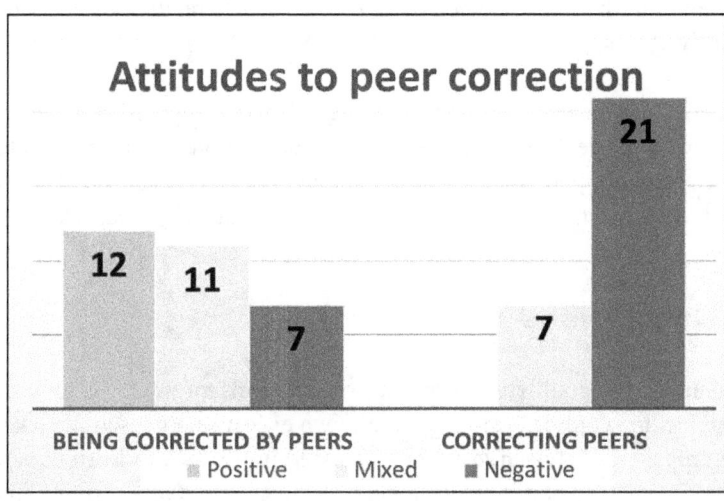

When asked about being corrected by peers, many participants indicated that feedback could be helpful provided it was undertaken tactfully ('positive'), but also expressed doubts about the reliability of the feedback ('mixed') and some thought that the expectation to correct peers places undue emphasis on accuracy and may even hinder communication and impede learning ('negative').

No-one was unreservedly positive about correcting others. Some participants stressed the need for feedback to be constructive and some thought it helped that they had had some training, for example, because they were themselves teachers ('mixed'). Most participants expressed reluctance or were strongly opposed to offering corrective feedback to others ('negative'). The main barriers were participants' lack of confidence in their own ability and a fear of triggering resentment, particularly given the absence of body language in the online environment and the cohort's cultural diversity. Some thought that it was 'not their place' to correct contributions by other learners who had done their best, or even that peer correction should not be touched 'with a barge-pole'. These attitudes were linked to an expectation to learn from the educators rather than from peers and a view that educators should take a more proactive role.

The discussion of peer corrective feedback led to the use of more negative emotive language ('annoying', 'conflict', 'upset', 'frustration') than any other discussion topic. For example, when talking about peer interaction more generally, most participants expressed appreciation for the opportunity to engage in a supportive way with their fellow learners from around the world. Some gave reasons for not contributing, but the kind of emotive language used in relation to peer correction was entirely absent.

On occasion, it appeared that cultural biases also led to conflicting expectations of who should correct and particularly how corrections should be undertaken. Some cultures were perceived to be more polite and sensitive, whilst others were perceived as less tactful. There is scope for further research in this area.

4. Conclusions

Participants reveal conflicting expectations in terms of wanting to learn from others but lacking confidence to share their own expertise. Focus group data further show discrepancies between learners' expressed preference to learn directly from the educators and the participatory nature of the course. Only a small number of LMOOC participants provide corrective feedback to their peers, and this receives mixed responses. Many respondents express strongly that they would not give corrections themselves.

As MOOC designers and educators, we need to consider how to foster the 'positive classroom atmosphere' (Philp, 2016) which is vital for successful peer learning and how to manage expectations in a large and culturally diverse cohort. We should explore ways of training our 'learners as teachers' so that the benefits of peer corrective feedback can be harnessed without causing anxiety or hindering meaningful interaction. The findings from this project can be used to develop strategies that promote constructive interaction, feedback, and error correction. These will be helpful to both participants and educators on LMOOCs.

5. Acknowledgements

Funded by PRAXIS, The Open University.

References

Martín-Monje, E., Bárcena, E., & Ventura, P. (2013). Peer-to-peer interaction in professional English MOOCs: a proposal for effective feedback. In *Proceedings of The European Conference on Language Learning*.

Philp, J. (2016). New pathways in researching interaction. In M. Sato & S. Ballinger (Eds), *Peer interaction and second language learning: pedagogical potential and research agenda* (pp. 377-395). John Benjamins . https://doi.org/10.1075/lllt.45.15phi

Sato, M. & Ballinger, S. (2016). Understanding peer interaction: research synthesis and directions. In M. Sato & S. Ballinger (Eds), *Peer interaction and second language learning: pedagogical potential and research agenda* (pp. 1-30). John Benjamins, https://doi.org/10.1075/lllt.45.01int

Sato, M., & Lyster, R. (2012). Peer interaction and corrective feedback for accuracy and fluency development: monitoring, practice, and proceduralization. *Studies in Second Language Acquisition, 34*(4), 591-626. https://doi.org/10.1017/s0272263112000356

Sokolik, M. (2014). What constitutes an effective language MOOC? In E. Martín-Monje & E. Bárcena (Eds), *Language MOOCs: providing learning, transcending boundaries*. Sciendo Migration, 16-32. https://doi.org/10.2478/9783110420067.2

Video assessment module: self, peer, and teacher post-performance assessment for learning

Matthew Cotter[1] and Don Hinkelman[2]

Abstract. Assessing student presentations can be made more reliable with video-recording and post-performance rating. Further, self assessment and peer assessment can aid in the learning process by students when using specific, easy-to-understand rubrics. A ten-year action research study involved video-recorded performance assessment tasks using a free, open-source Moodle module developed by Sapporo Gakuin University. The Video Assessment Module (VAM) allowed teachers to video record English presentations and upload them to the module for students for self and peer assessment on specific rubrics using qualitative and quantitative criteria. When compared to paper rubrics, the VAM reduced teacher management time and students could use out-of-class time to assess asynchronously without time pressure. Results showed that there was a higher difference in teacher variance for self assessment when compared to teacher variance with peer assessment. Qualitative and quantitative results reported value in using the tool by both students and teachers. This study also showed that students can be trained to use online rubrics to score presentations efficiently, giving further validity for using and developing online modules for video assessment.

Keywords: video assessment, presentation skills, performance assessment, rubrics, Moodle, self assessment, peer assessment.

1. Introduction

In performance-based learning, comprehensively assessing large numbers of students on given individual performances has long been a tedious and even unproductive

---

1. Hokusei Gakuen University Junior College, Sapporo, Japan; m-cotter@hokusei.ac.jp; https://orcid.org/0000-0003-0906-1400
2. Sapporo Gakuin University, Ebetsu, Japan; hinkel@sgu.ac.jp

How to cite this article: Cotter, M., & Hinkelman, D. (2019). Video assessment module: self, peer, and teacher post-performance assessment for learning. In F. Meunier, J. Van de Vyver, L. Bradley & S. Thouësny (Eds), *CALL and complexity – short papers from EUROCALL 2019* (pp. 94-99). Research-publishing.net. https://doi.org/10.14705/rpnet.2019.38.992

quest for educators throughout second language education. Furthermore, Gardner (2012) proposed that for learners to learn from the assessment, they needed to be part of the process. This led to practices such as self and peer assessment, both in score-giving and qualitative feedback.

Nicol, Thomson, and Breslin (2014) surveyed peer feedback research and observed that effects on both the receiver of peer feedback and the giver of peer feedback need to be examined. Based on these principles, the main research question of this study was whether online tools could be used and developed to aid in the process of post-performance self and peer assessment. Secondly, could participation in this type of self and peer assessment aid in improving future English as a Foreign Language (EFL) presentation performance for students? Other pertinent research questions such as the use of other feedback tools (paper, face-to-face), and timing of assessing (real time versus post-performance) are summarized in earlier action research by Rian, Hinkelman, and McGarty (2012), Rian, Hinkelman, and Cotter (2015), and Hinkelman and Cotter (2018). However, for the purpose of this study, results pertaining to the 2019 development cycle of online video assessment tools will be addressed.

2. Method

2.1. Course background

Each year, course participants comprise 50-60 second year English major students and two teachers at Sapporo Gakuin University. Students engage in a compulsory oral English presentation skills class titled 'Oral Communication C'. During weekly 90 minute classes over a single semester of 15 weeks, students were required to prepare for and deliver five presentations on varying themes such as giving instructions (speech to inform) or Hokkaido sightseeing recommendations (speech to persuade). Participation levels were high in these top two levels of classes (2019 n=34) with 87% in-class attendance rate and an average rate of nine out of ten out-of-class homework quizzes. The research question involved whether students could be trained to assess using online rubrics and whether they found value in the process.

After the decision in 2009 to move from paper rubrics to online tools for assessment, the teaching team of this course spent ten years researching, developing, improving, and reporting on assessment types (paper, verbal, online), assessment groupings (self, peer, class, teacher), and tools (Moodle learning management system, forum module, VAM) blended in an EFL speech communication class, as outlined in supplementary materials, part A. Funding for the module development was provided by internal university grants and seed funding by universities in the Moodle Association of Japan.

2.2. VAM functions

Using the Moodle VAM, teachers or students could upload presentation videos directly to Moodle and students could watch them while completing self and/or peer assessments on predetermined rubrics, simple at first, and becoming more complex late in the course. Comments could also be made for each criteria and or as a whole. The teacher could also assess and separate weightings for self, peer, and teacher scores respectively. Figure 1 below shows a screen with a video-recording playback window for both teacher and student viewing while rubric scales are checked and brief comments are made.

2.3. Data collection

Both quantitative and qualitative data were collected in 2019, as done in previous cycles. Overall scores could be downloaded from the Moodle gradebook and the VAM directly and statistical analysis performed via Excel as shown in Table 1 below.

In addition, end of course voluntary student satisfaction surveys (supplementary materials, part B) were given using the questionnaire module in Moodle. Qualitative data from students was also collected through the surveys and the Moodle Forum module helped collate qualitative data for the focus group of the teachers by recording weekly comments in a teaching journal.

Table 1. Self, peer, teacher, and overall assessment average scores (out of 100) with teacher variances

Presentation	Average Scores (Presentations 1-5)		
	2014 (n=55~63)	2017 (n=34~49)	2019 (n=34)
Self	66.0	75.9	77.8
Variance with teacher	-8.8	-9.0	- 8.2
Peer	73.6	N/A*	84.5
Variance with teacher	-1.3		- 1.5
Teacher	74.9	84.8	86.3

* In 2017, a timetable change required peer assessment to be dropped in order to reduce student workload

Video assessment module: self, peer, and teacher post-performance...

Figure 1. VAM rubric and comment feedback interface

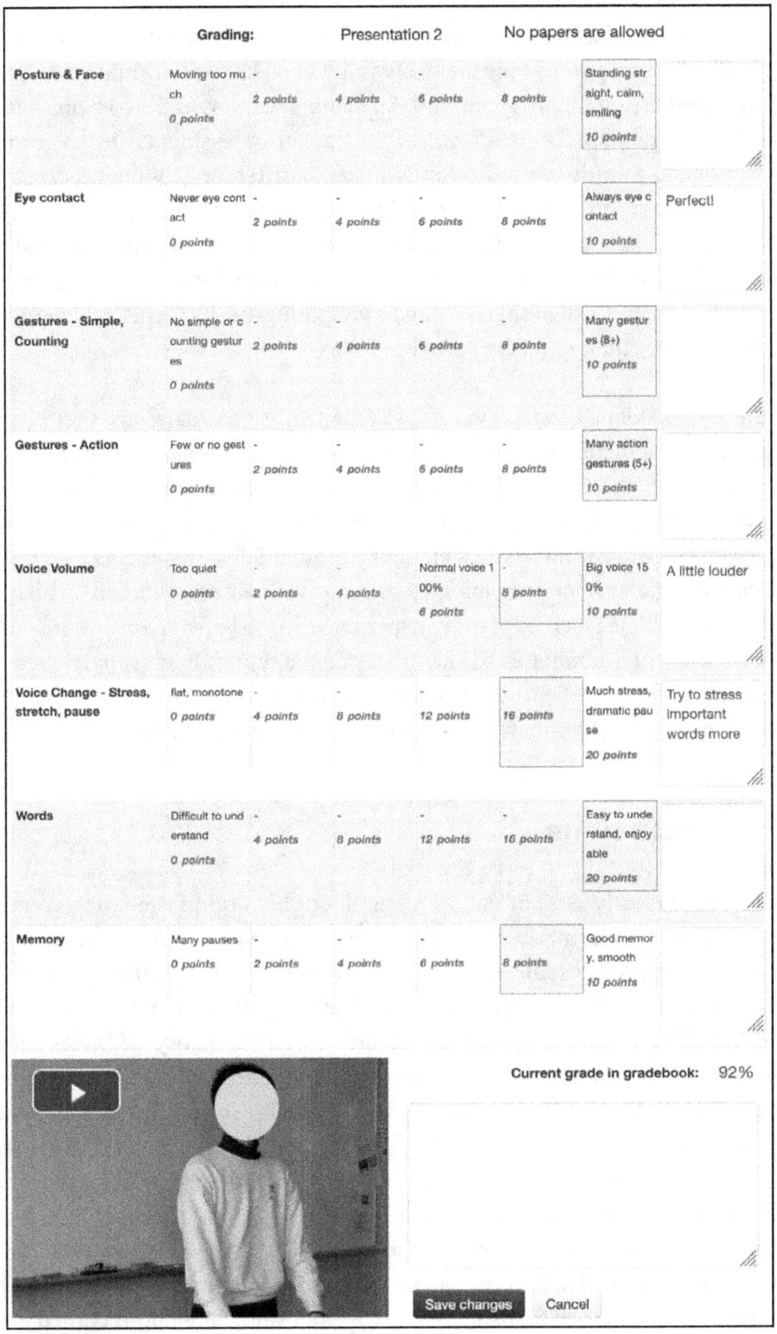

3. Discussion

Results from online learner assessment scores are consistent with those of previous years. Students continue to score themselves lower on post-performance assessment tasks than teachers on all presentations. An average total over the five presentations saw self assessments 8.2-9.0% lower than teacher assessments in the respective years, compared to only a 1.3-1.5 lower average difference by peers respectively. Students did not try to raise their score, but graded themselves more severely than their teachers. This is consistent with the general tendency of Japanese students to rate themselves modestly (Hinkelman & Cotter, 2018). Due to this high variance between teacher and self-ratings, a lower weighting of 20% was assigned to self assessment scores than to teacher scores (80%).

From the 2019 student satisfaction surveys (supplementary materials, part B) we can see that 92% of students responded positively (*agree* or *strongly agree*) to watching their own videos, and 77% valued rating their own presentations respectively. 73% found value in classmates rating their presentations, which shows strong support for using the VAM tool for assessment and learning. 92% of students also regarded feedback from the teacher as helping them improve their presentations which could portray perceived teacher expertise, experience, or comparatively more detailed feedback by teachers compared to classmates on the rubric. Interestingly, the highest value of 96% was achieved on the survey by students agreeing that watching live presentations of their classmates was helpful to improving their presentations.

4. Conclusions

Over the ten cycles (years) of action research on this oral presentation course, the evolution of post-performance video watching, along with self and peer assessment, has proven to be a successful formative tool. This most recent 2019 cycle has been no different, results showing that the VAM draws the students into a more learner-focused mode of assessment, putting Gardner's (2012) theory of 'assessment for learning' into practice. Students reported that being part of the assessment process through using the tool had helped them improve for future performances. Taking the role of 'evaluators' by using the VAM ultimately requires the students to first revisit the presentations again by viewing the videos, go through the cognitive process of scoring and giving feedback to their peers and to themselves, and finally reflect on all feedback received. We can also see that, as part of the assessment process, a complex rubric with specific criteria can be understood and used by intermediate-level students, in this case using their L2, to evaluate video-recorded student performances in an oral presentation course. Although some cultural modesty took place, students placed enough importance on the task as not to try and purposefully score themselves or their peers higher than teachers, or wantonly assign grades due to lack of motivation or time. The convenience of the VAM being able to be used during class or out-of-class, and having the ability to create rubrics to match the assessment criteria and level of students, may have had a part to play in this.

It is our view that future cycles of this research area need to concentrate on determining the most appropriate rubric language and rubric length to match learners and also to investigate whether students themselves have any ideas on how they would like to participate in the evaluation process.

5. Acknowledgments

We would like to thank all the teachers who have contributed to the teaching and curriculum of this course, the students themselves who did 'assessment for learning', and finally the plugin designers and programmers who continually updated this tool for ever changing video formats and standards.

6. Supplementary materials

https://research-publishing.box.com/s/w4ts3e0auk2pw6p60n8krb59tod4sxrd

References

Gardner, J. (2012). Assessment and learning. Sage. https://doi.org/10.4135/9781446250808

Hinkelman, D., & Cotter, M. (2018). Balancing real-time vs. post-performance feedback for EFL presentation classes. In P. Clements, A. Krause & P. Bennett (Eds), *Language teaching in a global age: shaping the classroom, shaping the world*. JALT.

Nicol, D., Thomson, A., & Breslin, C. (2014). Rethinking feedback practices in higher education: a peer review perspective. *Assessment & Evaluation in Higher Education, 39*(1), 102-122.

Rian, J. P., Hinkelman, D., & Cotter, M. (2015). Self-, peer, and teacher rubric assessments of student presentation videos. In P. Clemens, A. Krause & H. Brown (Eds), *JALT2014 Conference Proceedings* (pp. 688-697). JALT.

Rian, J. P., Hinkelman, D., & McGarty, G. (2012). Integrating video assessment into an oral presentation course. In A. Stewart & N. Sonda (Eds), *JALT2011 Conference Proceedings* (pp. 416-425). JALT.

Learning to design a mobile hunt on Actionbound: a complex task?

Carole Delforge[1], Julie Van de Vyver[2], and Alice Meurice[3]

Abstract. The research consisted in having an Actionbound mobile hunt for A1 learners of Dutch designed by a group of language Student Teachers (STs) within the framework of a second year course on foreign language teaching. The game was then implemented with two groups of fifth grade primary school pupils during their visit of the Hergé Museum in Louvain-la-Neuve, Belgium. These two steps allowed our multidisciplinary research team to analyse the use of the app from the perspective of not only the players but also the creators of the game. Research data was collected throughout the study via questionnaires, observations, and a focus group. A qualitative analysis of the STs' data allowed us to establish their digital profiles, thereby situating each of them in the digital integration process. The results suggest that integrating technology and content when designing a pedagogical activity is a complex task. Support and guidance from teacher trainers could therefore be recommended in order to propose a pertinent integration of technologies in the language classroom.

Keywords: mobile app, digital literacies, reading skills, gamification.

1. Context

In the framework of a government project funded by the Belgian French-speaking Community, our group of researchers in foreign language teaching and digital literacies from higher education institutions has designed a study that aims at analysing the use of the Actionbound mobile app in language learning – for further information, please refer to Meunier, Meurice, and Van de Vyver (2019). The study

---

1. Université de Namur, Namur, Belgium; carole.delforge@unamur.be; https://orcid.org/0000-0002-7212-9167
2. Université Catholique de Louvain, Louvain-la-Neuve, Belgium; julie.vandevyver@uclouvain.be; https://orcid.org/0000-0001-8820-8380
3. Université Catholique de Louvain, Louvain-la-Neuve, Belgium; alice.meurice@uclouvain.be; https://orcid.org/0000-0001-7892-1422

How to cite this article: Delforge, C., Van de Vyver, J., & Meurice, A. (2019). Learning to design a mobile hunt on Actionbound: a complex task? In F. Meunier, J. Van de Vyver, L. Bradley & S. Thouësny (Eds), *CALL and complexity – short papers from EUROCALL 2019* (pp. 100-106). Research-publishing.net. https://doi.org/10.14705/rpnet.2019.38.993

consisted in having ten language STs design both a mobile and a paper version of a hunt on L2-Dutch reading strategies in the Hergé Museum. The project was first introduced by the researchers to let the STs discover the tool and raise their awareness of various pedagogical aspects. The STs were then asked to create the two hunts and were accompanied by our research team throughout the process. The game was then implemented with 43 fifth-grade primary school pupils during their visit of the museum. The pupils were randomly distributed into two groups: a control group performed the hunt on paper (N=19); the test group played the game on tablets (N=24) after having discovered Actionbound through a short 'demo' hunt. The STs were in charge of welcoming and guiding the groups of pupils during the activity.

The present study intends to answer the following two research questions.

- What is the impact of the mobile hunt and the techno-pedagogical guidance on the ST's perceptions of the use of technology in a pedagogical context?

- What is the impact of the mobile hunt on the pupils' attitudes towards the activity?

2. Methodology

Figure 1. Data collection

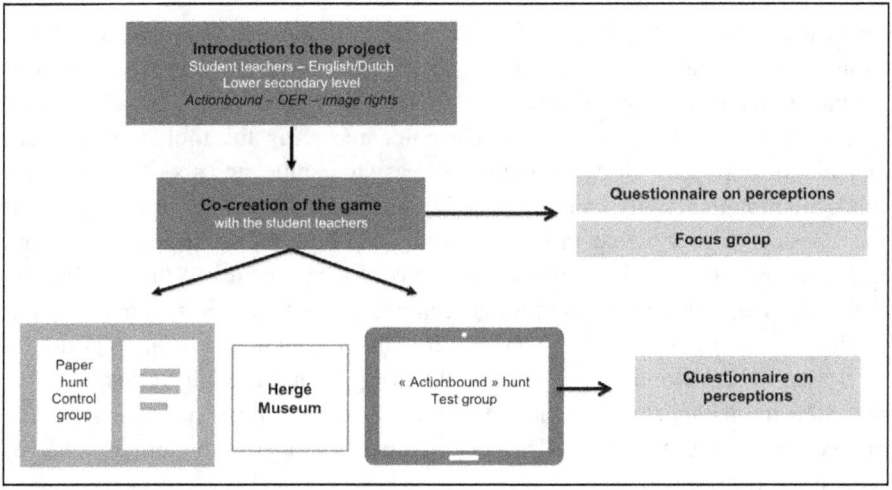

As depicted in Figure 1, different types of data were collected throughout the study. After the activity in the museum, the researchers held a focus group session with the STs. The discussion was organised very freely, with every ST expressing their opinions and impressions, and the researchers noting them down and sometimes directing the conversation. A post-questionnaire was also distributed to the STs to investigate their perception of the use of Actionbound and the integration of technology in the language classroom. The questionnaires had been built by the researchers based on Davis, Bagozzi, and Warshaw's (1992) Technology Acceptance Model (TAM), which predicts the intention of use of technology, and Niess et al.'s (2009) Technological Pedagogical Content Knowledge (TPACK) development model, which situates respondents on a scale of integration of technology, pedagogy, and content. The pupils filled in a short survey right after taking the hunt to give their opinion on the activity, and took a test on L2 reading strategies on paper the next day.

3. Results and discussion

3.1. What is the impact of the mobile hunt and the techno-pedagogical guidance on the STs' perceptions of the use of technology in a pedagogical context?

The STs' perceptions of the use of technology (based on TAM items) after the experimentation are on the whole positive, as shown in Figure 2. Teaching media education and Information and Communication Technology (ICT) is seen as important for the vast majority, and eight STs out of ten are motivated and intend to use the application in class. All of them believe Actionbound is useful for language teaching, although their attitude towards the ease of use of the tool is more nuanced. Three of them declare not mastering the tool, four of them consider an activity with Actionbound not easy to handle, and six of them do not think the mobile activity can easily be integrated into everyday practices. From these results, it seems that in our case, the usefulness of the tool plays a more important role in their intention to use it than its ease of use. When looking at the reasons why the use of the tool is seen positively by the STs, it appears that pupils' attitudes may be a key factor. While the vast majority of the STs do not think that Actionbound can help pupils learn better or more, all of them believe that their pupils appreciate their use of the app. Seven of them also assume the pupils can easily use the tool. The same number of STs view the tool as a way of reaching more pupils.

Learning to design a mobile hunt on Actionbound: a complex task?

Figure 2. STs' perceptions – four point Likert scale questions

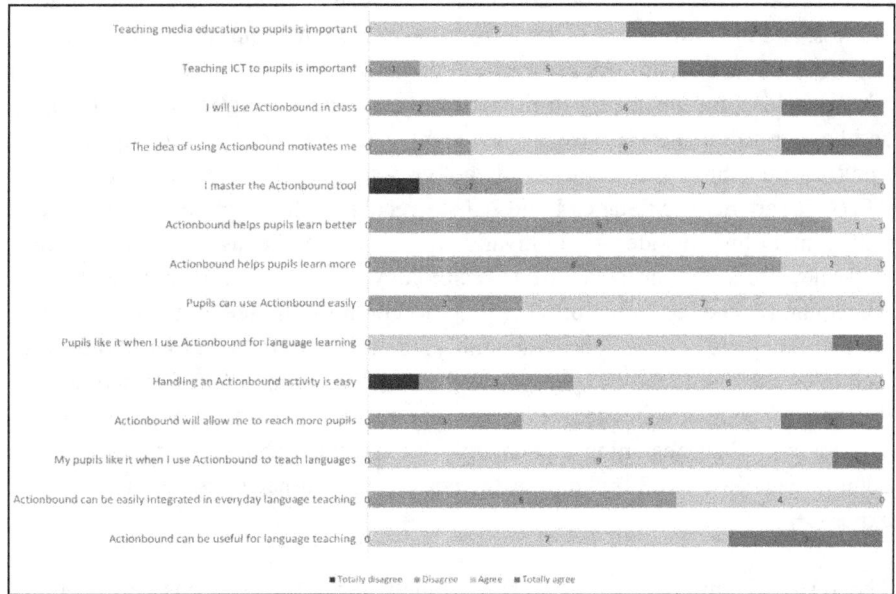

These figures show, in brief, some positive perceptions and acknowledgements of usefulness but no clear perception of the pedagogical added value of the tool. This is confirmed when examining the digital profile of each ST, illustrated in Figure 3.

Figure 3. STs' TPACK developmental profiles, based on Niess et al's (2009, p. 10)

All the STs' data was analysed to establish their digital profiles based on Niess et al.'s (2009) TPACK developmental model. Each ST is situated in the digital integration process, and more precisely in the integration of Actionbound. In Figure 3, one ST is at Stage 1, recognising the use of the alignment between technology and content when teaching but not being in favour or against the integration of technologies and having no intention of use. This student sees technology as a complement to traditional teaching and assumes it is not easy to use for pupils. The majority of STs (N=6) are between Stages 1 and 2. They recognise the alignment of technology with content but consider it a motivational tool with no pedagogical added value. Still, they are in favour of the use of technology and believe it is important to use it adequately. The last group of STs (N=3) accept the alignment of technology with content. They are between accepting and adapting. They are in favour of the use of technology and are ready to get involved in the integration of ICT in activities as they see its pedagogical added value. These results suggest that aligning technology and content when designing a pedagogical activity (Mishra & Koehler, 2006) is complex, at least for STs, and that it requires techno-pedagogical support from experts.

The results from the focus group session confirm the previous observations. According to the STs, the mobile hunt is motivating, fun, and is different from a traditional activity, and according to some of them, it also provides challenges to the pupils and offers new tasks such as video recording or taking pictures. The groups of pupils were seen as autonomous during the game even though they sometimes needed to be guided. On the whole, they need some computer skills to navigate the app or some technical support during the activity. Likewise, the teachers need computer skills to provide guidance and technical help if needed.

3.2. What is the impact of the mobile hunt on the pupils' attitudes towards the activity?

Figure 4 shows that the STs' hypotheses on the pupils' perceptions were on the whole correct, the only exceptions being that the young learners found the paper hunt easier and more useful than the STs thought they would. As for the answers of the pupils who did the hunt on paper and those who did it on a tablet, they are often similar. The most significant gap highlights that the mobile hunt seemed more stressful. This might be explained by the immediate feedback given by the app after each answer. During the focus group session however, some STs postulated that this stress was positive and seemed to be a motivation factor for the pupils to keep playing, which is further illustrated in the adjectives *original* and *fun*.

Figure 4. Comparison of the pupils' perceptions and the STs' hypotheses on these perceptions

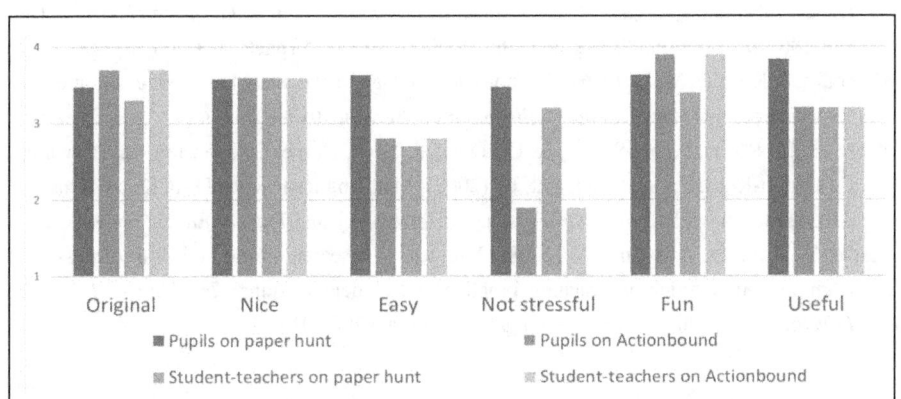

4. Conclusions

The results from the current study suggest that aligning technology and content in a pedagogical activity is a complex task which requires techno-pedagogical support from teacher trainers. An area for development would be to investigate the potential of professional learning communities (Vescio, Ross, & Adams, 2008) in raising STs' awareness and supporting them during the creation of ICT-integrated teaching sequences. The pupils' perceptions of the mobile and paper hunt did not differ greatly. This might be explained by our decision to make the two games almost identical, consequently not allowing for the full potential of ICT to unfold.

5. Acknowledgements

We would like to thank the research team of the modern languages Consortium as well as the STs from Vinci for their collaboration.

References

Davis, F. D., Bagozzi, R. P., & Warshaw, P. R. (1992). Extrinsic and intrinsic motivation to use computers in the workplace. *Journal of Applied Social Psychology, 22*(14), 1111-1132. https://doi.org/10.1111/j.1559-1816.1992.tb00945.x

Meunier, F., Meurice, A., & Van de Vyver, J. (2019). Empowering teachers and learners in and beyond classrooms: focus on OEPs in reading activities. In A. Comas-Quinn, A. Beaven & B. Sawhill (Eds), *New case studies of openness in and beyond the language classroom* (pp. 173-186). Research-publishing.net. https://doi.org/10.14705/rpnet.2019.37.974

Mishra, P., & Koehler, M. J. (2006). Technological pedagogical content knowledge: a framework for teacher knowledge. *Teachers college record, 108*(6), 1017-1054.

Niess, M. L., Ronau, R. N., Shafer, K. G., Driskell, S. O., Harper S., Johnston, C., Browning, C., Ozgun-Koca, S. A., & Kersaint, G. (2009). Mathematics teacher TPACK standards and development model. *Contemporary Issues in Technology and Teacher Education, 9*(1), 4-24.

Vescio, V., Ross, D., & Adams, A. (2008). A review of research on the impact of professional learning communities on teaching practice and student learning. *Teaching and Teacher Educatio, 24*(1), 80-91. https://doi.org/10.1016/j.tate.2007.01.004

■ UCLouvain

A pilot study of Alexa for autonomous second language learning

Gilbert Dizon[1] and Daniel Tang[2]

Abstract. Although initial research involving Intelligent Personal Assistants (IPAs) for language learning have yielded promising results, no study has examined their use in the context of Autonomous Second Language Learning (ASLL). Thus, the main goal of this pilot study was to investigate the use of an IPA, specifically Alexa, for ASLL. Two Japanese university second language (L2) English students participated in a four-week study, which involved the learners interacting with Alexa through the Echo Dot speaker in their respective homes. Learner usage data was collected via the Alexa website and the students' attitudes toward the IPA for ASLL were evaluated through a survey consisting of 12 Likert-scale items and four open-ended questions. It was found that while the L2 students had positive opinions toward the use of Alexa for ASLL, the learners did not make active use of the technology.

Keywords: intelligent personal assistants, autonomous language learning, L2 pronunciation, L2 speaking.

1. Introduction

While much of the focus on language teaching and research revolves around what happens in the classroom, what goes on outside the classroom is equally as important (Richards, 2015). Consequently, there has been a rise in the use of Computer-assisted Language Learning (CALL) to support ASLL. As Richards (2015) notes, the use of technology can "provide greater opportunities for meaningful and authentic language use than are available in the classroom" (p. 6). Considering this, IPAs may be potentially useful since they provide opportunities for L2 input and output. While initial studies have resulted in positive findings,

---

1. Himeji Dokkyo University, Himeji, Japan; gilbert.dizon.jr@gmail.com
2. Otemae University, Kyoto, Japan; dtang@otemae.ac.jp; https://orcid.org/0000-0002-6822-3011

How to cite this article: Dizon, G., & Tang, D. (2019). A pilot study of Alexa for autonomous second language learning. In F. Meunier, J. Van de Vyver, L. Bradley & S. Thouësny (Eds), *CALL and complexity – short papers from EUROCALL 2019* (pp. 107-112). Research-publishing.net. https://doi.org/10.14705/rpnet.2019.38.994

they were either feasibility studies which investigated the ability of IPAs to understand L2 speech (Dizon, 2017; Moussalli & Cardoso, 2016), or research centered on finding ways to use virtual assistants for classroom-based language learning (Underwood, 2017). No study has examined IPAs to promote ASLL; therefore, this case-study investigated the use of Alexa, a virtual assistant by Amazon, to support ASLL for two Japanese university students. Accordingly, the following research questions were addressed in the study; (1) to what extent do L2 learners use Alexa for ASLL?; (2) how do they use the IPA?; and (3) what are their views of Alexa for ASLL?

2. Method

2.1. Participants

Two fourth-year students at a Japanese university, who were selected based on volunteer sampling, agreed to participate in the pilot study and provided written informed consent. It is also important to note that it was clearly stressed to each participant that all commands given to Alexa would be stored in the cloud and accessed by the researchers. The learners had Test of English for International Communication (TOEIC) scores ranging from 720-770, which is equivalent to B1 on the Common European Framework of Reference for languages (CEFR) scale. Students were given a second generation Echo Dot, a smart speaker which features Alexa, and were allowed to use the device for four weeks from December 2018 to January 2019. A tutorial was given to familiarize the learners with the device because they had no prior experience with the smart speaker or Alexa.

2.2. Data collection and analysis

A mixed method case-study design was implemented to examine the use of Alexa for ASLL. Learner usage data was collected through the history page on the Alexa website, which lists all commands given to the IPA over the four-week intervention in text and audio form. Qualitative data concerning the students' attitudes toward Alexa for ASLL was obtained via two methods: a 12-item survey using a five point Likert-scale (strongly disagree=1 and strongly agree=5) adapted from Chen (2013), which examined three technology acceptance model variables (usefulness, effectiveness, and satisfaction), as well as four open-ended writing questions adapted from Lee (2011), which were explicitly designed to elicit responses related to autonomous learning.

Data concerning the learners' usage of Alexa was broken down into the types of commands given, as well as the frequency in which they were given. Mean and standard deviation (SD) values for each survey construct were provided. Lastly, the written responses were analyzed and thematically organized according to Hubbard's (2009) framework, which looks at how CALL can affect language learning through multiple perspectives.

3. Results and discussion

As shown in Table 1, the commands given were divided into eight different categories according to grounded theory. As outlined by Charmaz (1996), codes were developed based on the command data and these codes were arranged into categories. Music commands were the most commonly used type, which is unsurprising given the popularity of English music. More surprising, however, was the fact that commands related to getting to know Alexa were the second most frequent. This suggests that the students enjoyed having dialogues with Alexa, which links to one of the identified themes based on the students' written comments (see below). Nevertheless, Alexa was not used frequently by the learners over the four-week study. In fact, they only gave a total of 81 commands over the course of the intervention. One possible reason for this is the time of the year in which the students were given their Echos, which was over the New Year's break and end of the semester. Therefore, the students could have been too busy with holiday-related gatherings as well as studying for exams to use the IPA.

Table 1. Types and frequency of commands given

Command type	Command example	No.	%
Music	Play Taylor Swift 'Stay Stay Stay'	22	27.2%
Getting to know Alexa	Do you have any brothers or sisters?	13	16.0%
Humor	Tell me a joke.	11	13.6%
General info	What's the weather tomorrow?	10	12.3%
Language	How do you say good morning in Russian?	7	8.6%
News	What's my flash briefing?	7	8.6%
Story	Tell me a story.	6	7.4%
Other	Set an alarm for me.	6	6.2%
Total		81	100%

Table 2 depicts the mean results for each construct that was examined through the questionnaire. The students' responses indicate that they had favorable views of using Alexa for ASLL. In particular, both usability and satisfaction received mean totals of four, which indicates agreement with the statements. Therefore, it can be concluded that the learners believed the IPA was easy to use and that they enjoyed interacting with it for ASLL.

Table 2. Alexa survey results

Construct	M	SD
Usability	4.0	0.0
Effectiveness	3.8	0.3
Satisfaction	4.0	0.5

As Table 3 illustrates, three themes from Hubbard (2009) were identified from the students' written responses: (1) better *access* to dialogue in the L2; (2) improved *learning efficiency* through indirect pronunciation feedback; and (3) enhanced *learning effectiveness* through a promotion of self-awareness of gaps in the L2.

Table 3. Students' written responses

Theme	Student comments
Access – Better access to dialogue in the L2	S1: I asked many things that Alexa like a human such as 'What are you doing?' and 'How old are you?', because I wanted to get interesting answers.
	S2: I think the most interesting thing was having dialogue with Alexa, especially after I downloaded the Alexa app and its introductions helped me create better conversations with Alexa.
Learner efficiency – Improved learning efficiency through indirect pronunciation feedback	S1: By asking something in English, I could know my pronunciations were understandable or not for native speakers.
	S2: Alexa was like a real person who was having conversations with me... For example, it reminded me to pronounce correctly when I tried to give Alexa commands in English.
Learning effectiveness – Enhanced learning effectiveness through a promotion of self-awareness of gaps in the L2	S1: I couldn't pronounce some words correctly or find appropriate grammar though I've known enough knowledge.
	S2: I found the most difficult thing was talking to Alexa with a foreign accent could make Alexa misunderstand my commands.

These results further illustrate that the students had favorable opinions toward Alexa for ASLL. Particularly, they highlight the potential for IPAs to be used as simulated conversation partners to improve L2 speaking skills, especially pronunciation, which is significant given that many L2 learners lack speaking opportunities outside of class.

4. Conclusion

To sum up, although the L2 students did not interact with Alexa frequently, they did have positive perceptions toward its use for ASLL, which supports past positive findings on the use of virtual assistants in L2 contexts (Dizon, 2017; Moussalli & Cardoso, 2016; Underwood, 2017). Of particular importance are the learners' comments that indicated that the IPA could support L2 dialogue and pronunciation development. This is significant as many L2 learners, especially those in foreign language contexts, have few opportunities to use the target language in a productive and meaningful way. While this pilot study is obviously limited by its small sample size, it highlights the potential of IPAs such as Alexa to support ASLL due to the affordances they provide for L2 listening and speaking. Thus, future research ought to incorporate a greater number of participants from a variety of linguistic backgrounds to discover how IPAs can promote L2 development, especially in terms of languages other than English.

References

Charmaz, K. (1996). The search for meanings – grounded theory. In J. A. Smith, R. Harré & L. Van Langenhove (Eds), *Rethinking methods in psychology* (pp. 27-49). Sage Publications.
Chen, X.-B. (2013). Tablets for informal language learning: student usage and attitudes. *Language Learning & Technology, 17*(1), 20-36.
Dizon, G. (2017). Using intelligent personal assistants for second language learning: a case study of Alexa. *TESOL Journal, 8*(4), 811-830. https://doi.org/10.1002/tesj.353
Hubbard, P. (2009). *Computer assisted language learning: critical concepts in linguistics* (vols I-IV). Routledge.
Lee, L. (2011). Blogging: promoting learner autonomy and intercultural competence through study abroad. *Language Learning & Technology, 15*(3), 87-109.
Moussalli, S., & Cardoso, W. (2016). Are commercial 'personal robots' ready for language learning? Focus on second language speech. In S. Papadima-Sophocleous, L. Bradley & S. Thouësny (Eds), *CALL communities and culture – short papers from EUROCALL 2016* (pp. 325-329). Research-publishing.net. https://doi.org/10.14705/rpnet.2016.eurocall2016.583
Richards, J. C. (2015). The changing face of language learning: learning beyond the classroom. *RELC Journal, 46*(1), 5-22. https://doi.org/10.1177/0033688214561621

Underwood, J. (2017). Exploring AI language assistants with primary EFL students. In K. Borthwick, L. Bradley & S. Thouësny (Eds), *CALL in a climate of change: adapting to turbulent global conditions – short papers from EUROCALL 2017* (pp. 317-321). Research-publishing.net. https://doi.org/10.14705/rpnet.2017.eurocall2017.733

A case study of a learner's use of an online translator as a cognitive tool in a SCMC context

Morgane Domanchin[1]

Abstract. This study explores a language learner's screen while interacting from a desktop videoconferencing device as part of an intercultural telecollaboration exchange that connected teacher-trainees and French learners. Communicative tasks involving opinion exchanges require from language learners simultaneous speaking and listening comprehension skills, which may prompt linguistic difficulties. To compensate for their weaknesses, learners had access to online resources exposing them to various and complex language use. Based on Jonassen's (1992) work on 'cognitive tools' as intelligent resources that contribute to knowledge construction, the author draws on multimodal interaction analysis to question the uses of an automatic online translator in the context of Synchronous Computer Mediated Communication (SCMC). This study illustrates a learner's technical autonomy using Google Translate (GT) to search for vocabulary while interacting with his interlocutors. It reports the learner's emergence of a linguistic need which is followed by a search for vocabulary leading in some cases to the searched translation's integration within the pedagogical interaction. This study raises cognitive challenges that such a practice presents for language learning.

Keywords: learners' technical autonomy, knowledge construction, synchronised computer mediated communication, cognitive tools.

1. Introduction

In Desktop Video-Conferencing (DVC) environments, participants can benefit from technical autonomy which allows them to search on the Internet when looking for specific information. Yet due to time pressure, searching for information while interacting with a distant teacher involves technical complexity. Such a

---

1. University Lyon 2, Lyon, France; morgane.domanchin@univ-lyon2.fr; https://orcid.org/0000-0003-4053-0025

How to cite this article: Domanchin, M. (2019). A case study of a learner's use of an online translator as a cognitive tool in a SCMC context. In F. Meunier, J. Van de Vyver, L. Bradley & S. Thouësny (Eds), *CALL and complexity – short papers from EUROCALL 2019* (pp. 113-117). Research-publishing.net. https://doi.org/10.14705/rpnet.2019.38.995

practice requires the need to organise and structure one's screen environment to facilitate searches and to reduce processing time (Kirsh, 1995). As synchronous interactions impose a certain urge for communication, the use of online resources as 'cognitive tools' (Jonassen, 1992) was observed in our data. Cognitive tools are "computationally based tools that complement and extend the mind" (Jonassen, 1992, p. 2). Jonassen (1992) shows that they engage generative processing by exposing the learner to new information that (s)he can relate to prior knowledge.

In the case of our doctoral thesis, the use of the online translator GT was used as a cognitive tool to support a learner's need for vocabulary. As GT has been implemented in face-to-face education contexts (Vold, 2018), few studies consider the use of GT in a SCMC. Hence the following question raised in this paper: how is GT used by the language learner as a cognitive tool while interacting with a teacher-trainee?

2. Methodology

In 2014, the Cultura project allowed 24 teacher-trainees of French from the University of Lyon 2 (Lyon, France) and 16 students learning French at MIT (Boston, USA) to interact in order to practise the L2. As part of a hybrid course, the participants were first asked to chat using the Cultura platform. Then, three DVC sessions were organised to allow them to meet. As for the first DVC session, participants were able to introduce themselves freely whereas the other two sessions focused on particular topics.

To understand the use of the automatic translator, the analyses were based on a learner's dynamic screen captures. The analyses are drawn from Jozsef, a learner who used GT during the first two DVC sessions while interacting with a pair of teacher-trainees.

To understand the learner's onscreen use of GT, its time display was calculated on the learner's screen which was then crossed with the number of searched words and expressions. Then, in order to carry out a more fine-grained analysis on the learner's vocabulary searches, 'ELAN'[2] (Wittenburg et al., 2006) was used to transcribe onscreen actions (e.g. cursor's moves and clicks) and the participant's multimodal interactions (verbal and chat logs). These first annotations allowed to model the steps describing the learner's use of the automatic translator. What was

---

2. ELAN is an annotation tool "designed for the creation of text annotations for audio and video files" (Wittenburg et al., 2006, p. 1556).

first observed was the emergence of the linguistic need which gave rise to a lexical search on the automatic translator. Then, depending on the interaction context, the translator's suggested translation could be integrated within the learner's spoken utterance.

3. Results

3.1. GT onscreen

Table 1 summarises our results based on the onscreen use of the automatic translator. It shows a difference in the interaction time duration as the first DVC session lasted longer (40 minutes) than the second one (27 minutes). In total, 20 lexical searches were launched during the first session for a time display of 27 minutes (representing 66% of the total DVC time). For the second session, a decrease in the number of searches (n=9) was observed with an equal amount of onscreen display time totalling 27 minutes, which equals 100% of the session. Such results illustrate the cognitive tool's long display duration when it was occasionally used.

Table 1. Onscreen use of the automatic translator

	DVC session 1			DVC session 2		
Google Translate	Time display on the screen		Number of launched searches	Time display on the screen		Number of launched searches
	in minute	in percent	20	in minute	in percent	9
	27.15	66.11%		27.43	100%	
Interaction time duration	00:40:20 (100%)			00:27:43 (100%)		

3.2. The emergence of the linguistic need

Table 2 introduces the key results based on the emergence of a linguistic need. It presents the three main contexts in which it appeared in the interaction. The number below indicates the number of lexical searches.

Most lexical searches (n=18) emerged while Jozsef was interacting with his teacher-trainees (context 1). Our transcriptions showed that such a need was identified by a sudden interruption within the learner's turn. A pause was made in place of the missing word, followed by hesitation markers 'hm' stressing the need for help.

Table 2. Interactional contexts leading to the learner's emergence of his linguistic need

Context 1	Context 2	Context 3
In interaction	In interaction	In case of a temporary interruption within the interaction
during the learner's turn	during the teacher-trainee's turn	at the end of a turn
18	7	4

Some other lexical searches (n=7) were launched while his teacher-trainees were talking. In this second context, or in case of a silence within the interaction (context 3), his searches for vocabulary were silent, and mostly unknown to his teacher-trainees. At last, a minority of lexical searches (n=4) aimed at checking for a new topic of conversation to ensure the interactions' flow.

3.3. The search for lexical items on GT and their integration

Our analyses showed the integration of 23 searched vocabulary words out of 29. One of the main explanations for the non-integration of the searched item is the interaction's quick pace, which raises the question of choosing the appropriate moment to introduce it. In total, three lexical items were directly included within a sentence without any linguistic self-regulation. For the rest (n=20), three types of self-regulation – *linguistic* (e.g. reformulations, repetitions), *technical* (launching another search on GT), or *both* (e.g. use of the chat) – were observed.

4. Discussion

The use of an online translator as a cognitive tool allows to support language learners in need for vocabulary. As the lexical need mostly emerges while interacting, finding a translation appears fundamental to avoid disrupting the conversation flow. When finding a translation, the learner can integrate it directly within the interaction (if the word or expression is unknown for instance) or by processing the new information to prior knowledge. The latter can result in the implementation of self-regulations which may not guarantee the teacher-trainee's understanding of the learner's utterance. Indeed the integration of the new information depends on the grammatical structure in which it was inserted, but it also depends on the conversation topic that is discussed.

Our results furthermore showed a decrease in the number of searches launched. In the second DVC session, the implementation of hetero-regulations addressed to the teacher-trainees such as 'how do you say...' was observed. Such result would need further investigation in order to determine whether cognitive tools help learners reduce their anxiety in SCMC contexts.

5. Conclusion

This paper aimed at reporting a language learner's uses of GT as a cognitive tool in a SCMC context. Based on our limited data, our results are aligned with Jolley and Maimone (2015) who showed that machine translation could be used efficiently provided that learners have enough knowledge about the language and the tool. Indeed our results showed the implementation of linguistic and technical individual learning strategies, leading to knowledge construction. Yet such practice also adds complexity to a DVC learning situation. Not only does the online translator cause errors, it can potentially disturb the pedagogical interaction and affect the learner's feeling of social presence.

References

Jolley, J. R., & Maimone. L. (2015). Free online machine translation: Use and perceptions by Spanish students and instructors. In A. J. Moeller (Ed.), *Learn languages, explore cultures, transform lives. Paper presented at the 2015 Central States Conference on the Teaching of Foreign Languages* (pp.181-200). Robert M. Terry.

Jonassen, D. H. (1992). What are cognitive tools? In M. Kommers, D. H. Jonassen, T. J. Mayes & A. Ferreira (Eds), *Cognitive tools for learning* (pp. 1-16). Springer-Verlag. https://doi.org/10.1007/978-3-642-77222-1

Kirsh, D. (1995). The intelligent use of space. *Artificial Intelligence, Computational research on interaction and agency, 72*(1-2), 31-68.

Vold, T. E. (2018). Using machine-translated texts to generate L3 learner's metalinguistic talk. In A. Haukås, C. Bjørke & M. Dypedahl (Eds), *Metacognition in language learning and teaching* (pp. 67-97). Routledge. https://doi.org/10.4324/9781351049146-5

Wittenburg, P., Brugman, H., Russel, A., Klassmann, A., & Sloetjes, H. (2006). Elan: a professional framework for multimodality research. In *Proceedings of the 5th International Conference on Language Resources and Evaluation, LREC 2006* (pp. 1556-1559). http://www.lrec-conf.org/proceedings/lrec2006/pdf/153_pdf.pdf

The effects of an online learning management system on students' academic socialization: a qualitative study on a Chinese graduate course

Liu Dong[1], Li Cheng[2], Shixin Dong[3], and Guanzhen Wu[4]

Abstract. Blended learning which combines face-to-face instruction and online learning is increasingly important and pervasive in China. Guided by the theory of 'Language Socialization', the researchers explored the situated learning experiences of four Year 1 graduate students while they were adapting to the new academic environment through the graduate course of 'Second Language Acquisition' at a university in Beijing. In this course, a WeChat connected to the Blackboard learning system was used. Student-teacher interactions on the WeChat and Blackboard, classroom observations, and interviews were used for data collection. Results from four case studies illustrated that academic adaptation was a complex sociocultural phenomenon in which students gradually became competent members of the academic community. Moreover, Learning Management Systems (LMSs) were of great help for them in adapting to a new environment and developing negotiating competence in their new academic communities.

Keywords: blended learning, learning management systems, case studies, language socialization.

1. Introduction

Research on the use of LMSs suggest that the LMS had greatly influenced students' learning and educators' teaching (e.g. Rubin, Fernandes, Avgerinou, & Moore, 2010). An LMS can allow instructors and students to share study materials,

---

1. Beijing University of Posts and Telecommunications, Beijing, China; dongliu@bupt.edu.cn
2. Beijing University of Posts and Telecommunications, Beijing, China; licheng@bupt.edu.cn
3. Beijing University of Posts and Telecommunications, Beijing, China; dongshixin@bupt.edu.cn
4. Beijing University of Posts and Telecommunications, Beijing, China; wgzh111@bupt.edu.cn

How to cite this article: Dong, L., Cheng, L., Dong, S., & Wu, G. (2019). The effects of an online learning management system on students' academic socialization: a qualitative study on a Chinese graduate course. In F. Meunier, J. Van de Vyver, L. Bradley & S. Thouësny (Eds), *CALL and complexity – short papers from EUROCALL 2019* (pp. 118-123). Research-publishing.net. https://doi.org/10.14705/rpnet.2019.38.996

submit and return assignments, and exchange ideas online. Many platforms, like WeChat and Blackboard, have been useful tools for Chinese students to study and communicate in recent years. Studies on these tools suggest that they had a positive impact on the students' learning (Liu, Wang, & Tai, 2016).

Early studies on language socialization have investigated how newcomers would be socialized in the community (e.g. Duff, 2010). However, many studies have ignored that the use of technology also has great impact on students' learning while they adapt to a new environment.

In this study, we explored the perceived benefits and actual use of an LMS by instructors and students at a university in Beijing. We did a one year research to find out how they adapted to the new environment of postgraduate education with the help of the LMS. To be more specific, we aim to answer the following questions.

- How do the Year 1 graduate students adapt to the new academic environment with the help of LMS?

- What are the similarities or differences in their academic adaptation experiences in the course of second language acquisition supported by the LMS?

- What are the emerging effects of the LMS on the participants' adaptation experiences?

2. Method

2.1. Contextual background and participants

The study was conducted in a graduate course of 'Second Language Acquisition' at a university in China. This course is a compulsory course for graduate students to explore major issues in second language acquisition and English teaching. The course aims to help students improve their academic competence and learn academic English more deeply.

We focused on four Chinese participants: Gary, Lee, Andy, and Maria. With the permission of the instructor and volunteers, one of the researchers observed the participants in order to note their behaviors. The time span was from September 2018 to June 2019.

2.2. Research design

WeChat and Blackboard, which are regarded as learning resource centers, bulletin boards (posted messages or announcements), and chatrooms (exchanged ideas and provided group discussion), are the most popular learning and teaching tools in China (Wang, Fang, Han, & Chen, 2016).

The researchers conducted a multiple case study for one year. Data were collected from classroom observations, individual interviews, and interactive messages from WeChat and Blackboard (see Table 1). We took note of our observations. The interview data were first transcribed by the researchers and then double checked by the participants and the course instructor.

Table 1. Data collection

Method	Data collection period (September, 2018-June, 2019)	Data
Interviews with four participants	Interview 1: September 2018 Interview 2: December 2018 Interview 3: June 2019	Face-to-face interviews Total 12 interviews and 24 hours Audiotaped
Classroom observations	16 lessons in the first semester	32 hours of classroom observations Observation notes
LMS data collection		Handouts WeChat and Blackboard messages Online coursework

3. Results and discussion

Presented in this section are preliminary findings of the one-year study. During the first year of the participants' graduate studies, they all experienced a complex adaptation process and met different difficulties. The research data revealed two themes: peer effects and positive aspects of the online learning experience.

3.1. Peer effects

Academic adaptation is a dialogic and communal act that happens during the graduate studies (Seloni, 2012), so peer effects were evaluated within different communities: members in the same academic groups, classmates, and supervisors. Their behaviors may have a positive or negative effect on the students (Krasilnikov & Smirnova, 2017). We analyzed the data mainly from the interactions on WeChat and Blackboard. In this paper, we took Gary and Andy as examples.

The main challenge for Gary to adapt to the new academic environment was his worries about the differences between his previous and present degree. Therefore, he had to ask his supervisor and senior students for help through WeChat so that he could be familiar with the new environment. Through three interviews, we found that what his classmates or roommates did may have had a great influence on him. He repeatedly said that he used these online tools to communicate with friends, classmates, and supervisors. He gradually began to adapt to the new environment. He said,

> "since WeChat is the main tool for us to communicate, my supervisor sends me tasks about academic papers, writing skills and revising feedback in almost every day. Frequent communication comforts me and helps me be familiar with the academic environment " (interview, 20/12/2018).

The interaction between students and peers indicates that a tight community will give individuals more support and help them adjust quickly to new academic environments. Andy's social network was very simple. She always communicated with her classmates through the online tools. Andy remarked as below:

> "My supervisor and senior students care little for me, and I always envy other classmates, because they can get a lot of help from them. The only way for me to get help and information is to ask my classmates for help. Sometimes, I feel unhappy" (interview, 22/12/2018).

From Andy's interviews, we found that whether the supervisor and senior students can give help has a big influence on her adaptation experiences. It seemed that her attitude toward her social community had affected her performance negatively.

3.2. Positive aspects of the online learning experience

Previous researches have shown that the LMS is a complementary alternative to traditional tools on teaching method. The focal participants all adopted positive attitudes toward mobile learning. Gary remarked as below:

> "I think it's very useful. It provides an easier and more convenient way to learn new knowledge. It's easy to control" (interview, 20/12/2018).

In addition, Andy stated,

> "generally, it's good. The teacher knows how to use the online tools more efficiently. If there are some pictures or files which cannot be printed on time, or some students sit away from the Blackboard, the teacher will use the mobile phone and send these materials to the WeChat groups immediately. She will also put some materials on the Blackboard platform for us to review. However, I think it is essential that teachers should guide the students to focus on the study materials" (interview, 22/12/2019).

The focal participants all experienced the traditional teaching style before they went to the graduate school. The online learning management system was a new attempt for them to adapt to the academic environment. They could get more academic information from the WeChat and Blackboard platforms, which helped them adapt to the academic environment quickly.

4. Conclusion

In conclusion, the online LMS had a positive influence on the students' adaptation to the new academic environment, and peers played a significant role in the participants' academic socialization. Our results suggest that it is worthwhile to investigate the ways of strengthening students' social networks. Data also showed that educators should look for the best ways of using the LMS.

5. Acknowledgments

This research work was supported by two research funds (2018Y019 and BJSZ2019ZC12).

References

Duff, P. A. (2010). Language socialization into academic discourse communities. *Annual Review of Applied Linguistics, 30*, 169-192. https://doi.org/10.1017/S0267190510000048

Krasilnikov, A., & Smirnova, A. (2017). Online social adaptation of first-year students and their academic performance. *Computers & Education, 113*, 327-338. https://doi.org/10.1016/j.compedu.2017.05.012

Liu, C.-C., Wang, P.-C., & Tai, S.-J. D. (2016). An analysis of student engagement patterns in language learning facilitated by Web 2.0 technologies. *ReCALL, 28*(2), 104-122. https://doi.org/10.1017/S095834401600001X

Rubin, B., Fernandes, R., Avgerinou, M. D., & Moore, J. (2010). The effect of learning management systems on student and faculty outcomes. *The Internet and Higher Education, 13*(1-2), 82-83. https://doi.org/10.1016/j.iheduc.2009.10.008

Seloni, L. (2012). Academic literacy socialization of first year doctoral students in US: a micro-ethnographic perspective. *English for Specific Purposes, 31*(1), 47-59. https://doi.org/10.1016/j.esp.2011.05.004

Wang, Y., Fang, W.-C., Han, J., & Chen, N.-S. (2016). Exploring the affordances of WeChat for facilitating teaching, social and cognitive presence in semi-synchronous language exchange. *Australasian Journal of Educational Technology, 32*(4), 18-37. https://doi.org/10.14742/ajet.2640

Affordances for cultural adjustment of international students learning Chinese as a second language in a mobile-assisted learning environment

Shixin Dong[1], Li Cheng[2], Liu Dong[3], and Guanzhen Wu[4]

Abstract. The purpose of the study is to understand the mobile-assisted learning situation of international students in China from the perspective of cultural adjustment and explore the affordances for cultural adjustment of these students in this specific situation. This study investigated eight students learning Chinese as a second language in a university in Beijing and using mainly WeChat, a mobile technology. Qualitative methods were employed in this study. The researchers followed the students for three months (from September to November 2018) and collected all the online messages in the WeChat online group. Moreover, eight one-hour in-depth interviews with participants were conducted. Results showed that the characteristics of the international students' cultural adjustment in the mobile learning environment are universality, consciousness and unconsciousness, and interactivity. In addition, three affordances were identified: resources on Chinese linguistic and cultural knowledge, ways to obtain social support, and ways to relieve stress. Finally, two suggestions for international students are proposed.

Keywords: cultural adjustment, mobile learning environment, Chinese learning, international students.

---

1. Beijing University of Post and Telecommunications, Beijing, China; dongshixin@bupt.edu.cn
2. Beijing University of Post and Telecommunications, Beijing, China; licheng@bupt.edu.cn
3. Beijing University of Post and Telecommunications, Beijing, China; dongliu@bupt.edu.cn
4. Beijing University of Post and Telecommunications, Beijing, China; wgzh111@bupt.edu.cn

How to cite this article: Dong, S., Cheng, L., Dong, L., & Wu, G. (2019). Affordances for cultural adjustment of international students learning Chinese as a second language in a mobile-assisted learning environment. In F. Meunier, J. Van de Vyver, L. Bradley & S. Thouësny (Eds), *CALL and complexity – short papers from EUROCALL 2019* (pp. 124-129). Research-publishing.net. https://doi.org/10.14705/rpnet.2019.38.997

1. Introduction

Mobile-Assisted Language Learning (MALL) is an emerging research field undergoing rapid evolution (Duman, Orhon, & Gedik, 2015). In the past ten years, most researchers (e.g. Lu, 2008) have focused on how to use mobiles to improve the language levels and communication skills of second language learners. Few studies have been found investigating the process of learners' cultural adjustment. This study focused on the cultural adjustment of foreign students studying Chinese as a second language in a mobile-assisted learning environment.

Two theories guided this study: acculturation (Berry, 1989) and cultural shock (Oberg, 1960). Berry (1989) divides the cultural adaptation patterns of different groups into assimilation, separation, integration, and marginalization. Cultural shock was proposed by Oberg (1960). He indicates that "cultural shock is precipitated by the anxiety that results from losing all our familiar signs and symbols of social intercourse" (Oberg, 1960, p. 177). It is hoped that this research could help international students for better cultural adjustment in a MALL environment, and also provide references for future research.

2. Methods

The study was conducted in an undergraduate second-year intercultural communication class at a university in Beijing. The main mobile technology used in this study was WeChat, "a widely used instant messaging app used on mobile phones or/and computers and released by Tencent in 2011" (Wu & Miller, 2019, p. 6).

In the class, the international students used WeChat to participate in the course discussions on different topics. After class, the international students and Chinese students conducted a one-month cooperative learning activity entitled 'Discussion of Cultural Differences' through WeChat.

2.1. Data collection

The researchers followed eight international students from September to November 2018 for a total of three months. With the consent of the participants, the researchers collected all the online messages in the WeChat group for a total of 30,000 words in Chinese. Moreover, the researchers conducted eight one-hour in-depth interviews (see Figure 1 below) with the participants.

Figure 1. Interview outline

2.2. Research questions

The research questions are as laid out below.

(1) What are the characteristics of the international students' cultural adjustment in the mobile learning environment?

(2) Are there any similarities or differences in the participants' adjustment experiences?

(3) What are the affordances of MALL in cultural adjustment of international students?

2.3. Participants

In this study, eight participants were selected using a convenient sampling method. They were eight international students learning Chinese as a second language in a university in Beijing. Among the participants, there were four males and four females, all of whom were in the second year of undergraduate studies, and the average age was 22 years old. Moreover, they were from Greece, South Korea, Russia, Japan, Kazakhstan, Indonesia, Uzbekistan, and Venezuela. Seven participants passed Level V of the Chinese Proficiency Test (HSK) and one participant passed Level VI.

2.4. Data analysis

With a thematic analysis method (Braun & Clarke, 2006), two phases of data analysis were undertaken in this study. In the first phase, the researchers took a theoretically-informed and deductive approach to coding and looked for particular examples (e.g. the topic of communication and the role of participants in communication) and references (e.g. participants' feelings about using WeChat) to characteristics and affordances for cultural adjustment in the data. Then, the researchers categorized and coded them with distinct themes. In addition, timely discussions with the interviewees and each research group on summarized topics were carried out on October 20th, 2018.

3. Results and discussion

3.1. Characteristics of the international students' cultural adjustment in the mobile-assisted learning environment

The researchers summarized three characteristics of cultural adjustment. The first characteristic was universality. Data showed that seven out of eight participants said they used mobile devices frequently in their daily lives. Six participants clearly pointed out that mobile phones were good for their better cultural adjustment. Moreover, consciousness and unconsciousness was the second characteristic of the international students' cultural adjustment in the mobile-assisted learning environment. The researchers found that the participants' cultural adjustment in MALL environment was different in terms of consciousness. Four participants were able to take the initiative to use mobile phones to make cultural adjustments, while the other four participants did not realize their behavior of adjustment. Interactivity was a third important feature. For interview questions nine to 12, four participants mentioned the words 'communication' and 'feedback'. Mei Lin mentioned that when she had a problem with her studies, she could get a timely answer by asking the teacher through WeChat.

3.2. Affordances of MALL in cultural adjustment of international students

Three affordances were identified in the study. The first affordance of MALL in cultural adjustment of international students was the use of resources to learn the Chinese language and culture. Seven participants mentioned the use of mobile devices. For interview questions one to four, both Jane and Kim said that the improvement of Chinese proficiency had enhanced their confidence in communicating with Chinese people. Moreover, WeChat data showed that the content of collaborative learning was the most discussed topic. The Chinese students helped participants correct mistakes in their online communication and shared Chinese cultural knowledge, such as Chinese pop songs. Researchers indicated the finding seems similar to previous studies (e.g. Jin, 2018).

Second, the MALL approach afforded ways for participants to obtain social support. Interview data and WeChat messages showed that all eight participants expressed positive views on their interactions with the Chinese students in cooperative learning activities. Six participants thought that WeChat was beneficial to their exchanges with Chinese students. Jane and Kim said they had established friendships with Chinese students. However, three participants mentioned that differences in social software (e.g. Twitter and Line) had become obstacles to their interaction with Chinese students. Further research is however required to figure out whether participants can become real friends with Chinese students and obtain long-term social support.

Third, mobile tools also provided ways to relieve stress. For interview questions five to 12, two participants said that entertainment resources in WeChat relieved their pressure and helped them face the difficulties of cultural adjustment with a positive attitude. However, Ryo said he preferred to watch videos on YouTube because "most of the videos on WeChat are just for Chinese". It is suggested that it is necessary to develop entertainment content that is more suitable for international students.

4. Conclusions

This study focused on the cultural adjustment of foreign students studying Chinese as a second language in a mobile-assisted learning environment. Eight international students studying Chinese in China participated in the study. The study used qualitative research methods to analyze online messages of WeChat groups and personal in-depth interviews. The researchers identified three characteristics of the international students' cultural adjustment in the mobile-assisted learning environment. Three affordances that the MALL approach brought to students' cultural adjustment were found. Moreover, two suggestions were proposed. One is that emerging technologies could be applied to design Chinese apps that are more suitable for international students. The other is that mobile technology could be used to carry out activities in which Chinese and foreign students participate. Due to the limitations of the study, it is suggested that future research focus on the integration of emerging technologies and MALL, and the design of teaching activities in the MALL environment.

5. Acknowledgments

This research work was supported by two research funds (2018Y019 and BJSZ2019ZC12).

References

Berry, J. W. (1989). Psychology of acculturation. *Nebraska Symposium on Motivation, 37*, 201-234.
Braun,V., & Clarke, V. (2006). Using thematic analysis in psychology. *Qualitative Research in Psychology, 3*(2), 77-101. https://doi.org/10.1191/1478088706qp063oa
Duman, G., Orhon, G., & Gedik, N. (2015). Research trends in mobile assisted language learning from 2000 to 2012. *Recall, 27*(2), 197-216. https://doi.org/10.1017/s0958344014000287
Jin, L. (2018). Digital affordances on WeChat: learning Chinese as a second language. *Computer Assisted Language Learning, 31*(1-2), 27-52. https://doi.org/10.1080/09588221.2017.1376687
Lu, M. (2008). Effectiveness of vocabulary learning via mobile phone. *Journal of Computer Assisted Learning, 24*(6), 515-525. https://doi.org/10.1111/j.1365-2729.2008.00289.x
Oberg, K. (1960). Cultural shock: adjustment to new cultural environments. *Pract Anthropol, 7*, 177-182.
Wu, J. G., & Miller, L. (2019). Raising native cultural awareness through WeChat: a case study with Chinese EFL students. *Computer Assisted Language Learning, First View*, 1-31. https://doi.org/10.1080/09588221.2019.1629962

 ■ UCLouvain

Critical cultural awareness and learning through digital environments

James D. Dunn[1]

Abstract. Students with cultural and linguistic competence are needed to navigate an increasingly globalized society. This study collected and analyzed cultural awareness data from students who communicated with people of other cultures through Virtual Reality (VR) environments. Students from a private university in Japan engaged in directed communication with other students from the USA using an online virtual chat program. A questionnaire based on the Global Perspectives Inventory (GPI) was used by the students to self-report their views on the intercultural interactions and give a metacognitive analysis of their intercultural competence/knowledge of intercultural phenomena. In addition to directed communicative objectives, students were given the chance to engage in free conversation in the digital space created by the software to facilitate intercultural critical cultural awareness skills. Early findings show that students were able to improve critical cultural awareness through a virtual experience.

Keywords: virtual reality, critical cultural awareness, gamification, critical thinking.

1. Introduction

Japan's Ministry of Education, Culture, Sports, Science, and Technology (MEXT) has put forth a call for students to develop their cultural and linguistic skills to competently navigate an increasingly globalized society. Toward this end, MEXT has stipulated a goal for students to be developed as global human resources capable of being a valuable member of society in multiple cultural contexts (MEXT, 2011).

While communication tools such as Skype and other software have been used to help foster cultural awareness, non-VR methods of digital communication, while

---

1. Tokai University, Hiratsuka, Japan; james.d.dunn@outlook.com

How to cite this article: Dunn, J. D. (2019). Critical cultural awareness and learning through digital environments. In F. Meunier, J. Van de Vyver, L. Bradley & S. Thouësny (Eds), *CALL and complexity – short papers from EUROCALL 2019* (pp. 130-136). Research-publishing.net. https://doi.org/10.14705/rpnet.2019.38.998

useful for intercultural communication, have limitations, such as participants feeling disconnected and having no sense of physical presence with their partner (Gregersen & Youdina, 2009; Ip, 2011; Shachaf, 2008). This research was designed to collect and analyze students' perceptions of cultural awareness from students communicating with people of other cultures through the online virtual chat program, Big Screen. It was hypothesized that students who engaged in directed communicative tasks in a VR space with individuals from a variety of locations and cultures from around the world using an online virtual communication space would improve in their self-reported cultural awareness scores on the GPI-based questionnaire. Student answers to an intercultural communicative competence questionnaire were analyzed to elucidate their communicative competence and metacognitive-awareness development over multiple sessions of two directed communication tasks and one free conversation task.

2. Method

2.1. Context and participants

This study is being conducted over the spring and fall semesters of the 2019-2020 academic year at a private Japanese university. Professional contacts from the USA were sourced during the 2018-2019 academic year as a path to connect with high school and university students of other cultures. Two American students, one university and one high school, were chosen as participants as they each already possessed a VR headset and were willing to meet the standard three sessions minimum for the study. The students in Japan, all of whom were non-native English speakers, were recruited from compulsory second year English courses and aviation English courses respectively. Thus far, three student participants have successfully performed all communication sessions and completed the post-questionnaire (Table 1), with more students currently waiting to start their participation. The Japanese Participants (JPs) were paired with the same Foreign volunteers (FVs) throughout their culture-sharing session to normalize the development of questions and answers and to allow for the natural progression of information sharing through the three sessions. Based on recordings of the last interaction sessions, the information participants shared ranged from cultural knowledge in explaining a Japanese TV show to their partner, intracultural knowledge through asking their partner about their culture, and intercultural knowledge in answering the questions of the FV. All sessions were online utilizing a free VR gathering space software, Big Screen.

Table 1. Student participants

Participants in Japan				
Gender	Age	Self-Reported English Level	Area of Study	Nationality
JP1: Male	19-22	Advanced	Aviation	Japanese
JP2: Female	19-22	Advanced	Aviation	Japanese
JP3: Female	19-22	High-Intermediate	Physical Education	Japanese
Participants in The USA				
Gender	Age	Self-Reported English Level	Area of Study	Nationality
FV1: Male	15-18	Native	Psychology	USA
FV2: Male	15-18	Native	High School Student	USA

2.2. Questionnaire design and purpose

A questionnaire based on the GPI (http://www.gpi.hs.iastate.edu/) was used to allow students to self-report their views of the intercultural knowledge and cultural awareness along aspects such as understanding the other's culture, studying with people of other cultures, and the ability to work with people of other cultures. This questionnaire was chosen because it narrows the focus of interpersonal aspects into two sub-domains; knowledge of other cultures (Questions 1 and 2), and the ability to interact with people of other cultures (Questions 3, 4, and 5).

2.3. Questions

The questions utilized in the questionnaire are as follows:

- I feel that I know many things about other cultures;
- I feel that I can understand personalities of people from other countries well;
- I feel that I could study with people from other countries well;
- I feel that I could work with people from other countries well; and
- I feel confident in my ability to communicate with people in another country.

All questions were answered using a Likert Scale from 1, completely disagree, to 5, completely agree, with a 'no opinion' answer available on each question. All questions were input online using a Google Forms questionnaire. As part of the questionnaire, all students digitally signed a consent form that was provided in both English and Japanese. All sessions were attended by the Japanese student, a foreign student from the USA (virtually), and the researcher.

3. Data collection

At the outset of the study, the JPs were asked to complete a pre-study questionnaire based on the GPI created by the researcher. After the last session, the participants were asked to complete a post-questionnaire. The same questions were used in the pre- and post-questionnaires to help elucidate changes in the students' views on intercultural competence. Students were asked to spend three, 30-minute sessions in a private virtual conversation space created by the research leader utilizing the Oculus Quest VR headset (https://www.oculus.com/) which was obtained through an inter-departmental research grant from the researcher's university. The virtual space was created utilizing the free VR software, Big Screen (Figure 1), which allowed students to share and explain short clips of Japanese television variety shows that can be confusing to non-Japanese people.

Figure 1. Big Screen VR[2]

Students were paired according to their availability and students continued all three sessions with the same partner. Due to limitations in finding foreign participants, FV2 participated in two, three-session blocks.

These students then carried out initial introductions and an environment setup during the initial virtual chat session in a free talk manner. Student conversations were recorded and will be analyzed at a later date.

---

2. Reproduced with kind permission from © 2019 Bigscreen, Inc; https://bigscreenvr.com/

The second session consisted of engaging in a directed chat session where the JPs shared and explained Japanese cultural aspects through short Japanese television clips. These activities are in correlation with MEXT's (2011) guidelines for Japanese students to become cultural ambassadors. As such, the television clips from Japanese variety shows were chosen by the JPs according to their interest and existing knowledge. The participants were allowed to choose the clips to help minimize instances of silence that may have arisen if the JP was unfamiliar with the particular variety show.

The final session involved students explaining another Japanese television clip that consisted of a popular comedy show that was chosen by the researcher. After the final session, students were asked to complete the GPI-based questionnaire again. Due to the early nature of this data, scores were compared in the pre- and post-questionnaires for changes in attitudes. Once more data has been collected, and answers will be analyzed to measure changes in student self-perception of intercultural knowledge and development of cultural awareness.

4. Results

Preliminary analysis of questionnaire data suggests that students' exposure to intercultural communicative situations in a digital space could be both beneficial to the development of intercultural awareness, and helpful in developing the students' perspectives as global citizens. Across the five questions, all scores, except Question 3 ("I feel that I could study with people from other countries well"), scored higher in the post-treatment questionnaire than in the pre-treatment questionnaire (see Figure 2, Figure 3, and Figure 4).

Figure 2. JP1 results

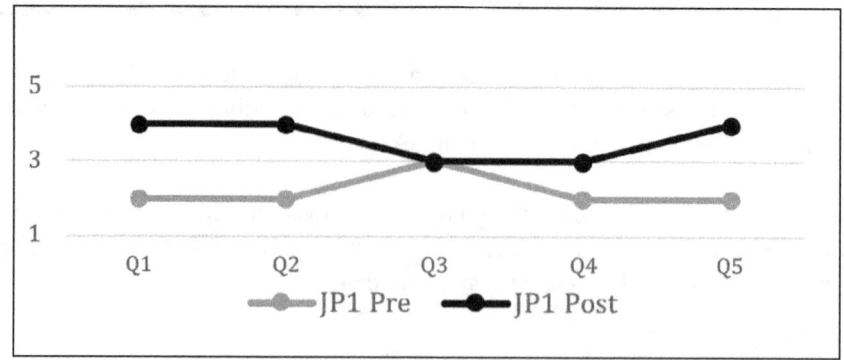

Figure 3. JP2 results

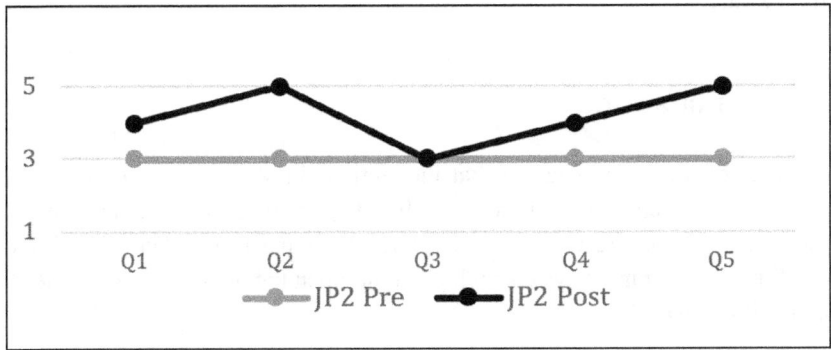

Figure 4. JP3 results

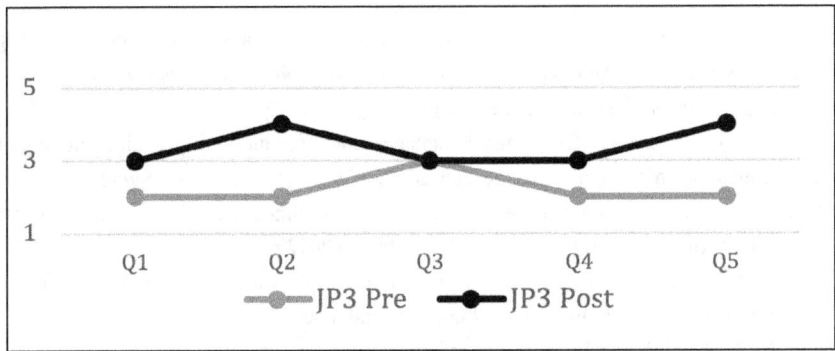

An analysis of the student questionnaires also suggests that student cultural awareness along the domains of knowledge of other cultures (Questions 1 and 2) and the ability to interact with people of other cultures (Questions 4 and 5) increased.

5. Discussion

The number of students in this study is still small due to a delay in the disbursement of grant funds, but the initial results are encouraging. Once data from a larger pool of participants can be collected, further analysis can be done to find trends and significance of changes due to the intervention. In the future, more questions will be added to further diversify and fine tune the information collected. Even though these results are still early, the initial findings suggest that VR can be a digital 'real-world' experience for students to interact with people of other cultures and expand cultural awareness.

6. Conclusions

The results of this study suggest that interactions in VR are potentially a viable pathway to intercultural competence building and global human resource development. Future research can explore the impact of other digital based intercultural development systems which could open the doors to new courses that span the globe digitally.

References

Gregersen, T., & Youdina, T. (2009). An intercultural communication event via video bridge: bringing Russian and American students together. *International Journal of Teaching and Learning in Higher Education, 20*, 262-266.

Ip, W. H. (2011). Video conferencing: advantages and limitations in teaching intercultural communication in foreign language education. *ICT for Language Learning Conference, Florence, Italy, July 9-10*. https://conference.pixel-online.net/conferences/ICT4LL2012/common/download/Paper_pdf/158-IBT31-FP-Ip-ICT2012.pdf

MEXT. (2011, February 24). English Translation of the MEXT Guidelines. *AJET.* http://ajet.net/announcement/english-translation-of-the-mext-guidelines/

Shachaf, P. (2008). Cultural diversity and information and communication technology impacts on global virtual teams: an exploratory study. *Information & Management, 45*(2), 131-142. https://doi.org/10.1016/j.im.2007.12.003

■ UCLouvain

Learner attitudes towards data-driven learning: investigating the effect of teaching contexts

Luciana Forti[1]

Abstract. Concordance-based Data-Driven Learning (DDL) aims to help second language learners infer language usage rules from language usage regularities. A number of DDL pedagogical treatments have focussed on phraseological units such as collocations, widely recognised as a central component of second language learning. This study evaluates DDL effects from an emic perspective, reflecting the learners' perceived usefulness of the approach, as opposed to etic perspectives, representing changes in language competence as a result of the approach. It compares a group of Chinese learners and a group of Belgian learners of Italian as a Second Language/Foreign Language (SL/FL). The findings indicate that the Belgian students seem to have gained familiarity with the approach faster than the Chinese, though the latter seems to perceive greater long-term benefits of the approach, and are more favourable to future mobile phone applications. The study aims to shed light on possible learner-related differences in DDL treatments and on the insightfulness of emic data in assessing DDL effects.

Keywords: data-driven learning, collocations, Italian.

1. Introduction

When investigating the effects of DDL, i.e. the direct and immediate use of corpus data by language learners (Leech, 1997; Meunier, 2010), one important perspective is the emic perspective, which aims to reflect the learners' personal attitudes towards the approach.

Previous research has highlighted the learners' positive attitudes towards the perceived relevance and authenticity of corpus data, and the empowering effect

---

1. University for Foreigners of Perugia, Perugia, Italy; luciana.forti@unistrapg.it; https://orcid.org/0000-0001-5520-7795

How to cite this article: Forti, L. (2019). Learner attitudes towards data-driven learning: investigating the effect of teaching contexts. In F. Meunier, J. Van de Vyver, L. Bradley & S. Thouësny (Eds), *CALL and complexity – short papers from EUROCALL 2019* (pp. 137-143). Research-publishing.net. https://doi.org/10.14705/rpnet.2019.38.999

of the inductive learning that is often associated with DDL (Chambers, 2007). Nevertheless, little attention seems to have been devoted so far to the potential effects that different teaching contexts may have when adopting DDL materials and strategies.

This paper examines learner attitudes towards DDL for learning collocations, comparing a larger sample of Chinese learners and a smaller sample of Belgian learners of Italian as an SL/FL.

2. Method

2.1. Participant samples and DDL treatment

All participants in this study were university students of Italian as an SL/FL. The larger sample of Chinese learners consisted of 123 participants, which were distributed in eight classes with a range of 13-17 per class. Their level, as assessed by the university placement tests, was pre-intermediate, and they were part of an eight-week long intervention, with one one-hour lesson a week. The smaller sample of Belgian learners consisted of 22 participants, divided into an elementary class of ten, and an intermediate class of 12, with an exposure of one one-hour lesson each. Various activities were developed for both samples on the basis of concordance lines extracted from the native Perugia Corpus (PEC) (Spina, 2014), and focussed on verb-noun collocations (see supplementary materials for a sample activity).

2.2. Questionnaire construction and administration

The questionnaire items analysed in this study are part of a larger questionnaire made of eight Likert scale items and four open questions. The results for the Chinese participant sample were partly published in Forti (2017). This paper reports on results for the four Likert scale items dealing specifically with features of the DDL treatment.

The Likert scale items were developed according to the recommendations contained in Dörnyei and Taguchi (2010), with items being formulated either positively or negatively in order to avoid single-sided choices. The values of the scale were operationalised as follows: 1, totally disagree; 2, disagree; 3, partially disagree; 4, partially agree; 5, agree; and 6, totally agree.

The questionnaire was distributed in class at the end of the pedagogical intervention, in pen-and-paper modality.

3. Results and discussion

Fifty questionnaires were collected from the Chinese students, while ten and 12 questionnaires were collected from the Belgian elementary and intermediate students respectively. For questionnaire items two and four, one Belgian intermediate student selected three values, so these two responses were removed.

Figure 1 shows a bar chart with response percentages and trend lines for each group. The figure relates to item one, focussing on whether the concordance-based work was deemed confusing. The Chinese group seems to exhibit the greatest difficulties ($M=3.60$; $SD=1.97$), followed by the Belgian elementary ($M=2.60$; $SD=1.57$) and the Belgian intermediate ($M=1.73$; $SD=1.67$) students. The different inclination of the trend lines characterising the Chinese and Belgian data indicate how the two groups differed in this respect.

Figure 1. Item 1: Reading groups of sentences containing the same combination confused me

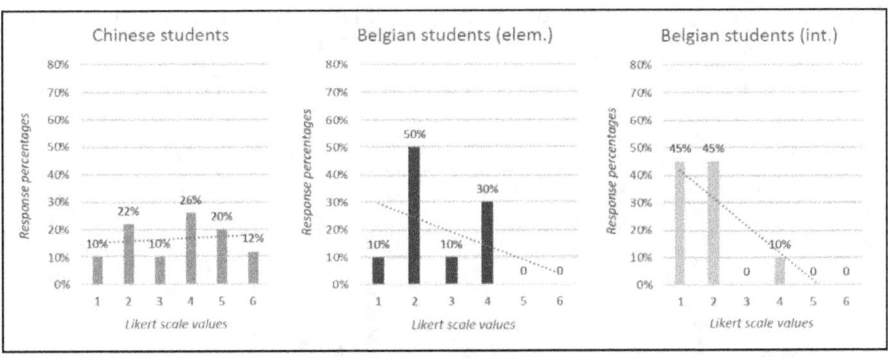

In Figure 2, we see the results dealing with whether observing the groups of sentences containing the same combination was perceived as helpful to understand how to use that combination in the future. In this case, we notice very similar trend lines in the three groups, with the starkest results obtained for the Chinese group ($M=5.20$; $SD=3.48$), followed by the Belgian elementary ($M=4.90$; $SD=2.90$) and the Belgian intermediate ($M=4.83$; $SD=2.48$) students.

Figure 2. Item 2: The observation of groups of sentences containing the same combination has helped me to understand how to use that combination in the future

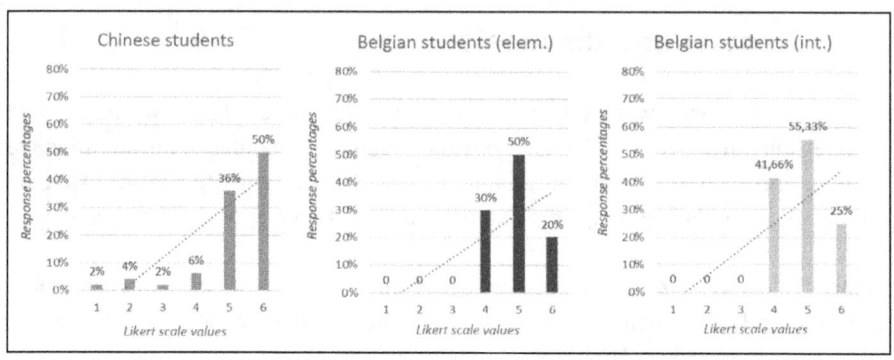

Figure 3 shows the results for the item dealing with the perception of DDL activities being able to help the students make fewer errors in the future. Once more, the trend lines in the three groups show a similar inclination, with the Chinese feeling more confident about the helpfulness of the approach (M=5.14; SD=3.24), followed by the Belgian intermediate (M=4.82; SD=3.02) and the Belgian elementary (M=4.30; SD=2.43) students.

Figure 3. Item 3: The groups of sentences will help me make fewer errors in the future

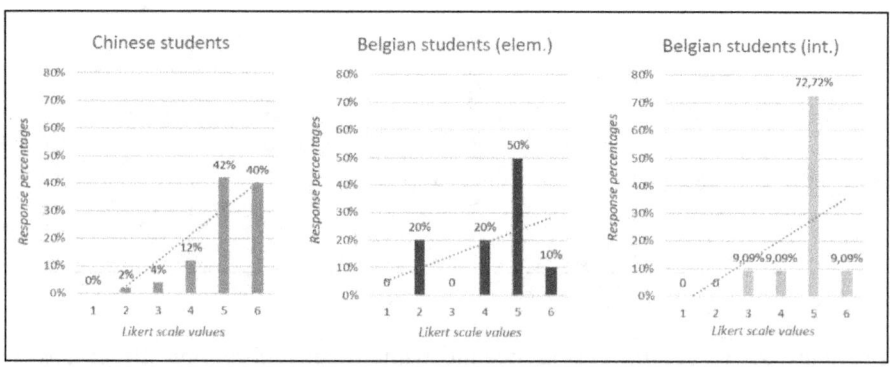

The last Likert scale item (Figure 4) was aimed at gaining insight into the perceived usefulness of a new app with groups of sentences as the output of a query involving word combinations. Here, we notice quite different trend lines in the response percentages, when comparing the Chinese (M=2.64; SD=2.54)

and the Belgian elementary ($M=4.20$; $SD=2.32$) students, with the Belgian intermediate students occupying more of a middle ground ($M=3.42$; $SD=1.29$).

Figure 4. Item 4: A new smartphone application with groups of sentences for word combinations would be useless

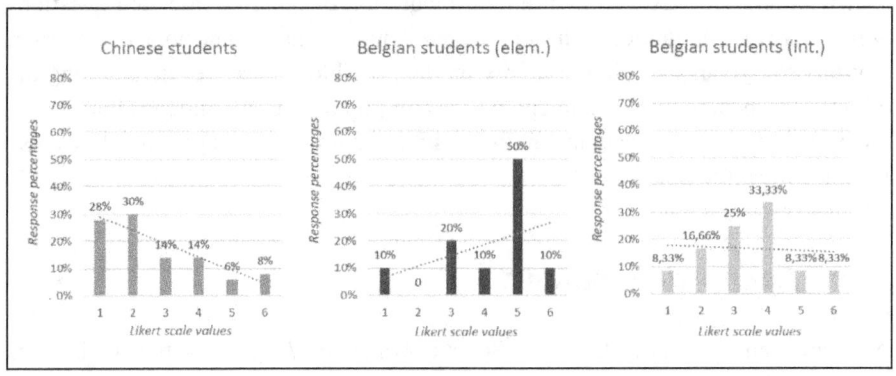

In sum, Belgian students have less trouble with the groups of sentences, as they seem to feel not as confused as the Chinese. This might be due to French belonging to a language family that is genealogically closer to Italian, especially in terms of reading system. However, the Belgian students do not seem to perceive DDL as useful as the Chinese do, which might also be due to the vicinity with the language being learned, and perhaps with the very limited exposure they had to the approach.

On the other hand, Chinese students seem to be more favourable to the idea of a concordance-based app in comparison to both groups of Belgian students. This might be due to a possible increased familiarity that the Chinese learners have with mobile phones, in comparison to the Belgian students.

4. Conclusions

In this paper, we briefly outlined some results related to a DDL pedagogical intervention which took place in two different teaching contexts. The results are based on emic data, aiming to elicit the learners' perceptions in relation to the usefulness of the approach.

The findings indicate that the Belgian learners were generally more comfortable with the proposed concordance work, although the Chinese perceived its usefulness more distinctly. Furthermore, the Chinese students seem more favourable to the idea of an app with a concordance-based version of DDL, in comparison to the Belgian students.

The study would definitely benefit from more fine-grained and sophisticated statistical analyses, as well as from an integration of other open-ended questions which were also contained in the administered questionnaire. The hope is, however, that this study can shed light not only on the possible differences in assessing the effects of a specific DDL treatment in different populations of students, but also on the importance of emic data in gaining insight into how DDL is perceived by those who it is meant to help.

5. Acknowledgements

A warm thank you goes to Laura Scarpa, *Maître de langues* at the Institut des Langues Vivantes of Université catholique de Louvain, for allowing the author to teach a DDL lesson in each of the two classes, and to Valerio Chiocchio for revising the French version of the questionnaire.

6. Supplementary materials

https://research-publishing.box.com/s/k87ww3zl2c0a3im0g4ykvo7dzarf8me3

References

Chambers, A. (2007). Popularising corpus consultation by language learners and teachers. *Language and Computers*, *61*(1), 3-16. https://doi.org/10.1163/9789401203906_002

Dörnyei, Z., & Taguchi, T. (2010). Questionnaires in second language research. Construction, administration, and processing (2nd ed.). Routledge. https://doi.org/10.4324/9780203864739

Forti, L. (2017). Data-driven learning and the acquisition of Italian collocations: from design to student evaluation. In K. Borthwick, L. Bradley & S. Thouësny (Eds), *CALL in a climate of change: adapting to turbulent global conditions – short papers from EUROCALL 2017* (pp. 110-115). Research-publishing.net. https://doi.org/10.14705/rpnet.2017.eurocall2017.698

Leech, G. (1997). Teaching and language corpora: a convergence. In A. Wichmann, S. Fligelstone, T. McEnery & G. Knowles (Eds), Teaching and language corpora. Addison Wesley Longman.

Meunier, F. (2010). Learner corpora and English language teaching: checkup time. Anglistik: International Journal of English *Studies, 21*(1), 209-220.

Spina, S. (2014). Il Perugia Corpus: una risorsa di riferimento per l'italiano. Composizione, annotazione e valutazione. In *Proceedings of the First Italian Conference on Computational Linguistics CLiC-it 2014 & the Fourth International Workshop EVALITA 2014litica* (Vol. 1, pp. 354-359). Pisa University Press.

ColloCaid: a tool to help academic English writers find the words they need

Ana Frankenberg-Garcia[1], Geraint Rees[2], Robert Lew[3], Jonathan Roberts[4], Nirwan Sharma[5], and Peter Butcher[6]

Abstract. This short paper summarizes the development of ColloCaid (www.collocaid.uk), a text editor that supports writers with academic English collocations. After a brief introduction, the paper summarizes how the lexicographic database underlying ColloCaid was compiled, how text editor integration was achieved, and results from initial user studies. The paper concludes by outlining future developments.

Keywords: collocation, EAP, writing, e-lexicography.

1. Introduction

Research has shown that less experienced users of academic English have a limited repertoire of collocations (Frankenberg-Garcia, 2018). Indeed, collocations like *REACH+conclusion* are among the most frequent look-ups among novice users of written academic English (Yoon, 2016).

There are a number of tools and resources that academic writers can use to search for such idiomatic combinations of words. These include general English dictionaries and more targeted ones like the *Longman Collocations Dictionary and Thesaurus* (Mayor, 2013) or the *Oxford Learner's Dictionary of Academic English* (Lea, 2014). Writers familiar with corpora can also consult general English corpora

1. University of Surrey, Guildford, United Kingdom; a.frankenberg-garcia@surrey.ac.uk; https://orcid.org/0000-0001-9623-7990
2. University of Surrey, Guildford, United Kingdom; g.rees@surrey.ac.uk; https://orcid.org/0000-0002-9204-8073
3. Adam Mickiewicz University, Poznań, Poland; rlew@amu.edu.pl; https://orcid.org/0000-0002-6772-210X
4. Bangor University, Bangor, Wales, United Kingdom; j.c.roberts@bangor.ac.uk; https://orcid.org/0000-0001-7718-3181
5. Bangor University, Bangor, Wales, United Kingdom; n.sharma@bangor.ac.uk; https://orcid.org/0000-0002-6576-3848
6. Bangor University, Bangor, Wales, United Kingdom; p.butcher@bangor.ac.uk; https://orcid.org/0000-0002-3361-627X

How to cite this article: Frankenberg-Garcia, A., Rees, G., Lew, R., Roberts, J., Sharma, N., & Butcher, P. (2019). ColloCaid: a tool to help academic English writers find the words they need. In F. Meunier, J. Van de Vyver, L. Bradley & S. Thouësny (Eds), *CALL and complexity – short papers from EUROCALL 2019* (pp. 144-150). Research-publishing.net. https://doi.org/10.14705/rpnet.2019.38.1000

like the BNC and COCA, and corpora of student papers like BAWE (Nesi, 2011) and MICUSP (Romer & Swales, 2010). Other useful tools include SkELL (Baisa & Suchomel, 2014), arguably the easiest to use English corpus available, FlaxLC (Wu, Fitzgerald, Yu, & Witten, 2019), a learner-friendly corpus-based collocation tool, and LEAD (Granger & Paquot, 2015), an academic English dictionary-cum-corpus.

However, writers may not know where or how to look up collocations (Frankenberg-Garcia, 2011), or may simply not realize that their emerging texts could be made more idiomatic (Frankenberg-Garcia, 2014; Laufer, 2011). Moreover, even when writers realize they need help, looking up collocations while writing can be distracting and disruptive (Yoon, 2016).

To address this challenge, we are developing a text editor that assists writers with academic English collocations (Frankenberg-Garcia et al., 2019a). ColloCaid provides writers with collocation suggestions as they write, helping them find idiomatic combinations of words and expand their collocational repertoire. ColloCaid can also be used to revise collocations in existing drafts.

2. Lexicographic database

The ColloCaid lexicographic database aims to address core collocations used across disciplines in general academic English. As detailed in Frankenberg-Garcia et al. (2019a), it draws on the noun, verb and adjective lemmas that occur in at least two of three well-known academic vocabulary lists: the Academic Keyword List (Paquot, 2010), the Academic Collocation List (Ackermann & Chen, 2013), and the Durrant (2016) subset of the Gardner and Davies (2014) Academic Vocabulary List.

The original selection of lemmas has been revised to (1) disambiguate polysemy (e.g. *figure* as image, as number and as person); (2) include homographs used in academic contexts (e.g. *aim* was initially only listed as a noun, but its less frequent verbal lemma was added to avoid the impression that only the noun was idiomatic); (3) discard lemmas that are not collocationally productive (e.g. *actual*); and (4) add high-frequency interdisciplinary academic lemmas like *paper* and *table*, which slipped through initial selection thresholds (Rees et al., 2019).

The database was populated with interdisciplinary collocates pertaining to the above lemmas extracted from corpora of expert academic English writing. As detailed in Frankenberg-Garcia et al. (2019a), this was undertaken using Sketch Engine (Kilgarriff et al., 2014), which automatically summarizes the main collocations of a lemma in a corpus. Issues with the extraction have been dealt with using lexicographic judgment on a case by case basis. This included, for example, overruling the classification of *regard* as a verb, since its primary use in academic texts is preposition-like, in contexts such as *decisions regarding safety*, or in prepositional phrases like *with regard to* (Rees et al., 2019).

The database was further populated with authentic examples of collocations in use, selected according to typicality, informativity, and intelligibility. Examples were also curated to address language production needs and maximize their potential for data-driven learning, as explained in Frankenberg-Garcia (2014). Figure 1 summarizes the lexical coverage of ColloCaid in its current 0.4 version (20 September 2019).

Figure 1. ColloCaid 0.4 lexicographic database

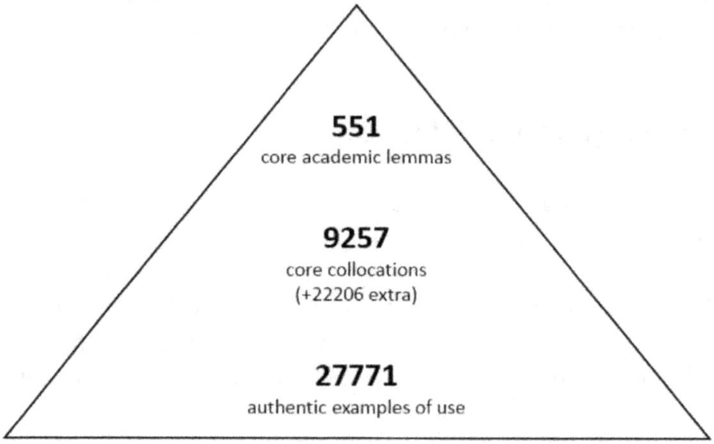

551
core academic lemmas

9257
core collocations
(+22206 extra)

27771
authentic examples of use

3. Text editor integration

Academic writers from different disciplines have their own preferred operating systems and text editors. In our interdisciplinary research team, for example, papers initiated by the linguists are normally drafted in a Windows environment using Microsoft Word, whereas the computer scientists prefer to use Macs and LaTeX editors. For developing a prototype and testing it with different users, we opted for an online editor that can be accessed from a normal browser compatible with multiple devices and operating systems, without the need to download additional software. TinyMCE (https://www.tiny.cloud/), a widely used open-source editor that looks like any regular editor was selected for this purpose (Figure 2: A).

We adopted a dynamic, data-driven learning approach to the integration of the lexicographic data into the editor. It is data-driven because collocations suggestions are shown rather than explained. It is dynamic because collocations are displayed only when wanted, and in as much detail as desired, via progressive interactive menus (Figure 2: B-E).

Figure 2.   ColloCaid editor

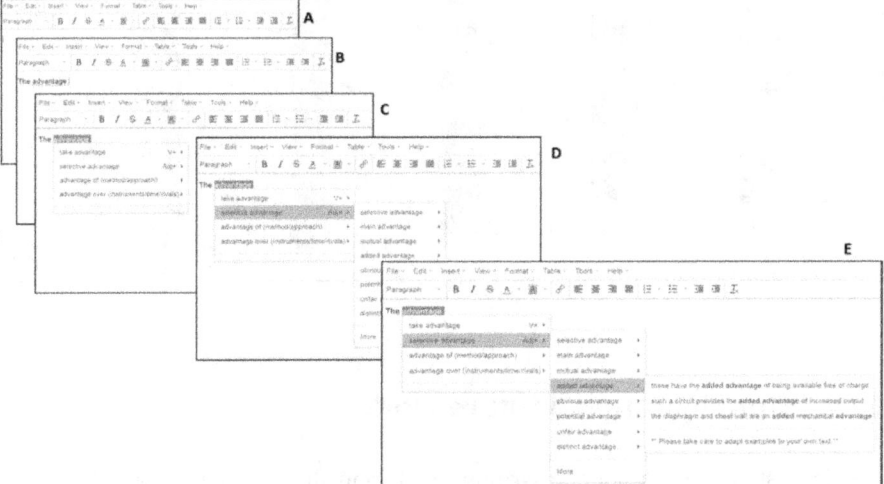

4.   Initial user studies

Development versions of ColloCaid have been tested during university writing workshops and seminars in Brazil, France, Poland, and Spain (Frankenberg-Garcia et al., 2019b). Participants (N=122) included novice and expert L2 English writers from a wide range of disciplines. Due to space restrictions, we are only able to present here the scores obtained on the Brooke (2013) System Usability Scale (SUS). The SUS is a standard for measuring the usability of systems (hardware, software, websites, etc.), with the advantage that its results can be compared on the same scale with hundreds of other systems. It comprises ten alternating positive and negative statements about system usability which users rate with a Likert-type scale. As shown in Figure 3, the SUS scores obtained for ColloCaid are between good and excellent (and above the SUS average of around 70), despite known bugs and minor issues with the lexicographic database.

Figure 3. Usability scores of ColloCaid v0.1 to v0.3 and interpretation of SUS values (right) according to Bangor, Kortum, and Miller (2009)

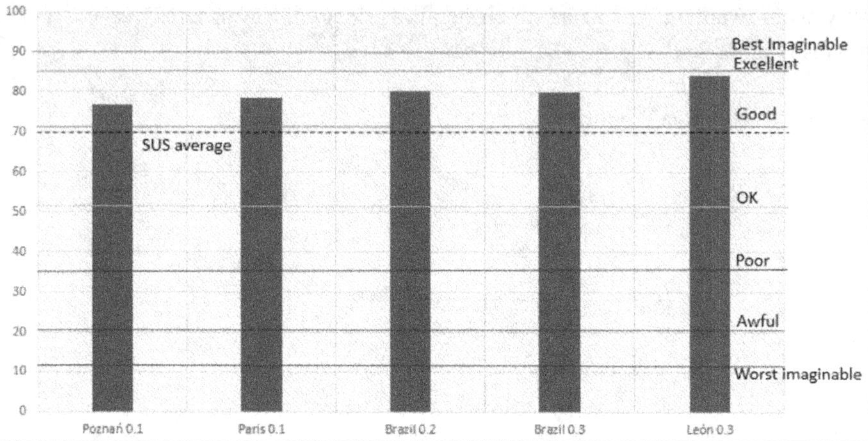

5. Conclusion and future work

Previous studies on academic writing needs and dictionary use have led us to develop a text editor integrated with a large, lexical database of general academic English collocation suggestions, enriched with corpus examples of collocations in use. Our prototype, which draws on the principle of dynamic data-driven learning, has been well received by L2 users of academic English, scoring between good and excellent on the SUS. Future development of ColloCaid includes adjustments to the lexical database (i.e. expanding and proofreading current coverage), experimenting with new ways of visualizing collocations, and further user testing with think-aloud and diary studies.

6. Acknowledgments

This research is funded by the UK Arts and Humanities Research Council (AH/P003508/1).

References

Ackermann, K., & Chen, Y. (2013). Developing the academic collocations list (ACL) – a corpus-driven and expert-judged approach. *Journal of English for Academic Purposes, 12*(4), 235-247. https://doi.org/10.1016/j.jeap.2013.08.002

Baisa, V., & Suchomel, V. (2014). SkELL: web interface for English language learning. In P. Rychlý (Ed.), *Proceedings of Recent Advances in Slavonic Natural Language Processing* (pp. 63-70).

Bangor, A., Kortum, P., & Miller, J. (2009). Determining what individual SUS scores mean: adding an adjective rating scale. *Journal of Usability Studies, 4*(3), 114-123.

Brooke, J. (2013). SUS: a retrospective. *Journal of Usability Studies, 8*(2), 29-40.

Durrant, P. (2016). To what extent is the academic vocabulary list relevant to university student writing? *English for Specific Purposes, 43*, 49-61. https://doi.org/10.1016/j.esp.2016.01.004

Frankenberg-Garcia, A. (2011). Beyond L1-L2 equivalents: where do users of English as a foreign language turn for help? *International Journal of Lexicography, 24*(1), 97-123. https://doi.org/10.1093/ijl/ecq038

Frankenberg-Garcia, A. (2014). The use of corpus examples for language comprehension and production. *ReCALL, 26*(2), 128-146. https://doi.org/10.1017/s0958344014000093

Frankenberg-Garcia, A. (2018). Investigating the collocations available to EAP writers. *Journal of English for Academic Purposes, 35*, 93-104. https://doi.org/10.1016/j.jeap.2018.07.003

Frankenberg-Garcia, A., Lew, R., Roberts, J., Rees, G., & Sharma, N. (2019a). Developing a writing assistant to help EAP writers with collocations in real time. *ReCALL, 31*(1), 23-39. https://doi.org/10.1017/s0958344018000150

Frankenberg-Garcia, A., Lew, R., Roberts, J., Rees, G., Sharma, N., & Butcher, P. (2019b). Collocations in e-lexicography: lessons from Human Computer Interaction research. Paper at *Collocations in Lexicography: existing solutions and future challenges*, 30 September 2019, Sintra, Portugal.

Gardner, D., & Davies, M. (2014). A new academic vocabulary list. *Applied Linguistics, 35*(3), 305-327. https://doi.org/10.1093/applin/amt015

Granger, S., & Paquot, M. (2015). Electronic lexicography goes local: design and structures of a needs-driven online academic writing aid. *Lexicographica - International Annual for Lexicography, 31*(1), 118-141. https://doi.org/10.1515/lexi-2015-0007

Kilgarriff, A., Baisa, V., Bušta, J., Jakubíček, M., Kovvář, V., Michelfeit, J., & Suchomel, V. (2014). The Sketch Engine: ten years on. *Lexicography, 1*(1), 7-36. https://doi.org/10.1007/s40607-014-0009-9

Laufer, B. (2011). The contribution of dictionary use to the production and retention of collocations in a second language. *International Journal of Lexicography, 24*(1), 29-49. https://doi.org/10.1093/ijl/ecq039

Lea, D. (Ed.). (2014). *Oxford learner's dictionary of academic English*. Oxford University Press.

Mayor, M. (Ed.). (2013). *Longman collocations dictionary and thesaurus*. Pearson Education.

Nesi, H. (2011). BAWE: an introduction to a new resource. In A. Frankenberg-Garcia, L. Flowerdew & G. Aston (Eds), *New trends in corpora and language learning* (pp. 213-228). Continuum. https://doi.org/10.5040/9781474211925.ch-013

Paquot, M. (2010). *Academic vocabulary in learner writing: from extraction to analysis.* Continuum.

Rees, G., Frankenberg-Garcia, A., Lew, R., Roberts, J., Sharma, N., & Butcher, P. (2019). Slipping through the cracks of e-lexicography: lessons from ColloCaid. Paper at *eLex 2019: Smart Lexicography*, 1-3 October 2019, Sintra, Portugal.

Romer, U., & Swales, J. (2010). The Michigan corpus of upper-level student papers (MICUSP). *Journal of English for Academic Purposes, 9*(3), 249-249. https://doi.org/10.1016/j.jeap.2010.04.002

Wu, S., Fitzgerald, A., Yu, A., & Witten, I. (2019). Developing and evaluating a learner-friendly collocation system with user query data. *International Journal of Computer-Assisted Language Learning and Teaching, 9*(2), 53-78. https://doi.org/10.4018/ijcallt.2019040104

Yoon, C. (2016). Concordancers and dictionaries as problem-solving tools for ESL academic writing. *Language Learning and Technology, 20*(1), 209-229.

Re-orienting CALL through the lens of complexity theory

Robert Godwin-Jones[1]

Abstract. Complexity Theory (CT) provides a useful framework for understanding Second Language Acquisition (SLA). Using an ecological model, CT studies the dynamic processes of change and emergent outcomes over time, tracing back how trajectories may have been affected by changes in and interactions among multiple variables and subsystems. Language learners do not follow linear learning paths, but rather their progress depends on a variety of interlocking variables. Developmental trajectories will look different for each learner. That is particularly the case for informal language learning, in which learners co-adapt from a wide variety of resources, leading to divergent outcomes (Godwin-Jones, 2018a). A CT approach emphasizes the dynamics of the interplay between learner variables and the people, artifacts, and services constituting the L2 learning system. It aligns well with usage-based linguistics. Viewing language learning from a CT perspective has a number of consequences for Computer Assisted Language Learning (CALL) research, explored here.

Keywords: complexity theory, SLA, CALL.

1. Introduction

SLA theories have difficult issues to account for (Atkinson, 2011). Some students make steady progress in the L2, but many will learn by fits and starts, feeling they have made insufficient progress compared to the time and effort spent. Those same learners may then have a positive encounter with a native speaker and suddenly realize that they have actually made a leap forward in proficiency. Learners might have mixed records in the classroom, but bloom with online L2 use through engagement with appealing content (video streaming, gaming, fanfiction) or

---

1. Virginia Commonwealth University, Richmond, VA, United States; rgjones@vcu.edu; https://orcid.org/0000-0002-2377-3204

How to cite this article: Godwin-Jones, R. (2019). Re-orienting CALL through the lens of complexity theory. In F. Meunier, J. Van de Vyver, L. Bradley & S. Thouësny (Eds), *CALL and complexity – short papers from EUROCALL 2019* (pp. 151-156). Research-publishing.net. https://doi.org/10.14705/rpnet.2019.38.1001

appealing peers (social media and fellow learners/L2 users). Language instructors are well aware of the reality that teaching does not necessarily lead to learning. Despite our best efforts and well-crafted curricula and lesson plans, some learners will prosper, and some will fail in the same classroom. At times, a teacher's random comment or slight word of praise will turn the motivational tide, which may come as an immediate reaction or occur much later. In summary, see below.

- SLA is highly variable with widely divergent individual learning trajectories even more so today than ever, due to access to a wealth of online materials, communities, and services.

- SLA is nonlinear, affected by myriad, shifting internal and external factors, with a complicated interplay between instructed and autonomous learning.

- SLA is unpredictable in its outcomes, with success or failure emerging over time through the intersections of learning goals, available resources, personal language history, external factors, and individual skills/knowledge/effort.

2. CT

The characteristics above align with a framework known as CT, also complex dynamic systems, which account for:

- the variability of learners (divergent 'initial conditions') and the uneven progress dependent on different dynamics of the learner with the learning environment;

- the peaks and valleys of SLA, through learners assembling resources on the fly and adapting them individually ('soft assembly' and 'co-adaptation'); and

- the unpredictability of SLA, with individually emergent learning outcomes over time.

The application of CT to SLA is not new, with Larsen-Freeman (1997) pioneering its use in applied linguistics. It has since been used in many areas within SLA, most recently for understanding the dynamics of L2 development through informal online resources (Kusyk, 2017; Sockett, 2014). A CT framework is also attractive because of its compatibility with views on the nature of language and language learning, which have been increasingly embraced by SLA researchers, namely usage-based linguistics (Ellis, 2017). This approach emphasizes patterns over rules. Supported by findings in corpus linguistics, usage-based views assert that L2 development occurs through the perception, use, and reuse of chunks of language, i.e. frequent combinations of lexis and syntax such as collocations, fixed expressions, or sentence frames. L2 users in the 'digital wilds' engaging in video streaming, gaming, or social media encounter multi-word constructions repeatedly in different contexts. Language and language learning are from this perspective open systems, with vocabulary and patterns learned over time (Godwin-Jones, 2018b).

3. Implications for CALL research

Assuming that language development is usage-based and that growth/interest in informal language learning will continue, a CT approach to CALL research might involve these realigned practices.

3.1. Emphasizing the learning context

Viewing language learning from such an ecological perspective places equal importance on learner characteristics and on the learning context, recognizing that their interaction is a constantly moving target, thus moving away from metaphors of linearity or mastery. CALL studies in naturalistic settings need to recognize the myriad intervening factors at play. Projects which focus on one particular online tool or service should take into consideration the likelihood of L2 learner-users engaging at the same time in other online L2 activities. Lin, Warschauer, and Blake (2016), for example, show gains in listening/speaking for users of LiveMocha, but the study does not take into account possible other online activities such as streaming L2 videos or engaging in private L2 chat. Furthermore, the learning context is crucial, i.e. a second language or foreign language context, providing or not local L2 affordances. Surveying study participants or collecting learning diaries on all L2-related activities would have supplied wider contexts for measuring L2 gains through LiveMocha.

3.2. Questioning simple causality

Rather than looking for cause-and-effect, CT calls for identifying emerging patterns within a wide realm of possible trajectories, affected by shifting variables and interactions. Results of pre- and post-tests need to be interpreted cautiously, as multiple factors beyond those assumed may exist. Task-based studies need to recognize that "a perfectly designed task cannot be seen as a closed system where learners follow a pre-ordained path to completion and learning" (Levy & Moore, 2018, p. 2). From a CT perspective, studies examining progress in complexity-accuracy-fluency might optimally treat these L2 features as interrelated subsystems, with learners alternatively allocating primacy to one or another of those aspects of language development. CT helps to recognize and document such trade-off dynamics (see Yang & Sun, 2015, for an example).

3.3. Focusing on individuals

CT places primacy on documenting and describing individual learning histories over time and tracing successful trajectories back to see patterns of emergence – discovering different enabling, disrupting, or inhibiting learner behaviors and resource uses. Narrative, qualitative, and mixed method research approaches are best suited for analyzing learning trajectories. These can be aggregated to point to patterns and possible best practices, always keeping in mind how contextual dynamics can affect individual outcomes. This entails a new approach to replication studies. In naturalistic settings where conditions cannot be duplicated, varied initial conditions and environmental factors can be examined instead, and their outcomes traced. However, such an emphasis on the diversity of individual development paths poses a research difficulty in CALL. The typical procedure is to examine variables in relative isolation and seek cause-and-effect relationships between isolated factors. General tendencies observed in a group may not yield useful information in terms of individual outcomes. That is demonstrated in a recent study on listening comprehension, in which a traditional L2 study was re-conceptionalized using a CT approach, yielding more informative results (Becker & Sturm, 2018).

3.4. Drawing themes from data

CT approaches CALL for collecting rich data over time and using a grounded approach to discover themes as they emerge from the data, rather than starting with a pre-defined set of research questions. Purely quantitative approaches can be helpful in providing a broad overview, but may not uncover individual development patterns. One option is to use clustering techniques to find revelatory sets of behaviors/outcomes. This can illuminate significant individual or group differences. Lee, Warschauer, and Lee (2019) re-examined a study by the same authors and this time used data-mining techniques to "shed light on unidentified learner types overshadowed by the average obtained through data analysis at the group level. The two learner types had distinctively different learning patterns, so combining them produced a poorly defined 'one-size-fits-all' conclusion" (p. 144). The conclusion was informative, namely, that in fact the different groups "might require different accommodations to maximize their L2 vocabulary learning potentials" (Lee et al., 2019, p. 146). Thus, the application of CT in CALL may lead to practical applications.

4. Conclusions

A CT/CALL approach to instructional practice echoes these themes, allowing for differentiated language goals over time, enabling individualized exploration of extramural resources, combining explicit/in-person instruction with implicit/online learning, and encouraging self-reflection through personal narrative.

References

Atkinson, D. (2011). *Alternative approaches to second language acquisition*. Routledge.
Becker, S., & Sturm, J. (2018). Using metacognitive strategies to induce phase shifts. In A. Tyler, L. Ortega, M. Uno & H. Park (Eds), *Usage-inspired L2 instruction: researched pedagogy* (pp. 165-185). Benjamins. https://doi.org/10.1075/lllt.49.08bec
Ellis, N. (2017). Cognition, corpora, and computing: triangulating research in usage-based language learning. *Language Learning, 67*(S1), 40-65. https://doi.org/10.1111/lang.12215
Godwin-Jones, R. (2018a). Chasing the butterfly effect: informal language learning online as a complex system. *Language Learning & Technology, 22*(2), 8-27.
Godwin-Jones, R. (2018b). Contextualized vocabulary learning. *Language Learning & Technology, 22*(3), 1-19.
Kusyk, M. (2017). The development of complexity, accuracy, and fluency in L2 written production through informal participation in online activities. *CALICO Journal, 34*(1), 75-96. https://doi.org/10.1558/cj.29513
Larsen-Freeman, D. (1997). Chaos/complexity and second language acquisition. *Applied Linguistics, 18*(2), 141-165. https://doi.org/10.1093/applin/18.2.141
Lee, H., Warschauer, M., & Lee, J. H. (2019). Advancing CALL research via data-mining techniques: unearthing hidden groups of learners in a corpus-based L2 vocabulary learning experiment. *ReCALL, 31*(2), 135-149. https://doi.org/10.1017/S0958344018000162
Levy, M., & Moore, P. J. (2018). Qualitative research in CALL. *Language Learning & Technology, 22*(2), 1-7.
Lin, C.-H., Warschauer, M., & Blake, R. (2016). Language learning through social networks: perceptions and reality. *Language Learning & Technology, 20*(1), 124-147.

Sockett, G. (2014). *The online informal learning of English*. Macmillan.

Yang, W., & Sun, Y. (2015). Dynamic development of complexity, accuracy and fluency in multilingual learners' L1, L2 and L3 writing. *Theory and Practice in Language Studies, 5*(2), 298-308. https://doi.org/10.17507/tpls.0502.09

ReDesigning intercultural exchanges through the use of augmented reality

Stella Hadjistassou[1], Maria Iosifina Avgousti[2], and Petros Louca[3]

Abstract. While the debate on breakthrough technologies has focused on inept, dexterous, and socially transforming technologies such as Artificial Intelligence (AI) assistants and robot dexterity, in second/foreign language learning, particular emphasis is placed on AI, Augmented Reality (AR) and Virtual Reality (VR). This study takes a closer look at the role of three newly developed AR applications in promoting a better understanding of complex concepts such as the Zone of Proximal Development (ZPD), strategies in dealing with disruptive students, and an immigrant's perspective in moving to a foreign country with no knowledge of the language(s) spoken in that country. The AR applications were developed and implemented during intercultural exchanges among students enrolled in academic institutions in the UK and Cyprus. The aim was to develop AR applications that were geared toward the learning needs of future language teachers and examine what students could achieve through the use of these applications during goal-driven tasks and activities.

Keywords: augmented reality applications, intercultural telecollaboration, multimodality.

1. Introduction

In the 'New Media Consortium (NMC) 2018 Horizon Report: Higher Education Edition' (Becker et al., 2018), it is acknowledged that AI, VR, and AR will have an impact on the assessment and planning of higher education institutions between 2018 and 2020. Educators are expected to explore the pedagogical value of novel technologies in different teaching, learning, and training contexts, but are rarely

---

1. University of Cyprus, Nicosia, Cyprus; shadjis@asu.edu; https://orcid.org/0000-0003-2963-8393
2. University of Cyprus, Nicosia, Cyprus; mariaiosifina@yahoo.co.uk; https://orcid.org/0000-0002-7678-8012
3. University of Cyprus, Nicosia, Cyprus; louca.petros@ucy.ac.cy; https://orcid.org/0000-0002-3616-1557

How to cite this article: Hadjistassou, S., Avgousti, M. I., & Louca, P. (2019). ReDesigning intercultural exchanges through the use of augmented reality. In F. Meunier, J. Van de Vyver, L. Bradley & S. Thouësny (Eds), *CALL and complexity – short papers from EUROCALL 2019* (pp. 157-162). Research-publishing.net. https://doi.org/10.14705/rpnet.2019.38.1002

offered opportunities to develop the required skills (Kessler, 2006). Further, in many cases digital tools are integrated into the curricula without a solid pedagogical value. The role of context-based AR applications and task-based learning have been investigated in several studies in second/foreign language learning, but this area is still in its early stages (Godwin-Jones, 2016). In the ReDesign project, an online platform, ReDesign, was developed to facilitate collaboration through joint lectures, tasks, and activities between academic institutions. QR codes, lectures, interactive activities, and AR applications were developed. The AR applications were designed to immerse students in a game-like environment by combining elements of the physical and virtual world and interacting with 3D objects and their peers, and engaging in pedagogically-driven activities (Bower et al., 2014; Yilmaz, 2016). Drawing on situative and ecological theory, the focus was placed on what students could do if they were offered the opportunity to interact with AR applications in particular contexts (Gresalfi, 2015). This step would also guide students in experimenting with technologies that are not commonly used in classroom contexts. The first AR application featured the ZPD animating in 3D the process of internalization. The second AR application featured three scenarios of a disruptive learner inviting students to select the best possible approach in dealing with disruptive behavior. The third AR application focused on an alien landing on earth, simulating the experience of immigrants moving to another country with no proficiency in the target language(s). Three research questions were addressed in this study.

(1) What are some of the pedagogical foundations upon which the AR applications were designed?

(2) What are the aims and objectives of each AR application?

(3) In what ways did students implement these AR applications in learning?

2. Method

Fifteen Greek-Cypriots experimented with the ZPD AR application during the fall of 2018. In the spring of 2019, three sets of students participated in the study: 14 students in their first year of their bachelor's degree in education in an academic institution in Cyprus and two sets of students from an academic institution in the UK, 13 students were enrolled in an Intercultural Communication course, and six graduate Chinese students were enrolled in a professional training course in Teaching

Chinese as a Second Language. The ReDesign platform was developed to mediate these collaborative lectures and activities. It featured live chat sessions, a wall, friends, groups, assignments, and multiple other tools. In this study, the platform was used to mediate students' written interactions. Prior to the development of the apps, IT professionals, applied linguists, and educational technologists exchanged views on the added pedagogical value of each AR application. Using Unity Engine, three AR applications were developed: (1) the ZPD, (2) a disruptive student, and (3) an alien application. The AR applications could be accessed individually or in groups using a mobile device.

The ZPD featured three 3D concentric circles: the inner circle indicating what 'learners can do unaided', the second circle noting what 'learners can do with guidance' and the largest one featuring what 'learner cannot do'. The second AR application featured three different approaches in dealing with disruptive student behavior: (1) ignoring a student's cell phone use in class, (2) acknowledging a student's cell phone use in class and pointing to his/her poor academic performance, and (3) kindly requesting the cell phone and placing it in a Ziploc bag. Figure 1 illustrates the disruptive student application.

Figure 1. The disruptive student AR application

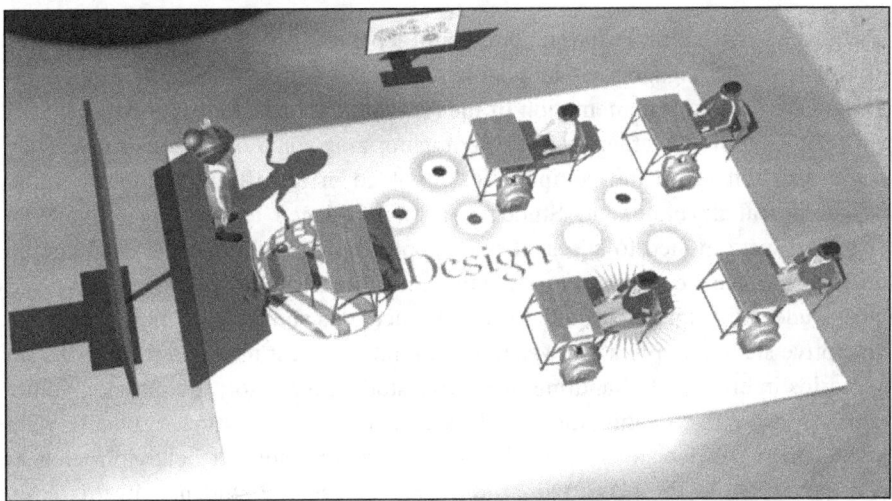

The third AR application featured an alien landing on earth with no proficiency in the target language. The three AR applications were designed to promote understanding the ZPD, exploring classroom management approaches, and provoking critical discussions on culturally and linguistically salient values. Students were invited to complete a set of tasks on each of these AR applications, such as exploring the concept of ZPD and identifying students' current knowledge and future prospects of building new knowledge. All tasks were posted on the ReDesign platform under 'Assignments' and shared on students' walls in order to be accessible to all their peers.

3. Discussion

The three questions addressed involved the pedagogical value driving the design of these AR applications, their aims and objectives, and students' implementations in different contexts. The first element driving the AR application design was their 'added pedagogical value'. Building on previous studies related to the implementation of tools and applications in the classroom context, the research team contemplated multiple principles, including (1) the contexts in which they would be implemented, (2) integration into the curricula across academic institutions, (3) relevance to students' learning, (4) practicality, (5) level of complexity and time required to navigate through the applications, (6) the enactment of affordances for engagement, (7) the promotion of interaction and intercultural collaboration, and (8) the promotion of conceptual understanding through goal-driven tasks.

The goal was to examine what students could achieve if the AR applications enacted affordances for engagement in goal-driven tasks and intercultural exchanges. During the actual implementation of the AR applications, students could interact with the ZPD in AR rather than simply memorizing some of its constructs. They could also reflect on the complexities involved in identifying students' future psychological development. Students were introduced to the target image in class and were invited to access the AR application. Some students encountered difficulties since the application was only accessible on Android devices. However, most students navigated through the AR applications and assisted their peers. The disruptive student application was more complex since it included three different scenarios in effectively handling disruptive student behavior; it combined audio, real and AR objects, animation, and user-interface information. Students were invited to make decisions in dealing with disruptive student behavior, such as cell phone use in the classroom, and engaging reserved students. In this case, it took a little bit longer to experiment with all three scenarios and understand both the written and oral conversation in the three scenarios. However, classroom management was a topic that students across academic institutions could relate to and enacted affordances for thinking more critically about the best approach possible in such cases.

The alien AR application was more ambitious than the rest of the applications. Students interacted with an alien that had just landed on Earth, contemplated on the role of language and culture, and identified salient cultural artifacts and posted their reflections on the ReDesign platform. Some of students' proffered cultural artifacts were created in AR, such as a bus and kolokasi (a sweet potato). This AR application enacted affordances for thinking more critically about the linguistic and cultural artifacts that are salient to each culture but which immigrants moving to a new country are not familiar with. Students implemented this AR application in a more creative and constructive way, providing artifacts that are rarely discussed.

4. Conclusions

In the case of AR technologies, challenges often emerge with the design of applications that are pedagogically sound, are developed with specific tasks in mind, and can be integrated into the curricula to promote understanding of complex constructs, interaction with artifacts and peers, collaboration, and learning in environments where virtual and real objects coexist. It is instrumental for AR applications to have specific aims and objectives and be explicitly conveyed to students. Applications can progress from simple to more complex ones, and students can be gradually involved in the process of interacting with the AR scenarios, making choices and contributing to the design process by identifying cultural artifacts that can be integrated into the AR applications. This step turns learning immersive and engaging and offers students an opportunity to reflect on their salient cultural values and artifacts.

5. Acknowledgments

We would like to thank all consortium partners for their invaluable contributions to the project and all the students who participated in the telecollaborative exchanges.

References

Becker, S. A., Brown, M., Dahlstorm, E., Davis, A., DePaul, K., Diaz, V., & Pomerantz, J. (2018). *The NMC 2018 Horizon report: 2018 higher education edition*. EDUCAUSE.

Bower, M., Howe, C., McCredie, N., Robinson, A., & Grover, D. (2014). Augmented reality in education – cases, places and potentials. *Educational Media International, 51*(1), 1-15. https://doi.org/10.1080/09523987.2014.889400

Godwin-Jones, R. (2016). Emerging technologies. Augmented reality and language learning: from annotated vocabulary to place-based mobile games. *Language Learning & Technology, 20* (3), 9-19.

Gresalfi, M. S. (2015). Designing to support critical engagement with statistics. *ZDM Mathematics Education, 47*(6), 933-946. https://doi.org/10.1007/s11858-015-0690-7

Kessler, G. (2006). Assessing CALL teacher training: what are we doing and what could we do better? In P. Hubbard & M. Levy (Eds), *Teacher education in CALL* (pp. 23-44). https://doi.org/10.1075/lllt.14.05kes

Yilmaz, R. M. (2016). Educational magic toys developed with augmented reality technology for early childhood education. *Computers in Human Behavior, 54*, 240-248. https://doi.org/10.1016/j.chb.2015.07.040

■ UCLouvain

Virtual exchange supporting language and intercultural development: students' perceptions

Eric Hagley[1] and Matthew Cotter[2]

Abstract. Foreign Language (FL) classrooms should be places where, at a minimum, communication is taking place in the foreign language being taught and intercultural understanding is also being developed. However, in countries where the majority of students are from a single cultural background, it is often difficult to keep students on-task if they do not have to use the language they are studying. Virtual Exchange (VE) ensures students interact with their online peers in the FL, as it becomes the lingua-franca. However, student attitudes toward such VE in the FL classroom are still not fully understood. This paper researches students' attitudes toward one VE, the International Virtual Exchange Project (IVEProject). Each iteration of the IVEProject is for eight weeks. Students interact asynchronously on Moodle forums in text, audio, and video. More than 15,000 students from 15 countries have participated in at least one of the VE carried out since 2016. Online surveys are carried out at the end of each exchange. Results suggest students have an overall positive attitude toward incorporating VE into FL and intercultural classes.

Keywords: virtual exchange, FL, IVEProject, intercultural understanding.

1. Introduction

VE has many forms and is used in many fields. It is of particular importance to FL and intercultural communication classes, as students see more relevance and need to apply what they are studying immediately. The importance of studying the FL becomes apparent when the FL needs to be used in real-world communicative activities and/or tasks where authentic communication and collaboration processes are at the very heart of the exchanges. O'Dowd and Lewis (2016) note that VE has

---

1. Muroran Institute of Technology, Muroran, Japan; hagley@mmm.muroran-it.ac.jp; https://orcid.org/0000-0002-4795-8043
2. Hokusei Gakuen University Junior College, Sapporo, Japan; m-cotter@hokusei.ac.jp; https://orcid.org/0000-0003-0906-1400

How to cite this article: Hagley, E., & Cotter, M. (2019). Virtual exchange supporting language and intercultural development: students' perceptions. In F. Meunier, J. Van de Vyver, L. Bradley & S. Thouësny (Eds), *CALL and complexity – short papers from EUROCALL 2019* (pp. 163-168). Research-publishing.net. https://doi.org/10.14705/rpnet.2019.38.1003

many benefits and research in the field is continuing to grow. However, in the same volume, O'Dowd (2016, p. 275) also notes there are some criticisms that need to be addressed, in particular: authenticity; creation of a false impression of universality, where students see other cultures through a prism of common humanity rather than appreciating the subtle and not so subtle differences therein; and a lack of opportunity to reflect on interactions.

Carrell and West (2010) noted that sometimes students are not the best judges of what is best for them. However, it is still important to discover if what they are studying is of interest to them. Helm (2015) noted research suggesting VE positively affects students' motivations, which leads to better learning outcomes. For this reason, we need to analyze participants' attitudes toward their participation in the IVEProject.

2. Method

2.1. The IVEProject

Hagley (2016) outlines the IVEProject in detail. Participating students from one country are partnered with students from at least one other country. The students interact asynchronously via Moodle forums using text, audio, and video. Interaction takes place in the focused discussion forum, run over an eight-week period, on four different assigned topics. The last of the assigned topics is a reflection task. Separate to the focused discussion forum is an open forum where students can interact on any topic they choose with students from multiple countries in the exchange (some 3,200 most recently).

One requisite is that teachers be involved and assist students with their interactions. Teachers and facilitators are important in all VE (INTENT, 2014). Participation is free-of-charge as the project is sponsored by a Japanese government Kaken grant.

2.2. Data from the project

At the end of each exchange, we survey students about their participation. In this paper, we concentrate on anonymous, optional replies from Japanese and Colombian students, the biggest participating groups in the most recent exchange. We used the Moodle questionnaire and groups function so only students from Japan answered the Japan-based questionnaire and the same for Colombian students. Questions were translated into Japanese and Spanish respectively. A series of questions, with answers on a six-point Likert scale, were asked in section one. Some statements related to technical aspects of the exchange. Only questions relating to this research are included here, with results outlined in Table 1. The percentages of students that answered positively 4-5-6 are noted with the means and standard deviation. Both Japanese and Columbian responses are shown there, but for the other two sections only Japanese students' responses are included as questions were open-ended and the authors cannot read Spanish. Columbian researchers will publish results at a later date.

3. Results and discussion

As shown in Table 1, students from both countries have a favorable view of their participation in the IVEProject. They clearly see it as being beneficial to the development of both their language learning and understanding of other cultures. Participation has also piqued the interest of participants in foreign countries and cultures and, as interactions were between students from different cultures, the use of English was necessary. This is a more authentic use of English than, for example, Japanese students in an English as an FL (EFL) class using English to carry out communicative tasks. Students appreciate this increase in the level of authenticity. In addition, students strongly state that they have changed their view of their partner countries, something that suggests they do not have a 'false impression of universality', emphasized by almost half of the respondents noting that their change in understanding of other cultures was a positive outcome.

Table 1. Students' attitudes toward the IVEProject

	Japan 2019 n=594			Colombia 2019 n=402		
	% of students' positive attitudes	Mean	SD	% of students' positive attitudes	Mean	SD
I think this online exchange is beneficial to learning English.	81	4.5	1.3	90	5.3	1.1
I didn't learn anything about the other country.	13	2.1	1.2	16	2.0	1.4
Compared to before starting the exchange, I now think English is an important language.	79	4.5	1.3	96	5.6	0.9

I'm more interested in the other country(ies) now because of the VE.	77	4.3	1.2	86	4.8	1.2
I changed my view of the other country because of the VE.	70	4.1	1.3	89	4.7	1.2

The second section addressed the following open question: "What were positive areas of the exchange?". The answers were separated into common themes and are outlined in Table 2. When more than two themes were covered in a response, they were added to both, hence the total number is greater than the number of respondents.

Table 2. Positive aspects of the exchange (n=594)

Sense of improving intercultural understanding	264
Sense of participation in a global community	227
Sense of linguistic improvement	171
Other (system ease of use, 'fun', could be done anywhere, etc.)	42
Motivation increase	31
No comment	12
Negative comment	1

In section two, one can see that close to half of the Japanese students started to 'feel' like they were part of a global community. This would suggest they see themselves as separate to, but part of that community, and hence not taking on feelings of universality. That many also believe it has improved their intercultural understanding is also positive; however, a better tool is required to check if their understanding really has improved. A large number believe the exchange has improved their language ability, though, again, this would need to be proven.

The final section included an open-ended question about the problems encountered and/or the parts of the exchange students disliked. Results are shown in Table 3 with common themes grouped.

Table 3. Type of problem or dislike (n=594)

'Nothing' or 'no problem'	257
System problems (such as difficulty in uploading pictures, etc.)	216
Dissatisfaction with other students' efforts	57
Time consuming	11
Topic choice	10
Demotivating	3
'Other' (slow reply time, assessment style, difficulty in understanding English, lack of synchronous exchange, etc.)	51

The results in Table 3 show that almost half of them had no negative comment and that most negative comments involved technical problems with the system we used such as having trouble uploading photos or other multimedia. Only three respondents (0.5%), stated the exchange was demotivating. Another area of dissatisfaction was that partner students did not reply often enough or fast enough. This shows students wanted to receive more replies and exchange with their partners in greater detail, which could actually be considered a positive outcome.

There were some comments of particular note. One student wrote "other students in my university didn't have to do this so, at first, I thought it was unfair that we had to do more work than them. However, after finishing the exchange, I thought it was unfair that the other classes couldn't participate in it too". Another wrote "I have always wanted to communicate with foreigners but have never been able to because I live in a regional area. This exchange was a great opportunity to do so".

4. Conclusions

Participating students appreciate this VE. It is a more authentic use of English than standard EFL communication in the Asian context. The results here suggest that when VE is done well, students do not acquire a false impression of universality nor lack opportunities to reflect on their interactions and can, in fact, learn from them. This would suggest that VE should become a part of EFL classes in general.

5. Acknowledgments

We would like to thank our VE team of Thom Rawson, Adam Jenkins, Yuka Akiyama, David Campbell, and Hideto Harashima, and also all the teachers and students that participated. This research has been carried out with the assistance of Kaken #19H01277.

References

Carrell, S. E., & West, J. E. (2010). Does professor quality matter? Evidence from random assignment of students to professors. *Journal of Political Economy, 118*(3), 409-432. https://doi.org/10.1086/653808

Hagley, E. (2016). Making virtual exchange/telecollaboration mainstream – large scale exchanges. In S. Jager, M. Kurek & B. O'Rourke (Eds), *New directions in telecollaborative research and practice: selected papers from the second conference on telecollaboration in higher education* (pp. 225-230). Research-publishing.net. https://doi.org/10.14705/rpnet.2016.telecollab2016.511

Helm, F. (2015). The practices and challenges of telecollaboration in higher education in Europe. *Language Learning & Technology, 19*(2), 197-217.

INTENT. (2014). Position Paper: Virtual Exchange in the European higher education area. *The INTENT consortium*. https://uni-collaboration.eu/sites/default/files/Position%20paper_1.pdf

O'Dowd, R. (2016). Learning from the past and looking to the future of online intercultural exchange. In R. O'Dowd & T. Lewis (Eds), *Online intercultural exchange: policy, pedagogy, practice*. Routledge.

O'Dowd, R., & Lewis, T. (Eds). (2016). *Online intercultural exchange: policy, pedagogy, practice*. Routledge. https://doi.org/10.4324/9781315678931

■ UCLouvain

Leveraging collaborative work for game-based language learning

Dirk Hansen[1], Carlee Arnett[2], and Ferran Suñer[3]

Abstract. Over the past few years, language teaching has progressively evolved from teacher-fronted classroom settings to more complex, learner-centered scenarios, allowing learners to explore authentic contents, work collaboratively, and create sophisticated and socially relevant products. In addition, these processes foster language learning, increase learner engagement, and support the acquisition of competences such as critical thinking and democratic competence. In spite of these positive results, previous research has not always suggested efficient ways to properly manage classroom interaction and potentially enhance learning outcomes. Against this backdrop, this paper explores the potential of cooperation scripts as a means to leverage collaborative work and classroom interaction in complex learning scenarios. In this paper, we report on the first phase of an intervention study that was conducted with 17 university learners of German at the B2-C1 level. Survey results show that most of the students found the addition of the cooperation script to be beneficial when engaging in a complex, game-based scenario.

Keywords: language learning, games, social media.

1. Introduction

The conception of this study was based on three core assumptions. First, students are best served by student-centered learning scenarios; second, a multimedia approach to learning has been shown to enhance learner engagement and outcomes; and lastly, we argue that the use of a cooperation script can leverage the potential of student-centered, media-based language learning.

---

1. Université catholique de Louvain, Louvain, Belgium; dirk.hansen@uclouvain.be
2. University of California, Davis, Davis, California; clarnett@ucdavis.edu; https://orcid.org/0000-0002-7190-0220
3. Université catholique de Louvain, Louvain, Belgium; ferran.suner@uclouvain.be

How to cite this article: Hansen, D., Arnett, C., & Suñer, F. (2019). Leveraging collaborative work for game-based language learning. In F. Meunier, J. Van de Vyver, L. Bradley & S. Thouësny (Eds), *CALL and complexity – short papers from EUROCALL 2019* (pp. 169-173). Research-publishing.net. https://doi.org/10.14705/rpnet.2019.38.1004

© 2019 Dirk Hansen, Carlee Arnett, and Ferran Suñer (CC BY)

There is a plethora of research on the benefits of student-centered learning in the second language classroom in a variety of languages (cf. Swain, 2006; Lantolf & Thorne, 2007). Therefore, socially based classroom activities that support cognitive development and learning are likely to be effective. Any number of activities would work well, but we chose Actionbound[4] (AB) for the extra benefit of the multimedia learning environment.

There are many studies on the benefits of using various types of media in the classroom (cf. Roche & Suñer, 2016). In this study, we intended to focus on the production phase in which students create something using the language they already know. The idea is that by engaging students in certain scenarios they will activate their language knowledge and in the virtual environment produce more accurate structures and a broader vocabulary. With AB, a website that can be used to create a mobile tour or scavenger hunt, students can create as a final product a game (Bound) that can be used by others. In order to route users in the Bound to the correct locations, students need to give directions and create a quiz or informational paragraph for each stop. In the case of German, the task is best done with the imperative and two-way prepositions. The task is complex and AB was new to the students, so we decided to use a cooperation script to guide their work.

In order to derive the most benefit from pair and small group activities, cooperation scripts can be given to the students to guide their discussion. In theory, cooperation scripts prevent learners from spending too much time in social interactions while learning collaboratively. In other words, cooperation scripts help learners organize their discussion quickly and guide them through the learning process so they can focus on learning and not how to structure their learning. We used a social cooperation script to help learners sequence interactions in the group. Although educational research has consistently provided evidence for the usefulness of cooperation scripts in classroom settings (Vogel, Wecker, Kollar, & Fischer, 2017), language teaching does not seem to use them.

2. Method

In this paper, we are concerned with the survey the students took about the use of the cooperation script. Participants in the study were 17 learners of German in an advanced German class at the University of California, Davis.

---

4. www.actionbound.com

Leveraging collaborative work for game-based language learning

The first session with AB consisted of explaining what the app does and how one can use it. Students also downloaded the app on their phone, which is how you use or test the app, and their computer, which is how you create a Bound. These tasks include writing an informational paragraph, developing a quiz with short answers, multiple choice, or loading a picture as the answers and using the phone's GPS to find a specific place. In order to make this fun, the app has a scoring system for quizzes, missions, and tournaments.

The next step was to give the students the first cooperation script which told them how to assign tasks to their group members and what they needed to create in their Bound. The design of the cooperation script was inspired by those used in the study by Stegmann, Weinberger, and Fischer (2007). They also were instructed to first choose a topic and location, before they started creating their Bound. Students made trial tasks in AB in order to see what was possible with the app. Over the course of two sessions, the class spent four hours creating their Bounds, which mostly used the quiz and mission features.

In the next session, the survey was administered by having the students fill it out during class. There were seven questions, six of which were on a Likert scale and one of which had a choice of three answers. The questions are given in Table 1 below.

3. Survey results

The post-test survey had six questions where the students could check one of six levels of a Likert scale, with completely disagree on the left and completely agree on the right. Question 7 gave the students three answers to choose from concerning the reasons why they liked using the cooperation scripts. Answers from three participants were discarded because they did not complete all data points in the tests. Table 1 below shows the results for the first six questions.

The first question asked students if *the AB app was difficult to manage*, and the students were fairly unified in their assessment that the app was easy to use. The second question asked participants whether they *liked working in a group*, and most of the students did. The third question asked if the *checklists were helpful*. Most students agreed in some form (9/13) and the SD shows that the students are fairly uniform in their assessment. The fourth question asked if the *AB graphics helped create the task*. The mean was 3.5, but the *SD* was 3.2, showing a wider distribution than the other questions. The fifth question asked if *the way the questions were asked in AB was clear*, and the students again showed uniformity in their answers. The sixth question asked if the *explanations in AB were sufficient*, and the students were positive in their responses.

The last question asked participants to choose from three options to complete the sentence *I liked using the checklists because...*. The first option *I have learned and understood the tasks better* was chosen by half of the 12 respondents. The second option, *the cooperation with other students was easier*, was chosen by less than half of the respondents (5/13), and this suggests that the students had to spend time clarifying among themselves the tasks on the checklist. The last option, *I was more motivated to work* was chosen by only one respondent, which suggests that these students were not motivated by visual acknowledgments of task completion.

Table 1.   Student responses

Questions	Strongly Disagree	Disagree	Rather Disagree	Rather Agree	Agree	Strongly Agree	Mean	SD
The AB app was difficult to manage	5	4	1	2	n/a	2	2.8	1.4
I liked working in a group	1	n/a	2	n/a	4	6	3.25	1.9
I found the checklists helped me	1	n/a	n/a	3	3	6	3.5	1.7
The graphics in AB helped you create the task	n/a	2	n/a	2	9	1	3.5	3.2
The way the questions were asked in AB was clear	n/a	1	n/a	2	8	3	3.0	1.8
The explanations on the app AB were sufficient and understandable	1	1	1	2	6	3	2.3	1.7

4.   Conclusion

Overall, the results show a positive picture of the implemented pedagogical intervention with regard to the usefulness and appropriateness of the materials used. This is an important first step toward the integration of cooperation scripts into language teaching, and more specifically in game-based language learning. However, further studies should investigate whether these predominantly positive learning experiences reported here go along with an increase in learning gains and higher task engagement, especially when compared with classroom settings without cooperation scripts. Research into this issue is already in progress.

References

Lantolf, J., & Thorne, S. L. (2007). Sociocultural theory and second language learning. In. B. van Patten and J. Williams (Eds), *Theories in second language acquisition* (pp. 201-224). Lawrence Erlbaum.

Roche, J., & Suñer, F. (2016). Metaphors and grammar teaching. *Yearbook of the German Cognitive Linguistics Association, 4*(1), 89-112. https://doi.org/10.1515/gcla-2016-0008

Stegmann, K., Weinberger, A., & Fischer, F. (2007). Facilitating argumentative knowledge construction with computer-supported collaboration scripts. *International Journal of Computer-Supported Collaborative Learning, 2*(4), 421-447. https://doi.org/10.1007/s11412-007-9028-y

Swain, M. (2006). Languaging, agency and collaboration in advanced second language proficiency. In H. Byrnes (Ed.), *Advanced language learning: the contribution of Halliday and Vygotsky* (pp. 95-108). Continuum. https://doi.org/10.5040/9781474212113.ch-004

Vogel, F., Wecker, C., Kollar, I., & Fischer, F. (2017). Socio-cognitive scaffolding with computer-supported collaboration scripts: a meta-analysis. *Educational Psychology Review, 29*(3), 477-511. https://doi.org/10.1007/s10648-016-9361-7

Integrating Xreading into class time using post-reading tasks

Peter Harrold[1]

Abstract. The Xreading website provides students with access to an extensive virtual library of graded readers. Teachers can then use it to keep track of which titles the students access, the total number of words they read, their reading speed, and also whether they have completed post-reading quizzes. However, an overreliance on monitoring student progress entirely outside of class using word targets or quizzes can potentially be circumvanigated by reluctant students who dislike reading regularly. This paper will share how the teacher integrated short creative post-reading tasks into the weekly digital reading assignment of a compulsory English language class in an attempt to ensure students were engaging with the stories and reading regularly. It was found that the tasks enabled students to interact and discuss their reading with their classmates and also helped demonstrate the value and importance of extensive reading to students by further integrating it into class time.

Keywords: extensive reading, Xreading.

1. Introduction

Xreading provides a complete digital solution to the implementation of an Extensive Reading (ER) programme. For an annual subscription, the students can access a substantial virtual library of graded readers, and teachers can monitor the books they have read, word counts, reading speeds, and ability to answer comprehension quizzes via Xreading's Learner Management System (LMS). This resource helps solve many of the long standing issues with setting up an effective ER programme, mainly stocking and managing a library with a sufficient range and number of readers, and being able to monitor whether the students are actually doing the assigned volume of reading. However, the convenience of assigning and tracking

---

1. Kyushu Sangyo University, Fukuoka, Japan; harrold@mail.kyusan-u.ac.jp

How to cite this article: Harrold, P. (2019). Integrating Xreading into class time using post-reading tasks. In F. Meunier, J. Van de Vyver, L. Bradley & S. Thouësny (Eds), *CALL and complexity – short papers from EUROCALL 2019* (pp. 174-179). Research-publishing.net. https://doi.org/10.14705/rpnet.2019.38.1005

reading outside of class using the Xreading LMS means ER is often relegated to exclusively a homework assignment unless the teacher finds useful ways to integrate it back into class time. Robb and Kano (2013) describe this approach as additive ER, when the reading occurs entirely outside of class and places the least burden on the teacher. However, what they label as replacement ER, that substitutes alternative class activities to further integrate ER into lessons, could potentially be the most beneficial approach for students (Bamford & Day, 2004).

Integrating ER into class time seeks to reinforce to students the value of reading, as well as the importance of completing the activity regularly. It also has many added benefits through establishing a reading community that can engage and interact with others regarding the titles they have read (van Amelsvoort, 2017). If ER is reduced to a homework task, then students might choose to engage with it only at a superficial level. For example, Xreading can be avoided by flipping through pages to reach the required word count whilst keeping within the target reading speed, or by choosing books based on movies they have seen to make the quizzes easier.

Furthermore, although it may be the case that quizzes are a useful method for testing reading completion that do not create more work for the instructor (Robb, 2015) and do not necessarily detract from reading enjoyment (Stoeckel, Reagan, & Hann, 2012), there are many more interesting and useful ways students can be challenged in post-reading tasks (Bamford & Day, 2004; Harrold, 2020). This paper will introduce a variety of short creative post-reading tasks that can be used to supplement and enhance Xreading by giving the students something to share in class, and also act as an additional tool for teachers to monitor whether the reading has actually been done. The tasks were chosen to be shorter and easier to complete than a book report and less repetitive than writing a weekly summary, whilst at the same time more interesting and engaging by requiring some creativity or imagination from the students. The tasks are split into two types: those done outside of class individually then shared in the next lesson, and those completed in class as a group having read the same book.

2. Participants and tasks

The class involved were first-year university students enrolled in a compulsory Reading and Writing class for all majors, studying at approximately Common European Framework of Reference for languages (CEFR) B1 level, who met for one 90-minute session each week over a 15-week semester. Based on the curriculum, students were expected to read at least 60,000 words monitored using the Xreading LMS. This target was broken down into a weekly reading goal, with students given the additional requirement of completing ten post-reading tasks over the course of the semester. These tasks had previously been trialled with books from a physical library (Harrold, 2020). In addition to the individual tasks, at three points in the semester students were assigned the same book to read for homework then completed a group task based on the assigned text.

2.1. Individual tasks

The class were provided with a list of 15 short post-reading tasks (Harrold, 2020):

- write a summary of the story;
- write a paragraph describing your favourite character;
- draw a picture of your favourite scene and write a caption to describe it;
- write an alternative ending, showing how the story could have finished differently;
- write a letter to a character;
- write three questions you would like to ask the author about the story;
- choose a gift you would like to give to a character and explain your reasons why;
- write a paragraph describing the setting of the book;
- compare examples of the culture in the story with your own country;
- write a diary entry from the perspective of one of the characters;
- draw a diagram showing the relationship between different characters in the book;
- choose your favourite line in the story, then write it in full using quotation marks ("...") and explain why you like it;
- make a movie poster for the book and choose actors to play each character;

- create a short comic book strip about the book; and
- create a timeline with details of key events in the story.

Students were provided with a reading journal handout with space for ten tasks (see Figure 1 for an example) to be completed over ten weeks. The teacher then explained how to complete it and provided the students with examples of each task. The students were asked to choose a different task to complete each week about one of the books they had read, and then bring their journal to share with classmates in the next lesson.

Figure 1.   Reading task template

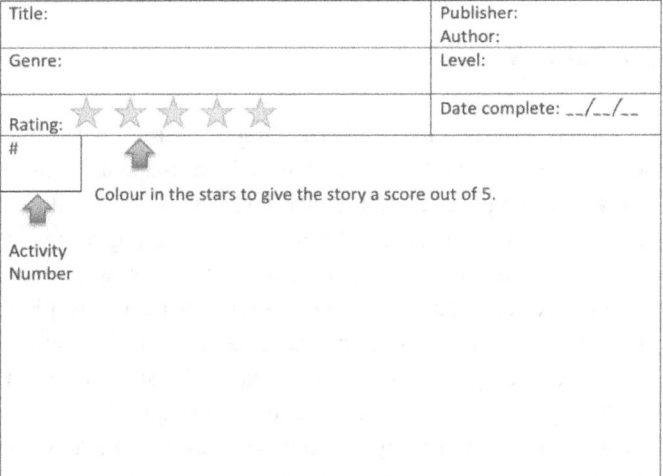

2.2.   Whole class tasks

Xreading enables all students to be assigned the same book to read. The whole class can read the same title, or each group can be assigned a different title. This can either be done inside of class or outside of class and enables a whole new variety of post-reading tasks to be completed as a group. The teacher decided to utilise this approach three times in the semester, once at the start of class when introducing students to Xreading for the first time, once in the middle, then again at the end of the semester after all the individual post-reading tasks had been completed. Students were once again provided with some autonomy in choosing which group task they would complete and were then expected to share it with the rest of the class at the end of the lesson. Group tasks were as below:

- write a script and act out your favourite scene from the story;
- create a prequel to the story, in which you describe what could have previously happened;
- create a sequel to the story, to continue on what might happen next;
- create a new character for the story;
- switch the genre of the story (e.g. romance to horror); and
- research information about the life of the author.

3. Discussion

The teacher monitored student usage of Xreading using the LMS and checked the completion of post-reading tasks. It was observed that the tasks provided creative and useful ways to reintegrate Xreading back into class time by allowing students to interact and discuss what they had been reading. Having a physical resource to show in class was a useful way for the teacher to track and remind the more reluctant readers. The individual tasks gave the teacher an easy platform to ask students follow up questions about their reading and identify those who were not reading regularly. The individual tasks could easily be shared with a partner or group without taking up much class time. Whole class activities required a greater allocation of class time but had many added benefits as they made reading a shared experience which allowed students to question and extend their understanding through collaboration and discussion. This interaction then produced both a written and oral outcome. The teacher found these tasks helped to establish reading as habitual behaviour amongst students and reinforced its value and importance as a component of the course that students were expected to complete to the best of their abilities.

4. Conclusions

The Xreading system is a useful digital resource that provides an extensive library of graded readers with an inbuilt LMS that makes tracking and monitoring students' progress easy for the teacher. However, the convenience of using this platform outside of class time has meant ER is often reduced entirely to a homework task.

This paper has hoped to introduce creative ways to reintegrate ER back into class time, not only to assist the teacher in monitoring students, but also to allow them to share their reading experiences and demonstrate the importance and value of ER as an integral part of the curriculum.

References

Bamford, J., & Day, R. (Eds). (2004). *Extensive reading activities for teaching language*. Cambridge University Press.

Harrold, P. (2020). *Creative post-reading tasks for extensive reading*. Manuscript submitted for publication.

Robb, T. (2015). Quizzes – a sin against the sixth commandment? In defense of MReader. *Reading in a Foreign Language, 27*(1), 146-151.

Robb, T., & Kano, M. (2013). Effective extensive reading outside the classroom: a large-scale experiment. *Reading in a Foreign Language, 25*, 234-247.

Stoeckel, T., Reagan, N., & Hann, F. (2012). Extensive reading quizzes and reading attitudes. *TESOL Quarterly, 46*(1), 187-198. https://doi.org/10.1002/tesq.10

Van Amelsvoort, M. (2017). Extensive reading onboarding: program design for increasing engagement. *Juntendo Journal of Global Studies, 2*, 98-106.

MOOCs as environments for learning spoken academic vocabulary

Clinton Hendry[1] and June Ruivivar[2]

Abstract. Massive Open Online Courses (MOOCs) are easily accessible for anyone in the world to study any given subject, often for free. However, there is some question as to whether they are comparable to their real-world counterparts. The Academic Spoken Word List (ASWL) created by Dang, Coxhead, and Webb (2017) was designed to create a word list that is more representative of spoken academic English. To contrast the real-world academic context to MOOCs, we created a MOOC academic corpus and compared it with the Michigan Corpus of Academic Spoken English (MICASE). Last, we used both to test the effectiveness of the ASWL. Overall, we found that the ASWL had similar coverage in both the MOOC and MICASE corpora but interestingly saw slightly more coverage in the MICASE dialogic sections. We believe future research should address the slight discrepancy between dialogic and non-dialogic academic situations.

Keywords: academic English, spoken academic English, corpus linguistics, online courses.

1. Introduction

There are considerable lexical differences between written and spoken academic English. For example, Biber et al. (2002) illustrate that classroom teaching, previously thought to be highly informational and persuasive, is in fact conversational and dialogic. Conversely, materials intended to be accessible to students, such as university brochures, were found to be informationally dense. To fully prepare second-language users for English-medium instruction, English for

---

1. Concordia University, Montreal, Canada; clinton.hendry@concordia.ca
2. Concordia University, Montreal, Canada; june.ruivivar@concordia.ca

How to cite this article: Hendry, C., & Ruivivar, J. (2019). MOOCs as environments for learning spoken academic vocabulary. In F. Meunier, J. Van de Vyver, L. Bradley & S. Thouësny (Eds), *CALL and complexity – short papers from EUROCALL 2019* (pp. 180-185). Research-publishing.net. https://doi.org/10.14705/rpnet.2019.38.1006

Academic Purposes (EAP) and similar language training courses need to include the variety of registers they are expected to encounter.

To this end, Dang et al. (2017) created the ASWL to identify words that are most useful for L2 students in English-medium universities. The ASWL serves to complement the previous Academic Word List (AWL; Coxhead, 2000), which was based on written texts. Although the ASWL has been validated across several corpora, the authors recognize the need to validate it across a variety of academic contexts.

The present study responds to this call by examining the ASWL's coverage of MOOCs, an increasingly popular mode of instruction (Lederman, 2018). Although MOOCs are primarily offered in English, many online students speak English as an additional language (Haber, 2014). Therefore, to be on par with in-person courses, English-language MOOCs must be accessible to learners of different proficiencies and provide them with opportunities for further language development. In many ways, the spoken component of MOOCs resembles that of in-person courses, but with video lectures making up most of the content. One notable difference is the lack of interactive elements such as classroom management and service encounters, which Biber et al. (2002) have found to have distinct register characteristics. This raises two questions. First, how accessible are MOOCs to students who have limited knowledge of academic English? Second, do MOOCs offer the same opportunities for incidental vocabulary learning observed in classroom tasks (e.g. Newton, 2013)?

2. Method

2.1. Corpora

This study compares the ASWL coverage between two corpora: MICASE (Simpson, Briggs, Ovens, & Swales, 2002) and a new corpus of online courses from edX, a MOOC platform offering courses from universities around the world. MICASE consists of 1.8 million words across various speech events, classified on a scale of interactivity from mostly monologic (e.g. presentations and speeches) to mostly interactive (e.g. advising and tutorials). Our MOOC corpus consists of video lectures, interviews, and live streaming sessions from 18 courses, totaling 733,431 words.

The MOOC corpus was compiled from transcripts from a wide range of MOOCs available on the edX platform. Our goal was to create a corpus that was representative of multiple academic fields from the natural sciences (247,247 words), social sciences and humanities (241,200), and vocational courses (126,000). Each transcript was individually cleaned of non-alphanumeric characters (e.g. @, #, $, etc.), html tags (i.e. < ... >), and onomatopoeic language (e.g. [boom!] [loud crash] etc.).

The ASWL was created by Dang et al. (2017) and consists of 1,741 word families. It was compiled based on overall frequency and dispersion across academic domains found in a 13-million-word academic spoken corpus. To be included in the list, each item had to occur at least once in each academic subcorpus (hard applied sciences, soft applied sciences, etc.), 50% of all discipline-specific subcorpora, and at least 350 times overall. The list was then validated using a different but similarly sized academic spoken corpus.

2.2. Analysis

Analysis was conducted using AntConc v3.4 (Anthony, 2018) using the 'Stop List' function which allows us to remove all instances of ASWL items from a given text. We then calculated coverage by computing the difference between the original corpus and the corpus with all ASWL families removed.

3. Results

Table 1 shows the breakdown of ASWL coverage for the entire MOOC corpus and the speech events of the MICASE corpus. The ASWL saw comparable coverage of 86% for the MOOC corpus and 87% overall for MICASE, indicating that the ASWL is useful for learners in both in-person and online contexts. It also suggests that MOOCs' vocabulary requirements are comparable to that of real-world universities, and that online environments can offer opportunities for incidental learning of academic vocabulary at least at par with in-person courses.

Table 1. ASWL coverage by speech event type

	# words	ASWL coverage
MOOC corpus	746,231	107,211 (86%)
MICASE speeches	26,563	2,593 (89%)
MICASE thesis defenses	53,980	6,124 (89%)
MICASE campus tours	22,734	2,325 (90%)
MICASE seminars	99,685	9,560 (90%)
MICASE lectures	505,281	55,089 (89%)

MICASE meetings	68,062	8,353 (88%)
MICASE discussion panels	92,183	11,098 (88%)
MICASE interviews	12,097	1,062 (92%)
MICASE tutorials	26,670	2,303 (91%)
MICASE workshops	14,252	1,044 (93%)
MICASE study groups	61,300	6.458 (89%)
MICASE laboratory sessions	58,557	8,229 (86%)
MICASE service encounters	25,054	2,183 (91%)
MICASE advising sessions	43,828	4,912 (89%)
MICASE office hours	76,084	8,529 (89%)

4. Discussion

Our analysis shows that there is similar coverage across different speech event types in MICASE. The lack of interactivity therefore does not appear to substantially affect MOOCs' lexical content and accessibility. However, coverage exceeded 90% in interviews, tutorials, workshops, and service encounters, all of which are dialogic or interactive contexts that are lacking in the MOOC environment. Other interactive speech events, such as meetings and discussion panels, may have received less coverage because they occur in more formal academic environments, making them more informationally dense. These contexts also tend to have one or more dominant speakers at a time and are thus less interactive and more persuasive in nature. Classroom lectures, which are the closest in format to the MOOC courses, also received slightly higher coverage than MOOCs (86% vs. 89%). These findings suggest that the ASWL can adequately prepare English as a Second Language (ESL) students for a broad range of linguistic encounters at university, both within and outside of academic contexts. Despite the slightly lower coverage, it also covers a substantial part of the vocabulary requirements of MOOCs.

5. Conclusions and future work

This study revealed that the ASWL (Dang et al., 2017) provides adequate coverage for MOOCs, as well as a variety of academic contexts that ESL learners are expected to encounter in English-medium universities. Our results indicate that MOOCs' vocabulary requirements are slightly lower but comparable to those of real-world universities, and that online environments can offer opportunities for incidental learning of academic vocabulary at least at par with in-person courses. However, it also revealed some differences in coverage among interactive speech events.

Notably, the ASWL offered the greatest coverage in highly dialogic and interactive contexts and the least in more typically formal speech events, indicating possible differences along a dimension of formality or topic. However, these results may be indicative of the overlap (approx. 85%) between the ASWL and the 2,000 most frequent words in English (Dang et al., 2017). Consequently, the slightly higher coverage in the interactive contexts might indicate a slightly lower use of more discipline-specific technical vocabulary.

Further research is called for to investigate such differences in more detail. Such research can, for example, identify specific linguistic markers in formal versus informal academic contexts, or create specific word lists for spoken encounters in different academic disciplines. Indeed, Hyland and Tse (2007) have argued that the AWL's usefulness varies across academic disciplines, and similar research might reveal similar patterns in the ASWL.

In terms of pedagogy, EAP courses using the ASWL can further support vocabulary learning by offering practice in a variety of registers and non-classroom speech events with confidence, of which the ASWL provides substantial coverage. Universities can also emphasize online courses to support ESL courses to enhance international students' preparation for in-person academic studies.

References

Anthony, L. (2018). AntConc (Version 3.5.7) [Computer Software]. Waseda University. http://www.laurenceanthony.net/software

Biber, D., Conrad, S., Reppen, R., Byrd, P., & Helt., M. (2002). Speaking and writing in the university: a multidimensional comparison. *TESOL Quarterly, 36*(1), 9-48. https://doi.org/10.2307/3588359

Coxhead, A. (2000). A new academic word list. *TESOL Quarterly, 34*(2), 213-238. https://doi.org/10.2307/3587951

Dang, T. N. Y., Coxhead, A., & Webb, S. (2017). The academic spoken word list. *Language Learning, 67*(4), 959-997. https://doi.org/10.1111/lang.12253

Haber, J. (2014). *MOOCs (The MIT Press Essential Knowledge Series)*. MIT Press.

Hyland, K., & Tse, P. (2007). Is there an "academic vocabulary"? *TESOL Quarterly, 41*(2), 235-253. https://doi.org/10.1002/j.1545-7249.2007.tb00058.x

Lederman, D. (2018, February 14). MOOCs: fewer new students, but more are paying. *Inside Higher Ed.* https://www.insidehighered.com/digital-learning/article/2018/02/14/moocs-are-enrolling-fewer-new-students-more-are-paying-courses

Newton, J. (2013). Incidental vocabulary learning in classroom communication tasks. *Language Teaching Research*, *17*(2), 164-187. https://doi.org/10.1177/1362168812460814

Simpson, R. C., Briggs, S. L., Ovens, J., & Swales, J. M. (2002). *The Michigan corpus of academic spoken English*. https://quod.lib.umich.edu/m/micase/

 ∎ UCLouvain

Effects of HVPT on perception and production of English fricatives by Japanese learners of English

Atsushi Iino[1]

Abstract. This study investigated the effects of High Variability Phonetic Training (HVPT) on beginner level English as a Foreign Language (EFL) Japanese learners' perceptions and productions of the English fricatives /f/, /v/ and /θ/. With the use of the computer program 'English Accent Coach' (EAC, Thomson, 2017), two groups of participants were engaged in learning the sounds in a two-syllable environment: target consonant + vowels (CV) and target consonant + vowels + consonant (CVC). The perception training with EAC was conducted for five weeks between a pre-test and a post-test in perception and production. Production was measured in the form of recorded reading aloud and was evaluated by native English speakers and a Japanese teacher of English. The results indicated the advantageous effects of CVC environments on perception as well as on production.

Keywords: pronunciation, HVPT, fricatives, perception, production.

1. Introduction

Training foreign language learners to perceive and produce sounds which have no equivalent sounds in their first language has always been an issue in pronunciation instruction. Particularly, HVPT has been regarded as an effective computer assisted pronunciation training which enriches robust sound images for L2 learners' perceptions, and hence intelligibility in production (Thomson, 2018).

Previous studies uniquely focus on /l/ and /r/ sounds for Japanese learners of English and suggest HVPT based on how perception affects production (Bradlow, Akahane-Yamada, Pisoni, & Tohkura, 1999, among others). Iino and Thomson

---

1. Hosei University, Tokyo, Japan; iino@hosei.ac.jp

How to cite this article: Iino, A. (2019). Effects of HVPT on perception and production of English fricatives by Japanese learners of English. In F. Meunier, J. Van de Vyver, L. Bradley & S. Thouësny (Eds), *CALL and complexity – short papers from EUROCALL 2019* (pp. 186-192). Research-publishing.net. https://doi.org/10.14705/rpnet.2019.38.1007

(2018) also focused on /l/, /r/, and /w/, and found computer assisted HPVT, namely EAC (Thomson, 2017), brought about progress in perception as well as progress in production.

However, there are few research studies that have investigated other consonants that Japanese learners have difficulty perceiving and producing. Lambacher, Martens, Nelson, and Bermen (2001) investigated the perception of voiceless fricatives for Japanese learners in a HVPT condition. They found /θ/ was the hardest to distinguish among other fricatives and the vowel environment had a strong influence. In the research, however, the variation of talkers seems to be limited. Iino (2018) investigated English sounds that are challenging for Japanese learners by using EAC. Among all the English consonants, fricatives such as /f/, /v/, and /θ/, were regarded as difficult sounds to perceive.

Thus, this paper focuses on the three fricative sounds: /f/, /v/, and /θ/, and I examined the effects of using computer assisted HVPT (i.e. EAC) under two different training environments: CV and CVC. My research questions are as follows.

> RQ1. What are the effects of HVPT on Japanese students' perceptions of the English /f/, /v/, and/θ/ over time depending on training environments?
>
> RQ2. What are the effects of HVPT on production of the target sounds over time depending on training environments?

2. Method

2.1. Participants

The learners who agreed to participate in this research were freshman students who were non-English majors in a university in Tokyo. They were enrolled in compulsory English courses consisting of two classes: Class A and Class B. By eliminating those who missed any of the assignments, pre-test, or post-tests, 33 students were eligible for data analysis as shown in Table 1. Their Test of English for International Communication (TOEIC) scores indicated they were categorized in the Common European Framework of Reference for languages (CEFR) A2 level (Class A: Mean (M)=342.5, Standard Deviation(SD)=11.5; Class B: M=265.4, SD=48.5).

2.2. Treatment

EAC (Thomson, 2017) was used for testing perception and training in two phonetic environments. In the program, users listened to randomly provided target sounds and chose one of the target phonetic symbols. The sound combinations were also randomized as were the 30 talkers' stimuli.

Treatment comprised three 100-item perceptual training sessions per week during the fall semester in 2018. Over five weeks, Class A received training in the CV phonetic environment in which the three target consonants were randomly provided as one syllable such as /fi /, /ve / or /θɑ/. Class B received the training in the CVC environment in single syllable words and word-like stimuli. The target sounds were always in syllable-onset position in both of the environments.

The participants practiced the first session of the training in class, and did the second and third sessions outside of class on their own within a week. They submitted three PDF feedback forms through Sakai, a course management system, every week. They could not do multiple sessions back-to-back in a day.

A pre-test and post-test design was adopted. The results of the first-week EAC training were used as a perception pre-test, and the ones in the fifth week were used as post-tests. In the first and the fifth week, the participants' productions were recorded by having them produce target items repeating the carrier phrases such as "The train runs valley to valley" and "Thirty-three people are thirsty" (see Table 1).

A total of five sentences included three assessment points for the target phonemes. The produced sounds were judged by two native speakers of English and one Japanese experienced English teacher. The raters listened to the data and rated together. When they disagreed on whether the sounds were correctly pronounced or not, they listened again, discussed, and decided on the judgment: correct (one point) or incorrect (zero).

Table 1. Sentences for production in reading aloud

The train runs valley to valley.
Let's face the facts.
Turn on Voice of America.
Fourteen friends follow my site.
Thirty-three people are thirsty.

*the underlined parts are the assessment points for the target sounds

3. Results

3.1. Perception

Progress was observed in all the sounds in more or less between 67% and 95% in the two training environments. Especially significant progress was found in /f/ in CV ($t(13)=2.58$, $p<.05$, $d=.90$) and /v/ ($t(18)=9.59$, $p<.01$, $d=3.36$), and /θ/ ($t(18)=3.42$, $p<.01$, $d=.95$) in CVC (Figure 1, Table 2).

Figure 1. **Left**: perception rate in CV training. **Right**: perception rate in CVC training

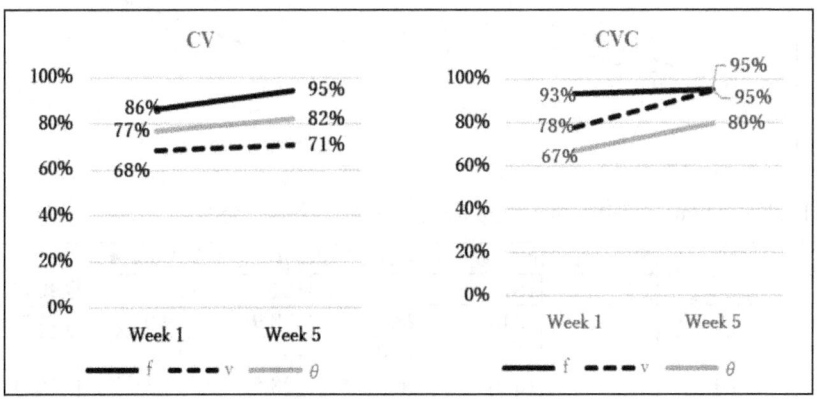

Table 2. Means of correct percentages in perception

		Week 1		Week 5		Progress	
		M	(SD)	M	(SD)	M	(SD)
CV (Class A) n=14	f	86.4	(12.3)	94.6	(4.8)	8.1*	(11.8)
	v	68.4	(11.4)	70.9	(9.7)	2.6	(11.9)
	θ	76.6	(8.6)	82.0	(6.3)	5.4	(9.6)
CVC (Class B) n=19	f	93.3	(3.8)	95.4	(4.4)	2.1	(5.8)
	v	77.6	(6.8)	94.8	(3.1)	17.3**	(7.9)
	θ	67.1	(13.8)	79.6	(13.2)	12.4**	(15.9)

** $p<.01$, * $p<.05$

3.2. Production

Statistically significant progress was found in /θ/ in CV ($t(13)=2.19$, $p<.05$, $d=.86$), /f/ ($t(18)=3.99$, $p<.01$, $d=.70$) and /v/ ($t(18)=2.47$, $p<.05$, $d=.60$) in CVC (Figure 2).

By overviewing the means, the majority of them remained as in low percentages, though the means in CVC were comparatively higher than those in CV (Figure 2, Table 3).

Figure 2. **Left**: production rate in CV training. **Right**: production rate in CVC training

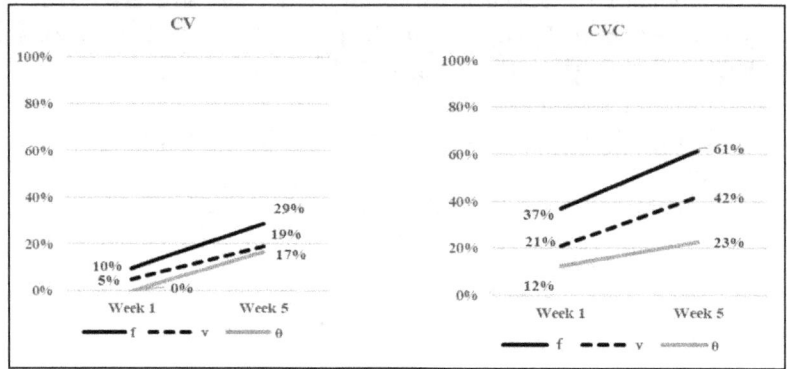

Table 3. Mean number of phonemes accurately produced

		Week 1 (3pts)		Week 5 (3pts)		Progress	
		M	(SD)	M	(SD)	M	(SD)
CV (Class A) n=14	f	9.5	(24.2)	28.6	(38.9)	19.0	(40.7)
	v	4.8	(17.8)	19.0	(33.9)	14.3	(31.3)
	θ	2.4	(8.9)	16.7	(28.5)	14.3*	(25.2)
CVC (Class B) n=19	f	36.8	(33.1)	61.4	(38.9)	24.6**	(26.9)
	v	21.1	(33.7)	42.1	(38.2)	21.1*	(37.2)
	θ	12.3	(27.7)	22.8	(29.5)	10.5	(25.0)

** p <.01, * p <.05

4. Discussion

4.1. Effects of HVPT on perception over time

The results in perception partially follow Lambacher et al. (2001) because perception of fricatives showed a high accuracy rate of over approximately 70%. Regarding the improvement in perception, /θ/ and /v/ showed significant progress in CVC, while they did not in CV. These results indicate the CVC environment helped improve perception more than the CV environment. Considering the ceiling effects in /f/ from the beginning, the CVC environment might have given more redundancy in perception potentially due to the length of stimuli and vocabulary knowledge the learners might have drawn on.

4.2. Effects of HVPT on production over time

HVPT was effective for improving all the sound articulations, particularly /θ/ in CV, and /v/ and /f/ in CVC. However, considering the fact that the majority of the scores were relatively low percentages particularly in the CV environment, the participants seemed to have struggled to articulate the target sounds. The gap between perception progress and production progress was also seen in different degrees in Iino and Thomson (2018). However, the gap in this study was larger, which indicates learning the articulation of those fricatives is quite challenging for Japanese learners of English in spite of the higher perception rates.

5. Conclusions

This study found positive effects of computer assisted HVPT on improving Japanese English learners' perception of English fricatives to some extent regardless of the training environments. The HVPT training was also effective in production in different levels to different degrees depending on target sounds and the training environments. Considering the participants' levels of proficiency (i.e. CEFR A2), these findings suggest that using the CVC environment, which provides single syllable words and word-like stimuli, leads to a better production rate.

6. Acknowledgments

I would like to thank Professor Ron Thomson (Brock University) for supporting the use of the program for this research. I also thank Brian Wistner (Hosei University) for examining the data. This study is supported by the Kakenhi Research Grant in Japan (No.17K02946).

References

Bradlow, A. R., Akahane-Yamada, R., Pisoni, D. B., & Tohkura, Y. (1999). Training Japanese listeners to identify English /r/and /l/: long-term retention of learning in perception and production. *Perception & Psychophysics, 61*(5), 977-985. https://doi.org/10.3758/bf03206911

Iino, A. (2018). Use of HVPT in CALL to assess less successfully recognized phonemes for Japanese EFL learners. *Hosei Univesity Tama Ronju, 34*,129-143. http://hdl.handle.net/10114/13827

Iino, A., & Thomson, R. I. (2018). Effects of web-based HVPT on EFL learners' recognition and production of L2 sounds. In P. Taalas, J. Jalkanen, L. Bradley,& S. Thouësny (Eds), *Future-proof CALL: language learning as exploration and encounters – short papers from EUROCALL 2018* (pp. 106-111). Research-publishing.net. https://doi.org/10.14705/rpnet.2018.26.821

Lambacher, S., Martens, W., Nelson, B., & Bermen, J. (2001). Identification of English voiceless fricatives by Japanese listeners: the influence of vowel context on sensitivity and response bias. *Acoustical Science and Technology, 22*(5), 334-343. https://doi.org/10.1250/ast.22.334

Thomson, R. I. (2017). English accent coach [Computer program]. Version 2.3. www.englishaccentcoach.com

Thomson, R. I. (2018). High variability [pronunciation] training (HVPT) --- A proven technique about which every language teacher and learner ought to know. *Journal of Second Language Pronunciation, 4*(2), 207-231. https://doi.org/10.1075/jslp.17038.tho

■ UCLouvain

Creating collaborative digital stories to promote community awareness

Bradley Irwin[1]

Abstract. The study presented in this paper explores the impact that a geographically situated digital storytelling project has on community awareness and engagement. A mixed method, exploratory case study approach was adopted for this study. Data was collected during in-class and fieldwork observations, with self-assessment surveys, open-ended questionnaires, and post-project individual debriefing sessions. Eighty-three first year undergraduate students at a rural Japanese university participated in the project. Seventy-nine (n=79) participants completed optional and anonymous self-assessment surveys and questionnaires. The results showed that participants' community awareness increased significantly after completing the project. Results also indicated that participants believed there was a strong likelihood that they would engage with the local community more in the future. Regarding L2 learning outcomes, data from the self-assessment surveys showed that students believed their English language ability improved alongside an increase in their motivation to study English.

Keywords: digital storytelling, community awareness and engagement, project-based language learning.

1. Introduction

The aim of the present study was to have students explore the local community in their university town to promote community awareness and engagement while at the same time improving their English communication skills. Working in small groups of three or four members, participants were tasked with creating digital stories about locations within their university town using only their smartphones. They were instructed to establish criteria for determining a historically or culturally

---

1. Nihon University, Mishima, Japan; irwin.bradley@nihon-u.ac.jp

How to cite this article: Irwin, B. (2019). Creating collaborative digital stories to promote community awareness. In F. Meunier, J. Van de Vyver, L. Bradley & S. Thouësny (Eds), *CALL and complexity – short papers from EUROCALL 2019* (pp. 193-198). Research-publishing.net. https://doi.org/10.14705/rpnet.2019.38.1008

significant location or place of interest within the town and to create a five-minute video highlighting the importance of the location. Students were required to use English during each phase of the project to develop communicative skills for effective collaboration and narrative techniques necessary to make their videos entertaining while also conveying complex ideas. In order to maximize potential English learning outcomes, students prepared for their projects by conducting research, creating storyboards, and drafting scripts, before finally traveling together to film their projects on-location.

A collaborative digital storytelling project was viewed as an ideal means to achieve these goals since research has shown that storytelling of community history can be used to increase community engagement and participation (Gaver, Dunne, & Pacenti, 1999). Carroll and Rosson (1996) also identified digital storytelling as a means to bond community members to one another and to foster a sense of engagement and attachment to a local community. In terms of language learning, several researchers have shown that students who participate in digital storytelling projects improve speaking and oral communication skills because of the narrative techniques required to complete the task (Hwang et al., 2016; Irwin, 2019; Razmi, Pourali, & Nozad, 2014). Listening ability has also been found to improve as a result of completing digital storytelling activities (Verdugo & Belmonte, 2007). Presently, the author is unaware of any published studies that explore the use of mobile devices to create collaborative digital storytelling projects in language learning contexts.

Although the full scope of this study investigated a broad range of areas of interest concerning language learning outcomes associated with collaboratively created digital storytelling projects made using only mobile devices, this paper briefly outlines the results of the following research questions:

- Can English language learners improve their English skills by creating collaborative digital storytelling projects using mobile devices?

- Can students increase community awareness and engagement through a geographically situated digital storytelling project?

2. Method

Eighty-three first year undergraduate students taught by the author of this study at a mid-sized liberal arts university in rural Japan participated in the digital storytelling project. All participants were enrolled in a compulsory English course and were assessed as having proficiency levels between A2 and B1 on the Common European Framework of Reference for languages (CEFR) scale. Of the 83 project participants, 79 completed the optional and anonymous self-assessment surveys and questionnaires.

In order to collect sufficient data to address the research questions, a mixed method, exploratory case study approach was adopted. Data was collected during in-class and fieldwork observations, with self-assessment surveys using 5-point Likert scale items, open-ended questionnaires, and post-project individual debriefing sessions. A pre- and post-project test was also conducted to assess whether creating the digital projects had an impact on local area knowledge and community awareness. Quantitative and qualitative data were combined to validate data through triangulation and provide a deeper understanding of the results.

3. Results and discussion

Data from the pre- and post-project test was analyzed using a paired samples t-test to compare differences in local area knowledge and community awareness before the digital storytelling project and after its completion. The results showed a significant increase in scores from before the digital storytelling project (M=24.94, SD=13.14) to after its completion (M=42.91, SD=5.39); $t(78)$=12.76, p=.00001. While these results suggest that participating in the digital storytelling project significantly increased local area knowledge and community awareness, it is difficult to account for any external factors that may have also contributed to this raise.

As meaningful community engagement is a repeated activity that occurs over a period of time, the time constraints of this study proved to be problematic. Participants were asked to assess the degree to which they believed they would engage with the local community in the future. The results of the self-assessment survey measuring potential future community engagement are displayed below (see Table 1 below).

Two notable results can be observed. First, participants strongly agreed that they would go to the places that their classmates had presented about in their video projects (M=4.5, SD=0.67). This finding indicated that the participants' interests were piqued about places they had not already visited within the town after watching their classmates' videos. Second, participants also strongly agreed that they would become more active in the community after having completed the digital storytelling project (M=4.4, SD=0.61). Thus, the results of the self-assessment survey indicated that there was an increased likelihood of future community engagement because of participating in the digital storytelling project.

Table 1. Self-assessment responses to statements measuring community engagement (n=79)

Statements	Strongly Agree				Strongly Disagree	Mean
	5	4	3	2	1	(SD)
I will go back to my location in the future.	28	34	14	3	0	4.2 (0.72)
I will go to the locations presented in my classmates' videos.	46	28	4	0	0	4.5 (0.67)
I will recommend the places presented in the videos to my family and friends.	27	38	12	1	1	4.2 (0.69)
I will become active in the community by participating in events and activities at video locations.	36	37	5	0	0	4.4 (0.61)

Students were also asked to assess the amount of English they used during each phase of the digital storytelling project, whether they believed their English had improved, and if their motivation to study English had increased. Table 2 shows their responses.

Table 2. Self-assessment responses to statements measuring English language use (n=79)

Statements	Strongly Agree				Strongly Disagree	Mean
	5	4	3	2	1	(SD)
I made an effort to use English to complete the research phase.	20	26	11	16	6	3.5 (1.28)
I made an effort to use English to complete the drafting phase.	36	27	12	4	0	4.2 (0.88)
I made an effort to use English to complete the filming phase.	18	29	21	8	3	3.7 (1.06)
My English has improved as a result of this project.	46	27	5	1	0	4.5 (0.68)
My motivation to study English has increased because of this project.	34	34	11	0	0	4.3 (0.70)

During the research and filming phases, students were less likely to make an effort to use English than during the drafting phase. During classroom observations it was apparent that students were more likely than not to search for information about their locations using Japanese. In some cases, there was actually very little online information in English about the places being researched. Because students were filming on-location, some of them were reluctant to use English in public in front of strangers. Students also strongly agreed that their English ability had improved as a result of the project (M=4.5, SD=0.68). Another important result was that students felt their motivation to study English had also increased because of their participation in the project (M=4.3, SD=0.70).

4. Conclusions

The present study investigated the impact of a geographically situated digital storytelling project using smartphones on language learning and community awareness. To address the first research question, results indicated that participants felt their English ability improved and that their motivation to study English had increased. Regarding the second research question, the results showed a significant increase in subjects' community awareness and potential future engagement. These findings were similar to those of Gaver et al. (1999) whose research showed that community history storytelling could be used to enhance community engagement and participation.

To improve English language use during the research phase, it would be useful for teachers in our context to select locations that have ample amounts of information in the target language. Also, to help improve target language use during the filming phase, students could be advised to go to their locations when there is less chance that others may be present. Finally, to build speaking confidence, it may also be worthwhile to have students practice the English narration by making mock videos before going to their locations.

References

Carroll, J. M., & Rosson, M. B. (1996). Developing the Blacksburg electronic village. *Communications of the ACM, 39*(12), 69-74. https://doi.org/10.1145/240483.240498

Gaver, B., Dunne, T., & Pacenti, E. (1999). Cultural probes. *Interactions, 6*(1), 21-29. https://doi.org/10.1145/291224.291235

Hwang, W.-Y., Rustam S., Hsu, J.-L., Huang Y.-M., Hsu, G.-L., & Lin, Y.-C. (2016). Effects of storytelling to facilitate EFL speaking using Web-based multimedia system. *Computer Assisted Language Learning, 29*(2), 215-241. https://doi.org/10.1080/09588221.2014.927367

Irwin, B. (2019). Mobile assisted project-based language learning: practical considerations and learning outcomes. *Studies in International Relations, 39*(2), 47-56.

Razmi, M., Pourali, S., & Nozad, S. (2014). Digital storytelling in EFL classroom (oral presentation of the story): a pathway to improve oral production. *Procedia - Social and Behavioral Sciences, 98*, 1541-1544. https://doi.org/10.1016/j.sbspro.2014.03.576

Verdugo, D. R., & Belmonte, I. A. (2007). Using digital stories to improve listening comprehension with Spanish young learners of English. *Language Learning & Technology, 11*(1), 87-101.

■ UCLouvain

Students' perceptions about the use of digital badges in an online English terminology course: a three-year study

Jun Iwata[1], Shudong Wang[2], and John Clayton[3]

Abstract. In e-learning environments, 'digital badges', often referred to as 'micro-credentials', are expected to function not only as valid indicators of learner's accomplishments but also as useful tools for motivational and reward purposes (Clayton, 2012). In this study, we investigated students' perceptions about the use of digital badges in an online terminology course we had developed (Iwata et al., 2017). We hypothesized that the badges which students earned for the course would not only function as an indicator of their achievement but also help enhance their learner autonomy. Through a three-year survey on students' perceptions of their course of study in this course, we found that a large majority of students (88.3%) were satisfied with their study through this course and that most of the students (69.7%) found the use of badges helpful in confirming their course achievements. The results also showed that two-thirds of them (64.3%) found that earning badges helped motivate them toward further autonomous study. These findings indicate that the use of digital badges can provide students with opportunities to enhance their learner autonomy.

Keywords: digital badges, micro-credentials, students' perceptions, medical English.

---

1. Shimane University, Shimane, Japan; j_iwata@med.shimane-u.ac.jp
2. Shimane University, Shimane, Japan; wangsd@soc.shimane-u.ac.jp
3. Institute for Indigenous Innovation, Whakatane, New Zealand; john.clayton@wananga.ac.nz

How to cite this article: Iwata, J., Wang, S., & Clayton, J. (2019). Students' perceptions about the use of digital badges in an online English terminology course: a three-year study. In F. Meunier, J. Van de Vyver, L. Bradley & S. Thouësny (Eds), *CALL and complexity – short papers from EUROCALL 2019* (pp. 199-205). Research-publishing.net. https://doi.org/10.14705/rpnet.2019.38.1009

1. Introduction

In today's e-learning environments, more and more learning tools and activities are available for learners. They have more choices for the time, like when they choose to learn and the place where they choose to learn. In these increasingly learner-centered, personalized learning environments, learners are expected to be more responsible for their learning outcomes. This means there is an increasing need for them to collect learning experiences or outcomes that matter to them (Aşık, 2010). Clayton, Iwata, and Saravani (2016) suggested that "a fundamental criterion for the success of self-motivated and self-directed English language learning environments is the ability of learners to make the appropriate connections between their existing skills, knowledge and experience, and expected skill, knowledge and behaviors" (p. 1340). Clayton (2012) and Clayton et al. (2016) also suggested that digital badges or micro-credentials function as valid indicators of accomplishment and they also function as a motivator by demonstrating their learning achievements through the display of endorsed digital badge collections.

In our study, we investigated students' perceptions about the use of digital badges in a 1,000 Basic Medical English Terminology course we had developed by using the badge function of Moodle, one of the most popular learning management systems in our previous study (Iwata et al., 2017). We hypothesized the use of digital badges would firstly help learners confirm their achievements and secondly help them engage with the courses available and participate autonomously in learning activities. Through a three-year study (2016-2018) on students' perceptions of implementation of digital badges in the course, we evaluated the effects of using them in the course.

2. Course details

2.1. Structure

The course we used in this study was a 1,000 Basic Medical English Terminology course on Moodle. This course was developed to help medical students in Japan to review the basic medical terms they learned at school. We applied the use of digital badges to this course by using the badge function of Moodle. The course consists of 13 sections, each of which includes three types of quizzes to check medical terms.

Students' perceptions about the use of digital badges...

2.2. Learning procedure

Figure 1. Learning procedure

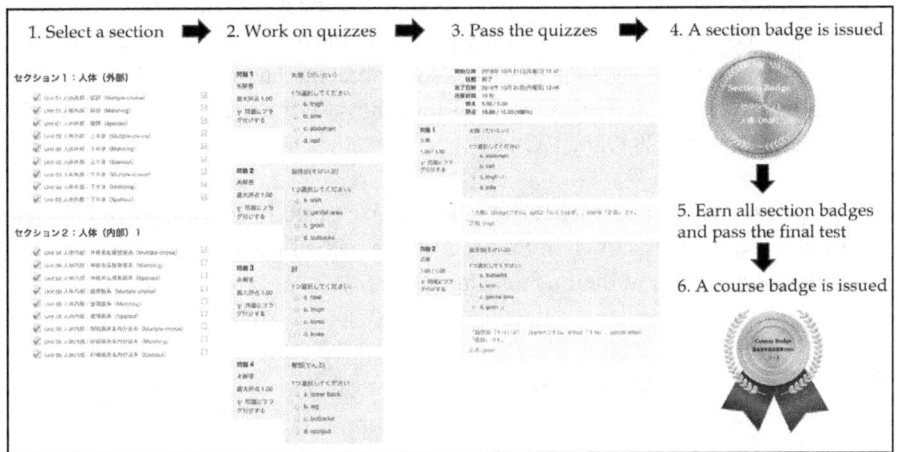

Figure 2. Portfolio

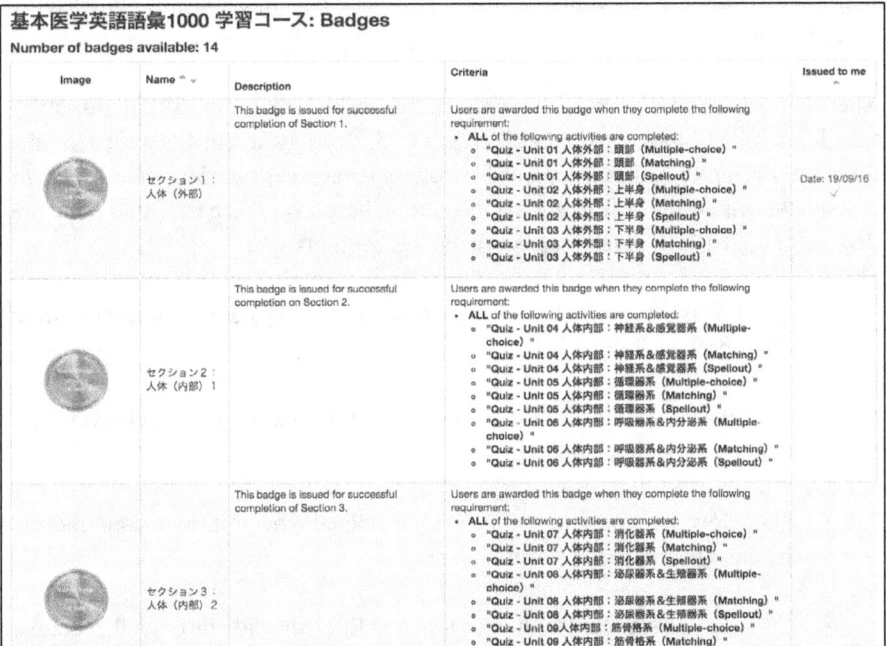

A typical learning procedure is shown in Figure 1 above. As explained in a previous paper:

> "[s]tudents first chose a section in the course and then worked on the quizzes in that section. To pass each quiz, they had to meet the criteria we set. When students successfully passed all the quizzes of each section, they were issued a 'section badge'. When students had earned all 13 section badges and had passed the final test, they were issued a 'course badge'" (Iwata et al., 2017, p. 172).

The badges students had earned during their course of study were displayed in their portfolio on Moodle as shown in Figure 2 above, which were expected to function as validated indicators of their achievements.

3. Course evaluation

We carried out a three-year research project to investigate students' perceptions for the course from 2016 to 2018. Each year, we made this course available on our Moodle site as a self-study review course and we encouraged first-year medical students to complete the course at their own pace during a four-month period in the fall semester.

After students had finished the course, we asked them to fill in an online questionnaire on Moodle using a Likert scale (5, strongly agree; 4, agree; 3, neither agree nor disagree; 2, disagree; and 1, strongly disagree) regarding their use of the course. We asked the following six questions based on the perceptual measures (Iwata et al., 2017) to investigate students' perceptions.

- Q1: Was the badge-based assessment system comprehensible? (Comprehensibility)

- Q2: Was the badge system helpful in checking your achievements? (Checking achievements)

- Q3: How do you think this course helped you improve your medical English vocabulary? (Usefulness)

- Q4: Are you satisfied with your medical English study through this course? (Satisfaction)

- Q5: Did the badges influence your learning motivation? (Learner motivation)

- Q6: Would you like to study English with online self-study courses like this course? (Further study)

4. Results

Three hundred students (RR=98.0%) answered the questions and the results of the six questions (Figure 3).

Figure 3. First results of the Likert scale questions about students' perceptions

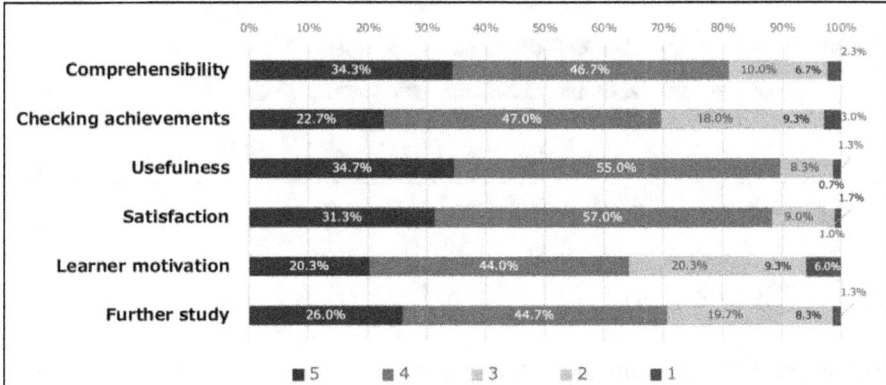

We regarded five (strongly agree) and four (agree) as positive results. The first two questions investigated whether the badge-based assessment was comprehensive and how digital badges helped confirm achievements. Eighty-one percent of the students found the badge-based assessment system comprehensible and 69.7% of them found the system helpful in checking their achievements. The next two questions investigated students' self-engagement: usefulness and satisfaction. A large majority of students (89.7%, 88.3% respectively) gave us positive responses to these criteria.

The last two questions investigated students' autonomy and their willingness to study further. About two-thirds of students (64.3%) found that earning badges helped motivate them toward further autonomous study. However, a third of them (35.7%) seemed unsure about the effect. Also, while about 70.7% of the students said that they would like to study English with online self-study courses like this course, about 30% of them said they were not willing to do so.

We also asked another series of questions about the structure and design of the course using a Likert scale. The results show that a majority of students seemed to find the course structure and design of badges satisfactory though there remained room for improvement in visual appeal and the design of badges (see Figure 4).

Figure 4. Second results of the Likert scale questions about students' perceptions

	5	4	3	2	1
Course structure	37.7%	49.3%		9.7%	2.3%
Accessability	46.7%	38.3%		9.3%	4.7%
Visual appeal	26.0%	47.0%		17.3%	6.7%	1.0%
Badge design (section)	31.0%	45.0%		21.3%	1.0%
Badge design (course)	32.7%	43.0%		20.0%	2.3%

5. Discussion

The initial findings from the survey on students' perceptions about the course seemed to indicate the use of badges functions well as an indicator (Clayton, 2012). As a whole, most of the students found the badge-based assessment was helpful in checking achievements. The data also has shown that the use of badges seemed to help students' engagement in the course. A large majority of the students found the course useful and they seemed satisfied with the course. As for the function of the use of badges as a motivational tool, two-thirds of the students found that earning badges helped motivate them with their study. However, there seems to be room for improvement because a third of them responded that the badges were not yet a motivating factor for them.

6. Conclusions

An investigation through three-year survey results on students' perceptions of the use of digital badges in a medical terminology course suggests that this digital badge system allows learners to create a holistic view of their achievements through a pictorial display of earned badges. The results also suggest that while there seems to be room for improvement, the digital reward system shows potential to help learners study autonomously.

7. Acknowledgments

We would like to thankfully acknowledge that this study was supported by KAKEN Grant C (2015-2017) from the Japan Society for the Promotion of Science (15K02718).

References

Aşık, A. (2010). Misconceptions on learner autonomy: a methodological and conceptual renewal. *Ekev Academic Review, 14*(43), 141-152.

Clayton, J. (2012). Mass-customisation and self-reflective frameworks: early developments in New Zealand. *Research in Learning Technology, 20*(Supp), 189-203. https://doi.org/10.3402/rlt.v20i0.19187

Clayton, J., Iwata, J., & Saravani, S. (2016). Designing e-learning environments to encourage learner autonomy: creating a framework for development. *Proceedings of the International Symposium on Education, Psychology and Social Science 2014* (pp. 1337-1346). http://irep.iium.edu.my/39044/2/201405-Kyoto_Proceedins-ICSSAM%26ISEPSS.pdf

Iwata, J., Telloyan, J., Murphy, L., Wang, S., & Clayton, J. (2017). The use of a digital badge as an indicator and a motivator. *Proceedings of the International Conference on Educational Technologies 2017* (pp. 171-174). https://files.eric.ed.gov/fulltext/ED579282.pdf

Complexity and tool selection for purposeful communication in telecollaborative encounters

Kristi Jauregi Ondarra[1]

Abstract. When organising TeleCollaboration (TC) encounters at primary or secondary schools, especially technological and organisational complexity, alongside pedagogical issues, plays an essential role in the degree of success of the exchanges. Within the European TeCoLa project, pilot experiences have been organised using innovative but 'simple' technologies, like Padlet or Voki to more demanding and complex ones like 3D virtual worlds in OpenSim. The present paper presents the experiences of three pilot exchanges differing in complexity and reports on learners' experiences.

Keywords: telecollaboration, learners' experiences.

1. Introduction

Task-based TC has been said to enrich foreign language curricula by providing learners with opportunities to get immersed in an intercultural dialogue with peers from other countries and in so doing develop intercultural, communicative, social, and digital competences (Canto & Jauregi, 2017, O'Dowd, 2016). The Erasmus+ TeCoLa project (2016-2019) originated from the wish to help schoolteachers to get familiarised with and learn how to integrate TC activities in their teaching in order to provide their students with these enriching learning opportunities. Teachers joining TeCoLa got trained and coached individually throughout the whole process of project preparation, execution, and evaluation.

---

1. Utrecht University, Utrecht, The Netherlands; k.jauregi@uu.nl

How to cite this article: Jauregi Ondarra, K. (2019). Complexity and tool selection for purposeful communication in telecollaborative encounters. In F. Meunier, J. Van de Vyver, L. Bradley & S. Thouësny (Eds), *CALL and complexity – short papers from EUROCALL 2019* (pp. 206-211). Research-publishing.net. https://doi.org/10.14705/rpnet.2019.38.1010

2. From simple to complex TC exchanges

When referring to TC in primary and secondary school contexts, complexity is present at different interrelated levels: the school context, the IT level, and pedagogical approaches to language teaching (Jauregi, 2018). In this paper we present the experiences of three pilot exchanges which differ in complexity.

2.1. Creating vlogs in Padlet

This pilot is an example of a successful, straightforward, and easy to conduct project. Since one of the two participating schools had old computers, a bad internet connection, and no IT support, the interactive wall Padlet was selected for sharing learners' vlogs asynchronously. Seventeen Dutch learners from a bilingual secondary school interacted in Spanish with 22 primary school learners from Spain, who carried out TC activities in English. The Dutch and the Spanish learners had an A2 proficiency level in their target language. Five groups were created in each school and subsequently paired up with parallel groups from the other country (Dutch Group A paired up with Spanish Group A, etc.) and separate Padlet walls were created for each international team.

Learners created four vlogs in groups, one per week in a period of a month, and uploaded them in their respective Padlet wall for the international peer group to view. In the first task, they introduced themselves and their school. In Task 2, they provided general information about their country/region. In Task 3, they informed their peers about tourist attractions in their region. In the last task, they provided cultural information about their region/country (how people live, what a regular day looks like, how they celebrate their birthday, etc.).

Tasks 1, 2, and 4 were carried out in the target language (Spanish for the Dutch learners and English for the Spanish learners). The topic of the third task was more complex and it was carried out in Spanish for the Spanish learners and in English for the bilingual Dutch learners (Jauregi & Melchor-Couto, 2018).

2.2. Multi-tool approach

In this pilot, various technologies were used for the exchanges with high levels of engagement and enthusiasm. Two state primary schools, one from London with limited resources and with access to Spanish language lessons during 40 minutes per week throughout the year and one bilingual primary school from Valencia, participated in the TC project. The participants were learners of English (B2 level) and Spanish (A1 level), ten to 12 years of age. The interactions took place between January and the end of June 2019, and age-appropriate and relevant topics were selected for each session, such as describing their own cities or favourite foods.

Different tools were used for the exchanges: Padlet to talk about topics such as Easter celebrations; Vokis for presenting themselves; and class-to-class video communication and weekly Moodle chat rooms.

Given the low proficiency in Spanish of the UK learners, it was decided to run the weekly chat sessions in English and allocate time at the beginning for these learners to be able to practise their Spanish by asking their peers to translate key vocabulary for them in Spanish. The tasks were carried out in school, either in lessons or at a dedicated time, even if this sometimes meant using the learners' play time.

2.3. TC in the virtual city of Saarburg

The third pilot was ambitious in many senses. It involved the use of the TeCoLa virtual world to facilitate synchronous oral communication in German among Dutch and French learners. Technologically speaking, the TeCoLa virtual environment is quite demanding. A viewer has to be installed and certain security ports opened in order to access and be immersed in the virtual world as an avatar and be able to speak and chat with other avatars. The interaction sessions were carried out at school. This implied finding a common time slot at both ends to be able to organise and carry out the weekly tasks, which proved to be quite challenging. The project was not viewed as an add-on activity, but as the main core of the curriculum.

Two teachers of German, one from a pre-vocational school in the Netherlands and the other one from a mainstream secondary school in northern France, offered their learners the possibility to experience TC in the 3D virtual world as a motivating way to work on their intercultural and communicative competences in German. Two full classes participated, in which 21 Dutch and 20 French learners all between 14 and 16 years of age and with an A2 proficiency level in German were paired up in international dyads (Figure 1). In the classroom, the teachers prepared the learners for the TC tasks, using pre-task activities: facilitating (new) vocabulary, practising communicative functions relevant for the tasks, and discussing communication and social strategies, etc. Then the learners carried out the TC tasks in international dyads. Finally, at the post-task phase learners and teachers reflected upon and evaluated the exchanges: what they had learned, the difficulties they had faced, etc.

Figure 1. International dyads

According to the carousel model we designed for the exchanges, seven international dyads met up in a given spot of the virtual Saarburg to carry out the task in time slots of 30 minutes (Figure 2). This model made it possible for all learners to participate every week during classroom hours (Dutch learners) or lunch break (French learners).

Figure 2. Seven meeting spots

In this first phase, learners carried out different TC tasks[2]: *Blind date*, *Frühstück*, and *Weihnachten in Frankreich und Niederlanden*. This first phase turned out to be quite challenging. Accordingly, the carousel model was adapted to make it more flexible: only seven dyads would participate per week for 45 minutes. The participating dyads would alternate per week. In this second phase, three additional tasks were carried out: *Gesund Leben*, *Meine Schule*, and *Carnival*.

3. Learners' experiences

Learners from the three exchanges were interviewed in their mother tongue at the end of the project. Overall, all the interviewed learners liked the TC exchanges, irrespective of their complexity. What learners liked most about the project was the possibility to meet with peers from a different country on a weekly basis and learn about their lives and culture. They also enjoyed the innovative character of the project: "to do other things than the typical classroom activities". The students valued the intercultural dimension of the experience: "I learnt about English, about their cultures and their city, London". Enjoyment was identified in the student interviews as a recurrent topic: "I loved the experience; it is very fun". Some students also referred to the positive effect that the experience had in their confidence: "Boosting your confidence speaking in Spanish". Learners reported to have learned about the other culture, to communicate in the target language, and to collaborate in teams. They would recommend the experience because "it is fun, interactive and they can learn lots of Spanish". They would like to continue with these projects as they get the chance to meet other people and learn about their lives.

Although learners in the three cases were enthusiastic about their experiences, learners faced some challenges in the first and third cases. In the first TC pilot, the younger Spanish learners were more positive than their Dutch peers. The Spanish learners valued the project with a mean value of 8.2 versus 6.8 of the Dutch peers. The Dutch learners were concerned about the lack of clarity about what they had to do, lack of time to carry out the activities, and the lack of feedback from their teacher. This made them uncertain. The teacher had organised the exchanges as an add-on activity and provided little or no coaching to learners. This clearly influenced their general evaluation of the project.

Regarding the third pilot in the virtual world, most of the learners liked being an avatar. But some found it scary ("freaky") and would have preferred to see their

---

2. Visit our TeCoLa Open Educational Resources Pool to access the tasks: https://sites.google.com/site/tecolaprojectoer/tasks?authuser=0

peer when carrying out the tasks. The technology did not always function properly, which was annoying for them. For the French learners, the time schedule was not satisfactory: they had to use their lunchtime break to carry out the TC tasks and in the long run they found it unpleasant.

4. Conclusions

One of the main conclusions of this paper advocates for the integration of TC exchanges in the languages curriculum irrespective of the IT situation of the school. TC does not seem to be more successful when complex technology, like 3D virtual worlds, is used. The lesson learned in these three exchanges suggests that learners appreciate more the possibility to engage and collaborate with peers abroad and carry out motivating tasks together than the sophistication of the tool being used for the exchanges.

5. Acknowledgements

We would like to thank all teachers and learners involved in the exchanges, and the coach of the second exchange: Eli Vilar.

References

Canto, S., & Jauregi, K. (2017). Language learning effects through the integration of synchronous socializing network opportunities in language curricula: the case of video communication and Second Life. *Language Learning in Higher Education Journal,* Special Issue: *Synchronous Technologies in Language and Intercultural Learning and Teaching in Higher Education,* 7(1), 21-53. https://doi.org/10.1515/cercles-2017-0004

Jauregi, K. (2018). Telecollaboration at secondary schools: challenges of open data. In J. Colpaert, A. Aerts & F. Cornillie (Eds), *CALL your data* (pp. 182-188). Antwerp University.

Jauregi, K., & Melchor-Couto, S. (2018). Successful telecollaboration exchanges in primary and secondary education: what are the challenges? In P. Taalas, J. Jalkanen, L. Bradley & S. Thouësny (Eds), *Future-proof CALL: language learning as exploration and encounters* (pp. 112-117). Research-publishing.net. https://doi.org/10.14705/rpnet.2018.26.822

O'Dowd, R. (2016). Emerging trends and new directions in telecollaborative learning. *CALICO Journal, 33*(3), 291-310.

Student perceptions of group writing processes and feedback

Kym Jolley[1]

Abstract. In this pilot study, two second year writing classes at a university in Japan completed two group writing tasks using Microsoft Word and Google Docs. After both tasks were completed, the students (N=45) completed a short survey containing Likert scale items about their preferences when writing under the different conditions. Willing individuals also answered a second survey containing open-ended questions to gain a deeper understanding about the first survey results. Findings showed that the students preferred using Google Docs for the writing tasks due to ease of use and submission of the final document, as well as the ability to understand online written feedback from the instructor.

Keywords: L2 writing, group writing, CALL, Google Docs.

1. Introduction

Compared with communicative classes, writing has traditionally been thought of more as an individual task (Storch, 2005). However, with modern technologies, collaborative writing tasks are becoming more common place in the L2 classroom. These kinds of activities have the potential to aid students' task completion, where collaborative writing can result in more linguistically accurate texts (Storch, 2013).

Furthermore, applications such as Google Docs allow for greater ease of collaboration and implementation of writing tasks (Slavkov, 2015), as groups can work on one document concurrently, as well as record all efforts from contributors. Thus, it also helps to alleviate concerns about unequitable workloads from participants.

---

1. Kwansei Gakuin Univeristy, Kobe, Japan; kymjolley@kwansei.ac.jp; https://orcid.org/0000-0002-9320-9297

How to cite this article: Jolley, K. (2019). Student perceptions of group writing processes and feedback. In F. Meunier, J. Van de Vyver, L. Bradley & S. Thouësny (Eds), *CALL and complexity – short papers from EUROCALL 2019* (pp. 212-217). Research-publishing.net. https://doi.org/10.14705/rpnet.2019.38.1011

However, how do students experience group writing tasks under a more traditional method, such as Microsoft Word, compared with online applications? This pilot study endeavors to understand which condition students prefer, with a focus on three key components: which condition they prefer to write under, which condition they prefer for submission, and under which condition is feedback easier to understand?

2. Method

2.1. Participants

Forty-five second year STEM[2] L2 English students from two classes at a university in Japan responded anonymously to a survey after completing two group essay writing tasks.

2.2. Writing tasks and survey

2.2.1. Writing tasks

In small groups of three or four, students completed two group argumentative essays of about 1,000 words each during one semester. Both essays contained five paragraphs and followed typical writing format processes. Each group was allowed to choose a current issue in science or technology as a topic, and required to follow the faculty formatting guidelines for documents. Groups completed a brief paper-based outline in class for feedback from the instructor before writing commenced. Furthermore, all groups sat together in class to aid the flow of collaboration.

The first essay was completed using Microsoft Word. Each student had access to a laptop computer within the classroom. In order to support an equitable division of work, students were advised to divide areas of the essay to take primary responsibility for. However, as a group they were instructed to, and given time to, reflect upon the essay as a whole in class. A printed copy of the first draft was then submitted. The instructor checked and offered handwritten feedback, primarily indirect and metalinguistic. Groups addressed the feedback before submitting a final paper-based copy.

---

2. Science, technology, engineering, and mathematics.

For the second essay, the instructor created separate Google Docs for each group. The appropriate document was shared with each group member. Groups again completed an outline, before working on the first draft in class as the instructor monitored their progress through Google Drive. The instructor then provided feedback by adding comments to the document. Again, feedback was primarily metalinguistic and indirect. Groups addressed the feedback together and completed final drafts. Throughout the writing process students were reminded that the history of their document would be viewed to ensure all students contributed to the writing of the essay.

2.2.2. Survey

After both essays were completed, students anonymously answered a short survey containing six-point Likert items (1=strongly disagree to 6=strongly agree) in class. The statements focused on the three previously mentioned key components and took about ten minutes to complete. Respondents were instructed both orally and within the survey itself to consider all experiences when writing with both Microsoft Word and Google Docs while responding to the Likert items. Respondents were also asked to share contact details if willing to answer further questions. A second survey asking respondents to choose their preference between Microsoft Word and Google Docs under the three key components and then answer open-ended questions asking why they preferred each condition was sent to those who volunteered their details.

3. Results

Survey results were analyzed using SPSS 25. Descriptive statistic results show that students preferred using Google Docs for all three conditions (see Table 1). The mean in each case was between 4.5 and 4.9, indicating agreement on the Likert scale. Furthermore, the standard deviation of each result was between 1.1 and 1.3, indicating at worst slight disagreement or just mere agreement.

Table 1. Survey results

	N	Mean	Standard deviation
I think it is easier writing in groups using Google Drive documents	45	4.69	1.240
I think it is easier to understand and read teacher comments using Google Drive documents	45	4.49	1.308

| I think it is easier submitting writing work using Google Drive documents. | 45 | 4.87 | 1.1.20 |

Frequencies of each response show that in each case (6) strongly agree was the most commonly selected response for each statement (see Table 2).

Table 2. Response frequencies

	1	2	3	4	5	6
I think it is easier writing in groups using Google Drive documents	0%	4.3%	17.4%	15.2%	28.3%	32.6%
I think it is easier to understand and read teacher comments using Google Drive documents	0%	6.5%	19.6%	21.7%	19.6%	30.4%
I think it is easier submitting writing work using Google Drive documents	0%	0%	17.4%	15.2%	28.3%	37%

Responses from the second survey attempted to gain deeper insight into student preferences. However, it should be noted that as only two responded, it is not possible to generalize these responses. Nonetheless, they may offer an interesting insight into student perceptions that can be further investigated in future research. Both respondents selected Google Docs as their preference in all three areas under investigation and elaborated on their choices. Their responses indicate that the affordances of Google Docs made it more convenient for these respondents during group writing (see sample comments below).

- Why did you prefer group writing with Google Docs?

    複数のメンバーが同時にでき、その同期が簡単にできるから (You can have multiple members at the same time and easily synchronize them).

- Why did you prefer feedback and comments with essays done on Google Docs?

    This is because its reply is online and it is easy to read anytime and anywhere on my smartphone.

- Why was it easiest to submit your group essays with Google Docs?

    提出するためにファイルを移動する必要がなかったから (I didn't have to move the file to submit).

4. Discussion

Though it has previously been found that Japanese students still realize the need both academically and professionally for writing skills using standard technological tools (Jolley & Donnellan, 2018), more modern approaches have been found favorable in this investigation. It is surmised that this has to do with the reduced cognitive load that Google Docs affordances allow. Indeed, Suwantarathip and Wichadee (2014) also found that students reported a good impression of collaborative writing with Google Docs when completing writing tasks outside of the classroom. They further posited that their results indicate Google Docs could have successful applications within the classroom, just as this study found in terms of student perceptions. Furthermore, as in Suwantarathip and Wichadee (2014), it is recommended that instructors thoughtfully implement such methods when conducting class writing activities. Indeed, in the case of this study the instructor controlled all documents using Google Drive to help students focus on the task at hand. However, as students become more familiar with new writing tools, less scaffolding would obviously be needed.

5. Conclusions

Results from this study indicate that when undertaking group writing, students value tools that facilitate collaboration most conveniently. This is an important consideration for instructors when planning group writing in the L2 classroom. This convenience may help lessen the cognitive load required by groups, thus, allowing students to focus on the task at hand.

Overall, this is an exploratory study which requires further development and wider investigation. However, as Limbu and Markauskaite (2015) assert, it is important to consider students' experiences with different technologies, as it helps to understand the learning environment from the students' perspective. This in turn helps to not only inform instructor task implementation and planning, but also very importantly, to improve learning for students.

6. Acknowledgments

I would like to thank the reviewers for their insightful comments in assisting with the completion of the final article.

References

Jolley, K., & Donnellan, M. (2018). Student uses and preferences of technology in the Japanese STEM classroom – PCs and smartphones. In *Proceedings of IAC 2018 in Budapest* (pp. 56-69). Czech Technical University.

Limbu, L., & Markauskaite, L. (2015). How do learners experience joint writing: university students' conceptions of online collaborative writing tasks and environments. *Computers & Education, 82*, 393-408. https://doi.org/10.1016/j.compedu.2014.11.024

Slavkov, N. (2015). Sociocultural theory, the L2 writing process, and Google Drive: strange bedfellows? *TESL Canada Journal, 32*(2), 80-94. https://doi.org/10.18806/tesl.v32i2.1209

Storch, N. (2005). Collaborative writing: product, process and students' reflections. *Journal of Second Language Writing, 14*(3), 153-73. https://doi.org/10.1016/j.jslw.2005.05.002

Storch, N. (2013). *Collaborative writing in L2 classrooms*. Multilingual Matters.

Suwantarathip, O., & Wichadee, S. (2014). The effects of collaborative writing activity using Google Docs on students' writing ability. *The Turkish Online Journal of Educational Technology, 13*(2), 148-156.

■ UCLouvain

Assessment of interculturality in online interactions: methodological considerations

Ana Kanareva-Dimitrovska[1]

Abstract. In this paper, methodological issues in tracing the evidence of Intercultural Competences (IC) in online intercultural exchanges or telecollaboration are examined. The possibilities and limitations of methods for analyzing IC occurrences are explored. By considering the complementarity of methods, the study contributes to advance the methodological reflections on identifying interculturality and intercultural learning processes in technology-mediated interactions.

Keywords: intercultural competence, online intercultural exchanges, telecollaboration, methodology.

1. Introduction

Despite the increased interest in IC in telecollaborative learning, few studies actually tackle the assessment of interculturality in interaction (O'Dowd, 2019). The assessment of IC is still problematic. First, IC as a concept is not transparent and universally understood. Second, there are two basic ways for examining intercultural learning in online settings: either exploring evidence of IC in post-online interaction reporting (i.e. diaries, portfolios, essays) or observing, examining, and tracking IC *in vivo* (i.e. chats or blog entries, Dervin, 2007).

This paper explores the possibilities and limitations of various methods for analyzing IC occurrences and intercultural learning in telecollaboration. Examples of written online exolingual interactions among Danish and French students are used. The aim is to go beyond the existing research methodology for interculturality in online intercultural exchanges. The study offers new insights to the field of IC

---

1. Aarhus University, Aarhus, Denmark; aekakd@cc.au.dk

How to cite this article: Kanareva-Dimitrovska, A. (2019). Assessment of interculturality in online interactions: methodological considerations. In F. Meunier, J. Van de Vyver, L. Bradley & S. Thouësny (Eds), *CALL and complexity – short papers from EUROCALL 2019* (pp. 218-222). Research-publishing.net. https://doi.org/10.14705/rpnet.2019.38.1012

through telecollaboration by going beyond Byram's (2000) omnipresent categories and guidelines for assessment of IC.

2. Analysis of intercultural discourse

We adapted Byram's (2000) and Dervin's (2007) guidelines for assessment of the IC to our context of online intercultural encounters and we developed them further by incorporating the criticisms addressed to Byram's work and postmodern thoughts (Holliday, Hyde, & Kullman, 2010; Kramsch, 1993). The guidelines are the following (please refer to Kanareva-Dimitrovska, 2018, pp. 168-199, for additional information):

- Savoir-faire I. Interest in other people's way of life and introducing one's own culture to others.

- Savoir-faire II. Knowledge about one's own and others' countries, states, and people.

- Savoir-faire III. Paying attention to discourses in the intercultural communication process.

- Savoir-réagir/agir I. Ability to take/shift perspective.

- Savoir-réagir/agir II. Ability to cope with living in another culture and with the interactions and reactions of people from other cultural communities in online context.

3. Methods and discussion

The methodological framework is based on discourse analysis combined with qualitative content analysis. The triangulation of data (pre- and post-questionnaires, written entries from the blog, discussion groups, Facebook, Skype chats transcripts, interviews, and students' reflection essays) was the central approach. Triangulation is a process that involves comparing multiple perspectives of the same phenomenon to increase the validity of the qualitative approach (Creswell, 2009). The triangulation method seems to be quite appropriate to examine mediated learning situations. The weakness/bias of any of the methods or data sources can be compensated for by the strengths of another.

The methodology to trace IC in telecollaboration described in this study is partially based on previous studies combined with our experience. To explore the potential and the limitations of methods for analyzing IC occurrences, we propose to trace the evidence of students' IC using three methods.

3.1. Showing evidence of IC

In the first stage of analysis, we tried to find traces of IC categories in all students' data. We provide below one example for illustration coded as *Savoir-faire I: (b) I know how to introduce my own culture to others*:

> "det er fordi at i Danmark der siger folk ikke deres mening, fordi de ikke vil fornærme nogen. Man taler ikke om politik, religion og samfundet med nogen man ikke kender rigtig godt. Selv min kæreste fortæller mig ikke hvilken politiker han stemmer på til valg. Det er meget privat. [That's because in Denmark people do not say their opinion because they don't want to offend anyone. You do not talk about politics, religion, and the society with someone you do not know really well. Even my boyfriend does not tell me which politician he is voting for at the election. It is very private]" (Danish student).

The potential of this approach to analyze online interactions is to identify the evidence of some or all components of IC. The main limitation is double coding, i.e. the difficulty of separation of IC components. All IC facets are strongly intertwined and sometimes coding in categories is artificial. The coding validity can be also problematic as very often only one researcher coded the data without having the possibility of consulting another opinion during the coding process. When one has to find traces of IC components, he/she does not necessarily have access to the context and consequently cannot be sure if some competences were developed before or are a result of that specific online interaction. One can also question the 'acquired' character of IC because, in our opinion, IC are not stable, and they are always closely linked to the situation. The last limitation is that this procedure does not provide the possibility of understanding how chronologically participants developed their IC or how categories are distributed per participants. Therefore, we combined this analysis procedure with the next described level of analysis.

3.2. Recording frequency of IC evidence

The main potential of this procedure is to give a clear visualization of all IC categories. It helps to detect the most or least present categories and/or to compare manifestations of IC traced in different groups of participants. Using both levels of data analysis was helpful to obtain a better insight into the relation between interculturality and the pedagogical scenario, i.e. given tasks and chosen computer-mediated communication tools (Kanareva-Dimitrovska, 2018).

There are several limitations with this analysis procedure: double coding, different interpretation of IC categories when several persons code the same data, and learning processes are not taken into account. To bridge these gaps, we have carried out a third level of analysis.

3.3. Microanalysis: tracking intercultural learning moments in interaction

Here we reconstructed interaction in chat-discussions as a rich source in terms of information exchange and meaningful negotiation. The microanalysis helped to identify evidence of intercultural learning processes. We suggest that the ability to take/shift perspective might be considered as a key performance able to reveal IC in interaction.

The potential of this procedure is that the analysis is based on processes and the researcher delivers a pure qualitative analysis to identify moments of intercultural learning. All entries are in a context. This procedure permits an analysis of students' communication strategies (e.g. conflict avoiding strategies) or a reconstruction of students' learning strategies. The most important limitation is the fact that the analysis and description are time-consuming. It is impossible to analyze all data and the researcher needs to select and focus the analysis on only a few sequences. The question that arises then is to what extent this analysis is only an exemplification or global understanding of the phenomena. Therefore, we need to be prudent without generalizing findings. The last limitation is whether sequences important in the researcher's eyes are the same that students considered important for intercultural learning.

In summary, these methods could be applied separately, but the potential of our approach lies in the complementarity of the various analytical methods.

4. Conclusions

This paper attempted to move beyond the methodological challenges in tracing evidence of IC and intercultural learning in online interactions by combining three analysis procedures. The significance of the study probably lies in the potential of analyzing interculturality as a complex construct by complementing methods, data, and theories. Future studies might consider the applicability and efficiency of our methodological approach. The results call for more extensive work on the issue of 'renewed' interculturality in (online) language education.

References

Byram, M. (2000). Assessing intercultural competence in language teaching. *Sprogforum, 18*(6), 8-13.

Creswell, J. W. (2009). *Research design. Qualitative, quantitative and mixed methods approaches*. SAGE Publications.

Dervin, F. (2007). Évaluer l'interculturel : problématiques et pistes de travail. In F. Dervin & E. Suomela-Salmi (Eds), *Évaluer les compétences langagières et interculturelles dans l'enseignement supérieur*. Publication du département d'études françaises, no.10, Université de Turku, Finlande, Åbo Akademi Tryckeri/Digipaino.

Holliday, A., Hyde, M., & Kullman, J. (Eds). (2010). *Intercultural communication: an advanced resource book for students* (2nd ed.). Routledge.

Kanareva-Dimitrovska, A. (2018). Reconsidering interculturality in online language education. In B. Mousten, S. Vandepitte, E. Arnó, & B. Maylath (Eds), *Multilingual writing and pedagogical cooperation in virtual learning environments* (pp.168-199). IGI Global. https://doi.org/10.4018/978-1-5225-4154-7.ch007

Kramsch, C. (1993). *Context and culture in language teaching*. Oxford University Press.

O'Dowd, R. (2019). A transnational model of virtual exchange for global citizenship education. *Language Teaching,* First View, 1-14. https://doi.org/10.1017/S0261444819000077

■ UCLouvain

Student perceptions of virtual reality use in a speaking activity

Samar Kassim[1], Neil Witkin[2], and Adam Stone[3]

Abstract. The aim of this study was to discover what potential benefits of Virtual Reality (VR) use students perceived in comparison to smartphone use in an English-speaking activity. Two surveys were conducted over three interventions in order to ascertain these student perceptions. Ten students enrolled in an elective English class at a Japanese university engaged in an English-speaking activity centered around the VR enabled application *Google Expeditions*. Student perceptions showed that the immersive nature of VR prompted communication, invoked a higher sense of presence, and greater enjoyment in this speaking activity. However, a majority of students did not perceive a difference in the amount of English spoken when comparing VR and smartphone use.

Keywords: virtual reality, speaking, immersion, presence.

1. Introduction

Online technology has been a way of providing more authentic opportunities for language students to practice their communication skills beyond the classroom (Jabbari et al., 2015) and virtual environments helped advance communicative competence without explicit classroom instruction and improve language acquisition (Tang, Sung, & Chang, 2016). These previous studies focused on the application of technology outside of the classroom (e.g. social media). On the other hand, VR is a technology that could be used in the classroom to benefit students. Thus far, VR has shown a potential to reduce distractions, and immersion has helped students make real-world connections between the subject matter and their lives (Bonner & Reinders, 2018; Gadelha, 2018). Classroom

---

1. Kyushu Sangyo University, Fukuoka, Japan; kassim@mail.kyusan-u.ac.jp
2. Kyushu Sangyo University, Fukuoka, Japan; witkin@mail.kyusan-u.ac.jp
3. Kyushu Sangyo University, Fukuoka, Japan; adamstone711@gmail.com

How to cite this article: Kassim, S., Witkin, N., & Stone, A. (2019). Student perceptions of virtual reality use in a speaking activity. In F. Meunier, J. Van de Vyver, L. Bradley & S. Thouësny (Eds), *CALL and complexity – short papers from EUROCALL 2019* (pp. 223-228). Research-publishing.net. https://doi.org/10.14705/rpnet.2019.38.1013

research conducted on VR as a teaching tool compared to two dimensional video viewers (iPods) has shown an increase in student enjoyment and interest (Lee, Sergueeva, Catangui, & Kandaurova, 2017). This study was not done in a language classroom.

While these previous studies showcase the features VR may have to help learners, there is still a lack of research using VR for speaking in the language classroom. This qualitative study seeks to explore what advantages of VR in contrast to smartphone use students perceived when practicing their speaking.

2. Method

2.1. Participants

Ten Japanese university students enrolled in an elective English course participated in this study. Their placement results show their English fluency is approximately A1 to B1 on the Common European Framework of Reference for languages (CEFR).

2.2. Technology

Google Expeditions is a smartphone application designed to allow teachers to take students on virtual field trips in either VR or a handheld 360° mode.

2.3. Instrument

Two Japanese language surveys were administered to the participants of this study, one after the first intervention and another after the third intervention. The first survey contained 19 questions in total. Seven questions utilized a four point Likert scale, allowing responses from *strongly disagree* (1) to *strongly agree* (4), to prevent overuse of the neutral response, which can occur often in a Japanese educational context (Dörnyei & Taguchi, 2009). The survey also contained four multiple-choice questions. Each of these was followed by open-ended questions, which allowed for further elaboration. Lastly, there were four open-ended questions.

The second survey was administered after the third intervention and was identical to the first, bar one exception. The first survey asked students to describe any past VR experiences.

The survey questions focused on student enjoyment in using VR and smartphones for the speaking activity, ease of use of the technologies, and the perceived usefulness of the two mediums.

2.4. Procedure

During each intervention, students participated in the same speaking activity utilizing the application *Google Expeditions*. Students were placed in pairs and each student visited two specific locations. The first partner (Partner A) viewed their designated location on their smartphone and described it to their partner (Partner B). Partner B, who could not see what Partner A saw, had to ask follow-up questions to receive more information about the location within two minutes. Partners A and B then switched roles. The same task was then conducted with VR. Each intervention lasted approximately 60 minutes. Three interventions were conducted in order to examine VR use after the novelty had lessened.

2.5. Data analysis

The Likert scale questions were analyzed along with survey comments that were translated from Japanese to English. They were then coded by the researchers into seven categories in Table 1.

Table 1. Number of student comments to open-ended questions

	Intervention 1		Intervention 3	
	VR	Smartphone	VR	Smartphone
Immersion-Prompted Communication (IPC)	5	0	9	0
Presence	6	0	7	0
Enjoyment	5	1	4	1
New Experience	3	1	3	2
Visual Appeal	1	1	3	2
Ease of Use	1	3	0	0
Technical Difficulties	7	0	1	0

3. Results and discussion

As seen in Table 1, by the third intervention, many students attested to VR's IPC, which is the ability to create a sense of immersion which prompted communication.

Presence, a product of VR immersion which produces a sense of existing within the virtual world (Mütterlein, 2018), was also featured frequently.

Nine out of ten students had never used VR before. Their unfamiliarity with the technology may explain why the first intervention prompted many technical problems. The results may signal that VR needs to be used more than once for students to be able to focus on the benefits of its usage.

Table 2. Students' perception changes

Likert Scale Question	Number of Changing Students	
Q1. VR should be used more for speaking education.	+4	-1
Q2. VR is a tool that contributes to improving speaking skills.	+3	-1
Q3. During this activity, it was easy to use VR.	+5	-2
Q4. I enjoyed speaking English while using VR.	+2	-1
Q5. I enjoyed speaking English while using a smartphone.	+3	0

+=change on the scale toward Strongly Agree;
- = change on the scale toward Strongly Disagree

Table 2 illustrates the changes in student perceptions in relation to VR and smartphones between the interventions. The most striking perception change was after the third intervention, four students rated Q1 higher while one student rated it lower. In the open-ended question portion, one student had explained that at first VR was *difficult to use* but now *it looks fun*. Two students attributed their perception change to IPC, while another thought that it made *learning intuitively fun*. The one negative change in perception was due to one student feeling that VR would be *difficult to make common*. Given these results, it hints at ease of use and accessibility being a hurdle for VR. Nevertheless, the student perceived benefits of VR for speaking education seemed to be due to higher enjoyment and IPC.

Similarly, the other measures of student perception increased in positive changes over the course of the interventions. Notably, Q3 increased the most dramatically, which reinforces the idea that as students experience less difficulties with using VR, they can then perceive more value from it.

Overall, Table 3 implies that after students have gained experience using VR, there is no difference between these two mediums. Student comments show that the reason they had chosen smartphones in the first intervention was a result of experiencing difficulty with VR usage.

Table 3. Which equipment helped you speak more English?

	Smartphone	VR	No Difference
First Intervention	3 students	2 students	5 students
Third Intervention	0 students	3 students	7 students

Table 4 demonstrates that smartphones received no positive responses and thus VR use may better contribute toward the improvement of their English-speaking abilities. Four students attributed it to VR's IPC feature, while one student did not leave a comment as to their reasoning.

Table 4. Which equipment will help improve your English-speaking abilities?

	Smartphone	VR	No Difference
First Intervention	0 students	3 students	7 students
Third Intervention	0 students	5 students	5 students

4. Conclusions

This study found that the potential benefits of VR are IPC, students feeling more present within the speaking activity, greater enjoyment, and the perception that VR can possibly help students improve their speaking abilities more effectively than smartphones due to the aforementioned qualities. Additionally, the biggest constraint to VR was found to be the ease of use and technical difficulties, which were overcome with more user experience.

Future research would benefit from the use of a wider range of VR applications and speaking tasks, as well as a quantitative study utilizing the findings presented above with a larger sample size.

5. Acknowledgments

We would like to thank Shuhei Mitsuyasu for all of his translation work.

References

Bonner, E., & Reinders, H. (2018). Augmented and virtual reality in the language classroom: practical ideas. *Teaching English with Technology, 18*(3), 33-53.

Dörnyei, Z., & Taguchi, T. (2009). *Questionnaires in second language research: construction, administration, and processing.* Routledge. https://doi.org/10.4324/9780203864739

Gadelha, R. (2018). Revolutionizing education: the promise of virtual reality. *Childhood Education, 94*(1), 40-43. https://doi.org/10.1080/00094056.2018.1420362

Jabbari, N., Boriack, A., Barahona, E., Padron, Y., & Waxman, H. (2015). The benefits of using social media environments with English Language Learners. In *Society for Information Technology & Teacher Education International Conference* (pp. 2382-2386). Association for the Advancement of Computing in Education (AACE).

Lee, S. H., Sergueeva, K., Catangui, M., & Kandaurova, M. (2017). Assessing Google Cardboard virtual reality as a content delivery system in business classrooms. *Journal of Education for Business, 92*(4), 153-160. https://doi.org/10.1080/08832323.2017.1308308

Mütterlein, J. (2018). The three pillars of virtual reality? Investigating the roles of immersion, presence, and interactivity. In *Proceedings of the 51st Hawaii International Conference on System Sciences* (pp. 1407-1415). https://doi.org/10.24251/hicss.2018.174

Tang, J. T., Sung, Y. T., & Chang, K. E. (2016). Action research on the development of Chinese communication in a virtual community. *Computer Assisted Language Learning, 29*(5), 942-967. https://doi.org/10.1080/09588221.2015.1113184

Pedagogical frameworks and principles for mobile (language) learning to support related teacher education

Ton Koenraad[1]

Abstract. In this paper results of the EU projects 'Designing and Evaluating Innovative Mobile Pedagogies' (DEIMP, http://www.deimpeu.com/) and 'Mobilising and Transforming Teacher Educators' Pedagogies' (MTTEP, http://www.mttep.eu/) are presented. Two key outputs, the Mobile Learning Toolkit and its iPAC framework (MTTEP) and the principles for innovative mobile learning (m-learning, DEIMP), both targeted at stimulating pedagogically sound m-learning practices in teacher education and schools, are highlighted. To enhance these general pedagogical resources for use in professional development activities specifically for language teachers and teacher educators, I refer to some currently available frameworks and guidelines for Mobile Assisted Language Learning (MALL) and teaching.

Keywords: MTTEP, mobile learning, iPAC framework, MALL, DEIMP.

1. Introduction

The Erasmus+ projects DEIMP (2017-2020) and its predecessor MTTEP (2014-2017) could contribute both to implementing m-learning in (language) teacher education and to enhancing the innovative quality of current and future practices using mobile devices in schools.

---

1. TELLConsult, Vleuten, Netherlands; ton.koenraad@tellconsult.eu; https://orcid.org/0000-0002-7353-4164

How to cite this article: Koenraad, T. (2019). Pedagogical frameworks and principles for mobile (language) learning to support related teacher education. In F. Meunier, J. Van de Vyver, L. Bradley & S. Thouësny (Eds), *CALL and complexity – short papers from EUROCALL 2019* (pp. 229-235). Research-publishing.net. https://doi.org/10.14705/rpnet.2019.38.1014

2. The projects' outputs

2.1. The MTTEP project[2]

The key result of the MTTEP project is the Mobile Learning Toolkit (http://www.mobilelearningtoolkit.com/). It is designed for teacher educators and trainers to support teachers in better understanding how they can pedagogically enhance the learning activities they design by including the use of features and functionalities specific for mobile devices. Its core content is a pedagogical model (the iPAC framework) supporting the design and evaluation of meaningful and authentic m-learning pedagogies.

2.1.1. The iPAC framework

The iPAC framework, based on an internationally validated model for m-learning (Kearney, Schuck, Burden, & Aubusson, 2012), identifies the specific pedagogical features or affordances of mobile devices that make learning distinctive (Figure 1). These are referred to as the 'signature pedagogies' of m-learning and they consist of three principal constructs: personalisation, authenticity, and collaboration. Below I briefly describe these principal constructs and their respective operational subconstructs.

Figure 1. The iPAC framework (http://www.mobilelearningtoolkit.com/ipac-framework.html)

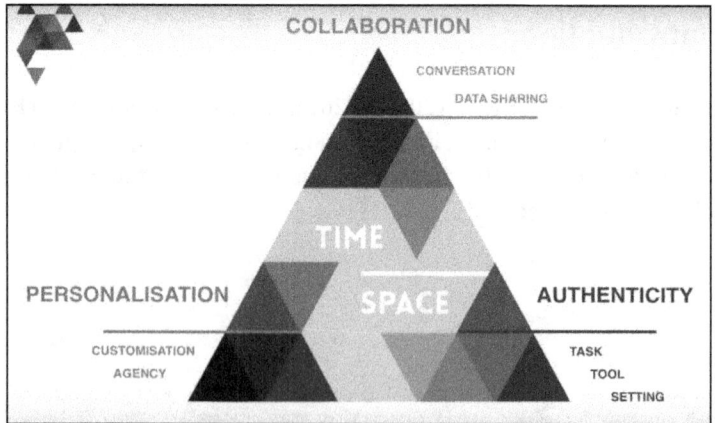

---

2. The iPac framework and constructs are reproduced with kind permission of Kevin J. Burden (http://www.mobilelearningtoolkit.com/ipac-framework.html).

2.1.2. The iPAC constructs

A. Personalisation (and the subconstructs agency and customisation)

Personalisation, a key benefit of m-learning, includes pedagogical features such as learner choice, agency, self regulation, and customisation. In well designed m-learning activities, students have greater control over the place (physical or virtual), pace and time they learn, and can enjoy autonomy over their learning content. Goals are set by learners making the learning activity more personalised (agency) and therefore more engaging (c.f. non formal mobile activities such as game-playing. Apps and context awareness of mobile devices are used to tailor the learning experience to the needs of individual learners (customisation).

B. Authenticity (and the subconstructs setting, task, and tool)

Mobile technologies support authentic learning through the setting, the task, and the tool. Settings can be both physical (field trip, museum visit) and virtual (networked activities) enabling learners to experience what it is like to learn *in situ*. Setting is closely linked to both the task and tools learners are engaged with. Task authenticity refers to the extent to which tasks are realistic and offer problems encountered by real-world practitioners. Tool authenticity relates to the apps and tools students are using and how far they replicate those of real-world practitioners.

C. Collaboration (and the subconstructs conversation and data sharing)

M-learning allows students to enjoy a high degree of collaboration by making rich connections to other people and resources mediated by a mobile device. Social interaction, conversation, and dialogue are fundamental to Vygotskian learning. Sharing conversational spaces mediated by mobile devices can be conducive to timely, personally tailored feedback from teachers, as well as rich peer interactions, leading to learners' negotiated meaning-making (conversation). In shared, socially interactive environments, learners can consume, produce, and exchange information and (self generated) resources with peers, teachers, and other experts (data sharing).

Other components of the toolkit are: explainer videos; a survey tool enabling practitioners to measure their current use of mobile technologies and their students' experiences of m-learning; exemplar eBooks that illustrate the use of mobile technologies in teacher education; and a rubric for evaluating the value and use of apps in different educational contexts.

Combined, these Mobile Learning Toolkit materials offer a rich set of resources to design professional development activities for initial and inservice teacher education to deepen understanding of the proposed constructs and promote related teachers' design and evaluation competences.

2.2. The DEIMP project

The Erasmus+ project DEIMP (2017-2020) aims to research the concepts of innovative and disruptive design for m-learning (for a discussion see Kearney, Burden, & Schuck, 2018) by means of action research on m-learning scenarios in diverse educational contexts (Figure 2). Planned outputs include a systematic literature review, a MOOC, and an app to explore and share inspirational practices. The literature review and its related Delphi research show "that innovation can occur to varying degrees across […] four criteria to result in effective student learning outcomes and engagement" (Burden, Kearney, Schuck, & Hall, 2019, p. 96). The criteria likely to be useful to practitioners as a basis for designing effective mobile activities concern the nature of the task, its context, the relationship between teacher and student, and student agency (Burden et al., 2019, p. 96).

Figure 2. Visualisation of principles for innovative m-learning[3]

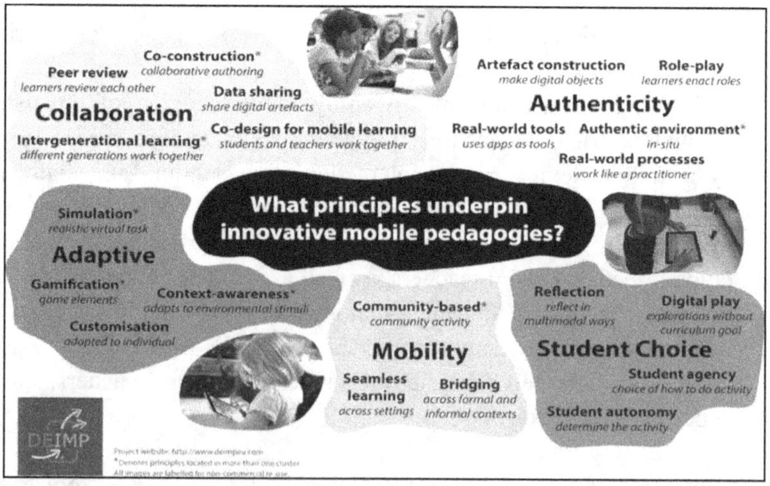

3. http://www.deimpeu.com/principles-of-innovative-mobile-learning.html

3. MALL specific resources

To meet the professional development needs of (student) teachers of specific disciplines/content areas, further contextualisation of the m-learning principles presented above is needed. Below a number of relevant resources for m-learning in modern language education are listed. Evidently, as also reported by the authors of these resources, discipline-specific frameworks incorporate insights from a number of related knowledge domains, such as general instructional design principles and pedagogical approaches. In the case of MALL, these are general principles for m-learning (such as the iPAC framework), computer assisted language learning, and Second Language Acquisition (SLA) insights.

Due to space limitations I only briefly summarise key contents and characteristics of these MALL guidelines. The ten MALL principles proposed by Stockwell and Hubbard (2013) raise awareness of relevant issues across three (interrelated and overlapping) domains: physical, pedagogical, and psycho-social implications and considerations when introducing m-learning in language education. These guidelines and caveats can support the planning and implementation of mobile language learning initiatives.

In Kukulska-Hulme, Norris, and Donohue (2015), an activity design framework is described aiming to support "the language teacher [in redefining] the 'language lesson' and the teacher-learner relationship when the boundaries between the classroom and the outside world are dissolving" (p. 7). Kukulska-Hulme et al.'s (2015, p. 8) proposed model contains four 'spheres' (Figure 3 below) and their connecting concepts (reflection, rehearsal, inquiry and outcomes) with the central question: how does the activity exploit these aspects?

- *teacher wisdom*: the teacher's personal role and experience in enacting pedagogy (effective teaching strategies and task design);

- *device features*: enabling multimodal communication, collaboration, and rehearsal;

- *learner mobilities*: places and times for learning, students' personal goals, contexts, and cultural settings; and

- *language dynamics*: the dynamic character of language, with technology facilitating new opportunities for teaching and communication.

Figure 3. Presentation version[4] of a pedagogical framework for MALL (based on Kukulska-Hulme et al., 2015, p. 8)

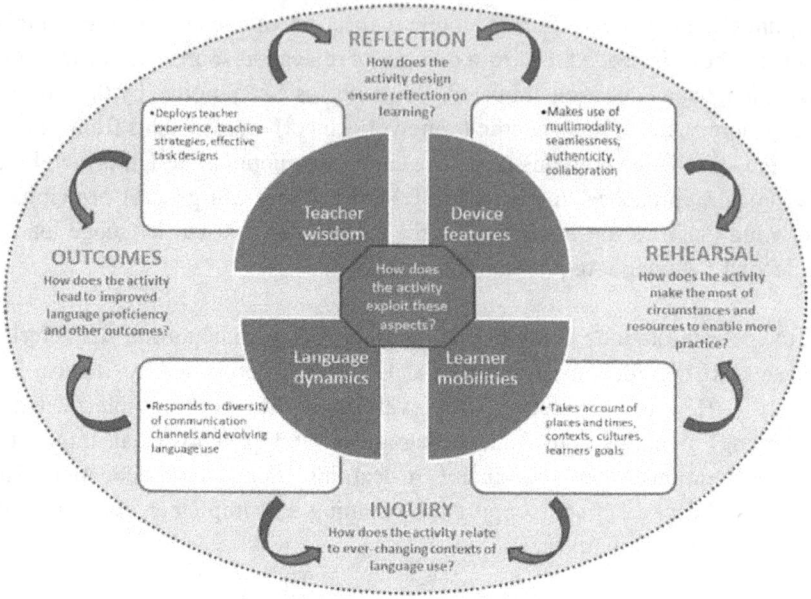

Other resources described in the publication include a further explanation of the concept 'mobile pedagogy', mobile activities to try out, a template for mobile activity design, and examples of useful apps.

Although usable for developmental purposes Reinders and Pegrum (2015) designed their framework primarily to support the evaluation of MALL resources. The framework offers rubrics to evaluate the learning designs of both mobile materials (such as dedicated web services and content-specific apps) and mobile activities (activities designed around websites or apps) with respect to five categories:

- category 1: exploitation of the potential educational affordances of mobile devices;

- category 2: correspondence to general pedagogical approaches;

- category 3: correspondence to specific L2 pedagogical approaches;

---

4. Reproduced here with the kind permission of © 2019 Agnes Kukulska-Hulme, all rights reserved.

- category 4: correspondence to SLA principles; and
- category 5: implementation of affective principles.

In their article, the authors elaborate on these categories and provide an exemplary peer evaluation of a practice case.

4. Conclusion

Several iPAC framework constructs and principles for innovative m-learning (e.g. authenticity, collaborative learning, student choice) are also part and parcel of current pedagogical approaches in modern foreign language education. In our view they can support both cross curriculum and discipline-specific approaches to professional development of educators on m-learning when relevant elements from related discipline-specific domains (*in casu*, SLA and language learning pedagogy, e.g. rehearsal) are included when using them for designing or evaluating practice.

References

Burden, K., Kearney, M., Schuck, S., & Hall, T. (2019). Investigating the use of innovative mobile pedagogies for school-aged students: a systematic literature review. *Computers & Education, 138*, 83-100. https://doi.org/10.1016/j.compedu.2019.04.008

Kearney, M., Burden, K., & Schuck., S. (2018). Disrupting education using smart mobile pedagogies. In L. Daniela (Ed.), *Didactics of smart pedagogy* (pp. 139-157). Springer. https://doi.org/10.1007/978-3-030-01551-0_7

Kearney, M., Schuck, S., Burden, K., & Aubusson, P. (2012). Viewing mobile learning from a pedagogical perspective. *Research in Learning Technology, 20*(1), 1-17. https://doi.org/10.3402/rlt.v20i0.14406

Kukulska-Hulme, A., Norris, L., & Donohue, J. (2015). Mobile pedagogy for English language teaching: a guide for teachers. The British Council. http://oro.open.ac.uk/43605/1/__userdata_documents3_lemn3_Desktop_E485%20Mobile%20pedagogy%20for%20ELT_FINAL_v2.pdf

Reinders, H., & Pegrum, M. (2015). Supporting language learning on the move. An evaluative framework for mobile language learning resources. In B. Tomlinson (Ed.), *Second language acquisition research and materials development for language learning* (pp.116-141). Taylor & Francis. https://hdl.handle.net/10652/2991

Stockwell, G., & Hubbard, P. (2013). Some emerging principles for mobile-assisted language learning. The International Research Foundation for English Language Education. http://www.tirfonline.org/wp-content/uploads/2013/11/TIRF_MALL_Papers_StockwellHubbard.pdf

Quality for online language courses – a coaching program for teachers

Kirsi Korkealehto[1]

Abstract. Finnish universities of applied sciences are building a shared digital course offering, and therefore, digital pedagogy and teachers' competences are being developed via the eAMK project which provides a nationwide coaching program. The program started early in 2018 to ensure that the staff competence in digital pedagogy is timely and that the quality of the courses offered through CampusOnline.fi is consistent and as high as possible. Language teachers take part in the coaching program as a subgroup in which the focus is on language specific topics and issues. The aim was to cover all language competences and to offer suitable digital solutions for them all. The coaching program includes webinars, online and face-to-face meetings, and guidance and workshops. The participating language teachers considered the coaching program beneficial; especially peer feedback, webinars, and workshops were regarded as supportive. The sessions were arranged according to the teachers' timetables which enabled regular participation.

Keywords: digital pedagogy, higher education, professional development.

1. Introduction

Finnish universities of applied sciences are building shared digital courses which "enable open, year-round studying and more flexible specialization and cross-studying opportunities between the educational institutions for the students" (https://www.eamk.fi/en/project2/). Furthermore, students nowadays tend to combine work and study, and therefore flexible study opportunities are needed. The digital course aims "to shorten [study] times, make study paths more versatile and, ultimately, secure better employment. The new educational solutions meet with the competence needs of the future and ensure smooth [e-learning] study paths for

---

1. Häme University of Applied Sciences, Hämeenlinna, Finland; kirsi.korkealehto@hamk.fi

How to cite this article: Korkealehto, K. (2019). Quality for online language courses – a coaching program for teachers. In F. Meunier, J. Van de Vyver, L. Bradley & S. Thouësny (Eds), *CALL and complexity – short papers from EUROCALL 2019* (pp. 236-240). Research-publishing.net. https://doi.org/10.14705/rpnet.2019.38.1015

students" (https://www.eamk.fi/en/project2/). The year-round digital courses offer will work under the name CampusOnline.fi.

2. Coaching program

The coaching program is based on the quality criteria for online implementations, which consists of 11 topics: target group and users, learning objectives, learning process and pedagogical solutions, assignments, contents and materials, tools, interaction, guidance and feedback, evaluation, development, usability and visuals, and support services. The quality criteria were developed in the eAMK project, which was funded by the Finnish Ministry of Culture and Education. In creating the criteria, the expert team utilized the already existing Finnish and European online quality criteria, such as quality cards (Aarreniemi-Jokipelto et al., n.d.) and EOCCS (2019) standards and criteria cards.

The quality criteria are available online in several languages and it is free of charge. It can be used for organization-wide development work as well as for self-assessment by teachers. The coaching program engages participants to experiment with practical ways to use the quality criteria. In addition to the coaching program, several Finnish universities of applied sciences have utilized the quality criteria in their internal quality development.

In the autumn term 2018, 77 teachers and 24 higher education institutes participated in the program, resulting in 60 e-learning courses. In the Finnish education system, higher education is provided by traditional universities and universities of applied sciences, and in this program, 23 universities of applied sciences and one university were involved. The number of language teachers was ten and they formed a subgroup of the coaching program. The coaching program provided five webinars, two nationwide training days, four subject-specific video conference sessions, and two face-to-face meetings for the participants. The duration of the program was six months and the teachers for the training program were selected via applications.

In the first webinar, the whole training program and the quality criteria were introduced, and the notion of the pedagogical model was presented. Further, the importance of visualizing the learning process with deadlines and tools at the beginning of the course or module was emphasized. The first assignment was to (1) evaluate participant's own course according to the criteria, (2) choose the important elements of the criteria in order to develop a course for the CampusOnline offer, (3) set one's own goals, methods to reach them, and describe needed support, (4) write down questions and ideas on development points, (5) ask questions e.g. in the small group or in the LinkedIn group, and (6) in the upcoming webinars write down new ideas.

The second webinar provided information on task design and the aspects that should be taken into account, and suitable learning material was discussed. The second assignment was given: the teachers were to estimate their digital pedagogy competence and create a Padlet-virtual wall and use it as a reflective tool for their own development. A week after the second webinar, the language teachers had a Zoom meeting where Padlets were presented and discussed.

The topics of the third webinar were guidance, feedback, and evaluation according to the quality criteria. Team teaching, evaluation of a collaborative project, and a five step model of guiding was presented (Salmon, 2013). Regarding guiding, the importance of scheduling and tools were highlighted and examples of pedagogical scripts with activities, timing, guiding, and assessment were provided. Various tools and types of evaluation were covered: self-evaluation, peer-evaluation, and teacher evaluation. For the third assignment, the teachers were asked to continue with their own Padlets and post a question in the LinkedIn group of the project.

The fourth webinar focused on interaction, communality, collaboration, and gamification in e-learning. The benefits of synchronous and asynchronous interaction were presented as well as relevant tools for interaction. The participants were asked to prepare themselves for peer assessment and to present their own plan or implementation. After the webinar there was the subgroup meeting on Zoom where the teachers presented the phase of their own course and peers provided valuable feedback.

Thereafter, a two day face-to-face seminar with all participants was organized in Helsinki. Besides workshops and subgroup meetings, the program included topics such as learning analytics, context, and materials, as well as tools for guidance. In their own subgroup, language teachers presented their own courses with pedagogical scripts and implementation plans. They also gained teacher and peer feedback.

The fifth and last webinar covered the topics: tools, usability, and visuals. In addition, students' workload and timing of the assignments were discussed. It was stressed that the teacher needs to schedule time for guidance sessions throughout the course which should be taken into consideration when planning the teachers' workload for the term. The last assignment for the teachers was to make a development plan of their own course in relation with the quality criteria, and to finalize their own course according to the received peer and trainer feedback.

In the last subgroup online meeting, the language teachers presented their finalized courses and implementation plans. In addition, the benefits of the training program were discussed and development ideas were gathered.

During the spring term 2019, the created courses were implemented in the CampusOnline platform and student feedback was collected from the pilot courses. The teachers were also asked to conduct self-evaluation and further development plans of their courses.

The final webinar of the eAMK project was organized in June 2019, six months after the training program had finished. The topics covered CampusOnline student feedback, the current news from CampusOnline, and perceptions and feedback of the coaching program. In addition, the concept of badges was introduced.

3. Feedback

In the last webinar, the advantages and disadvantages of the coaching program were discussed. According to the feedback, the language teachers considered the coaching program beneficial for their digital pedagogy competence improvement. In addition, the design of the program with its various phases and subject-related online guidance sessions were appreciated. The trainer and peer feedback and expertise were valued. All participating language teachers would recommend the coaching program for their colleagues. However, the teachers complained that alongside with their work they had limited recourses to concentrate on the program. The language teachers in turn had received positive feedback from their students on the courses created or improved during the eAMK project. The students appreciated especially the flexibility online courses provided, enabling the students to combine their studies with working life.

4. Conclusions

The nationwide coaching program, the eAMK project, improved language teachers' digital pedagogical competences. Further, the coaching program scaffolded the teachers to create or improve already existing online language courses with field-specific webinars, seminars, and video conference guiding and feedback sessions.

The implemented language courses received positive feedback from the students. The feedback from the participating teachers and their students will be analyzed in more detail.

References

Aarreniemi-Jokipelto, P., Leppisaari I., Rajaorko P., Tervonen P., & Törmänen, M. (n.d). *Uutta avointa energiaa - hankkeen laatukortit.* https://agileamk.wordpress.com/materiaalit/laatukortit/

EOCCS. (2019). *EOCCS standards and criteria.* EFMD Global Network. https://efmdglobal.org/wp-content/uploads/EOCCS_Standards_and_Criteria.pdf

Salmon, G. (2013). *E-tivities: the key to active online learning* (2nd ed.). Routledge.

■ UCLouvain

Towards sustainable language learning in higher education – engagement through multimodal approaches

Kirsi Korkealehto[1] and Vera Leier[2]

Abstract. This project was conducted in a five credit course in English as a Foreign Language, which was a compulsory module in first year business administration studies. The data includes students' learning diaries and a post-course online questionnaire (N=21). The data were analysed using a content analysis method. The results indicate that the students perceived the multimodal task design as enjoyable and students' engagement was fostered by course design, teacher's activity, student's activity, and collaboration.

Keywords: multimodality, language learning, student engagement, higher education, blended learning.

1. Introduction

This study investigates how a multimodal approach affects student engagement in a first year business administration English course. As higher education institutes offer online and blended learning courses, they attract an increasing number of non-traditional students, often professionals who combine working life with studying. Online courses cater to this student type by offering flexible study options (Chen, Lambert, & Guidry, 2010). Although online-learning provides flexibility for students, balancing between studies and external commitments can cause stress and scheduling issues which can lead to a higher rate of interrupted or even dropped studies.

---

1. Häme University of Applied Sciences, Hämeenlinna, Finland; kirsi.korkealehto@hamk.fi
2. University of Canterbury, Christchurch, New Zealand; vera.leier@canterbury.ac.nz

How to cite this article: Korkealehto, K., & Leier, V. (2019). Towards sustainable language learning in higher education – engagement through multimodal approaches. In F. Meunier, J. Van de Vyver, L. Bradley & S. Thouësny (Eds), *CALL and complexity – short papers from EUROCALL 2019* (pp. 241-246). Research-publishing.net. https://doi.org/10.14705/rpnet.2019.38.1016

© 2019 Kirsi Korkealehto and Vera Leier (CC BY)   241

Technologies that afford multimodal communication enhance interaction. Multimodality defined by Kress and van Leeuwen (2001) is "the use of several semiotic modes in the design of a semiotic product or event, together with the particular way in which these modes are combined" (p. 20). Students should get opportunities to engage with complex communicative models to understand that communication is layered action and that different modes complement or reiterate each other to convey social action (Jewitt, 2013; Kress & van Leeuwen, 2001).

Multimodal online environments encourage collaboration (Leier & Korkealehto, 2018), which leads to agency. *Agency* is defined by Chik (2014) and van Lier (2004, 2007) as active learning where learners utilise resources in the environment to advance their competence based on individual requirements. *Agency* can be developed by interaction and self-reflection, which the virtual environment affords. Teacher and peer-support help to build agency in distance and face-to-face teaching. *Agency* is closely associated with *authenticity* (Chik, 2014; Gee, 2004), which refers not only to how the learner perceives the learning environment and how its resources can be harnessed, but also to how competence acquired in the learning context can be applied in real life situations (Chik, 2014; Lave & Wenger, 1991).

This study investigates how students perceived a collaborative learning environment afforded by a multimodal course design. The study contributes to the discussion of communication using multimodality. Our research question is:

- What are the students' perceptions of factors to enhance student engagement in a blended[3] learning course?

2. Method

This qualitative research study was conducted and data were collected in an English course in higher education in Finland. The participants were first year students (N=21) with heterogeneous educational backgrounds and their ages ranged from 20 to 51 years. Their level of English proficiency ranged from A2 to B1. The data includes sources as shown in Table 1.

---

3. This study is a blend of five online sessions and five face-to-face meetings over a period of 16 weeks.

Table 1. Data collection

Source	Participants	Method	Words
Questionnaire	21 students	Content analysis	2,017
Diaries	21 students	Content analysis	31,077

The reflective learning diaries included weekly entries with a length between 335 to 2,626 words, an average learning diary comprised of 1,700 words. The diaries were sent to the teacher after completing the course. Student reflections over a period of time help the teacher to get a better understanding of how the students' perceived the tasks.

3. Course design

The target was to support student engagement and oral interaction and therefore the course material and the assignments were carefully planned following a pedagogically sound model (Long, 1985; Swain, 1997) which was in line with the guidelines of the institution promoting field specific, context-aware language learning.

The duration of the course was 16 weeks with five face-to-face sessions and distance learning sessions. The students used various educational tools to conduct their assignments. A questionnaire was used to ask the students about the course design. The eight questions were open-ended and were accessible online. The data were analysed using content analysis (Schreier, 2012).

4. Findings

The study provided insights on students' perceptions of the blended learning course. The results show that the students' engagement was fostered by the following factors: course design, teacher's activity, student's activity, and collaboration. The students appreciated the clearly structured course design with information about the timetable, assignments, and tool instructions. The students enjoyed the assignments which were to be conducted utilising various educational technology tools:

"The tools were awesome, I utilised them in my other studies and work".

Furthermore, the students appreciated the course material which was authentic and supported their working life. Moreover, the students considered themselves taking an active role in the course, they developed their own agency which in turn contributed to engagement:

> "I prepared myself by learning the new material and after that it was easy to conduct the weekly oral tasks via WhatsApp video call with my pair".

Further, the students stated that the feeling of progress and overcoming challenges had a positive impact on their engagement. In addition, the students appreciated the teacher's guidance, support, and personal feedback on distance and contact teaching periods:

> "I really liked the teacher's style, it was relaxed but consistent and engaging".

Further, the students regarded the weekly discussions with their assigned partners as beneficial for their engagement; they appreciated peer feedback and support. Weekly pair discussions were also utilised as a forum to discuss off-task issues:

> "Once again, my partner helped me with a difficult task, and we were able to have a proper conversation afterwards".

5. Discussion

This blended learning course was developed using technology-enhanced course material. The students were engaged both with the course material and with their classmates. The results show that the factor contributing to student engagement in this English course was the course design, which encouraged both the teacher and students to learn actively and collaboratively.

Course design using different technology is essential to cater for a partly online taught course. The applications were carefully chosen to support the course objectives. The multimodal course design (Hauck & Youngs, 2008), with its collaborative tasks, afforded interaction with peers and promoted agency, which resulted in engaged learning.

The students perceived themselves as active learners and regarded their own studying as contributing positively to engagement, which led to feelings of agency as defined by Chik (2014); active learning where learners utilise resources in the environment to advance their competence based on individual requirements.

The authentic learning content with its multimodal activities was designed to relate to students' real life situations which enhanced engagement. The design provided a platform to perform genuine social interaction and collaboration, as Gee (2004) claims that agency and authenticity are closely related.

Students answered in the questionnaire that they regarded the teacher's availability and flexibility to solve issues and to provide support throughout the course as beneficial. It fostered students' engagement and coactions, and also helped to build a pleasant course atmosphere, which is essential for learning (Chik, 2014).

6. Conclusions

This research study has implications for language learning in the tertiary sector since it reminds educators to utilise educational technology creatively and it encourages students to be creators instead of consumers of technology. Furthermore, the study urges teachers to design online courses to support oral language competence.

7. Acknowledgements

We would like to thank the students who participated in the study.

References

Chen, P. S. D., Lambert, A. D., & Guidry, K. R. (2010). Engaging online learners: the impact of web-based learning technology on college student engagement. *Computers & Education, 54*(4), 1222-1232. https://doi.org/10.1016/j.compedu.2009.11.008

Chik, A. (2014). Digital gaming and language learning: autonomy and community. *Language Learning and Technology, 18*(2), 85-100. http://llt.msu.edu/issues/june2014/chik.pdf

Gee, J. P. (2004). *Situated language and learning: a critique of traditional schooling*. Routledge.

Hauck, M., & Youngs, B. L. (2008). Telecollaboration in multimodal environments: the impact on task design and learner interaction. *Computer Assisted Language Learning, 21*(2), 87-124. https://doi.org/10.1080/09588220801943510

Jewitt, C. (2013). *The Sage handbook of technology research*. Sage.

Kress, G., & van Leeuwen, T. (2001). *Multimodal discourse: the modes and media of contemporary communication.* Arnold.

Lave, J., & Wenger, E. (1991). *Situated learning, legitimate peripheral participation.* Campbridge University Press.

Leier, V., & Korkealehto, K. (2018). *Antipodal communication between students of German in Finland and in New Zealand.* In P. Taalas, J. Jalkanen, L. Bradley & S. Thouësny (Eds), *Future-proof CALL: language learning as exploration and encounters – short papers from EUROCALL 2018* (pp. 160-164). Research-publishing.net. https://doi.org/10.14705/rpnet.2018.26.830

Long, M. (1985). A role for instruction in second language acquisition: task-based language teaching. In K. Hylstenstam & M. Pienemann (Eds), *Modelling and assessing second language acquisition* (pp. 77-99). Multilingual Matters.

Schreier, M. (2012). *Qualitative content analysis in practice.* Sage.

Swain, M. (1997). The output hypothesis and beyond: mediating acquisition through collaborative dialogue. In R. K. Johnson & M. Swain (Eds), *Immersion education: international perspectives* (pp. 98-115). Cambridge University Press.

Van Lier, L. (2004). *The ecology and semiotics of language learning: a sociological perspective.* Kluwer Academic.

Van Lier, L. (2007). Action based teaching, autonomy and identity. *Innovation in language learning and teaching, 1*(1), 46-65. https://doi.org/10.2167/illt42.0

■ UCLouvain

'So close, yet so different' – reflections on the multicultural course of Slavic languages

Anna Kyppö[1]

Abstract. The complexity of language learning may be expanded to learning the languages belonging to the same language family, for example, Slavic languages. This paper reports on the reflection-on action research aimed at the increase of learners' multicultural competence and enhancement of critical thinking at the interdisciplinary, blended course of Slavic languages and cultures. The course organized in modules is implemented in Moodle. Course content is designed by the teacher; however, Slavic languages are presented by native speakers of these languages. Learners have an opportunity to get familiar with Slavic languages, history, and culture from the presenters' perspective, what generally results in the increase of learners' multicultural competence and enhancement of critical thinking. Learning experience is intensified through reflective learner logs, which serve as a knowledge-sharing medium and cognitive learning.

Keywords: Slavic languages, multicultural competence, critical thinking, reflective learner logs.

1. Introduction

This paper reports on the reflection-on action research aimed at the enhancement of learners' multicultural competence (awareness of one's own cultural values and biases; Mio, Barker, & Tumambing, 2012) at the interdisciplinary, blended course of Slavic languages and cultures. The course has been designed and developed at the Centre for Multilingual Academic Communication, University of Jyväskylä, Finland.

---

1. University of Jyväskylä, Jyväskylä, Finland; anna.kyppo@jyu.fi; https://orcid.org/0000-0002-9044-374X

How to cite this article: Kyppö, A. (2019). 'So close, yet so different' – reflections on the multicultural course of Slavic languages. In F. Meunier, J. Van de Vyver, L. Bradley & S. Thouësny (Eds), *CALL and complexity – short papers from EUROCALL 2019* (pp. 247-251). Research-publishing.net. https://doi.org/10.14705/rpnet.2019.38.1017

The course provides basic information about all Slavic nations and languages, including Slavic micro languages, such as Kashubian, Carpathian Rusyn, or Upper and Lower Sorbian. The purpose is to learn about Slavic languages from the linguistic and socio-cultural perspective and raise learners' interest in learning Slavic languages. In addition to a brief outline of the history and an update of the socio-political situation, the focus is on phonetic and morphological features of Slavic languages as well as some characteristics of phonological and writing systems that are interestingly related to the religious and cultural divisions of Slavic nations. Moreover, lexical features, such as code switching, language variation, and borrowings, which are often the consequences of historical language contacts, are also included. In addition, the concept of linguistic intelligibility – the occurrence of similarities and differences between the languages of the same language family – is tested in practice. Figure 1 below describes the course content and structure.

Figure 1. Structure of the course

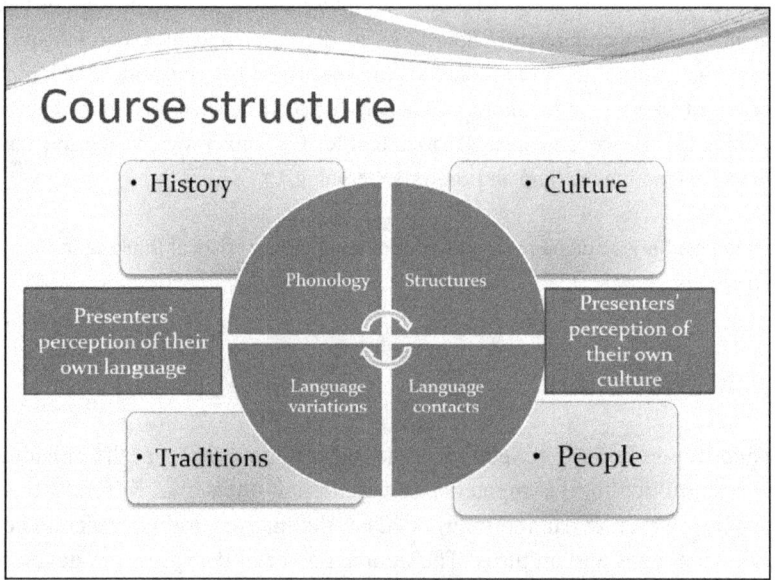

2. Method

The course consisted of 30 contact sessions and 20 hours of independent learning. Course participants were both persons with a Finnish degree and exchange students.

The course is module-based and implemented in Moodle. Every module provides basic linguistic and socio-cultural information about one Slavic group, for example, West Slavic, East Slavic languages, etc. Modules offer a variety of sources, including online presentations, links to web-based material such as Slavic web portals, online courses of Slavic languages, videos, and quizzes. However, the firsthand information on language and culture (traditions, people, etc.) was obtained from the presentations delivered by native speakers of Slavic languages, who presented their language and culture from their own perspective, which resulted in the increase of learners' multicultural competence and critical thinking.

Conclusions and findings presented in this paper are based on the teacher's perceptions and observations, analyses of learner logs, and course evaluations and informal class interviews. To find out which themes and topics occurred most frequently in learner logs, thematic analysis (Braun & Clarke, 2006) was used.

The learning experience is intensified through reflective learner logs – learners reflect on the topics brought up in class after every lesson. Individual entries are commented on by the teacher and other course participants. In accordance with the constructivist models of learning, learner logs serve as a knowledge-sharing medium and a cognitive learning tool (Du & Wagner, 2007), thus in addition to reflections on the matters brought up in class, new topics are occasionally discussed. Reflective learner logs are part of the interactive multimodal learning environment, since they enable multidirectional communication (student-teacher, student-student) and knowledge construction.

3. Discussion

The format of the course – language and culture modules offering a static approach to cultural learning (Liddicoat, 2005) – and, on the other hand, personal engagement with linguistic and cultural diversity obtained through Slavic presentations on contact sessions offer a unique learning experience (intercultural approach to cultural learning; Liddicoat, 2005). In addition to Slavic presentations, the concept of mutual intelligibility[2] of Slavic languages, a relationship between languages in which speakers of different languages can understand each other without special effort, is tested in practice, for example, Slovak and Czech, Russian and Ukrainian, Ukrainian and Belarusian, and Serbian and Croatian, etc. Culture clashes cannot always be avoided, nevertheless, they may result in generating a more dynamic

---

2. https://www.academia.edu/4080349/Mutual_Intelligibility_of_Languages_in_the_Slavic_Family

intercultural communication practices and finally foster more effective multicultural thinking (Hamedani & Markus, 2019).

Learners' reflections in learner logs revealed not only their awareness of learning, but also the increase of multicultural awareness that involves understanding, sensitivity, and appreciation of the history, values, experiences, and lifestyles of Slavic people. Reflections were generally related to the conceptual exchange of information, for example, cultural identity, intelligibility of Slavic languages, values, history, etc. The most frequently discussed topics referred to the future of Slavic micro languages and the historical, social, and political background of bilingualism/multilingualism of Slavs (Serbian, Croatian, Bosnian, and Montenegrin; Bulgarian and Macedonian; Sorbian, both Upper and Lower; and Slovak and Czech).

Experiential learning – learning through reflection on doing (Kolb, 1984) – resulted in an evident increase of multicultural competence and critical thinking, as well as in the acquisition of new interpersonal skills based on reflective observation. An excerpt from a learner's log describes the process of (reflective) learning best.

> "I noticed that on this course I started to think about something I have never known – how little I know about these countries and languages. I cannot claim I know much now, however, even the 'little' I know is the beginning of developing toward something new".

As revealed in learner logs, the multicultural and multilingual environment of the course, and above all the presence of Slavic guests, strengthened not only learners' motivations to learn Slavic languages, but also their intercultural competence and critical thinking.

4.   Conclusion

The primary purpose of this course is to increase learners' interest in learning Slavic languages, especially those lesser known. Due to various, mostly economic reasons, educational institutions cannot offer language programs in these languages. Thus, multilingual and multicultural courses of this type are welcome. The format of the course supports cultural and reflective learning. Learning about the language and culture may be as motivating as learning the language itself, as pointed out by a student.

"When we cannot learn the language, we can learn ABOUT the language… and perhaps one day I will learn the language".

What are the challenges of learners of Slavic languages today?

Despite various facilities, which are meant to simplify the use of keyboards in writing diacritics, maintaining the language awareness – awareness of learning how to employ the diacritical marks – seems to be challenging, especially in West Slavic languages (Kyppö, 2017).

Nonetheless, new mobile technologies and social media offer possibilities for the development of dynamic multiple learning spaces appropriate for courses of this type. In addition to blended learning, often adopted in learning less commonly taught languages, basic information about linguistic and cultural settings presented in an inspiring way may enhance the increase of learners' multilingual and multicultural awareness and finally result in raising their motivation to learn these languages.

References

Braun, V., & Clarke, V. (2006). Using thematic analysis in psychology. *Qualitative Research in Psychology, 3*(2), 77-101. https://doi.org/10.1191/1478088706qp063oa

Du, H. S., Wagner, C. (2007*).* Learning with weblogs: enhancing cognitive and social knowledge construction. *IEEE Transactions on professional communication, 50*(1), 1-16. https://doi.org/10.1109/tpc.2006.890848

Hamedani, M. Y. G., & Markus, H. R. (2019). *Understa nding culture clashes and catalyzing change: a culture cycle approa ch. Front iers in Psychology.* https://doi.org/10.3389/fpsyg.2019.00700

Kolb, D. (1984). *Kolb's experiential learning cy cle.* https://www2.le.ac.uk/departments/doctoralcollege/training/eresources/teaching/theories/kolb

Kyppö, A. (2017). *Climbing a mountain.* Learning Slovak in new language learning environments. Department of Language and Communication Studies, University of Jyväskylä.

Liddicoat, A. J. (2005). Teaching languages for intercultural communication. In D. Cunningham & A. Hatoss (Eds), *An international perspective on language policies, practices and proficiencies* (pp. 201-214). Fédération Internationale des Professeurs de Langues Vivantes.

Mio, J. S., Barker, L. A., & Tumambing, J. S. (2012). *Multicultural psychology: u nderstanding our diverse communities* (3rd ed). Oxford University Press.

MALL tools tried and tested

Bruce Lander[1], Valentina Morgana[2], Jaime Selwood[3], Tim Knight[4], Robert Gettings[5], Mari Yamauchi[6], Julie Van de Vyver[7], and Carole Delforge[8]

Abstract. In 2013, Stockwell and Hubbard published an article on emerging principles in Mobile Assisted Language Learning (MALL). In that article, they mentioned three issues that could perhaps impede learning in the domains of the physical, pedagogical, and pyscho-social. The physical issue they imply, refers to the general size of screens, which at the time were deemed small, or not big enough to have an impact on learning. The pedagogical issue involved with MALL, according to Stockwell and Hubbard (2013), is to ensure that tasks introduced with mobile tools are suited to the affordances of the devices. They questioned the need for mobile devices for language learning and whether tasks that were being introduced were suitable and worthwhile and not simply replicating what could normally be done without them, with pen and paper for example. The psycho-social issue they refer to implies that the primary function of mobile devices is generally regarded as one for "personal and social purposes, as opposed to work or study purposes" (Stockwell & Hubbard, 2013, p. 4). In this short paper, we would like to argue this point by introducing seven tools currently available for free on mobile applications that can be adapted to foreign language learning in several ways.

Keywords: mobile assisted language learning, mobile apps for learning, apps for presentations, web tools for EFL.

1. Matsuyama University, Matsuyama, Japan; blander@g.matsuyama-u.ac.jp
2. Università Cattolica del Sacro Cuore, Milan, Italy; valentina.morgana@unicatt.it
3. Hiroshima University, Higashihiroshima, Japan; jselwood@hiroshima-u.ac.jp
4. Shirayuri University, Tokyo, Japan; tknight@shirayuri.ac.jp
5. Hokusei Gakuen University, Sapporo, Japan; bgettings@mac.com
6. Chiba University of Commerce, Chiba, Japan; yamauchi@cuc.ac.jp
7. Université Catholique de Louvain, Louvain-la-Neuve, Belgium; julie.vandevyver@uclouvain.be; https://orcid.org/0000-0001-8820-8380
8. Université de Namur, Namur, Belgium; carole.delforge@unamur.be

How to cite this article: Lander, B., Morgana, V., Selwood, J., Knight, T., Gettings, R., Yamauchi, M., Van de Vyver, J., & Delforge, C. (2019). MALL tools tried and tested. In F. Meunier, J. Van de Vyver, L. Bradley & S. Thouësny (Eds), *CALL and complexity – short papers from EUROCALL 2019* (pp. 252-256). Research-publishing.net. https://doi.org/10.14705/rpnet.2019.38.1018

1. Introduction

The MALL Special interest Group (SiG) symposium introduced a selection of seven mobile apps, or webtools, that have been tried, tested, and approved by our expert instructors in three different countries. Each tool will be introduced, and key features of each highlighted. This short paper is a summary of the MALL SiG symposium with the same title, held on August 28th, Day 1 of the conference. It should present readers with further details on the benefit that each of these tools can provide the teacher and the student with regards to MALL.

The use of mobile technology, especially with the younger generation, has become second nature and is no doubt ubiquitous in their everyday life. In the education settings in which these trials were conducted, our students though may not yet associate their mobile device as a potential tool that can enhance their learning. Hopefully this short summary will provide you with a list of MALL tools that we know have worked well for us and can help to change the perception of our students.

2. MALL tools

2.1. SpeakingPhoto

The first tool is a free mobile voice recording app called SpeakingPhoto. This tool allows users to record their voice over photos and is perfect as a substitute to class presentations which can take up time and be difficult to manage. SpeakingPhoto can help students who may not appear confident in class when giving presentations by encouraging them to use mobile devices to speak the target language in a more comfortable environment. Recorded presentations can then be saved and uploaded to a Learning Management System (LMS) of your choice, or sent via email. Students who were given the freedom to record in their own time and submit online showed a higher quality of presentation almost every time. A survey after conducting trials indicated that 70% of students (n=162), if given the choice, would prefer to use SpeakingPhoto to record in a location of their choice as opposed to in class presentations.

2.2. Showbie

Showbie allows teachers to instantly distribute written assignments to students and manage them by providing immediate and multimodal feedback (e.g. comments, voice messages, pictures). The sample of the study consisted of 43 English as a Foreign Language (EFL) secondary school students from Italy. The presentation demonstrated how students and teachers used the app inside and outside the language classroom. Participants were divided into two sections: an iPad group and a pen and paper group. Data was collected through classroom observations, students' written assignments on Showbie, and through individual interviews. Written assignments were analyzed for accuracy and complexity using t-unit measures. Results provide patterns of use and show significant differences between the two groups, mainly related to the potential of the Showbie app and the immediate and personalized feedback that allowed iPad students to easily edit their written assignment based on the teacher's comments. Results indicated that Showbie can help students' overall writing skills with particular attention to vocabulary and complex sentence writing.

2.3. Moxtra

Moxtra is a tool made for collaboration in the business world, but was used by a Tokyo based EFL educator for collecting digital portfolios from students, and for facilitating feedback both directly from a teacher to a student, and collectively between students. Available on all smartphone and computer platforms, the free app is a smooth way for language learners to practice speaking and listening, especially in conjunction with visual aids made for presentations. Students can actively participate in the benefits of multimedia learning (Mayer, 2009) by sharing presentations beyond the classroom. It is especially useful for extending a presentation project outside class time when students have been unable to see everyone else's presentations because they had made presentations in small groups rather than to the whole class. Thus, Moxtra is particularly beneficial when students need a confidence-building environment. Post-class surveys indicated that students enjoyed using the app as a way to practice speaking and learning collaboratively.

2.4. Clips

The fourth tool is a video app produced by Apple called Clips, free on iOS devices. Clips was chosen in this case as it is free and could offer useful language learning skills while also not distracting from the main purpose of the course: to improve oral communication skills with a specific emphasis on fluency, intonation, and non-verbal communication. Students often feel pressured to talk in front of others in class, but this tool allows students to be creative while giving presentations in a setting they feel comfortable with. Clips offers the opportunity to record video using a variety of backgrounds for effect, with the added advantage of any spoken word being transcribed and displayed on screen. In classes of 25 to 35, students were instructed to use Clips to create short, one to three minute videos about their impressions of various global issues raised in class. These videos were then exchanged online using Blackboard, the university wide LMS. As the majority of students in the setting were iPhone users, the video editing process was very smooth. Access to footage was instant. For Android users though, students used university owned iPads to transfer footage to and create videos with.

2.5. MyMobileWorld

MyMobileWorld (MMW) is a Moodle-based online site 'optimized for mobile devices' integrated with the Pearson student textbook series 'English Firsthand' . Sixty students were surveyed and five interviewed about their patterns of MMW use and their preferences for desktops or smartphones. Most students felt that MMW was easy to use, well integrated with the textbook, and that it facilitated their EFL learning. Almost all students felt MMW had successfully adjusted learning materials from the A4 size of the textbook to the narrower mobile screen format using Moodle Quiz activities and Quizlet flashcards. However, some students complained that text input activities only accepted one answer when there were several correct alternatives. Most students preferred desktop use in the classroom and mobile use in their free time, such as when commuting. Most also preferred desktops for activities with longer text input. Students' positive reactions to MMW suggest it might be of interest for teachers who are thinking of flipping their EFL classroom or as a model for content developers creating mobile materials that intentionally, closely follow a textbook.

2.6. Duolingo

Duolingo is a game-like app and webtool for foreign language learning. The presenter here used 'English for Japanese speakers', with a group of 30 university students in spring, 2019 consisting of 56 skills (Duolingo defines a skill as a set of lessons that focuses on a particular topic). Students were set an assignment every week to study and open at least two new 'skills'. Lessons to be covered varied from student to student, depending on proficiency levels. Self-study with Duolingo was not directly linked to classwork but provided the opportunity to introduce MALL to students, allowing them to learn at a place and pace that suits. According to the activity log available in Duolingo for schools, the number of days students studied with Duolingo over the course of a 13 week semester was 17.3 days on average. The estimated study time per day varied widely, providing a daily average of about 30 minutes. Student feedback on their Duolingo experience was fairly positive:

74% agreed that Duolingo helped them learn English while 65% claimed it helped them to continue learning independently.

2.7. Actionbound

The final tool, Actionbound, allows users to create their own scavenger hunt for mobile devices. This tool was chosen for its interactive features (e.g. audio and video recording as a type of answer), its gamification features, and the possibility for the learners to experience contextualized and situated learning. In the framework of this study, a hunt was designed by ten pre-service language teachers with the help of a research team for use in the Hergé Museum in Louvain-la-Neuve, Belgium. It displayed one potential use of the app for language learning. The game De avonturen van Hergé focuses on L2 reading strategies and was created for 43 fifth grade primary school learners of Dutch at the beginner level. The one-hour mobile activity takes the learners through the eight rooms of the museum and addresses various daily life topics relating to the life of the father of Tintin. The learners are invited to implement different reading strategies (e.g. visual discrimination, connecting the text to my experience, transfer from L1) to answer questions, win points, and move forward. The hunt has become an open educational resource as it is now available to any user of the Actionbound app who visits the museum.

3. Conclusion

We, in the MALL SiG, believe that the potential for learning with tools such as those introduced here is an opportunity not to be missed. We will endeavor to discover new tools that can be used in our educational setting and plan on introducing more at future EuroCALL related meetings.

References

Mayer, R. E. (2009). Multimedia learning (2nd ed.). Cambridge University Press.
Stockwell, G., & Hubbard, P. (2013). Some emerging principles for mobile-assisted language learning. *The International Research Foundation for English Language Education*, 1-15. https://www.tirfonline.org/publications/mobile-assisted-language-learning/some-emerging-principles-for-mobile-assisted-language-learning/

Connecting extensive reading to TOEIC performance

Paul A. Lyddon[1] and Brandon Kramer[2]

Abstract. Although Extensive Reading (ER) has been shown to increase reading fluency and comprehension, such benefits are generally slow to appear. The present study investigated the possible contribution of ER to single-semester Test of English for International Communication (TOEIC) reading gains. The participants were 497 first-year students from two annual cohorts at a tertiary institution in Japan. All took a preliminary TOEIC before enrolling in the online ER system *Xreading*, which awarded them a word count for successfully completing a short quiz on each book they read for homework. Hierarchical linear regression analyses of end-of-semester ER words read and TOEIC reading scores showed a consistent positive relationship between the two. However, semester increases in the former were not reflected by proportional gains in the latter, a finding possibly explained by greater consistency in ER's implementation across course sections over time. In short, ER words read might in fact be a proxy for general compliance in homework completion rather than a direct cause of TOEIC reading score improvement.

Keywords: extensive reading, reading fluency, reading comprehension, TOEIC.

1. Introduction

Though long-term benefits of ER, such as greater reading speeds and comprehension, are well established, its short-term effectiveness has been far less obvious (see Nakanishi, 2015). Moreover, as the researchers in the present study discovered within the context of an all-female private tertiary institution in Japan, even program-level adoption of ER is no guarantee of individual teachers' and students' valuation of it without clear evidence of its immediate worth. Consequently, this

---

1. University of Shizuoka, Shizuoka, Japan; palyddon@u-shizuoka-ken.ac.jp; https://orcid.org/0000-0002-1782-9769
2. Osaka Jogakuin University & Junior College, Osaka, Japan; Brandon.L.Kramer+eurocall@gmail.com; https://orcid.org/0000-0003-3910-0810

How to cite this article: Lyddon, P. A., & Kramer, B. (2019). Connecting extensive reading to TOEIC performance. In F. Meunier, J. Van de Vyver, L. Bradley & S. Thouësny (Eds), *CALL and complexity – short papers from EUROCALL 2019* (pp. 257-262). Research-publishing.net. https://doi.org/10.14705/rpnet.2019.38.1019

investigation sought to correlate ER with short-term standardized reading score gains.

One popular standardized measure of English proficiency in Japan is the TOEIC. Its most commonly administered form is the Listening and Reading Test, on which the average reading section scores are comparatively much lower for test takers not only in Japan but worldwide (Educational Testing Service, 2019). Arguably contributing to this discrepancy are the demands this section places on sufficient fluency to read the many required text passages, much less fully comprehend them. Given the relevant attested benefits of ER, the present study sought to link it positively with TOEIC reading performance.

Researchers previously investigating a possible connection between ER and TOEIC have reported mixed results. Whereas studies such as Nishizawa, Yoshioka, and Fukada (2010) and Rutson-Griffiths and Rutson-Griffiths (2018) concluded a positive relationship between them, Carney (2016) and O'Neill (2011), for example, found no support for such conclusions. Complicating matters further, these and similarly motivated studies generally evince either limitations in sample size or shortcomings in methodology, diminishing their claims. Thus, the aim of the present study was to rigorously analyze a sufficiently large dataset to statistically verify the existence of even a small correlation between the two target variables.

2. Method and results

Two semesters' worth of data were collected from separate cohorts of first-year Japanese university students in 2017 (N=360) and 2018 (N=370). Each student had taken a TOEIC Institutional Program (IP) pre-test and enrolled in an online ER system known as *Xreading* (xreading.com). Though participation in the ER program was compulsory, the ER software allowed the learners to individually select digital books according to their comfort level and awarded them a word count for scoring 60% or above on a short multiple-choice quiz at the end of each book they read. With the exception of a brief initial in-class demonstration of the system, all ER was treated as homework, with evaluation points (i.e. grades) assigned for final numbers of words read.

Only non-repeating students who successfully completed the academic year and sat for all three compulsory TOEIC administrations were included in the data analysis. Table 1 shows the relevant descriptive statistics.

Table 1. Means, standard deviations, and intercorrelations for TOEIC reading scores and predictor variables

Year	Semester	Variable	M	SD	1	2
2017	Spring	Post-semester TOEIC Reading	156.71	65.82	.79***	.52***
		Predictor Variable				
		1. TOEIC Reading Pre-test	137.34	60.28	---	.45***
		2. Current Semester ER Words Read	42,273	51,429	---	---
	Fall	Post-semester TOEIC Reading	171.39	69.33	.84***	.31***
		Predictor Variable				
		1. Pre-semester TOEIC Reading	156.71	65.82	---	.30***
		2. Current Semester ER Words Read	32,744	41,386	---	---
2018	Spring	Post-semester TOEIC Reading	156.69	64.23	.82***	.19**
		Predictor Variable				
		1. TOEIC Reading Pre-test	137.07	61.58	---	.12*
		2. Current Semester ER Words Read	90,150	72,797	---	---
	Fall	Post-semester TOEIC Reading	167.29	69.08	.84***	.16**
		Predictor Variable				
		1. Pre-semester TOEIC Reading	156.69	64.23	---	.05
		2. Current Semester ER Words Read	80,035	86,093	---	---

*p<.05. **p<.01. ***p<.001.

A hierarchical linear regression analysis was conducted for each semester. For the first half of each year, post-semester (i.e. end-of-spring) TOEIC reading scores were regressed on reading pre-test scores and spring semester words read. For the second half, post-semester (i.e. end-of-fall) TOEIC reading scores were regressed on pre-semester (i.e. end-of-spring) reading scores and fall semester words read.

Despite a decrease from .0003 in spring of 2017 to .0001 in every semester thereafter, in each analysis ER accounted for a statistically significant proportion of the shared variance equivalent to at least one TOEIC point per 10,000 words read (see Table 2).

Table 2. Hierarchical regression analysis summary for variables predicting post-semester TOEIC reading scores in 2017 (N=248) and 2018 (N=249)

Year	Semester	Variable	Model 1			Model 2		
			B	SE B	β	B	SE B	β
2017	Spring	y-intercept	39.90***	6.46		41.59***	6.21	
		TOEIC Reading Pre-test	.86	.04	.76***	.76	.05	.69***
		Current Semester ER Words Read				.0003	.00005	.20***
		R^2		.62			.65	
		F for ΔR^2		396.77***			22.96***	
	Fall	y-intercept	33.19***	6.24		32.82***	6.21	
		Pre-semester TOEIC Reading	.88	.04	.84***	.86	.04	.82***
		Current Semester ER Words Read				.0001	.00006	.07
		R^2		.70			.71	
		F for ΔR^2		576.66***			3.33	
2018	Spring	y-intercept	39.83***	5.7		33.71***	6.12	
		TOEIC Reading Pre-test	.85	.04	.82***	.84	.04	.81***
		Current Semester ER Words Read				.0001	.00003	.10**
		R^2		.67			.68	
		F for ΔR^2		497.18***			7.17**	
	Fall	y-intercept	26.69***	6.39		20.27**	6.55	
		Pre-semester TOEIC Reading	.90	.04	.83***	.89	.04	.83***
		Current Semester ER Words Read				.0001	.00003	.11**
		R^2		.70			.71	
		F for ΔR^2		565.83***			11.10**	

*p <.05. **p <.01. ***p <.001.

3. Discussion

The best predictor of TOEIC reading scores in every analysis was prior performance, which accounted for 48% to 69% of the variance. Even with that portion removed, the number of ER words read showed a small but consistent positive contribution. However, this relationship should be interpreted with caution.

As seen in Table 1, the mean number of words read from spring 2017 to spring 2018 more than doubled, but mean TOEIC reading scores remained nearly identical. The fall semester disparity was even greater, with reading scores slightly decreasing. In Table 2, however, the explanatory power of the regression equation (i.e. R^2) is virtually the same in corresponding semesters of each year. The difference is expressed as a drop in the y-intercept, indicating a downward shift of the regression line: a student with a TOEIC reading score of 100 and zero words read in the fall of 2018 would be expected to earn approximately ten points fewer than an analogous student in the same semester of 2017.

One possible explanation for this finding is increasingly consistent ER implementation across the institution. As Table 1 shows, the correlation between ER words read and prior TOEIC scores steadily decreased semester by semester, from a statistically significant $r=.45$ in the first half of 2017 to a non-significant $r=.05$ at the end of 2018. Students were streamed into their course sections on the basis of a placement test, and instructors in the higher tiers, perhaps more invested in ER from the start, might have therefore held their students more strictly accountable for it. Industrious students in the lower tiers at that time, on the other hand, might have been engaged in other kinds of out-of-class efforts (e.g. work with TOEIC practice materials) to improve their reading. Now that ER is being more uniformly implemented across all course sections, ER words read can still serve as a predictor of TOEIC reading performance – students who read more will almost certainly outperform those who read less – but it might have more to do with general diligence in completing homework assignments than with numbers of words read.

4. Conclusion

This study found a small but statistically significant relationship between ER words read and TOEIC reading scores. However, a lack of proportional increase in these two variables over time suggests mediation by a third variable, such as relative out-of-class diligence. Thus, while ER might have other valuable short-term benefits, improving TOEIC reading gains does not appear to be one of them.

References

Carney, N. (2016). Gauging extensive reading's relationship with TOEIC reading score growth. *Journal of Extensive Reading, 4*(4), 69-86.

Educational Testing Service. (2019). *2018 report on test takers worldwide: TOEIC listening and reading test.* https://www.ets.org/s/toeic/pdf/2018-report-on-test-takers-worldwide.pdf

Nakanishi, T. (2015). A meta-analysis of extensive reading research. *TESOL Quarterly, 49*(1), 6-37. https://doi.org/10.1002/tesq.157

Nishizawa, H., Yoshioka, T., & Fukada, M. (2010). The impact of a four-year extensive reading program. In A.M. Stoke (Ed.), *JALT2009 Conference Proceedings* (pp. 632-640). Tokyo, Japan: JALT.

O'Neill, B. (2011). Investigating the effects of extensive reading on TOEIC reading section scores. *Extensive Reading World Congress Proceedings, 1*, 30-33.

Rutson-Griffiths, A., & Rutson-Griffiths, Y. (2018). The relationship between extensive reading and TOEIC score gains. *Hiroshima Bunkyō Joshi Daigaku Kōtō Kyōiku Kenkyū*, 41-50.

UCLouvain

Understanding the complexities associated with conceptualising pedagogical scenarios for online multimodal interaction between two languages and cultures

Oneil N. Madden[1] and Anne-Laure Foucher[2]

Abstract. The complexity surrounding the design of collaborative pedagogical scenarios can allow foreign language learners to develop intercultural and linguistic skills; however, careful consideration must be given when conceptualising telecollaborative projects. Many research studies have been conducted which led to significant discoveries, but only few studies examine the intricacies of developing pedagogical scenarios for online multimodal interaction and the outcomes of these complexities. This paper reports on a Franco-Jamaican telecollaborative project, ClerKing, which took place in two phases between Applied Foreign Languages (AFL) students of English from University Clermont Auvergne (UCA), France, and Modern Languages students of French from Shortwood Teachers' College (STC), Jamaica. Each phase had a different pedagogical scenario, with the first being restricted and the second being more open. Using the exploratory method, various parameters of online pedagogical scenarios were identified and examined with varying degrees of granularity. Preliminary findings show that a less restricted and more flexible pedagogical scenario allowed for students to develop language and intercultural competencies, while strengthening negotiation skills.

Keywords: complexity, pedagogical scenario, multimodal interaction, clerking, telecollaboration.

---

1. University Clermont Auvergne, Clermont-Ferrand, France; oneil.madden@uca.fr
2. University Clermont Auvergne, Clermont-Ferrand, France; a-laure.foucher@uca.fr

How to cite this article: Madden, O. N., & Foucher, A.-L. (2019). Understanding the complexities associated with conceptualising pedagogical scenarios for online multimodal interaction between two languages and cultures. In F. Meunier, J. Van de Vyver, L. Bradley & S. Thouësny (Eds), *CALL and complexity – short papers from EUROCALL 2019* (pp. 263-269). Research-publishing.net. https://doi.org/10.14705/rpnet.2019.38.1020

© 2019 Oneil N. Madden and Anne-Laure Foucher (CC BY)

Oneil N. Madden and Anne-Laure Foucher

1. Introduction

One way to prepare our students to communicate successfully with people from varying backgrounds is to foster their development of linguistic and intercultural competence; this can be achieved through telecollaborative projects. Helm (2015) defines telecollaboration as the "practice of engaging classes of geographically dispersed learners in online exchange using Internet communication tools for the development of language and/or intercultural competence" (p. 197).

Critical to telecollaborative projects is a pedagogical scenario. This is a plan that outlines the expectations of and instructions for the learner. It includes the objectives of the project, prior and targeted skills, and resources and tools made available for accomplishing proposed activities and tasks (Nissen, 2006).

Closely associated with the pedagogical scenario, or even sometimes included in it, is the communication scenario. Nissen (2006) explains that this entails all the possible forms of interactions that the learner has at his disposal and which are clearly communicated to him as part of his online project. Nissen (2006, p. 4) also identities five variables for defining the type of communication scenario in an online project: the prospective conversation partners (who communicates with whom?), the status of the learner and his interlocutors (novice, expert), the purpose of the interaction (e.g. practice of the language), the temporality of the exchanges (duration, frequency, rhythm), and the communication tools used (the choice of platform may lead to more synchronous or asynchronous exchanges). To this list, Foucher (2010, p. 86) adds the following: the language(s) of interaction (native, foreign, third language), the objective of the exchanges (collaborative realisation of a final task or 'simple' communication), and the number of interlocutors possible (in a chat session, for example). All these elements play an essential role in regard to how the learner will position himself throughout the project.

Pedagogical scenarios can either be restraint or open. Pernin and Lejeune (2004) explain that the former describes precisely to the learner the activities to be executed. This type of scenario leaves a low degree of initiative to the actors of the learning situation. Conversely, they note that the latter outlines the activities to be achieved, leaving the actors in the learning situation varying degrees of freedom to organise the activities or determine their course (Pernin & Lejeune, 2004, p. 6).

Several studies have found that there are multiple interactional factors that could impact the success of telecollaboration and the benefits it brings to language learning. Kötter (2002) underlined delays in asynchronous communication. Kern

(2006) noted challenges regarding mismatched language levels. O'Dowd and Ritter (2006) established areas such as low participation and motivation, negative evaluations of the target culture, and failed opportunities for cross-cultural exchange. They also cited methodological aspects such as task design which can significantly influence the outcome of telecollaboration.

Using the exploratory approach, we are particularly interested in the complexity associated with the following elements of pedagogical and communication scenarios: language(s) of exchanges and communication platforms.

2. Method

ClerKing, a Franco-Jamaican project, was conducted in two phases for ten weeks in the second semester between AFL students of English from UCA, and Modern Languages students of French from STC. There was a total of 50 participants of mixed genders, between the ages of 18 and 33. A restrained pedagogical scenario was used in the first phase, while the second phase was more open (see Table 1 for differences). Participants were paired based on their profiles submitted before the start of the project. The main objective of this project was for students to practise the target language(s) studied and to improve their linguistic and cultural competencies in said language(s) based on their respective levels (Jamaican students were between Common European Framework of Reference for languages levels A2-B2 in French, while French students were B2-C1 in English). Students discussed different intercultural topics weekly, and specific instructions were given concerning communication tools, language choice, and outcome of each session.

Table 1. Differences in pedagogical choices between the two scenarios

Elements of pedagogical and communication scenarios	Scenario 1	Scenario 2
Language of exchange	English and French (Imposed by teacher) Some tasks in French and others in English	English or French (Free choice of the students)
Types of communication	Pairs (one Clermontois and one Jamaican)	Groups of four (two Clermontois and two Jamaicans)
Communication platforms	Facebook, Moodle, Skype, WhatsApp	WhatsApp

265

Tasks and topics given	All topics imposed	Choice of two out of ten topics
	Complete guided and systematic tasks	Complete tasks in a personal manner
	One imposed final task	Choice of one out of two final tasks

The data collection for this study included all the types of interactions that took place within ClerKing as well as two questionnaires: the first one administered at the start of the project, which gathered data on the participants' biography, linguistic competencies, usage of communication tools, and elements related to intercultural communication. The second one examined the same elements but in the context of the project at the end.

3. Discussion of preliminary results

In assessing the objectives of the project, findings show that students declared greater improvement in culture compared to linguistic gains in both scenarios. As illustrated in Table 2, the less restricted scenario seemed to have allowed for more cultural development.

Table 2. Students' declaration of linguistic and cultural gains in percentage

	Linguistic gains	**Cultural gains**
Scenario 1	60%	66%
Scenario 2	55%	88%

In citing examples of cultural gains on the second questionnaire, students provided the following responses in Figure 1 below.

3.1. Choice of language

It was observed that even though students were instructed in Scenario 1 to use a specific language at given points, most of the exchanges happened in English as this was the more comfortable mutual language within each pair.

In Scenario 2, the non-imposition of language not only led to the development of linguistic skills, but also negotiation skills. On many occasions, students had to agree on which language to choose to discuss the given topics (see Figure 2).

Understanding the complexities associated with conceptualising pedagogical...

Provisions were also made on both ends to utilise both languages to facilitate adequate practice.

Figure 1. Excerpts of declarations of students' cultural gains in both scenarios

Scenario 1	Scenario 2
"France is a very beautiful country and the government takes care of its citizens by offering free healthcare and education."	« Au niveau du créole jamaïcain et de leurs coutumes traditionnelles ou encore sur l'histoire du pays. »
"Certain stereotypes were cleared up. I learnt that the youth of France don't drink as much wine as their predecessors. I also learnt that religion doesn't play an important role in government in France."	« Le créole jamaïcain, le night life en Jamaïque, Anansi, les espaces touristiques de la Jamaïque. »
« L'importance de la religion en Jamaïque. »	« A propos des rastafaris et qu'ils sont très croyants. »
« Le système éducatif, la façon de vivre, l'éducation religieuse... »	"French people are not religious, more free-minded."
	"I learnt about the protest culture in France."

Figure 2. Screenshots of excerpts from conversations in Scenario 2

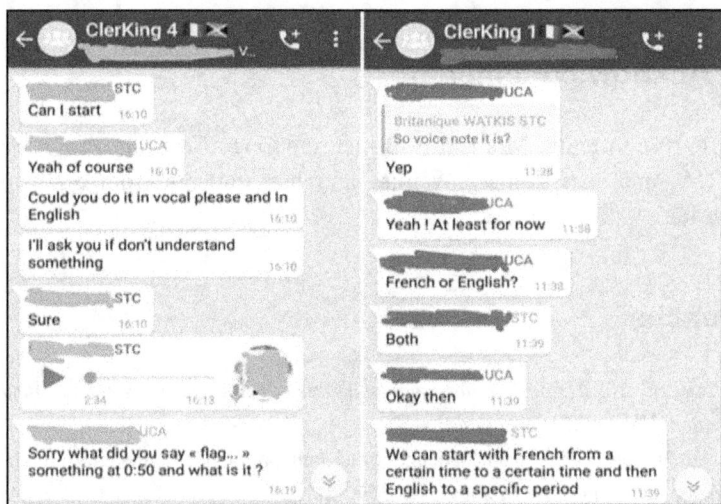

3.2. Communication platforms

Even though there were four communication platforms in Scenario 1, it was found that only two of them were given priority, WhatsApp and Skype. Students attested that these two platforms were the most feasible for communication: Skype for video and WhatsApp for chat.

Students from Scenario 2 also confirmed that WhatsApp was, indeed, an ideal platform because of its features; however, certain functionalities such as voice and video call proved difficult in a group of four people.

4. Conclusions

As O'Dowd and Ritter (2006) and Pernin and Lejeune (2004) noted, we have observed that the design of a pedagogical scenario plays an important role in telecollaboration. Open scenarios seem to allow for the development of linguistic but more so cultural and negotiation skills in foreign languages.

It is also noteworthy that Skype and WhatsApp are suitable communication platforms for telecollaborative projects. Therefore, it would be wise not to use multiple tools, but to choose the pertinent ones that require less cognitive manipulation from the students because they are already familiar with them.

5. Acknowledgements

We would like to thank Mrs Emily Butler and Open Learning Project students from UCA, and Mrs Kathey Wanliss and her students from STC for their participation.

References

Foucher, A.-L. (2010). *Didactique des langue-cultures et tice : scénarios, tâches, interactions. Education.* Université Blaise Pascal .

Helm, F. (2015). The practices and challenges of telecollaboration in higher education in Europe. *Language Learning & Technology, 19*(2), 197-217.

Kern, R. (2006). La communication médiatisée par ordinateur en langues : recherches et applications récentes aux USA. In C. Degache & F. Mangenot (Eds), *Les échanges en ligne dans l'apprentissage et la formation. Le français dans le monde : recherches et applications* (vol. 40, pp. 17-29). CLE International.

Kötter, M. (2002). Tandem learning on the internet: learner interactions in virtual online environments (MOOs) (Vol. 6). Peter Lang.

Nissen, E. (2006). Scénarios de communication en ligne dans des formations hybrides. In C. Degache & F. Mangenot (Eds), *Les échanges en ligne dans l'apprentissage et la formation. Le français dans le monde : recherches et applications* (vol. 40, pp. 44-58). CLE International.

O'Dowd, R., & Ritter, M. (2006). Understanding and working with 'failed communication' in telecollaborative exchanges. *CALICO Journal, 23*(3), 623-642. https://doi.org/10.1558/cj.v23i3.623-642

Pernin, J.-P., & Lejeune, A. (2004). Modèles pour la réutilisation de scénarios d'apprentissage. http://www-clips.imag.fr/arcade/User/jean-philippe.pernin/recherche/download/PerninLejeune_TiceMed04_Article.pdf

Second language learning in knowledge forums: an analysis of L2 acquisition of students participating in the knowledge building international project

Marni Manegre[1] and Mar Gutiérrez-Colón[2]

Abstract. This study presents the results of an experiment designed to determine whether knowledge building can facilitate foreign language acquisition. We examined how groups of Catalan students in secondary schools worked together on collaborative writing tasks in English, their foreign language. The students were participating in the Knowledge Building International Project (KBIP), which is based on the concept that students can learn while working together in computer-assisted learning environments. The quantitative data was collected through a pre-test and post-test. The pre- and post-tests were divided into four sections, which were grammar, vocabulary, long answer, and multiple-choice. The results show an increase overall in the performance of the foreign language, English. In particular, the analysis determined that the comprehension of the subject matter and writing abilities in the L2 showed an increase at high confidence levels, however, there are challenges in determining whether the students have acquired new vocabulary or developed a better understanding of grammatical rules, since it is difficult to predict which words and sentence structures they will use when participating in this project.

Keywords: collaborative writing, computer-assisted language learning, online language learning, knowledge building.

1. Introduction

This study has been designed to analyze and address foreign language acquisition in online collaborative learning environments. An analysis has been done on the

---

1. Universitat Rovira i Virgili, Tarragona, Spain; marnilynne.manegre@estudiants.urv.cat; https://orcid.org/0000-0002-6021-521X
2. Universitat Rovira i Virgili, Tarragona, Spain; mar.gutierrezcolon@urv.cat; https://orcid.org/0000-0001-8479-4933

How to cite this article: Manegre, M., & Gutiérrez-Colón, M. (2019). Second language learning in knowledge forums: an analysis of L2 acquisition of students participating in the knowledge building international project. In F. Meunier, J. Van de Vyver, L. Bradley & S. Thouësny (Eds), *CALL and complexity – short papers from EUROCALL 2019* (pp. 270-274). Research-publishing.net. https://doi.org/10.14705/rpnet.2019.38.1021

use of English as a foreign language among secondary students using a knowledge forum as part of the KBIP. More specifically, do the students' performances show evidence of increased knowledge of vocabulary acquisition, grammar rules, syntactic structure, and basic comprehension of the topic in the foreign language?

Knowledge building occurs when students collaborate by sharing their ideas and creating expertise collectively (Bereiter & Scardamalia, 2010, 2014; Bielaczyc & Collins, 2005). It is the creation of knowledge through building ideas out of ideas (Bereiter & Scardamalia, 2014). Students can create knowledge when they work together (Bereiter & Scardamalia, 2010), and they do so while addressing problems in various topics, including when conversing in a foreign language. The KBIP allows for international collaboration online where students ask questions and share their ideas in a forum. Their classmates contribute to the ideas by researching the questions, adding information, and participating in discussions until they collectively reach a conclusion that answers the initial questions posed. Further information on the KBIP can be found on the Learning Exchange website[3].

Students create knowledge unintentionally when they participate in digital collaborative activities (Thorne, Black, & Sykes, 2009). Not only do the students show gains in literacy, but they also show evidence of stronger collaborative writing skills with enhanced content and organization, especially in foreign language contexts (Yim & Warschauer, 2017). These findings suggest that knowledge forums would assist in second language acquisition.

2. Method

2.1. Participants

Two classes of grade nine students in a Catalan secondary school participated in this study. There were 30 students in each class (N=60). The students were all 14-years-old and at an A2-B1 level of English when they participated.

2.2. Procedure

At the onset of the study, the students were given a pre-test. The students then participated in the KBIP where they worked in groups to create questions they

---

3. https://thelearningexchange.ca/itl-project-home/itl-project-knowledge-building/

wanted to be answered. Once the questions were determined, they were posted in the forum using the scaffold *I need to understand*. They then worked in groups to respond to and answer the questions using scaffolding to provide an opinion (*My theory* or *This theory cannot explain*), explain the answer based on research (*New information*), then summarize what they had learned (*Putting our knowledge together*). Upon completion of the writing task, the students then took a post-test.

The pre- and post-tests are divided into four sections: grammar, long answer, vocabulary, and multiple-choice. The grammar, vocabulary, and multiple-choice sections followed a forced-choice paradigm where the long answer follows a free answer paradigm. The forced-choice sections only had one possible answer for each question and were graded based on whether the correct answer was provided. The grammar section measured their understanding of modal verbs, and the vocabulary section included words typically taught in L2 texts relating to the topic. The multiple-choice section measured comprehension. The long answer section was graded based on whether the syntax was correct and whether the students understood the question and responded appropriately in the L2. The tests followed relevant common European framework of reference for languages texts for B1 English related to the topic of discussion, which was the United Nations Sustainable Goal of Climate Action.

3. Results

Through in-class observation, it was noted that the students in the two classes had different levels of engagement when participating in this task. While the students in Class B appeared to be more distracted throughout the semester, they also posted less in the forum. For this reason, the two classes were analyzed separately to see whether the amount of engagement within the forums influenced the results (see Table 1).

The pre- and post-test results were compared using a t-test. The results of the test show the alternative hypothesis to be effective at a 95% confidence level for both classes (see Table 2).

Table 1. Engagement levels of Class A and Class B

Class	# of Posts	% of Posts	Classroom Observations
Class A	142	61 %	Higher Engagement
Class B	90	39 %	Lower Engagement

Table 2. Overall results

Class	Tstat	Tcrit
Class A	-4.74	-2.045
Class B	-2.595	-2.045

When looking at the sections of the test, for Class A, two of the sections reject the null hypothesis in favor of the alternative hypothesis, while the other two sections are in favor of the null hypothesis. For Class B, only one section, the long answer section, rejected the null hypothesis in favor of the alternative hypothesis, while three of the sections reject the alternative hypothesis in favor of the null hypothesis (see Table 3 and Table 4).

Table 3. Class A results

Section	Tstat	Tcrit	Cohen's D
Total Test	-4.74	-2.045	Medium (0.364)
Grammar	-0.163	-2.045	Low
Long Answer	-5.375	-2.045	High (0.7924)
Vocabulary	-0.188	-2.045	Low
Multiple-Choice	-2.23	-2.045	Medium (0.2683)

Table 4. Class B results

Section	Tstat	Tcrit	Cohen's D
Total Test	-2.595	-2.045	Medium (0.3033)
Grammar	-0.8063	-2.045	Low
Long Answer	-4.821	-2.045	High (0.5791)
Vocabulary	-0.66	-2.045	Low
Multiple-Choice	-1.688	-2.045	Medium (0.3382)

4. Discussion

From this study, the analysis has determined that participating in the KBIP is effective for foreign language acquisition. However, when looking at the specific sections of the tests, we can conclude that participating in forums is useful for developing writing skills in the foreign language and for comprehension of the material in the foreign language. However, our testing does not show that this method of instruction is effective for grammar or vocabulary acquisition. When looking at the vocabulary words tested, very few of these words were used in the forums. The students are likely acquiring vocabulary in their foreign language; however, the challenge is that it is difficult to predict which words the students will use. The interesting findings with these tests are the responses for the long answer section. Class A was more engaged throughout the process and posted 50% more responses in the forum than Class B. Class A showed a mean increase in the long answer section by 26.9%, while Class B showed a mean increase of 17.3%.

5. Conclusions

The present study analyzed foreign language acquisition, where the participants were writing and collaborating using their L2. We were able to determine that using collaborative writing tasks in a foreign language classroom is effective in developing the comprehension of the subject matter and improving L2 writing skills.

6. Acknowledgments

We would like to thank the participating students of Sant Pau School in Tarragona and the faculty of Sant Pau, in particular, Père Bolunda for his assistance and contribution.

References

Bereiter, C., & Scardamalia, M. (2010). Can children really create knowledge? *Canadian Journal of Learning and Technology / La revue canadienne de l'apprentissage et de la technologie, 36*(1), 1-15. https://doi.org/10.21432/t2zp43

Bereiter, C., & Scardamalia, M. (2014). Knowledge building and knowledge creation: one concept, two hills to climb. In S. Chee Tan, H. Jeong So & J. Yeo (Eds), *Knowledge Creation in Education* (pp. 35-52). Springer. https://doi.org/10.1007/978-981-287-047-6_3

Bielaczyc, K., & Collins, A. (2005). Technology as a catalyst for fostering knowledge-creating communities. In A. M. O'Donnell, C. E. Hmelo-Silver & J. van der Linden (Eds), *Using technology to enhance learning*. Lawrence Erlbaum Associates.

Thorne, S., Black, R. W., & Sykes, J. M. (2009). Second language use, socialization, and learning in internet interest communities and online gaming. *The Modern Language Journal, 93*(1), 802-821. https://doi.org/10.1111/j.1540-4781.2009.00974.x

Yim, S., & Warschauer, M. (2017). Web-based collaborative writing in l2 contexts: methodological insights from text mining. *Language Learning & Technology, 21*(1), 146-165. https://doi.org/10125/44599

■ UCLouvain

Brazil and Colombia virtual exchange project: the Brazilian view

Claudia Beatriz Martins[1] and Maristela Werner[2]

Abstract. The objective of this paper is to report the preliminary results of a telecollaborative project between a Brazilian university (UTFPR) and a Colombian university (Universidad de Pamplona) that both offer a Licentiate degree in English. The project had two purposes: a pedagogical one to show student-teachers how they can develop their communication skills in English in a collaborative way by sharing information with other student-teachers from a different culture, and a technological one to put future teachers in contact with some technological tools. The paper is divided into three parts: (1) a brief description of the context and the participants; (2) the project itself – the first steps, the objectives, and the tasks; and (3) the Brazilian view of the whole process/project as well as the students' feedback.

Keywords: virtual exchange, telecollaboration, pre-service teachers, CALL teacher education.

1. Introduction

Teacher education for Computer Assisted Language Learning (CALL) is a challenging area. There are many unanswered questions on how future language teachers should be prepared for using technology in their practice. What should be taught? What duration/quantity? One course? Or should it be spread across all subjects? Studies show that language teachers are graduating with little or no formal training on the use of technology in language teaching (Hubbard, 2008). However, there is evidence that language teachers with technological skills are the ones that educational institutions request the most. The market wants qualified teachers in CALL, but teacher-training courses are not meeting the demand.

---

1. UTFPR, Curitiba, Brazil; claudiab@utfpr.edu.br; https://orcid.org/0000-0002-1046-5894
2. UTFPR, Curitiba, Brazil; pugsley@utfpr.edu.br; https://orcid.org/0000-0003-3536-6750

How to cite this article: Martins, C. B., & Werner, M. (2019). Brazil and Colombia virtual exchange project: the Brazilian view. In F. Meunier, J. Van de Vyver, L. Bradley & S. Thouësny (Eds), *CALL and complexity – short papers from EUROCALL 2019* (pp. 275-279). Research-publishing.net. https://doi.org/10.14705/rpnet.2019.38.1022

Besides that, language teachers need to be equipped with knowledge and skills not only about new technologies. They must also have foreign language competence, for example. One way of helping these future teachers to develop some of these language and technology skills simultaneously is telecollaboration or, using the umbrella term, virtual exchange. Research has shown the important contributions that this kind of activity can make to the language learning process (O'Dowd, 2013, 2018). By taking part in it, students will be exposed to online collaborative approaches to learning and teaching and will have semi-authentic experiences of communicating in the foreign language as well as a focus on the pedagogical and technical applications of new technologies. If we want them to be innovative when they become teachers, first they themselves need to have this kind of experience.

Based on this, a telecollaborative project between UTFPR and Universidad de Pamplona was developed by the end of 2018. The objective of this paper is to report the preliminary results of this project.

2. The context and participants

This project involved two professors from Brazil – Claudia and Maristela – and two professors from Colombia – Antonio and Gabriel. The two universities offer a *Licenciatura* in English (a teacher-training program). So, the participants were pre-service English teachers: 30 from Brazil and 35 from Colombia. In Brazil, Claudia had 25 students in the subject English Language Basic 1 (A2 students – focus on listening/speaking), and Maristela had 25 students in the subject English Reading and Writing 1 (A2 students). Both subjects are in the second semester and complement each other to cover the four skills. Twenty of these students were the same for both teachers and five others attended only one or the other. Antonio had ten students in one of his groups and 25 in the other (A2 students) and he worked the four skills with the groups. Gabriel coordinated the project.

3. The project

3.1. The first steps

This project was the result of an initial contact that professors Gabriel and Claudia had in 2016. By the end of 2018, the idea was to conduct a project involving the students from both universities in the first semester of 2019. To guide the project, we used documents from the EVALUATE project[3] (Müller-Hartmann & O'Dowd, 2018) as well as other authors from the CALL area, mainly O'Dowd (2013, 2018).

We initially communicated using Skype. The objective was to get to know each other and also to establish a working plan. Brazil is two hours ahead of Colombia and this and the fact that the four professors had several other activities besides their classes made it difficult to have the meetings. The solution later was to create a WhatsApp group and that worked perfectly.

Another difficulty that we faced were the differences in academic schedules. This had some impact because we realized the project should last less than what we had initially planned. Another consequence was that we had to adjust the deadlines of the activities, taking into consideration the exam periods of both groups.

It took us a good amount of time to decide what exactly we would do taking into account the constraints mentioned before. We then agreed that this would be a 'pilot study' for future projects and in this way we had to simplify it. The platform used was Edmodo.

3.2. The objectives

The project had two purposes: a pedagogical one to show student-teachers how they can develop their communication skills in English in a collaborative way by sharing information with other student-teachers from a different culture, and a technological one to put future teachers in contact with some technological tools. We also agreed to conduct a survey with both the professors in charge and the student-teachers from both countries to have the necessary feedback.

3.3. The tasks

We decided to have two activities, each one lasting about a month to be done. The activities had to be complementary so that they could be used by the two disciplines in Brazil. Participation was mandatory for the Brazilian students and the activities were used as part of their final grades for both subjects. In both tasks students had to use English.

---

3. See http://www.evaluateproject.eu/ for more information.

Activity 1. First students had to record a one-minute video introducing themselves to their international partners. They had to use their own devices, and could not read. Then they had to upload it to a Google Drive folder. After watching the partner's video they had to write a short text describing him/her. Detailed instructions were given on the platform and in class. A list with the pairs of students had to be prepared so that they knew whose video to watch.

Activity 2. For the second activity, they had to also record a video and write a short text, but this time about a topic they chose after talking to their partners. They had to use WhatsApp, Skype, or Facetime – any app to talk and see the partner.

4. Preliminary results: the Brazilian view of the project and students' feedback

Despite all the preparation and even some previous experience, reality was more complex than expected. The interaction between Brazilian and Colombian professors went very well and it was easy to reach an agreement. This kind of collaboration worked and will probably continue. Nonetheless, time management was our biggest issue.

Some misunderstandings concerning the first instructions happened and it was not clear why. Detailed instructions were given about the activities, however, some students had difficulties understanding them and even uploading the videos. For Activity 2, the number of students changed and other arrangements had to be made. Unfortunately, the interaction using an app to decide on the topic did not happen for all the pairs/groups; writing messages was the option they preferred.

The survey created is still receiving responses, but the first answers show that students would like to continue taking part in projects like this. The biggest difficulty was their partners' accent. Several suggestions have been made and most of them mention that they would like to have more contact with the other group: live video sessions with the whole class, for example.

5. Conclusions

There are many barriers and problems that still make telecollaboration be on the periphery in higher education. It takes time and teachers have to be absolutely committed to it. Students do benefit from this kind of exchange but also require attention and have to be constantly motivated. Autonomy is an issue that still has to be developed so that students become more independent and responsible for their own learning.

Nevertheless, our final goal is to have a long-term project involving other professors from other subjects from our course and partners from other countries. This is the starting point to try to raise awareness in our teaching community as well as in our Latin American colleagues of the advantages of telecollaboration. By sharing these results here we aim to engage others from the foreign language community. As teacher trainers, it is important to get to know the reality of colleagues all over the world who are also preparing future English teachers and to share our realities, challenges, strategies, and expectations.

References

Hubbard, P. (2008). CALL and the future of language teacher education. *CALICO Journal, 25*(2), 175-188. http://www.jstor.org/stable/calicojournal.25.2.175

Müller-Hartmann A., & O'Dowd, R. (2018). A training manual on telecollaboration for teacher trainer. https://www.evaluateproject.eu/evlt-data/uploads/2018/07/Training-Manual_Final_EVALUATE.pdf

O'Dowd, R. (2013). Telecollaborative networks in university higher education: overcoming barriers to integration. *The Internet and Higher Education,18*, 47-53. https://doi.org/10.1016/j.iheduc.2013.02.001

O'Dowd, R. (2018). From telecollaboration to virtual exchange: state-of-the-art and the role of UNICollaboration in moving forward. *Journal of Virtual Exchange, 1*, 1-23. Research-publishing.net. https://doi.org/10.14705/rpnet.2018.jve.1

Assemblage theory: coping with complexity in technology enhanced language learning

Blair Matthews[1]

Abstract. Language classrooms are complex systems, but theory often simplifies these processes making researching effectiveness difficult. Assemblage theory – a theory of complexity in the social sciences – allows us to examine complexity in the language classroom. In this paper, I present an account of the language classroom that captures the complexity, subjectivity, and temporality of technology enhanced language learning.

Keywords: complexity, theory, assemblage theory, technology enhanced language learning, TELL.

1. Theoretical background

The technology enhanced language classroom is a complex system combining technical processes (i.e. teaching) with natural, biological ones (e.g. the cognitive processes of learning). Theories of learning help us align these processes, providing frameworks for "intelligent and reasoned strategy selection" (Ertmer & Newby, 2013, p. 44) which are "useful for evaluating the quality of technologies for language learning" (Chapelle, 2016, p. 159).

But theories are like bricks: they "can be used to build [a] courthouse of reason [or they] can be thrown through the window" (Deleuze & Guattari, 1988, p. xiii). Theory necessarily simplifies complex processes, sorting objects into epistemological categories that are not real. These categories are subsequently generalised into abstractions and granted concrete properties (a process known as *reification,* Bewes, 2002). Concepts such as *student autonomy* and *social*

---

1. University of St Andrews, St Andrews, Scotland; bm221@st-andrews.ac.uk

How to cite this article: Matthews, B. (2019). Assemblage theory: coping with complexity in technology enhanced language learning. In F. Meunier, J. Van de Vyver, L. Bradley & S. Thouësny (Eds), *CALL and complexity – short papers from EUROCALL 2019* (pp. 280-284). Research-publishing.net. https://doi.org/10.14705/rpnet.2019.38.1023

constructivism are used to explain complex learning processes and underpin the practices and routines of language teaching, though they may be understood and applied in very different ways.

Distinctions between various applications of theories lead to methodological differences, where effectiveness is quantified using different techniques. Quantifying effectiveness and making direct comparisons between technological interventions becomes difficult to do. As a consequence, technology enhanced language learning has never been systematically investigated (Golonka et al., 2013; Hew et al., 2019).

This is not an argument to reject current theory – teachers and learning designers need to know learning theories as a lawyer needs to know the law. Instead, there needs to be a set of parameters within which language learning and technology can be explored. This paper's contribution is to present an account of the language classroom that is unshackled by reification and captures its complexity, subjectivity, and temporality.

2. Assemblage theory

Assemblage theory (DeLanda, 2016) draws on *dynamic systems theory* to explain self-organisation and self-regulation in the social and cultural world. DeLanda (2016) presents a material account of the social world, arguing that assemblage theory avoids reification by emphasising the fluidity of objects. An assemblage is comprised of objects and their connections, which combine to make up interconnected arrangements with their own functional properties and capacities. An object can be anything that has an effect on the world: humans, technology, animals, policies, or opinions. An assemblage can be any arrangement of objects: a football team, a zoo, a large-multinational, or a language classroom.

Key to an assemblage is its co-functioning; that an object's capacities only become realised in relation to other objects. For example, a teacher may use a mobile device to revise a particular language point. The technology on its own does not have the capacity to be used for language teaching. Only when it is used in combination with the students, the teachers, the software, the hardware, theories of learning, the task, and cognitive processes in the brain can its functional capacity be realised. Remove any of these objects, and the functional capacity of the device is lost. However, an assemblage cannot be reduced to these objects; all the component parts can be replaced by others, yet the functionality remains.

There are infinite possibilities and arrangements of an assemblage. In order to make sense of this complexity, DeLanda (2016) observes a series of formal operations that assemblages share, arranged along three continua:

- material-expressive;

- territorialisation-deterritorialisation; and

- coding-decoding.

First, assemblages can be defined by their material or expressive properties. The material components refer to the concrete properties of the assemblage. The language classroom comprises an array of material objects: technology, people, institutions, schemes of work, processes, methods, and policies that all interact to facilitate language learning. The expressive components meanwhile refer to the subjective properties of the assemblage. An example of expressivity can be found in the work of Stockwell (2013), who observes the importance of technology in motivating students. Motivation is an expressive component, an object may be motivating to some or not to others, or with different activities. Expressivity can help explain the dynamic nature of the language classroom.

A second continuum describes the processes of formation of an assemblage (territorialisation-deterritorialisation). Territorialisation refers to the extent to which an assemblage is bound together. Interaction between the constituent parts generates consensus, as parts find ways of working with each other. These processes determine the routines and limits of the assemblage (for example, setting up a subscription, defining roles, and establishing a designated online space are all examples of territorialisation of digital language learning). Deterritorialisation on the other hand refers to the processes of disassembling. For example, if a technology is replaced by another, then this is an example of deterritorialisation. Digital technologies have the effect of deterritorialising physical spaces, as it becomes possible to do more with digital devices. In this respect, *flipped learning* may be an example of deterritorialisation of language classrooms, taking learning outside designated spaces and times.

Related to the concept of territorialisation-deterritorialisation is the continuum of coding-decoding. Coding refers to the rituals, language, and routines of an assemblage. Formal assemblages such as a classroom tend to be highly coded, its language and routines are often clearly defined and prescribed through decades of practice and theory building. An example of coding is the language of teaching methodologies, which are introduced and reinforced in teaching qualifications, Continuing Professional Development (CPD) training, conferences, and publications. Decoding meanwhile refers to changes in routines, habits, or practices. The introduction of new technologies have a disrupting effect that can change the way we talk about language learning and teaching. Concepts such as *gamification* or *multimodality* codify new practices.

Finally, while an assemblage has its core functions (for example to facilitate the teaching of languages), its influence extends far beyond this. These influences are known (perhaps a little abstractly) as *lines of flight* and serve to link the assemblage to the external world (ie. other assemblages). These lines of flight include links to external actors such as education boards, immigration bodies, and assessment companies – e.g. International English Language Testing System (IELTS) –, all of which influence the practices and routines of the assemblage. Big data is an example of how technology may exert an influence on the practices within a classroom. A teacher may use a platform such as ClassDojo to track students. However, there have been a number of criticisms on the reach and influence of the ClassDojo platform through the collection of data on students (Williamson, 2017). The algorithms ClassDojo uses as part of its platform reflect the worldview of San Francisco tech companies. Concepts such as grit, character, or perseverance are coded into the functioning of the platform, imposing on users particular classroom practices and behaviours that perform the values of the platform.

3. So what?

The perennial problem of the relationship between theory and practice is how theory can be practically applied in the language classroom. Assemblage theory allows us to unpick the objects and their relations in a systematic way, helping us to understand how processes or functions work. One practical application is the process of *mapping*. Mapping refers to a technique whereby designers identify all the objects, participants, and actions involved in a task. Typically this involves identifying the material objects in a system. Assemblage theory also allows us to map on lines of flight (such as assessment bodies) or expressive components, such as the attitude towards technology, or the time of day, all of which may exert an influence on practices. Concepts of territorialisation and deterritorialisation also allow us to understand the dynamic processes of language classrooms. Learning a new language point or a new skill has the effect (over time) of deterritoritalising and reterritorialising the language classroom, as new abilities allow for new powers and opportunities for creativity.

Assemblage theory also provides a frame of reference to explore other theories, such as student autonomy. Student autonomy is often reified into a series of *ideal behaviours* that successful language learners have been observed doing. By situating the student in the context of a socio-technical system, we can explore how autonomy may be constrained or enabled and how it takes shape over time.

References

Bewes, T. (2002). *Reification, or, the anxiety of late capitalism.* Verso.

Chapelle, C. A. (2016). CALL in the year 2000: a look back from 2016. *Language Learning & Technology, 20*(2), 159-161.

DeLanda, M. (2016). *Assemblage theory.* Edinburgh University Press.

Deleuze, G., & Guattari, F. (1988). *A thousand plateaus: capitalism and schizophrenia.* Bloomsbury Publishing.

Ertmer, P. A., & Newby, T. J. (2013). Behaviorism, cognitivism, constructivism: comparing critical features from an instructional design perspective. *Performance improvement quarterly, 26*(2), 43-71. https://doi.org/10.1002/piq.21143

Golonka, E. M., Bowles, A. R., Frank, V. M., Richardson, D. L., & Freynik, S. (2013). Technologies for foreign language learning: a review of technology types and their effectiveness. *Computer assisted language learning, 27*(1), 70-105. https://doi.org/10.1080/09588221.2012.700315

Hew, K. F., Lan, M., Tang, Y., Jia, C., & Lo, C. K. (2019). Where is the "theory" within the field of educational technology research? *British Journal of Educational Technology. Advance online publication, 50*(3), 956-971. https://doi.org/10.1111/bjet.12770

Stockwell, G. (2013). Technology and motivation in English-language teaching and learning. In E. Ushioda (Ed.), *International perspectives on motivation* (pp. 156-175). Palgrave Macmillan, London. https://doi.org/10.1057/9781137000873_9

Williamson, B. (2017). Decoding ClassDojo: psycho-policy, social-emotional learning and persuasive educational technologies. *Learning, Media and Technology, 42*(4), 440-453. https://doi.org/10.1080/17439884.2017.1278020

■ UCLouvain

Learners' emotional response to a complex video-creation task

Alice Meurice[1], Véronique Henin[2], and Marie Van Reet[3]

Abstract. We are three teachers of business English in higher education who have developed a project for our second-year management students to co-create their own video document, exploring a business question. Our intention is to determine whether the complexity of our entire teaching sequence, and more specifically the use of Information and Communication Technology (ICT) tools for the co-creation of problem-solving content, allowed our learners to experience positive emotions, i.e. *enjoyment* – vs. *anxiety* – in the process of Second Language Acquisition (SLA), and whether they perceived the *usefulness* of the project for their future personal or professional life. Our project took place over the second semester of the 2018-2019 academic year, after which the students answered a questionnaire in their mother tongue with both Likert-scale and open questions. The current paper uses a mixed-methods approach to analyse the results and report on the emotional effect of the teaching sequence on the students.

Keywords: SLA, CALL, emotions, enjoyment.

1. Introduction

Interest for the emotional aspects of language learning has been growing among researchers over the years (De Smet et al., 2018; Dewaele, Witney, Saito, & Dewaele, 2018). Two major concepts have been highlighted as being complementary in the learners' experience of SLA, i.e. 'anxiety' and 'enjoyment'. We made use of Dewaele and MacIntyre's (2014) Foreign Language Enjoyment (FLE) scale and Foreign Language Classroom Anxiety (FLCA) scale to analyse the learners'

---

[1]. Université Catholique de Louvain, Louvain-la-Neuve, Belgium; alice.meurice@uclouvain.be; https://orcid.org/0000-0001-7892-1422
[2]. Université Catholique de Louvain, Louvain-la-Neuve, Belgium; veronique.henin@uclouvain.be
[3]. Université Catholique de Louvain, Louvain-la-Neuve, Belgium; marie.vanreet@uclouvain.be

How to cite this article: Meurice, A., Henin, V., & Van Reet, M. (2019). Learners' emotional response to a complex video-creation task. In F. Meunier, J. Van de Vyver, L. Bradley & S. Thouësny (Eds), *CALL and complexity – short papers from EUROCALL 2019* (pp. 285-290). Research-publishing.net. https://doi.org/10.14705/rpnet.2019.38.1024

emotional experiences. We also assessed their perceived usefulness (De Smet et al., 2018) of the whole project. Also, Romero's (2015) model suggests that the most complex but also engaging way of integrating technology in pedagogy consists in having the learners use ICT for the 'participative co-creation of knowledge' (our translation). To do so, the learners must be engaged in the understanding or solving of problems shared by the class, which is then considered as a learning community. The aim of this study is to determine whether, when faced with a complex, ICT-integrated task, our learners experienced a positive emotional relationship with the target language.

2. Methodology

The project took place throughout the second semester of the 2018-2019 academic year and involved 94 second-year management students aiming at a B2 level of proficiency in oral skills (CEFR, 2001, p. 27). The students were divided into four groups and taught by three different teachers. The majority of the work on the project was done in class, and the students were asked to work in groups of three or four on the creation of a video exploring a real-life business question of their choice. Each group then had the entire class reflect upon their question during a thirty-minute activity including their video. By the end of the semester, all the videos were compiled into a data bank, which the students were prompted to browse with a view of discussing a new question during their end-of-year oral examination. The learners were also asked to complete a questionnaire in French, reflecting upon their enjoyment, anxiety, and perceived usefulness of the tasks throughout their experience. The questionnaire submitted to the students at the end of the year contained nine sections of five-point Likert-scale questions – from 1, disagree, to 5, agree – and open questions, based on Dewaele and MacIntyre's (2014) FLE and FLCA scales. The questions on perceived usefulness were based on De Smet et al.'s (2018) questionnaires. The answers we received from 67 – out of 94 – students allowed us to conduct a mixed-methods analysis.

3. Results and discussion

In this section, we will first address the Likert-scale questions quantitatively for each emotional item separately – i.e. *anxiety*, *enjoyment*, and *perception of use*. The graphs show the mean and standard deviation. Questions for which the expected answer is the opposite of the others are represented in orange. We will then further refine our analysis qualitatively by focussing on the open questions.

Figure 1. Anxiety – Mean and SD – "Throughout the project..."

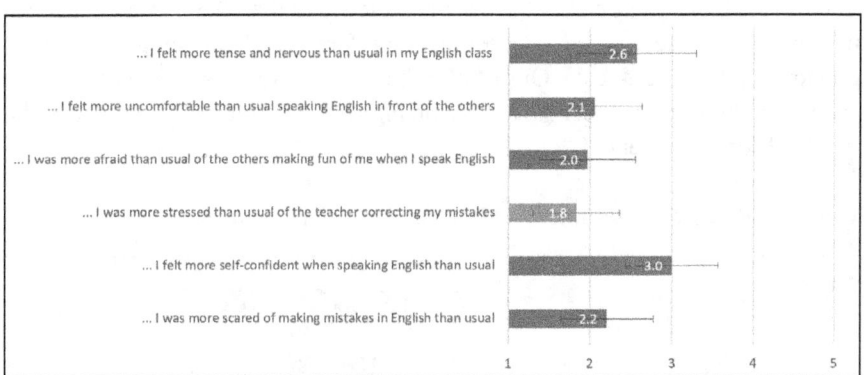

As depicted in Figure 1, the students' answers show that they did not feel any more tense, uncomfortable, or stressed than usual throughout the project. When asked whether they felt more self-confident expressing themselves in the target language, they answered neutrally. The whole project, however complex, does therefore not seem to have generated more anxiety than usual among the students.

Figure 2. Enjoyment – Mean and SD – "Throughout the project..."

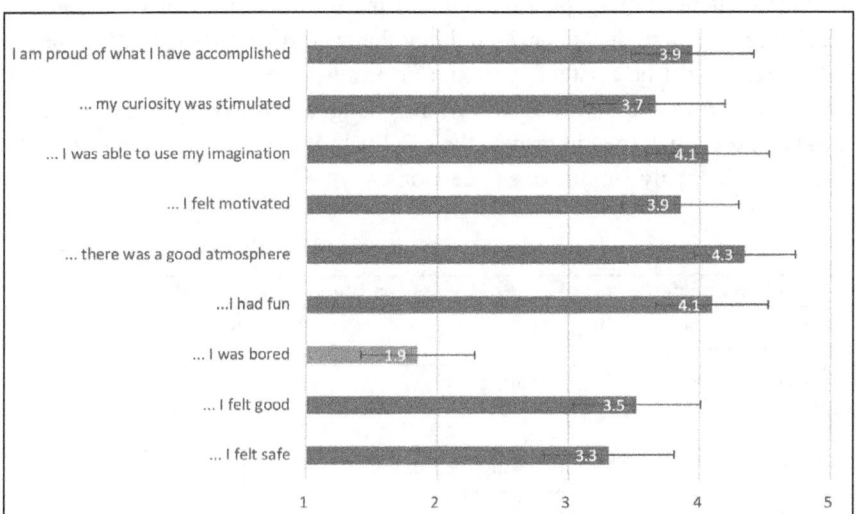

Enjoyment-related questions prompted clearly positive results – cf. Figure 2 – with high scores in terms of atmosphere, how much fun the students had, and how much they were able to use their imagination. They also quite agreed on the fact that they felt motivated, that their curiosity was stimulated, and that they felt good and safe throughout the project. The one question that referred to them being bored scored quite low on the Likert-scale. Our results show that, in the case of our project, the students felt both low anxiety (or at least no higher than usual), all the while feeling high levels of enjoyment.

Figure 3. Perceived usefulness – Mean and SD – "This project..."

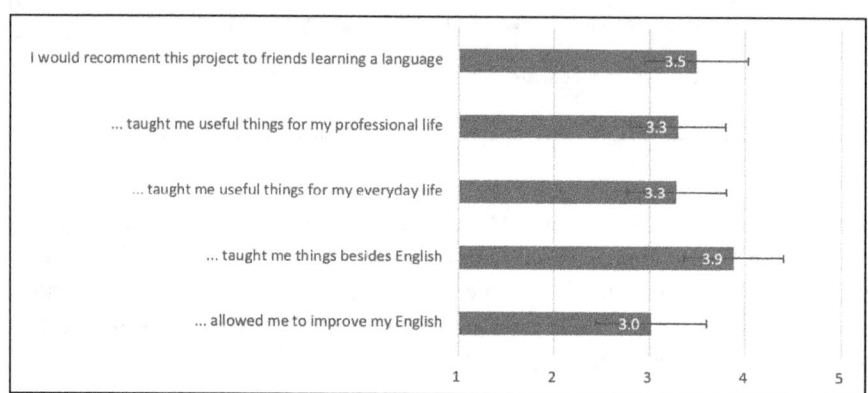

The third variable showed positive but less prominent results than the other two – cf. Figure 3. The students considered that the project taught them things besides English, whether it be for their personal or professional life, and they would, on the whole, recommend it to friends learning a language. Nevertheless, they remain neutral on how much they improved their English. We will shed a brighter light on these results by analysing the open questions.

Table 1. Open questions, categorised by item and number of occurrences

What did you prefer?		What did you least like?		What did you learn?	
Creativity/originality/ freedom/imagination	30	Time	14	Video/editing/ shooting/technology	16
Video(s)/shooting/ editing	21	'Nothing'	12	Communication / speaking/English/ non-verbal	10
Fun/enjoyment	16	Planning /beginning/ preparations/ portfolio	9	Topics	8
Group/interaction	12	Video/editing/ shooting	9	Group/ collaborating	4
Serious	5	Topic	2	Different	2

To analyse the open questions, we have tagged them with key words, which we later categorised into concepts using grounded theory (Cohen, Manion, & Morrison, 2013), and then counted the number of times they were mentioned. The main concept is identified in bold in Table 1 above, along with its associated keywords. Any concept that was mentioned only once is not represented.

Creativity and associated terms were mentioned 30 times as the thing the students preferred throughout the project. Many also mentioned how they were able to deal with a serious (5) topic in a fun (16) way, while enjoying a certain degree of freedom. Group work and interaction (12) were also highlighted as a plus, as well as ICT aspects such as shooting, editing, and the videos themselves (21).

The least liked items focussed on how time-consuming (14) the project was, which is confirmed by elements such as the portfolio, preparations, planning, and beginning (9). Some students disliked technical aspects like editing and shooting of their video (9). Finally, 12 students out of 64 did not mention anything they disliked.

The students considered they had learned about editing and shooting or videos and technology in general (16). Eight students also mentioned learning about the topics that were addressed in class, in their own group, or by the others. Language-wise, they mentioned learning about English, and more specifically speaking and non-verbal communication (10). The students have also improved their group work and collaboration (4) skills, while learning to work in a different (2) way.

These results corroborate and further detail the answers to the Likert questions. It seems the low anxiety and high enjoyment can be attributed to a good atmosphere, which allowed the students to use their creativity and learn about ICT and communication skills to learn about serious topics, in a fun way. The feedback received is also encouraging in terms of reaching the highest level of complexity and engagement via a 'participative co-creation of knowledge' while working with ICT (Romero, 2015), since the students highlight group work, collaboration, and ICT skills, in combination with their interests in the topics covered.

4. Conclusion

As mentioned, our main aim was to determine whether our learners experienced positive emotions, and whether they perceived the usefulness of the project for their future life. Results tend to show that the complexity of the task required from the students did not create any more anxiety than usual. They felt a high level of enjoyment throughout the semester and, even though they did not feel strongly about the use of the project for their everyday life and their future careers, they considered they learned a variety of things from ICT skills, to communication and collaborating competences. Should we replicate this study, we would work with a control group, on a full-year project, which would allow us to integrate and be more explicit on linguistic objectives.

References

CEFR. (2001). *Common European framework of reference for languages: learning, teaching, assessment*. Council of Europe.
Cohen, L., Manion, L., & Morrison, K. (2013). *Research methods in education*. Routledge. https://doi.org/10.4324/9780203720967
De Smet, A., Mettewie, L., Galand, B., Hiligsmann, P., & Van Mensel, L. (2018). Classroom anxiety and enjoyment in CLIL and non-CLIL: does the target language matter? *Studies in Second Language Learning and Teaching*, *8*(1), 47-71. https://doi.org/10.14746/ssllt.2018.8.1.3
Dewaele, J.-M., & MacIntyre, P. D. (2014). The two faces of Janus? Anxiety and enjoyment in the foreign language classroom. *Studies in Second Language Learning and Teaching*, *4*(2), 237-274. https://doi.org/10.14746/ssllt.2014.4.2.5
Dewaele, J.-M., Witney, J., Saito, K., & Dewaele, L. (2018). Foreign language enjoyment and anxiety: the effect of teacher and learner variables. *Language Teaching Research*, *22*(6), 676-697. https://doi.org/10.1177/1362168817692161
Romero, M. (2015, December 4). *Usages pédagogiques des TIC : de la consommation à la cocréation participative*. VTÉ - Vitrine Technologie Éducation. https://www.vteducation.org/fr/articles/collaboration-avec-les-technologies/usages-pedagogiques-des-tic-de-la-consommation-a-la

Learner-adaptive partial and synchronized captions for L2 listening skill development

Maryam Sadat Mirzaei[1] and Kourosh Meshgi[2]

Abstract. Many language learners have difficulty practicing listening skills using authentic materials, and thus use captions to map text with speech, and they benefit from reading along while listening to comprehend content. However, many learners over-rely on reading the text and many have difficulty in dividing their attention to the multimodal input. We have proposed a captioning tool, Partial and Synchronized Captions (PSC), which detects the useful words to be shown in the caption for addressing learners' listening difficulties. To handle individual learner demands, PSC should adapt its word selection criteria. This study proposes an Adaptive PSC (APSC), which improves its word selection and retrains itself on-the-fly by applying learner feedback on the generated caption to provide individualized and effective assistance that satisfies the learners' requirements. Preliminary results revealed that the system was relatively successful to adapt itself to the demand of the L2 learner, which raised learner satisfaction on the resultant captions.

Keywords: partial and synchronized captions, adaptive captions, individualized assistance, second language listening.

1. Introduction

One popular tool used for developing L2 listening skills, especially when it comes to listening to authentic materials, is captioning (Vandergrift, 2011). Captioning facilitates listening comprehension by providing the text along with the audio/video. However, many learners, especially beginners, struggle with cognitive load and split attention, while attending to caption text together with other modes of input (Leveridge & Yang, 2013; Sweller, 1994). Mirzaei, Meshgi, Akita, and

---

1. RIKEN AIP/Kyoto University, Kyoto, Japan; maryam.mirzaei@riken.jp; https://orcid.org/0000-0002-0715-1624
2. RIKEN AIP/Kyoto University, Kyoto, Japan; kourosh.meshgi@riken.jp; https://orcid.org/0000-0001-7734-6104

How to cite this article: Mirzaei, M. S., & Meshgi, K. (2019). Learner-adaptive partial and synchronized captions for L2 listening skill development. In F. Meunier, J. Van de Vyver, L. Bradley & S. Thouësny (Eds), *CALL and complexity – short papers from EUROCALL 2019* (pp. 291-296). Research-publishing.net. https://doi.org/10.14705/rpnet.2019.38.1025

Kawahara (2017) proposed PSC to provide selective text in the caption for reducing textual density and encouraging more listening than reading. PSC synchronizes text and audio at word-level to facilitate text-to-speech mapping. The selection of words to appear in the caption is based on lexical and speech difficulty. The former considers factors such as frequency and specificity, whereas the latter incorporates the use of automatic speech recognition on the system's errors to detect difficult speech segments (e.g. breached boundaries).

The main challenge is the word selection for learners with different proficiencies. While the full caption may bring too much text that sometimes negatively affects the comprehension (Leveridge & Yang, 2013), partial captioning may provide insufficient text for beginners or too much text for highly-advanced learners. One solution is to make an interactive environment where learners can provide feedback to the system on selected words. Meanwhile, the system should be able to learn from learners' feedback to address individual's needs.

This paper proposes a machine learning approach that uses learner's feedback on-the-fly to adapt the word selection criteria of PSC with the ever-changing user preferences and video stream. Therefore, we asked the learners to mark the hidden words that they wanted to see in PSC and to omit shown words that were easy for them. The system is then trained based on the learner's feedback and adapted its word selection accordingly (Figure 1).

Figure 1. Learner feedback on the caption to hide a word (top) and to show a masked word (bottom) by clicking on it. The classifier's labels and the decision boundary (dashed line) change according to the learner feedback

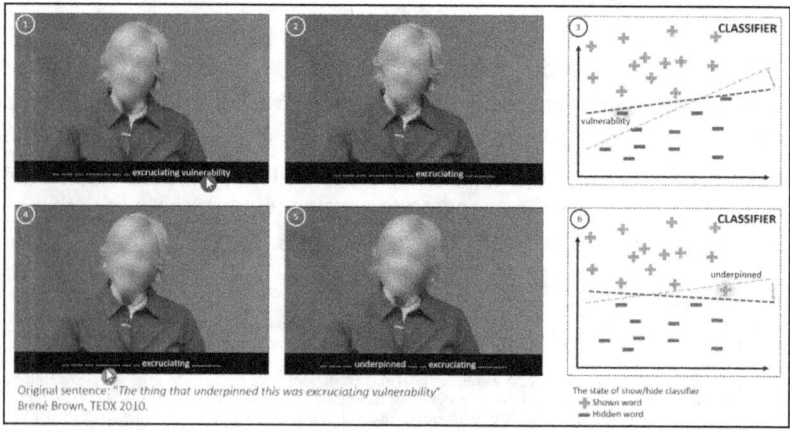

2. APSC

Different lexical, acoustic, and content-based features are considered in PSC. The features are extracted for each word, classifying it as either easy or difficult. A word is classified as difficult when its feature value exceeds some thresholds. Mirzaei et al. (2017) proposed using learners' vocabulary and listening test scores to adjust the thresholds for filtering words and making a caption for learners of similar proficiency groups. However, such a method ignores individual differences within each proficiency group, the limitation of the tests to measure the different listening difficulty features, and the effect of learners' background on their listening comprehension (e.g. engineers listening to medical talks). Moreover, the fixed threshold does not reflect the gradual improvement of learner's listening skills.

Previous analyses revealed that some learners need additional factors to be considered when generating PSC (e.g. speech disfluencies) and others gradually adapt to the listening material (e.g. getting used to vocabulary and speech rate of the speaker), hence no longer needing some words in the caption. To this end, we developed the APSC (Figure 2), in which an online machine learning module receives the feedback from the learners and adjusts the thresholds of the system on-the-fly. The feedback includes user clicks either on a masked word they wish to see or on a shown word that is too easy. The system reacts by showing/hiding the word and learns to intelligently classify words with similar features in the future.

Figure 2. System components and process flow: TED talks are fed to the forced aligner for text-to-speech synchronization. Knowledge bases (e.g. corpora) are used for detecting listening difficulty features. The classifier applies the rules and learner feedback for word selection

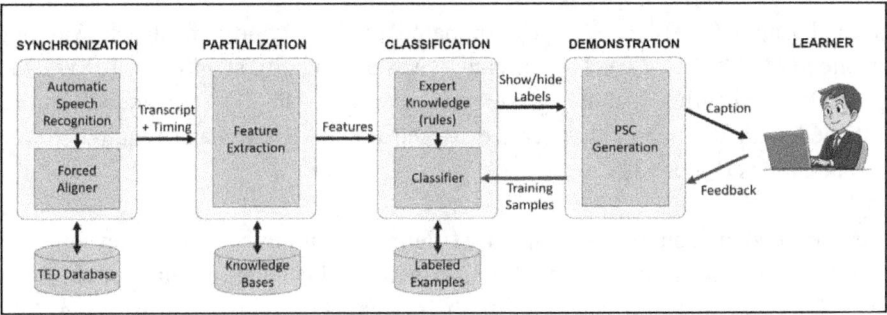

Rather than defining rules, our classifier is trained by giving several examples for each category of words in context. Therefore, it can easily expand to support other

types of listening materials (e.g. daily conversations, news) that require different rules, features, and thresholds. Additionally, the system can detect and learn the discriminative features of the learners' feedback. Such feedback serves as a bag of examples for retraining the system, which can be easily obtained from the learners and used to their advantage. The learner feedback acts as new labels for words that the system misclassified, and the classifier is re-trained with such data to learn about individuals' problems, backgrounds, vocabulary reservoirs, and possible sources of listening difficulties.

3. Preliminary evaluation and discussion

Twenty-four pre-intermediate learners of English, graduate students of Kyoto University with engineering and humanities backgrounds, used our system and provided feedback. They were divided into two groups and were asked to: (1) watch a series of videos captioned by using baseline PSC and provide feedback by clicking on difficult words masked (to be shown), and on the easy words that were shown (to be hidden); and (2) watch another set of videos and provide feedback in a similar way, however, this time the first group received baseline PSC (i.e. their feedback was received but not applied in the PSC), whereas the second group received APSC trained by their annotations in the previous phase.

For each set, learners were given five different two to three minute TED Talk clips delivered by native English speakers. Learners were also asked to do a five-point Likert scale questionnaire on the use of system.

Analysis of the number of modifications for the first and second sets of videos revealed that learners who received APSC required fewer modifications in the second round (M=14.2, SD=1.6) compared to those whose feedback was not applied (M=9.8, SD=2.0). The difference was statistically significant, [$t(8)$=3.74; p=0.006], indicating that the group who received APSC were generally more satisfied with the captions generated by the trained system and required fewer modifications (Figure 3).

Learner feedback on the questionnaire (Figure 4) demonstrated that they enjoyed having control over the captions (Q1, Q4), benefited from individualized captions (Q3, Q5), and were motivated to use the system (Q6) with less frustration (Q7, only asked from the second group). Most learners also believed that this system can be more interesting and useful if it challenges them with more difficult cases (Q2).

Detailed analysis revealed that words with different British and American pronunciations were selected more frequently to be included in the caption. The learners also demanded to show idioms and sentences with complex grammar. Moreover, talks delivered by specific speakers raised more feedback, perhaps due to many speech disfluencies. Additionally, learners with certain backgrounds chose to hide certain words in the captions that were familiar to them.

This system aims to overcome the shortcomings of keyword or partial captioning on ignoring different learner's requirements (Guillory, 1998). Furthermore, unlike the full caption, this system reduces text to facilitate ingesting the multimodal input (Vandergrift, 2011), provides learner control over the generated captions, and tailors the captions for different learners to increase satisfaction.

Figure 3. Analyzing the number of modifications requested in the captions by the learners as an indicator of learner satisfaction of word selection in PSC

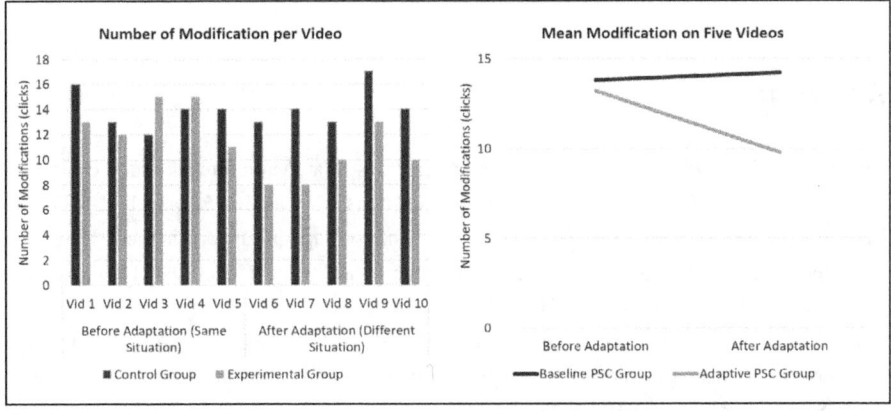

Figure 4. Learner feedback on the questionnaire (APSC group only)

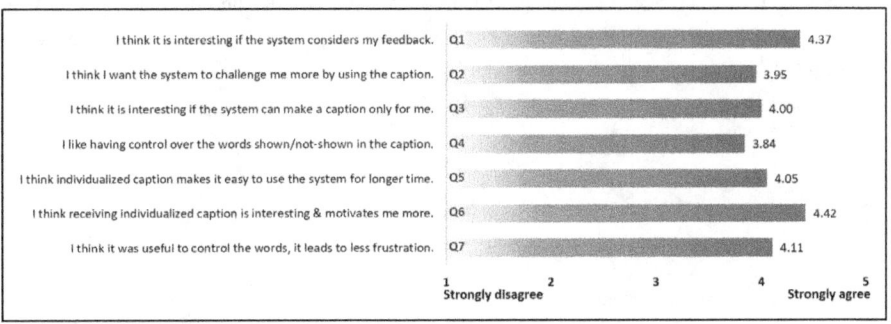

4. Conclusions

We developed an APSC system that considers learner feedback on the word selection, trains itself based on such feedback, and provides more individualized captioning for each learner. The system uses machine learning to identify the listening difficulties of learners by using their feedback as example cases and provides effective scaffolding by selecting necessary words for the captions. System evaluation revealed that our approach is successful in providing tailored captions to the listeners, thus increasing learner satisfaction, while the effectiveness of the system largely depends on the amount of feedback each learner provides.

5. Acknowledgments

This paper was supported by Japan's Ministry of Education, Culture, Sports, Science and Technology (MEXT) Kakenhi grant #17K02925.

References

Guillory, H. G. (1998). The effects of keyword captions to authentic French video on learner comprehension. *Calico Journal*, *15*(1-3), 89-108. https://doi.org/10.1558/cj.v15i1-3.89-108

Leveridge, A., & Yang, J. (2013). Testing learner reliance on caption supports in second language listening comprehension multimedia environments. *ReCALL*, *25*(2), 199-214. https://doi.org/10.1017/s0958344013000074

Mirzaei, M. S., Meshgi, K., Akita, Y., & Kawahara, T. (2017). Partial and synchronized captioning: a new tool to assist learners in developing second language listening skill. *ReCALL*, *29*(2), 178-199. https://doi.org/10.1017/s0958344017000039

Sweller, J. (1994). Cognitive load theory, learning difficulty, and instructional design. *Learning and Instruction*, *4*(4), 295-312. https://doi.org/10.1016/0959-4752(94)90003-5

Vandergrift, L. (2011). Second language listening: presage, process, product, and pedagogy. In E. Hinkel (Ed.), *Handbook of research in second language teaching and learning* (455-471). Routledge.

Collaborative learning through story envisioning in virtual reality

Maryam Sadat Mirzaei[1], Qiang Zhang[2], Kourosh Meshgi[3], and Toyoaki Nishida[4]

Abstract. We developed a story creation platform that allows for collaborative content creation in a 3D environment by utilizing avatars, animations, objects, and backgrounds. Our story envisioning platform provides a shared virtual space that promotes collaborative interaction for story construction, involving a high degree of learner input and control. It allows the L2 learners to perform as actors and directors to create the story and supports offline or online collaboration (online chatting). Using state-of-the-art technologies, the system creates 3D stories from text to be presented in virtual reality. The learner can choose premade assets and input the story script for conversion into story elements and timelines. Experiments with 35 intermediate learners of English on the usability of the system and user engagement confirmed the system's effectiveness to promote learner collaboration, peer support, negotiation, opinion exchange, and critical thinking. Learners found the system to be a powerful tool to visualize their thoughts, and revise/expand their stories, according to questionnaire results. This system brings an interesting and intense language practice that encourages learners to actively participate in the learning process through collaboration.

Keywords: digital story creation, collaborative learning, natural language processing.

---

1. RIKEN AIP/Kyoto University, Kyoto, Japan; maryam.mirzaei@riken.jp; https://orcid.org/0000-0002-0715-1624
2. Kyoto University, Kyoto, Japan; qiang.zhang@riken.jp
3. RIKEN AIP/Kyoto University, Kyoto, Japan; kourosh.meshgi@riken.jp; https://orcid.org/0000-0001-7734-6104
4. Kyoto University, Kyoto, Japan; nishida@i.kyoto-u.ac.jp

How to cite this article: Mirzaei, M. S., Zhang, Q., Meshgi, K., & Nishida, T. (2019). Collaborative learning through story envisioning in virtual reality. In F. Meunier, J. Van de Vyver, L. Bradley & S. Thouësny (Eds), *CALL and complexity – short papers from EUROCALL 2019* (pp. 297-303). Research-publishing.net. https://doi.org/10.14705/rpnet.2019.38.1026

1. Introduction

Storytelling is an effective language practice that promotes learners' literacy skills, motivation, creativity, communication skills, and critical thinking (Ohler, 2013; Yang & Wu, 2012). Developments in multimedia technologies have led to the emergence of digital storytelling, which provides learners with accessible tools to create multimodal stories (Brunvand & Byrd, 2011; Russell, 2010). Such platforms (e.g. Second Life) are increasingly utilized in the Computer Assisted Language Learning (CALL) domain, making learning through storytelling a practical reality (Ribeiro, 2015; Sanchez, 2009).

With technology advancements, digital stories have entered into a new level of immersion and engagement with extensive freedom and control over the content generation. We developed a story creation platform that uses state-of-the-art technologies to receive learners' scenarios as input and convert them into 3D animated stories for further presentation in virtual reality (see the following section). This platform visualizes the story content made by the learners, enables role-play to modify or generate new content, and orchestrates the presentation of the story to control the tone, narration, and perspective. It also allows the learner to envision the story by adding meta-explanations about the characters' feelings and mental states (Figure 1).

Figure 1. Screenshot of a story generated by the system in the 3D environment (Meta-explanation about the character's feeling is added by the learner)

This platform can be utilized to (1) create personalized stories for sharing with others, (2) collaborate with peers to generate an integral story, (3) expand the storyline by building on top of each other's stories, (4) work on disjoint parts of a story in a group and integrate them, and (5) work in different groups to make multiple stories for a given situation. It reinforces self-expression and practical knowledge use by providing personally meaningful practice and feelings of self-inclusion.

Moreover, learners are engaged in meaning construction and content generation, and are encouraged to collaborate not only to generate the stories, but also to play the roles in their stories, to traverse back and forth in the storyline, to navigate between branches of the story, and to expand/revise those branches. Learners can switch between first-person and third person views to experience the story from different perspectives. The platform supports content and language integrated learning as well as situated and experiential learning, where learners are immersed in a virtual situation and interact to generate the content using the L2 (Coyle, Hood, & Marsh, 2010).

This paper investigates the platform's effectiveness in promoting collaboration, motivation, and engagement as well as the system's usability by inviting learners to create stories, observing their interactions with the platform, and asking them to give qualitative feedback via a questionnaire.

2. Story creation tool

Our proposed system analyzes the input from the user to extract different pieces of information that form the story (Figure 2). It extracts the characters of the story and assigns proper avatars to them, resolves their relative location based on the scene description and its arrangement, identifies the actions, and retrieves proper animations. It also handles character interaction in the form of speech and gestures, and classifies the mental process, feelings, and thoughts of the characters provided by the learner as meta-explanations. It allows for the selection of the cameras' point-of-view (first or third person) and cinematography profile to effectively convey the intended message and enable experiencing the situation.

The storyline is then formed as the succession of sequential and parallel actions, enabling learners to create alternative storylines as branches of the main story. Using such features, the system creates a 3D story in Unity3D®, supporting virtual reality to provide a sense of immersion (Figure 3).

Figure 2. System components and process flow

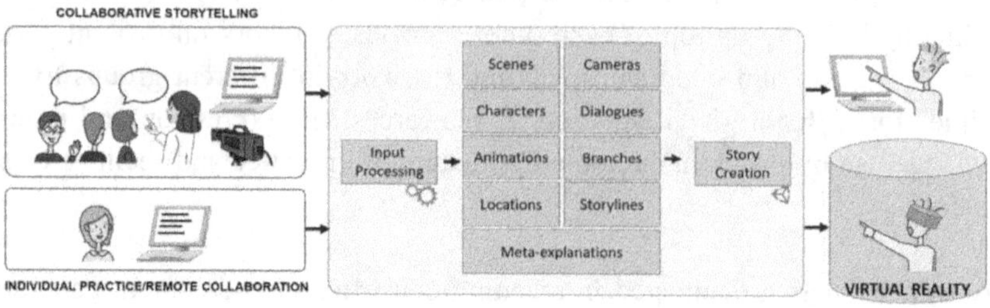

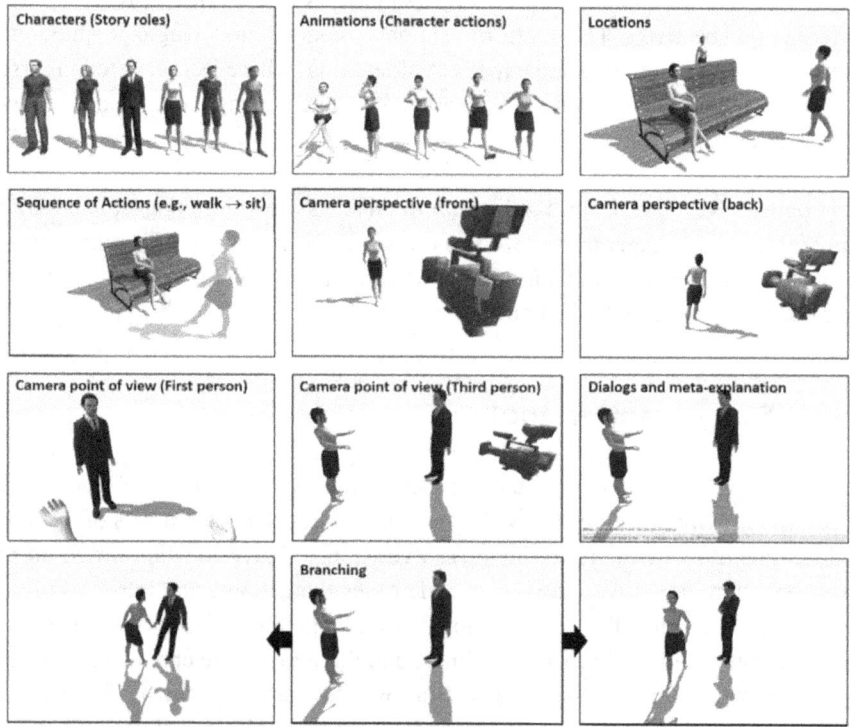

Figure 3. Characteristics of the system

3. Preliminary evaluation and discussion

We asked 35 intermediate learners of English who were graduate students of Kyoto University to use our system in a CALL class and provide feedback. The participants were divided into seven groups and were asked to collaborate to complete a short story. They were given a short opening of the story and the instructions on using the system. The story consisted of five characters and each participant was supposed to play one role. The participants were asked to discuss within the group to draft the final story including characters, actions, dialogs, and meta-explanation. They were instructed to use our tool for generating 3D animated stories and control the camera to make cinematic scenes as a director. The participants then shared their 3D stories with other groups. Finally, learners were asked to do a 5-Likert scale questionnaire, followed by an open-ended question (Figure 4).

As the data suggests, overall, learners were satisfied with the design of our system (Q1-2) and found it easy to use (Q3-5). Participants enjoyed it as the system visualized their imagination, allowed them to act as a director, and enabled inputting meta-explanations (Q6-8). Learners' feedback on Q9-12 showed a high level of learner engagement. Finally, learners acknowledged that they benefited from collaboration in creating stories (Q13-17).

Figure 4.   Learner feedback on the questionnaire

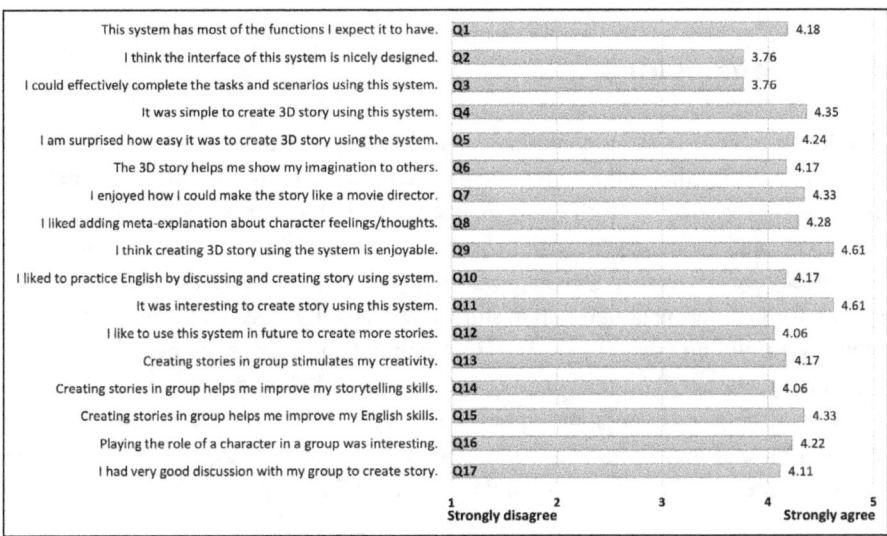

In the open-ended question about using the system, learners repeatedly linked their motivation to the system's ability to create 3D stories and giving life to the characters (e.g. "It is so fun to see characters move", "I like such an easy system to make a 3D story"). The system provided an atmosphere of collaboration, creativity, and critical thinking, with interesting instances of attempting to reach an agreement (e.g. "I don't think she should be kind to him because he was so mean to her"), negotiation of meaning (e.g. "What do you mean by he is unconscious?"), self-expression (e.g. "If I were her, I would leave him"), and especially creative reflection using the system's ability to include meta-explanations (e.g. "I think she felt heartbroken, but not angry"). Moreover, the learners enjoyed watching other groups' stories (e.g. "I liked their storyline", "Surprising idea, it was very original").

Monitoring the session, we observed a high level of learner engagement and motivation as they began to co-construct meaningful scenarios and using the system together. The degree of control over the system's input motivated the participants to actively use this tool for the whole session by generating branches of the story and using different features to direct their story. Moreover, learners actively collaborated to create meaningful and realistic scenarios and used the system as a means of self-expression (Sanchez, 2009). Most learners emphasized that they enjoyed practicing English through story creation using our system. However, they had certain demands that the system could not fulfill at this stage, such as adding voice to the characters, modifying the main scene, and including effects (e.g. explosions).

4. Conclusions

We developed a 3D story creation system to convert learners' scenarios into 3D animations using the scene as the environment, avatars as characters, animations as actions, cameras as different perspectives, dialogs or meta-explanations as narratives, and sequences of actions as the storyline. Learners' feedback revealed a high degree of learner satisfaction, engagement, and motivation in using the system for generating collaborative stories. Moreover, the system promotes learner input by providing control over the story content, stimulates learner creativity by visualizing learner thoughts in 3D, and fosters collaborative learning to create and direct the stories. It is anticipated to be used as a platform for collaborative storytelling and story creation. Future work is to provide synthesized character voices, scene modifications, and adding fine-tuned actions.

References

Brunvand, S., & Byrd, S. (2011). Using VoiceThread to promote learning engagement and success for all students. *Teaching exceptional children, 43*(4), 28-37. https://doi.org/10.1177/004005991104300403

Coyle, D., Hood, P., & Marsh, D. (2010). *Content and language integrated learning*. Ernst Klett Sprachen.

Ohler, J. B. (2013). *Digital storytelling in the classroom: new media pathways to literacy, learning, and creativity* (2nd ed.). Corwin Press. https://doi.org/10.4135/9781452277479

Ribeiro, S. (2015). Digital storytelling: an integrated approach to language learning for the 21st century student. *Teaching English with technology, 15*(2), 39-53.

Russell, A. (2010). ToonTastic: a global storytelling network for kids, by kids. *In Proceedings of the fourth international conference on Tangible, embedded, and embodied interaction* (pp. 271-274). ACM. https://doi.org/10.1145/1709886.1709942

Sanchez, J. (2009). Pedagogical applications of Second Life. *Library Technology Reports, 45*(2), 21-28.

Yang, Y.-T. C., & Wu, W.-C. I. (2012). Digital storytelling for enhancing student academic achievement, critical thinking, and learning motivation: a year-long experimental study. *Computers & education, 59*(2), 339-352. https://doi.org/10.1016/j.compedu.2011.12.012

The use of Quizlet to enhance vocabulary in the English language classroom

Salvador Montaner-Villalba[1]

Abstract. This research focuses on vocabulary acquisition in foreign language learning. The latest trends of teaching as well as the huge advance of technology allow teachers to utilize online and mobile applications through diverse apps. This quasi-experimental design research investigated Quizlet, in its mobile version, on vocabulary acquisition in English as a Foreign Language (EFL). One group of A2 (according to the Common European Framework of Reference for Languages) EFL learners at a state secondary school in Valencia (Spain) (N=24) participated in this study. Learners from the Treatment group (henceforth, T-group) underwent a pre-test and a post-test to assess their acquisition of the assigned vocabulary lessons which were extracted from the course syllabus. After utilizing Quizlet for vocabulary learning for the academic year 2017-2018, the results proved that these learners improved significantly their level of EFL vocabulary at the post-test. Accordingly, this research recommends utilizing Quizlet in its mobile version at secondary education.

Keywords: MALL, vocabulary, EFL, Quizlet.

1. Emergence of Mobile Assisted Language Learning (MALL)

Technology-enhanced language learning has widened the field of language teaching and learning (Abdollapour & Maleki, 2012). This modification, according to Fageeh (2013), is shown by the latest technologies which revolutionized teaching and learning through scaffolding and complementing traditional classroom learning tasks and materials. The increasing use of mobile learning has become relevant in education since it is causing a new generation

---

1. UNED, Madrid, Spain; smontaner@invi.uned.es; https://orcid.org/0000-0002-2742-5738

How to cite this article: Montaner-Villalba, S. (2019). The use of Quizlet to enhance vocabulary in the English language classroom. In F. Meunier, J. Van de Vyver, L. Bradley & S. Thouësny (Eds), *CALL and complexity – short papers from EUROCALL 2019* (pp. 304-309). Research-publishing.net. https://doi.org/10.14705/rpnet.2019.38.1027

of Technology-Enhanced Language Learning (TELL) to emerge (Fageeh, 2013; Kimura, Obari, & Goda, 2011).

By 2015, there were seven billion mobile users in the world (International Telecommunication Union, 2015), representing around 96% of the world population. This widespread use of mobile phone usage makes MALL an inevitable extension of TELL since the mobile phones control all aspects of life (Chinnery, 2006).

MALL is believed to increase second language learning through the real world (Palalas, 2011) and transform the learning process into an informal, interactive, and ubiquitous experience (Kimura et al., 2011; Taj, Sulan, Sipra, & Ahmad, 2016), offering solutions to learning obstacles concerning time and place (Miangah & Nezarat, 2012). Latest applications allow learners to interact through the use of customizable e-flashcards, engaging games, and collaborative tasks. This research is necessary to help learners improve their vocabulary. Quizlet is an interesting example.

As an e-learning app, the efficacy of Quizlet on improving vocabulary is attributed to the increasing role of information and communication technology in all aspects of life. Teenagers are used to utilizing smart devices linked to the internet to perform most of their daily tasks. Moreover, Quizlet enhances active learning both inside and outside the classroom. Within the classroom, the *Live learning* mode offers students collaboration, since learners share information, so that learning becomes cooperative. For this, Quizlet is regarded as the perfect tool for learners to improve vocabulary.

2. Method

2.1. Aim of this study

Quizlet is a mobile and web-based application which utilizes learning modules composed of concepts and their definitions or descriptions. These study sets are introduced to learners through various learning modes which include flashcards, games, collaborative tasks, and quizzes that help learners master different topics and, particularly, languages and vocabulary. This research aims to analyze Quizlet as a tool to learn EFL vocabulary by learners whose L1 is Spanish. To achieve this, this paper pretends to verify that Quizlet improves learners' acquisition of EFL vocabulary.

2.2. Sample

One group of A2 level EFL learners participated in the research. The participants were chosen randomly. There was only the T-group, which included 24 learners who, aged between 14 and 15 years old, were studying their fourth year of compulsory secondary education at the time this experiment developed. These learners were studying at a state secondary school in Valencia.

Both the nature and content of the class was communicative since the teacher aimed to help learners become fully competent. The learners studied the English language for three sessions during the week at school, each session consisting of 45 minutes. Outside the school, the learners were required to limit exposure to English to, at least, between six and eight hours a week to make sure that no vocabulary gains were made outside of the treatment.

2.3. Research tools

This study utilized a quasi-experimental research design including a pre-/post-test group design. Thus, two tests were administered to the learners participating in this experiment. Each test covered five different types of tasks: written, matching, multiple choice, true/false, and spelling. These two tests assessed learners' acquisition of nine units of the course syllabus. The top score of each test was 15 marks divided between the five tasks.

2.4. Procedures

The pre-test was administered after the first three units of the course, and before utilizing Quizlet. The learners' outcomes were recorded for further correlation to the scores of the post-test, which was offered at the end of the academic year after the last three units were taught. During the year, the learners were required to study the three units, which were previously assigned, utilizing Quizlet both outside and inside the EFL classroom. These students attended lessons for three weeks where the same units were taught utilizing *Learn*, *Flashcards*, and *Live learning* modes. Additionally, they were asked to install Quizlet in its mobile version and learn the assigned units outside the school through other learning manners (*Write*, *Test*, *Match*, and *Spelling*).

The researcher designed a learning set for each unit where illustrations, paraphrasing, and L1 annotation are employed to explain the meaning of the new words. Next, a diagram is shown to make clear the organization and timeline of the different tasks (Figure 1).

Figure 1. Organization and timeline of the different tasks

```
Units 1, 2, and 3 were taught in traditional manner.
                    ⇓
The pre-test was administered.
                    ⇓
Quizlet was utilized to review vocabulary from Units 1, 2, and 3 both outside and inside the classroom.
                    ⇓
Units 4, 5, and 6 were taught in a traditional way.
                    ⇓
Quizlet was used to review vocabulary from Units 4, 5, and 6 both outside and inside the classroom.
                    ⇓
Units 7, 8, and 9 were taught in a traditional manner.
                    ⇓
Quizlet was employed to review vocabulary from Units 7, 8, and 9.
                    ⇓
The post-test was administered through the *test* mode in Quizlet.
```

The outcomes of both the pre-test and the post-test were then analyzed in order to verify the hypothesis research.

3. Outcomes

The learners achieved the outcomes which are shown in Table 1 below. It should be mentioned that the t-tests were paired samples since we are measuring changes in the same students.

Table 1. Mean scores and t-test outcomes of the scores (Cohen's *d*)

	Measure, mean (SD)		t-Student		d
	Pre	Post	t(23)	p-value	
TOTAL	5.98 (1.22)	7.39 (1.05)	-14.035	< 0.001	2.86
WRITTEN	5.75 (1.57)	7.21 (1.72)	-7.669	< 0.001	1.56
MATCHING	5.67 (1.55)	7.25 (1.65)	-15.402	< 0.001	3.14
MULTIPLE CHOICE	5.46 (1.77)	6.83 (1.52)	-6.382	< 0.001	1.30
TRUE/FALSE	5.67 (1.79)	7.21 (1.59)	-7.73	< 0.001	1.58
SPELLING	7.38 (1.79)	8.46 (1.32)	-3.844	0.001	0.78

The written variable is lower in the pre-test than in the post-test. The matching variable is lower in the pre-test than in the post-test. This happens again with the multiple choice. The same occurs with the true/false variable and, lastly, outcomes of the spelling variable are higher in the post-test than in the pre-test.

4. Discussion and conclusion

In general, the mean scores implied that there was a significant improvement of the outcomes of this group. The media of the post-test is 7.39, significantly higher than the pre-test (5.98). However, the Standard Deviation (SD) of the scores of this group at the post-test was only 1.11, which is slightly lower than the SD at the pre-test (1.22). The difference in SD between both tests was very small. This suggests that their scores were more homogenous after studying with Quizlet, and hence involved that the effect of the application on all participants was more consistent in comparison with the classic methods where a huge modification between the learners' outcomes were witnessed.

Related to the outcomes of the different variables in Table 1, we can clearly see that the results improved significantly at the various post-tests in comparison with the corresponding pre-tests. Moreover, the total media of the post-test is notably higher than the pre-test. This means that the participants in the experiment improved their level of EFL vocabulary through Quizlet. This significant improvement of the outcomes in the various post-tests may result from the mobile version specifically, such as out-of-class exposure as well as immediate feedback. For this reason, it is recommended that learners practice vocabulary through Quizlet.

References

Abdollapour, Z., & Maleki, N.A. (2012). Second language vocabulary acquisition in CALL and MALL environments and their effect on L2 vocabulary retention: a comparative study. *Australian Journal of Basic and Applied Sciences, 6*(9), 109-118.
Chinnery, G. M. (2006). Emerging technologies: going to the MALL: mobile assisted language learning. *Language learning & technologies, 10*(1), 9-16.
Fageeh, A. A. I. (2013). Effects of MALL applications on vocabulary acquisition and motivation. *Arab World English Journal, 4*(4), 420-447.
International Telecommunication Union. (2015). *ICT facts & figures: the world in 2015.* ITU.
Kimura, M., Obari, H., & Goda, Y. (2011). Mobile technologies and language learning in Japan. In M. Levy, F. Blin, C. B. Siskin & O. Takeuchi (Eds), *WorldCALL: international perspectives on computer-assisted language learning* (pp. 38-54). Routledge. https://doi.org/10.4324/9780203831762

Miangah, T. M., & Nezarat, A. (2012). Mobile-assisted language learning. *International Journal of Distributed and Parallel Systems, 3*(1), 309-319. https://doi.org/10.5121/ijdps.2012.3126

Palalas, A. (2011). Mobile-assisted language learning: designing for your students. In S. Thouësny & L. Bradley (Eds), *Second language teaching and learning with technology: views of emergent researchers* (pp. 71-94). Research-Publishing.net. https://doi.org/10.14705/rpnet.2011.000007

Taj, I. H; Sulan, N. B.; Sipra, M. A., & Ahmad, W. (2016). Impact of mobile assisted language learning (MALL) on EFL: a meta-analysis. *Advances in language and literary studies, 7*(2), 76-83. https://doi.org/10.7575/aiac.alls.v.7n.2p.76

Designing tasks for developing complex language skills and cognitive competence in the distance learning of Slovak as a foreign language

Michaela Mošaťová[1] and Jana Výškrabková[2]

Abstract. The Slovak language is one of the less commonly taught languages, and its learners worldwide have few options in terms of its study and practice. One of them, however, is the www.e-slovak.sk e-learning platform provided by the Studia Academica Slovaca Centre at the Comenius University Faculty of Arts in Bratislava, Slovakia. This article summarises a two year experience teaching Slovak in two tutored e-learning courses of e-slovak levels A1 and A2 (CEFR, 2001). The article focusses mainly on the tasks contributing to the development of productive communication skills (speaking and writing). We explored to what extent various language learning tasks are efficient in terms of developing complex language skills and engaging students' cognitive skills in accordance with Anderson et al.'s (2001) revised Bloom's taxonomy of teaching objectives.

Keywords: e-learning, language learning tasks, cognitive competence, revised Bloom's taxonomy.

1. Introduction

Learning a language usually means gradually developing all four fundamental language skills, i.e. receptive – listening comprehension and reading comprehension – and productive speaking and writing. It is crucial to provide sufficient space to students' balanced and complex development, which is a great challenge when designing and managing online language courses. For the purposes of this paper, we used an e-learning platform for Slovak as a foreign language, available at

---

1. Comenius University, Bratislava, Slovakia; michaela.mosatova@uniba.sk
2. Comenius University, Bratislava, Slovakia; vyskrabkova2@uniba.sk

How to cite this article: Mošaťová, M., & Výškrabková, J. (2019). Designing tasks for developing complex language skills and cognitive competence in the distance learning of Slovak as a foreign language. In F. Meunier, J. Van de Vyver, L. Bradley & S. Thouësny (Eds), *CALL and complexity – short papers from EUROCALL 2019* (pp. 310-313). Research-publishing.net. https://doi.org/10.14705/rpnet.2019.38.1028

the website www.e-slovak.sk. Learners have to use various general knowledge, abilities, and skills to handle varied communication situations effectively (CEFR, 2001). We also consider as important the development of cognitive skills based on Anderson et al.'s (2001) revised Bloom's taxonomy. Thus, the research question in this study is which variables of tasks support the development of learners' speech and written production, and simultaneously stimulate their cognitive competence.

The data in this research are collected from the e-learning portal of the Slovak language in which tutor-supported courses for levels A1 and A2 are available. Data represent students' essays and recordings. We analysed the task and its impact on students' assignments. Both courses approximately correspond to the textbooks *Krížom-krážom – slovenčina A1* and *Krížom-krážom –slovenčina A2*. They consist of ten topic-based units, and each of them contains dialogues with new words, phrases, illustrations, and reading and listening, followed by self-evaluation exercises, a short final test, as well as two assignments, one recording and one essay. There are no course fees associated with the work in the e-slovak course.

2. Method

The participants of the research were 22 adults enrolled in the tutor-supported course e-slovak A1 in 2017, 62 people in the tutor-supported course e-slovak A1 in 2018, 17 people in the tutor-supported course e-slovak A2 in 2017, and 38 students in the tutor-supported course e-slovak A2 in 2018. They completed ten units in ten months. It means each group was supposed to write ten essays and create ten recordings, although the number of students in each group decreased during the course – the course finished with 50% of the students.

Tasks were bilingual (in Slovak and English) in the A1 course and monolingual (in the target language) in the A2 course. Tasks were appropriate for learner language skills (basic vocabulary and simple morphologic and syntactic features).

In our research, we compared the parameters of the recording and essay tasks and the resulting student assignments. We were inspired by the cognitive hypothesis (Robinson, 2005; Robinson & Gilabert, 2007) according to which pedagogic tasks should be designed, and then sequenced, for learners on the basis of increasing their cognitive complexity.

Anderson et al.'s (2001) revised Bloom's taxonomy provided a framework to think about the tasks and helped us to analyse them as far as teaching objectives and aims were concerned. Within this framework, we analysed the tasks and how the instructions influenced students' essays and recordings using qualitative methods. Mostly, we aimed at two parameters: the length of the texts or recordings and the extent of developing the topic of the tasks. On the basis of this analysis the following criteria emerged.

3. Discussion

As we were focussed on designing tasks in order to support communicative language skills, based on the analysed recordings and essays, few criteria proved significant. We consider the following standards to be the most relevant.

Open-ended questions concerning the content provide a broad range of possibilities and ways in which students can answer them. There are no sub-questions which can incite the students to reply unequivocally and briefly. For instance, in the type of task such as *Introduce yourself* (*What is your name?*, *Where are you from?*, *How old are you?*, *What is your profession?*, *How are you?*), which contains few specific sub-questions, students tend to answer more stereotypically in comparison with the task, for example, *Who are you?*. This allows students to respond creatively in many ways.

Another type of question oriented to the students, that is learner-oriented tasks, offers students a huge space for self-expression. Students can compare their own life with others, and moreover, in intercultural-oriented questions, their own culture with the target culture. These kinds of tasks supported learners' motivation, as well as their language skills. Students are aware of the meaningfulness and usability of these tasks, which is also a strong motivational factor. Regarding this, using real sources, e.g. searching for information on the actual websites, publications, etc. is also efficient.

To simulate real communication situations in our courses, a tutor is in the course as a 'communication partner'. This claim supports the tasks from the e-slovak course, for example, *Napíšte svojmu tútorovi/svojej tútorke, čo ste robili včera* [write to your tutor what you did yesterday]. Feedback from the tutor acts as an elemental communication with students, and it also includes the evaluation of assignments or other tasks, and explaining problems in grammar. Addressing recordings and essays directly to the tutor was for students a motivational factor, which students' final questionnaires proved.

The level of cognitive demands of the task is another factor which influences the successfulness of students in learning a language. In compliance with Anderson et al.'s (2001) revised Bloom's taxonomy, we assume that the higher level of cognitive demands supports the motivation and involvement of students in no small extent. However, it is essential that the tasks are not overly demanding, because in such a case it causes a reverse effect on learning. Therefore, in the e-slovak courses, we included tasks corresponding to various levels of cognitive demands, going from 'remembering' to 'creating' in the cognitive process dimension, and from 'factual knowledge' to 'procedural knowledge' in the knowledge dimension according to Anderson et al.'s (2001) revised Bloom's taxonomy. Regarding the last level of the knowledge dimension, 'metacognitive knowledge' in the e-slovak courses is implicitly included within the whole course. However, the essays and recordings are not individually focussed on it.

4. Conclusions

This study has outlined possibilities and conditions in which designers and teachers can support the improvement of productive communication skills and build a complex and balanced communication competence in an e-learning environment. The involvement of recordings and essays in the tutor-supported e-slovak courses A1 and A2, and written or audio feedback by tutors for each assignment, proved to be motivating and beneficial in online teaching and learning. Tasks which cover all levels of Anderson et al.'s (2001) revised Bloom's taxonomy support the betterment of all language skills and help to acquire a language more effectively.

References

Anderson, L. W., Krathwohl, D. R., Airasian, P. W., Cruikshank, K. A., Mayer, R. E., Pintrich, P. R., Raths, J., & Wittrock, M. C. (2001). *A taxonomy for learning, teaching and assessing. A revision of Bloom's taxonomy od educational objectives* (Abridged edition). Longman.

CEFR. (2001). *The common European framework of reference for languages: learning, teaching, assessment*. Cambridge University Press. https://rm.coe.int/1680459f97

Robinson, P. (2005). Cognitive complexity and task sequencing: a review of studies in a componential framework for second language task design. *International Review of Applied Linguistics in Language Teaching, 43*(1), 1-33. https://doi.org/10.1515/iral.2005.43.1.1

Robinson, P., & Gilabert, R. (2007). Task complexity, the cognition hypothesis and second language learning and performance. *International Review of Applied Linguistics in Language Teaching, 45*(3), 161-176. https://doi.org/10.1515/iral.2007.007

■ UCLouvain

An iCALL approach to morphophonemic training for Irish using speech technology

Neasa Ní Chiaráin[1] and Ailbhe Ní Chasaide[2]

Abstract. A key benefit in intelligent Computer Assisted Language Learning (iCALL) is that it allows complex linguistic phenomena to be incorporated into digital learning platforms, either for the autonomous learner or to complement classroom teaching. The present paper describes (1) complex phonological/ morphophonemic alternations of Irish, which are problematic for many learners; (2) an iCALL platform, *An Scéalaí*, which uses speech technology and Natural Language Processing (NLP) prompts to train writing and aural skills – in this paper the target is the morphophonemic alternations of (1); and (3) a perception experiment to guide how the platform might be used for prompt-based self-correction. The perception experiment has been carried out using newly built synthetic voices based on deep neural network technology.

Keywords: iCALL, text-to-speech synthesis, Irish, phonological contrasts, morphophonemics, linguistic complexity.

1. Introduction

Learning a second language may entail dealing with complex linguistic phenomena which have no parallel in the first language. In the case of Irish, there are complex phonological and morphophonological aspects which present numerous difficulties to learners and which are not common to other 'familiar' Western European languages. As detailed below, inadequate mastery of these structural elements impacts greatly on written accuracy as well as pronunciation accuracy.

---

1. Trinity College Dublin, Dublin, Ireland; neasa.nichiarain@tcd.ie; https://orcid.org/0000-0002-4669-5667
2. Trinity College Dublin, Dublin, Ireland; anichsid@tcd.ie

How to cite this article: Ní Chiaráin, N., & Ní Chasaide, A. (2019). An iCALL approach to morphophonemic training for Irish using speech technology. In F. Meunier, J. Van de Vyver, L. Bradley & S. Thouësny (Eds), *CALL and complexity – short papers from EUROCALL 2019* (pp. 314-320). Research-publishing.net. https://doi.org/10.14705/rpnet.2019.38.1029

In this paper, we are concerned with how an iCALL platform can serve as a vehicle for the training of these specific language skills, training not only the phonological and morphophonological processes, but also their realisation in the written language. The platform under development, *An Scéalaí* (the storyteller), uses speech technology – here text-to-speech (TTS) synthesis – to ensure that all four language skills are nurtured together and that the spoken language is at the heart of all learning activities. It functions as an intelligent tutor: the learner first composes a piece of text and is then guided through prompts, both auditory and textual, with the goal of enabling self-correction. Being speech-based, it seems ideally suited to the training of the morphophonological aspects of the language, which are the focus here. This platform incorporates NLP capacities where the prompts being offered to the learner are based on linguistic-phonetic knowledge, drawing in many cases on linguistic modules that are core components of the TTS system. It also draws on pre-existing resources such as online dictionaries and spelling and grammar checkers (Scannell, 2013).

2. Complex phonological and morphophonemic targets

The sound system of Irish contrasts palatalised and velarised pairs of consonants. For example, 'leon' /lʲo: nʲ/ (*lion*) and 'lón' /lˠo: nˠ/ (*lunch*). This contrast is of fundamental importance for lexical differentiation but also for grammatical differentiation, for example the morphophonological alternation of velarised and palatalised final consonants is used to signal number and case (e.g. bád /bˠa: dˠ/ (*boat*), báid (/bˠa: dʲ/ (*boat: plural and genitive case*)). In this paper we focus on noun number.

The orthographic conventions of Irish are rather complex in how the contrast is signalled. The consonant is not marked, but the palatalisation-velarisation (*slender* and *broad* in vernacular parlance) difference is shown by the adjacent vowel letter used – front vowel letters (i, e) marking palatalisation and back vowel letters (a, o, u) marking velarisation. A spelling rule, '*broad-with-broad and slender-with-slender*', dictates that the vowel letters before and after a consonant letter have to come from the same set, front or back.

Unfortunately, the phonic basis of the spelling rule is not appreciated by learners or by most teachers. Rather, the consonantal difference is entirely missed (at least consciously) by learners. The spelling rule is rather vacuous and understood to be something simply to do with the visual written forms, rather than a basic rule of pronunciation.

3. An Scéalaí as a personal intelligent tutor

An Scéalaí works as a personalised intelligent platform (see Ní Chiaráin & Ní Chasaide, 2018). After initial registration and personal profile creation, the learner writes a story (Figure 1).

Figure 1. *An Scéalaí* user interface where learners compose their story

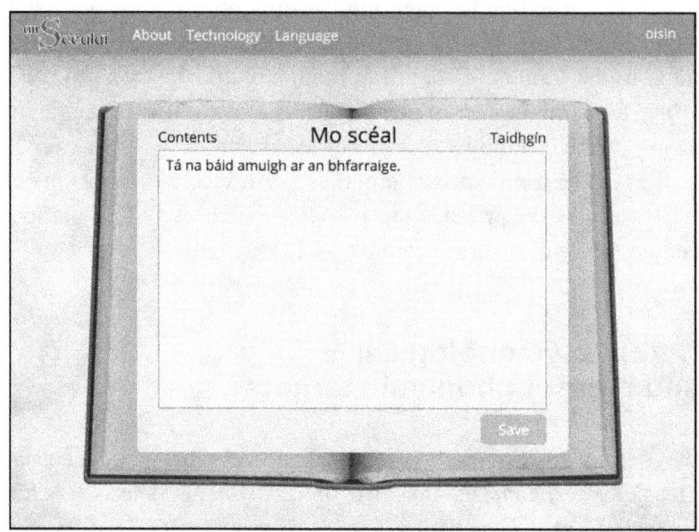

Figure 2. How to use the platform

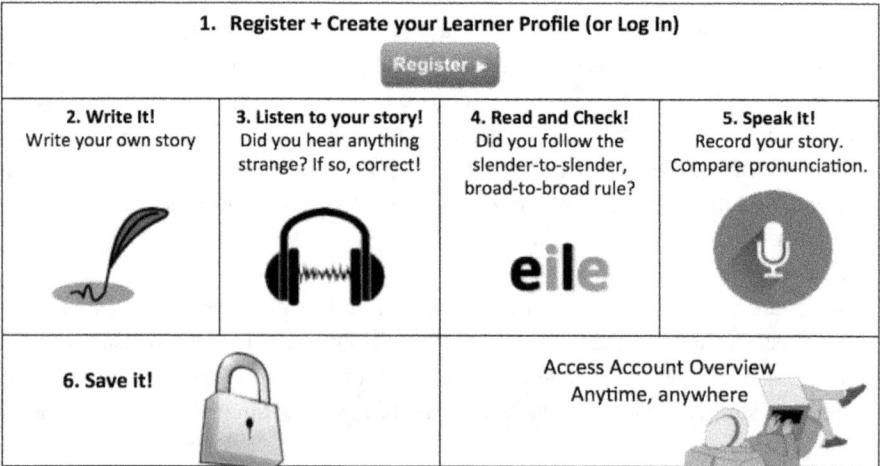

An iCALL approach to morphophonemic training for Irish using speech technology

Learners are then directed to follow specific steps to improve the piece (see 2-5 in Figure 2 above):

- write a story;

- listen back to the story (using TTS), and correct;

- read back over the story (using NLP prompts), and correct; and

- record yourself reading the story aloud (compare recording with native-like TTS).

3.1. Present problem

The focus here is on the morphophonemic alternation of palatalised versus velarised consonants to differentiate singular and plural. However, when an error appears, it is not necessarily obvious whether this is the result of (1) a simple typo, (2) a lack of discrimination (phonological awareness) on the part of the learner (do they *hear* the difference?), or (3) a lack of understanding of the grammatical role in signalling plurals. The prompting process can help illuminate which of the above is the case for a particular learner in a particular instance.

The second step in *An Scéalaí* requires learners to listen to their written text spoken by the TTS voice. This proof listening step may be all that is required for proficient learners in that they can simply hear errors because they 'sound wrong'. However, if the targeted errors fail to be corrected, the learner is then prompted in two ways. First, a chatbot intervenes and points out that they have failed to indicate (in this case) the plural form. If this does not suffice, a text version is also provided and the learner's written text is highlighted with colour coding that signals precisely where the rule has been contravened. For example, the learner writes « Tá **na bád** amuigh ar an bhfarraige » (*The *boat (definite article plural + noun singular) are at sea*). (Note the correct version is '**na báid**' (*definite article plural + noun plural*)).

- Step 1, the learner listens and self corrects; if the error is missed they move on to Step 2.

- Step 2, the chatbot says "An bád amháin nó níos mó na bád amháin atá i gceist agat?" (*Are you referring to one or to more than one boat?*); if the error is missed the learner moves on to Step 3.

- Step 3, the text feedback says "Tá *na* bád amuigh ar an bhfarraige" (red/italics (slender indicator) should match red and not blue/bold (broad indicator)).

3.2. Justifying use of prompt

The goal is to use auditory and visual feedback to reinforce the phonological contrast and train its morphophonological (grammatical) usage. However, in order to examine to what extent the prompts are effectively used in the learning process, certain tests are required, as follows:

(1) Pre-test the synthetic voices:

- Does the TTS adequately produce the contrast so it is clearly audible (test proficient speakers)?

(2) Learner Phonological Awareness (PA) test:

- Is the particular learner/cohort aware of (discriminating) the consonantal contrast?

(3) Efficacy of prompting test:

- Auditory prompting: can the TTS prompting (listening only) lead to the ability to hear the error (when the slender consonant is not produced)? This suggests the PA is OK, and that the grammatical rule is understood.

- Written prompting: is it only the written prompt that leads to correction (as a vacuous spelling rule)? This suggests the PA is not OK, and the grammatical rule is meaningless as it involves only the written 'correct' form, and lacks phonic basis. There is a need to go back to PA training.

The following section describes a perception experiment to test (1) above.

4. Perception experiment

This experiment is designed to ascertain that the TTS voice is producing sufficiently clear differentiation of the contrast in the context where plurality is expressed. The experimental setup involved:

- materials in which a set of words was compiled to cover all final velarised consonants (and many final consonant clusters) which should yield palatalised counterparts in plural forms (all first declension masculine nouns, n=38); and

- participants (n=25) were presented with a survey interface (*Limesurvey*) where they hear either the singular or plural form of the noun and are asked to transcribe the word they hear. In the event that they hear the difference but misspell the answer they are also asked to specify whether the form they heard was singular or plural. They are further asked to rate the ease with which each item was judged (see results in Figure 3). Before the task begins, they enter their biographical information and level of Irish.

The experiment was advertised to proficient speakers of Irish via Twitter and was carried out online. The first 25 responses are analysed for this paper.

5. Results

Results were overwhelmingly positive. The majority of transcriptions were accurate. Unsurprisingly, the items deemed most difficult were those where very few instances exist in the language, i.e. finals in -b/ and -f/ (Figure 3).

Figure 3. Limesurvey responses displaying one to eight of 25 results for final consonant 'g' in 'clo(i)g' *(clock(s))* where participants transcribed the TTS output and specified it was 'uatha' *(singular)* or 'iolra' *(plural)*

Déan trascríobh ar an bhfocal ...	An san uimhir uatha nó san uim...	Bhí sé...
clog	Uatha (an...) [A1]	An-éasca le tuiscint [A2]
Clog	Uatha (an...) [A1]	An-éasca le tuiscint [A2]
clog	Uatha (an...) [A1]	Réasúnta soiléir le tuiscint [A4]
clog	Uatha (an...) [A1]	An-éasca le tuiscint [A2]
Clog	Uatha (an...) [A1]	Éasca le tuiscint [A3]
clog	Uatha (an...) [A1]	Éasca le tuiscint [A3]
Clog	Uatha (an...) [A1]	Réasúnta soiléir le tuiscint [A4]
clog	Uatha (an...) [A1]	Éasca le tuiscint [A3]

Déan trascríobh ar an bhfocal ...	An san uimhir uatha nó san uim...	Bhí sé...
cloig	Iolra (na...) [A2]	An-éasca le tuiscint [A2]
Cloig	Iolra (na...) [A2]	An-éasca le tuiscint [A2]
cloig	Iolra (na...) [A2]	Éasca le tuiscint [A3]
cloig	Iolra (na...) [A2]	Éasca le tuiscint [A3]
Cloig	Iolra (na...) [A2]	Réasúnta soiléir le tuiscint [A4]
cloig	Iolra (na...) [A2]	Éasca le tuiscint [A3]
Cloig	Iolra (na...) [A2]	Éasca le tuiscint [A3]
cloig	Iolra (na...) [A2]	An-éasca le tuiscint [A2]

6. Conclusion

This experiment eliminates one fundamental source of uncertainty that could arise from prompting this morphophonological process of Irish. Since the participants successfully transcribed the prompts, it is clear that the phonological distinction is robustly carried in the synthetic output. Current research is directed at the second and third steps outlined in the section above.

7. Acknowledgement

This research is funded by the Department of Culture, Heritage, and the Gaeltacht, Government of Ireland (ABAIR project).

References

Ní Chiaráin, N., & Ní Chasaide, A. (2018). An Scéalaí: synthetic voices for autonomous learning. In P. Taalas, J. Jalkanen, L. Bradley & S. Thouësny (Eds), *Future-proof CALL: language learning as exploration and encounters – short papers from EUROCALL 2018* (pp. 230-235). Research-publishing.net. https://doi.org/10.14705/rpnet.2018.26.842

Scannell, K. (2013). An Gramadóir: an open source grammar checking engine, Version 0.70. https://cadhan.com/gramadoir/

■ UCLouvain

Children's perspectives on the use of robotics for second language learning in the early years of primary education: a pilot study

Susan Nic Réamoinn[1] and Ann Devitt[2]

Abstract. This paper explores how floor programmable robotics can be used during play to promote language development. This paper describes a two-day pilot in two early years classrooms and presents data collected on children's perception of the Irish language and using robotics. A sample of 48 children (age range six to seven years) took part in a robotics activity using a bee-shaped robot, called Beebot. The activity was orientated around the children's second language, Irish. The children took part in a questionnaire before and after the activity about the language and the use of the robot in promoting their use of the language. Data was also collected through video, photos, a focus group, and the teacher's observations. The main finding of the pilot study was an increase in children's positive responses towards using the language when integrated into a robotics play activity.

Keywords: language, learning, robotics, early years, play.

1. Introduction

This research is situated in the Irish curriculum framework of play, known as Aistear (NCCA, 2009). The activity integrates the language curriculum, specifically the children's second language, Irish, and a technology resource: programmable floor robots. Language lessons are taught every day and the Irish language is used informally throughout the day. Play in the context of the Aistear curriculum framework is the perfect opportunity to develop that living language for young children. This study looks at the development of the second language during play.

1. Trinity College Dublin, Dublin, Ireland; nicramos@tcd.ie
2. Trinity College Dublin, Dublin, Ireland; devittan@tcd.ie; https://orcid.org/0000-0003-4572-0362

How to cite this article: Nic Réamoinn, S., & Devitt, A. (2019). Children's perspectives on the use of robotics for second language learning in the early years of primary education: a pilot study. In F. Meunier, J. Van de Vyver, L. Bradley & S. Thouësny (Eds), *CALL and complexity – short papers from EUROCALL 2019* (pp. 321-326). Research-publishing.net. https://doi.org/10.14705/rpnet.2019.38.1030

Robotics provides a playful way for teachers to integrate curriculum content with the development of meaningful projects (Bers, Seddighin, & Sullivan, 2013). While using robotics, children are given the opportunity to experiment with engineering concepts as well as telling stories by narrating contexts for their projects (Bers, 2008). By engaging in these types of robotics projects, young children play to learn while learning to play in a creative context (Bers et al., 2013; Resnick, 2003). In this study, children are developing their language skills by making meaningful connections through play and robotics. This study explores the use of robotics in a play environment for language learning, and how the intervention can both motivate children to learn and use Irish. This area is an identified gap in the research literature on robotics in early years education.

2. Method

The pilot study explores the following research questions.

- What are children's perspectives of using robots during play-based learning as an opportunity to use their new language?

- Can robots facilitate language learning in the early years of primary education?

- Do programmable floor robots motivate children to learn and use a new language?

To answer these questions, 48 children from two schools participated in this study. Day 1 took place in a boy's school (27 participants; age range six to seven years), and Day 2 took place in a girl's school (21 participants; age range six to seven years). Written consent was obtained from participants' parents/guardians and written assent from the children. An interview took place with the teacher on Day 1 and a focus group with two groups of children on Day 2.

On both days, the children completed a questionnaire about learning Irish before and after the activity. A focus group was conducted with two groups on Day 2. Their language lesson lasted for 30 minutes and then they were asked to participate in a play activity in a small group using a programmable robot, Beebot (see Figure 1), for a twenty-minute period. Beebot is a programmable floor robot that looks like a bee. The robot can move forward and backwards 15 cm, turn at 90-degree angles, and can pause. The code to move the robot can be inputted by pushing the directional buttons on his back and the robot can take up to 40 commands. Once Beebot has completed its route, it will make a sound alerting the children to the end of the program they have inputted. Beebot was designed to move around on a floor map and, during the activity for this study, the floor map was designed for this specific context by the researcher and the classroom teacher. This map displays pictures and words that children have been learning in the Irish language lesson.

Figure 1.   Beebot

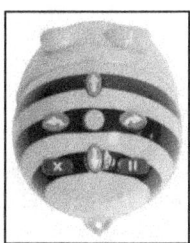

3.   Results

3.1.   Questionnaire

The children answered two questionnaires. One prior to the activity and one after. The questionnaire after the activity had an additional four questions about the robot. Children responded by colouring a cartoon face associated with yes, no, or maybe (see Table 1).

Table 1.   Pre and post-intervention questionnaire

Pre-intervention questions	Post-intervention questions
I like learning Irish.	I like learning Irish.
I like using my Irish words.	I like using my Irish words.
I have lots of chances to use my Irish words.	I have lots of chances to use my Irish words.
We use technology to learn Irish.	We use technology to learn Irish.
Technology makes me want to learn more.	Technology makes me want to learn more.
	I talk to the robot in Irish.
	Is using robots to learn Irish fun?
	Robots help me to learn more Irish.
	Robots make me want to use more Irish.

As shown in Figure 2, the results of the questionnaire showed an increase of yes answers in the post-questionnaires on both days across the first four questions while there was a decrease in yes answers on Day 2 for Question 5.

Figure 2. Comparison of yes responses from boys and girls

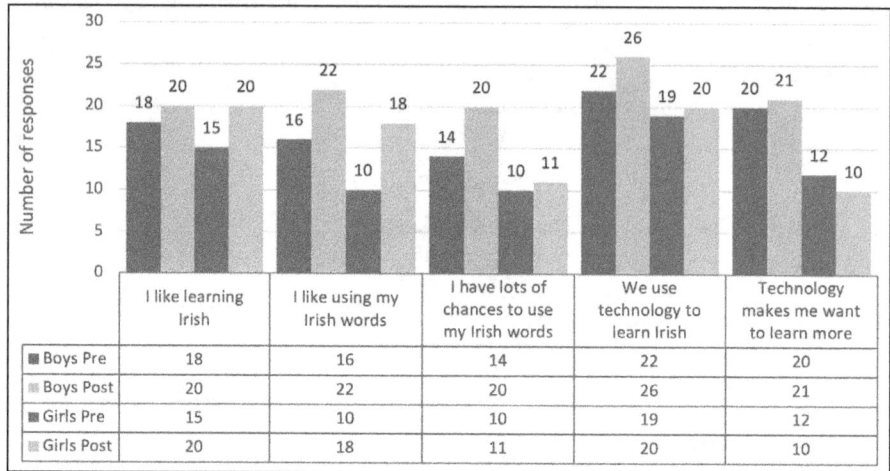

The additional four questions after the activity which focused on the robot produced positive responses across both days of the pilot.

The boys on Day 1 gave more yes responses to the question 'robots make me want to use more Irish' (22 yes responses, five no responses and zero maybe responses), while the girls' responses on Day 2 were the same between yes and maybe (nine yes responses, three no responses, and nine maybe responses).

3.2. Focus group

A focus group took place on Day 2 of the pilot study with two groups of six children. The children were asked about using Beebot for learning Irish. The resounding comments from both groups were positive about using the robot and the impact it had on their learning. One child commented, "well they move lots of ways and make some noise. Yeah we really enjoy them because it helps us with our Irish".

At the end of the focus group, the children were asked for any additional comments on using the Beebot. The children compared the activity to other activities that were available to them during the play-based activities session. One child commented on how the Beebot activity also included maths, it was more stimulating, and gave them an opportunity to use their imagination more: "there's lots of maths and cause of maths it helps get our imagination better instead of just going to blocks. When we're at blocks everything was really boring".

3.3. Teacher

The classroom teacher on Day 1 was interviewed after the activity. The teacher observed one child in the class who she would describe as having very little interest in Irish generally and who was more enthusiastic and engaged in the language because of the activity: "his behaviour and everything would have been a lot calmer than he normally would be – a lot more focused". She was surprised at the child's language production and their positive behaviour during the activity. When asked would this be an activity she would incorporate into the classroom the teacher commented:

> "I could see myself being able to cover loads of topics and loads of language. I just thought that they were really motivated. I don't see their motivation dwindling that quickly I would imagine, you could get a long time out of them [Beebots], and they would still be highly motivated and then obviously because you can change the language on the maps that you're using".

4. Discussion and conclusions

This study addresses an important gap in the research literature on the use of robots for language learning with young children. It echoes the findings of previous studies in other domains that children find the use of robots in learning motivating (Kazakoff, Sullivan, & Bers, 2013).

This pilot study would suggest that the functional context of robotics provides a functional context for the use of the language – another critical factor in Irish language learning as the language is not widely spoken as a community language (Devitt et al., 2018). The children themselves comment on the benefits of integrating other curriculum areas (in this case maths) to build interest. Future research, however, would need to include a larger population and statistical analysis to confirm or refute our preliminary results.

References

Bers, M. U. (2008). Engineers and storytellers: using robotic manipulatives to develop technological fluency in early childhood. In O. N. Saracho & B. Spodek (Eds), *Contemporary perspectives on science and technology in early childhood education* (pp. 105-125). Information Age Publishing.

Bers, M., Seddighin, S., & Sullivan, A. (2013). Ready for robotics: bringing together the T and E of STEM in early childhood teacher education. *Journal of Technology and Teacher Education, 21*(3), 355-377.

Devitt, A., Condon, J., Dalton, G., O'Connell, J., & Ní Dhuinn, M. (2018). An maith leat an Ghaeilge? An analysis of variation in primary pupil attitudes to Irish in the growing up in Ireland study. *International Journal of Bilingual Education and Bilingualism, 21*(1), 105-117. https://doi.org/10.1080/13670050.2016.1142498

Kazakoff, E., Sullivan, A., & Bers, M. U. (2013). The effect of a classroom-based intensive robotics and programming workshop on sequencing ability in early childhood. *Early Childhood Education Journal, 41*(4), 245-255. https://doi.org/10.1007/s10643-012-0554-5

NCCA. (2009). *Aistear - the early childhood curriculum framework. Guidelines for good practice*. National Council for Curriculum and Assessment.

Resnick, M. (2003). Playful learning and creative societies. *Education Update, 8*(6), 1-2.

Improving the English skills of native Japanese using artificial intelligence in a blended learning program

Hiroyuki Obari[1] and Stephen Lambacher[2]

Abstract. A constructivist approach to language learning can motivate students by activating their brains to create new knowledge and reflect more consistently and deeply on their language learning experience. The present study focused on assessing the use of the Artificial Intelligence (AI) speakers Google Home Mini and Amazon Alexa as part of a Blended Learning (BL) environment to improve the English skills of two groups of native Japanese undergraduates. The participants were 47 native speakers of Japanese, all third-year business majors at a private university in Tokyo. Pretest and posttest Test of English for International Communication (TOEIC) scores, as well as results from a post-training survey, were used in evaluating the overall effectiveness of the program. Gains in TOEIC scores indicated the BL program incorporating AI speakers improved the students' overall English skills, particularly listening comprehension. The results suggest the integration of AI, along with social media and 21st-century skills, may be an effective way to improve the English language proficiency of adult L2 learners.

Keywords: AI speakers, blended learning, intercultural awareness, mSNS, 21st-century skills.

1. Introduction

Recently, AI speakers can be experienced efficiently and smoothly using hand-held devices, which can enhance the construction of broader learning environments and viewpoints (Kepuska & Bohouta, 2018). AI/mobile technologies have succeeded in transforming learning methodologies. One such methodology adopted successfully in recent years is BL (Obari & Lambacher, 2014). BL combines

---

1. Aoyama Gakuin University, Tokyo, Japan; obari119@gmail.com; https://orcid.org/0000-0002-9203-6785
2. Aoyama Gakuin University, Tokyo, Japan; steve.lambacher@gmail.com; https://orcid.org/0000-0001-8216-5543

How to cite this article: Obari, H., & Lambacher, S. (2019). Improving the English skills of native Japanese using artificial intelligence in a blended learning program. In F. Meunier, J. Van de Vyver, L. Bradley & S. Thouësny (Eds), *CALL and complexity – short papers from EUROCALL 2019* (pp. 327-333). Research-publishing.net. https://doi.org/10.14705/rpnet.2019.38.1031

traditional face-to-face classroom methods with computer-mediated activities, resulting in a more integrated approach to language learning. AI, mobile devices, and social media are key components of the next generation of this novel wave of educational instruction. Digital content is also transforming and expanding as AI and mobile technologies continue to develop and improve. The growth of mobile Social Networking Sites (mSNS) has enabled teachers to considerably increase the number of ideal learning opportunities through experiential learning activities with the help of these emerging technologies (Wong, Tan, Loke, & Ooi, 2015).

The main purpose of this study is to introduce two case studies carried out with the goal of ascertaining the effectiveness of a BL training program incorporating the AI speakers Google Home Mini and Amazon Alexa to improve the English proficiency of native Japanese, including 21st-century learning for developing intercultural awareness.

The following research questions were targeted:

- Could the participants improve their English proficiency and understanding of 21st century skills after exposure to the AI/BL activities?

- Was the application of AI/mobile learning helpful in improving the participants' English skills?

Pedagogy of 21st century skills with AI

Harvard researcher Tony Wagner identified the '7 Survival Skills' necessary for the modern workplace (Wagner, 2014):

- critical thinking and problem solving;
- collaboration;
- agility and adaptability;
- initiative and entrepreneurialism;
- effective oral and written communication;
- accessing and analyzing information; and
- curiosity and imagination.

In addition to the above 7 survival skills, we added another skill referred to as 'Coexistence with AI' – resulting in 8 survival skills for 21st-century education. In this study, we attempt to integrate these 8 survival skills for developing English proficiency and intercultural awareness.

2. Method

2.1. Participants

The study was conducted over a period of two semesters (September 2018 to July 2019). A total of 47 undergraduates participated, all native speakers of Japanese. Participants were divided into two groups: Group 1 (n=24) during the first training period (September 2018 to January 2019) and Group 2 (n=23) during the second training period (April 2019 to July 2019).

2.2. Training procedure

Technologies utilized in training included Google Home Mini, Amazon Alexa, ATR CALL Brix, mSNS programs Facebook, Twitter, and Line, as well as a number of other English language programs and applications. TOEIC was used as a measure to determine if the students' English skills improved and to help ascertain the overall effectiveness of the BL program. TOEIC was administered to Group 1 as a pretest in September 2018 and posttest in January 2019, and to Group 2 as a pretest in April 2019 and posttest in July 2019.

During AI speaker training, participants of both groups were divided into eight subgroups, with half using Google Home Mini and the other half using Amazon Alexa. The AI speakers were literally integrated into the daily lives of the participants over the four-month training period. A timer was regularly set while interacting with the AI speakers to practice English listening, speaking, and vocabulary skills with a variety of software programs.

Group 1 used Google Home Mini daily to improve English listening and speaking skills using the following programs: Best Teacher, Travel English, Let's play around with English, and BBC/CNN news. Group 2 used Alexa daily to improve their listening comprehension and vocabulary skills using the following programs: Kikutan, English Quiz by Arc, Liberty English, and Kindle. Participants of both groups used virtual reality goggles for interaction in a variety of authentic L2 learning environments.

While studying with the AI speakers, participants recorded short movie clips of their learning experiences, which they uploaded to Facebook. The participants also periodically maintained written diaries of their observations about the contents and duration of their studies, recording their thoughts using a smartphone.

At the completion of training, participants from all eight subgroups delivered presentations of their experiences and impressions of the BL-lesson training using the AI speakers, with a majority indicating the training had a positive effect on their English language learning.

In conjunction with the above AI training procedure, the following additional tasks were incorporated during training.

(1) Practice English using the AI speakers Google Home Mini and Amazon Alexa (as mentioned above).

(2) Watch online TED Talks, including Rick Warren's 'Purpose-Filled Life' (Warren, 2012) and other popular subjects, using their mobile devices; write 300-word summaries, create PowerPoint (PPT) presentations, and discuss summaries with a group of English native speakers.

(3) Study worldviews after viewing online lectures by several Oxford University scholars, which focused on ontological and epistemological issues, and deliver PPT presentations and create digital stories with iPads.

(4) Use ATR CALL Brix to practice TOEIC.

(5) Study the theory behind 21st century skills and with iPads deliver PPT presentations summarizing the contents.

(6) Interact with English native speakers who assessed the presentations and discussed worldviews and cultural issues with the participants – the native speakers were eight university students from the US.

(7) Periodically participate in supplementary interactions and discussions.

3. Results and discussion

3.1. Pretest/posttest TOEIC

The TOEIC pretest and posttest results of Group 1 (n=24) during the first training period (September 2018 to January 2019) increased from a mean score of 422 (*SD*:115) to 617 (*SD*: 114), or equivalent to B1 CEFR[3].

Figure 1.   Group 1 pretest vs. posttest TOEIC scores

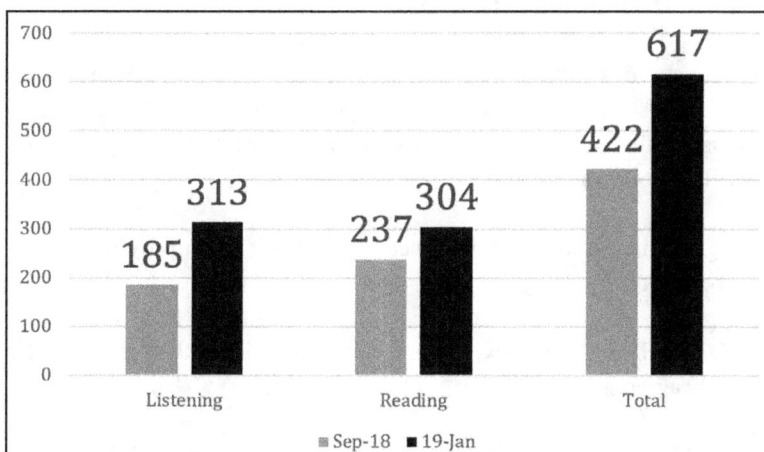

Figure 2.   Group 2 pretest vs. posttest TOEIC scores

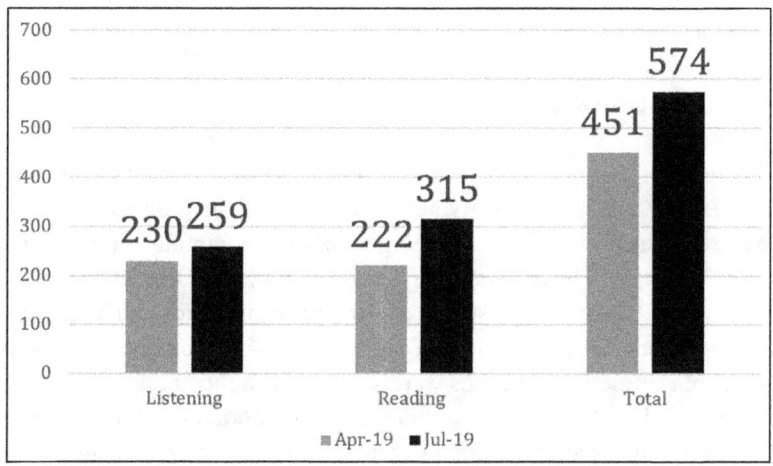

As shown in Figure 1, Group 1 improved both their listening and reading scores. Their listening scores, in particular, increased from a mean of 185 (*SD*=55) to 313 (*SD*=76). Similarly, the overall TOEIC scores of Group 2 (n=23) participants

---

3. CEFR (Common European Framework of Reference for languages) – language competencies defined at six levels from beginner to near native fluency: level A1 (the lowest) through A2, B1, B2, C1, and C2 (the highest).

331

increased from a mean of 451 (*SD*:125) to 574 (*SD*:93), or equivalent to B1 CEFR (Figure 2). The pre/posttest TOEIC results were analyzed using a series of t-tests, indicating these differences were statistically significant (p<.01).

3.2. Post-training questionnaire

Post-training surveys (n=47) were administered to both groups at the end of their respective AI/BL training period for the purpose of ascertaining their overall impressions of the program. Responses to a few of the survey questions are summarized as follows:

> (Q1) The online lectures were beneficial in improving my English proficiency: 88% agreed.

> (Q2) mSNS (Facebook, Line, Twitter) was helpful in studying English: 92% agreed.

> (Q3) This program was useful in learning 21st-century skills: 90% agreed.

> (Q4) The AI speaker assisted in improving my English skills: 84% agreed.

4. Conclusions

An assessment of the pretest and posttest TOEIC scores revealed the combination of the AI/BL lessons had a positive effect on students' overall English language learning experience. Students' listening and oral communication skills were improved, which may have been due to the integration of the language learning activities which focused on a social constructivist approach while utilizing the AI smart speakers Alexa and Google Home Mini. Additionally, the post-course questionnaire revealed both groups were satisfied with the online course materials and motivated by the AI/BL environment incorporating 21st-century skills. Students cited improved recognition of ambiguities within cross-cultural contexts and improved global communication skills. Students' oral summaries improved through interaction with the AI smart speakers and native English speakers. Taken as a whole, these results would seem to indicate the integration of AI smart speakers into the BL training program played a role in improving the students' overall language proficiency and in expanding their worldviews. Nevertheless, we should not fail to mention this study was merely a start with further research required, including a more controlled experiment utilizing AI speakers exclusively during training, to more accurately evaluate noticeable gains in participants' improvement.

5. Acknowledgments

This work was supported by a grant from the Japan Society for the Promotion of Science (JSPS) KAKENHI Grants-in-Aid number JP19K00798, and The SOKEN Research Institute.

References

Kepuska, V., & Bohouta, G. (2018, January). Next-generation of virtual personal assistants (Microsoft Cortana, Apple Siri, Amazon Alexa and Google Home). In *2018 IEEE 8th Annual Computing and Communication Workshop and Conference* (CCWC) (pp. 99-103). IEEE. https://doi.org/10.1109/ccwc.2018.8301638

Obari, H., & Lambacher, S. (2014). Impact of a blended environment with m-Learning on EFL skills. In S. Jager, L. Bradley, E. J. Meima & S. Thouësny (Eds), *CALL design: principles and practice - proceedings of the 2014 EUROCALL Conference, Groningen, The Netherlands* (pp. 267-272). Research-publishing.net. https://doi.org/10.14705/rpnet.2014.000229

Warren, R. (2012). *The purpose driven life: what on earth am I here for?* Zondervan.

Wagner, T. (2014). *The global achievement gap: why even our best schools don't teach the new survival skills our children need-and what we can do about it.* Hachette UK.

Wong, C.-H., Tan, G. W.-H., Loke, S. P., & Ooi, K.-B. (2015). Adoption of mobile social networking sites for learning? *Online Information Review, 39*(6), 762-778. https://doi.org/10.1108/oir-05-2015-0152

■ UCLouvain

Time to evaluate: the students' perspective of an online MA in CALL programme

Salomi Papadima-Sophocleous[1] and Christina Nicole Giannikas[2]

Abstract. Despite the critical importance of Computer Assisted Language Learning (CALL) Teacher Education (CTE) programmes, L2 practitioners often report that there are not many such onsite/online programmes, and the ones that exist may not directly meet their specific needs. Moreover, there seems to be a lack of systematic evaluation studies of such courses. As a result, problems in such courses cannot be diagnosed, and they are left unresolved. This paper presents a study undertaken to evaluate an online Master's of Arts (MA) in CALL programme in the Republic of Cyprus. The investigation was based on a conceptual multidimensional e-learning evaluation model rated by the students. Data were collected from 25 graduate students via an online anonymous survey. This focussed on the participants' perceptions of the value of the following aspects: (1) their engagement; (2) the course and its organisation, teaching mode, and materials; (3) course strengths; (4) course aspects most helpful to learning; and (5) course aspects which were obstacles to learning. This paper discusses the findings and offers some first recommendations for further improvement to the MA in CALL programme.

Keywords: evaluation research, CALL teacher training programme evaluation, higher education, students' perspectives.

1. Introduction

In the last decades, substantial research has been dedicated to CTE. The research of Hubbard and Levy (2006), Torsani (2016), Hauck and Kurek (2017), and Jordano de la Torre (2019) are indicative. However, a brief review in the area of CTE programme evaluation reveals that this area still "warrants considerably more

---

1. Cyprus University of Technology, Limassol, Cyprus; salomi.papadima@cut.ac.cy; https://orcid.org/0000-0003-4444-4482
2. Cyprus University of Technology, Limassol, Cyprus; christina.giannikas@cut.ac.cy; https://orcid.org/0000-0002-5653-6803

How to cite this article: Papadima-Sophocleous, S., & Giannikas, C. N. (2019). Time to evaluate: the students' perspective of an online MA in CALL programme. In F. Meunier, J. Van de Vyver, L. Bradley & S. Thouësny (Eds), *CALL and complexity – short papers from EUROCALL 2019* (pp. 334-339). Research-publishing.net. https://doi.org/10.14705/rpnet.2019.38.1032

professional – and international – attention" (Hubbard & Levy, 2006, p. ix). This paper presents a study undertaken to evaluate an online MA in CALL programme in the Republic of Cyprus. The investigation was based on a conceptual multidimensional e-learning evaluation model rated by the students.

2. Method

The present investigation concentrates on the evaluation of an online MA in CALL programme (running since September 2015) from the students' viewpoint. The paper presents the results of the research study implemented at the end of the academic year 2018-2019.

2.1. Participants

Nineteen students (80% of the total programme population over a period of four years) from Cyprus University of Technology, ranging between 22 to 60 years old, participated in this study. The grade point average mean of females was 2.80, while that of males was 2.52, out of a possible 4.00.

2.2. A conceptual multidimensional e-learning evaluation model

The investigation proposed a conceptual multidimensional e-learning evaluation model focussing on: (1) their engagement; (2) the course and its organisation, teaching mode, and materials; (3) course strengths; (4) course aspects most helpful to learning; and (5) course aspects which were obstacles to learning

2.3. Procedure

The data collection was conducted between May and June 2019. The online survey was distributed to 25 students. Nineteen participants submitted a signed consent form and completed the online survey anonymously.

2.4. Instrument and data collection

The online survey contained questions on the eight modules:

- LCE510 Second Language Acquisition;
- LCE511 Teaching Methodologies;
- LCE512 L2 Instructional Technologies;

- LCE513 L2 Curriculum Review and Improvement and Evaluation;
- LCE514 Research Methodologies in Applied Linguistics;
- LCE515 Computer Assisted Language Assessment and Testing;
- LCE516 Mobile Assisted Language Learning;
- LCE517 CALL from the Student Perspective.

The survey consisted of 58 questions and supported quantitative and qualitative elements. Likert scale closed-ended questions were applied. Respondents were presented with a set of verbal answer options – Disagree (D), Strongly Disagree (SD), Neutral (N), Agree (A), Strongly Agree (SA) – to cover a range of opinions, and 32 open-ended questions. Open-ended questions were also included and covered three aspects: (1) course strengths; (2) course aspects most helpful to learning; and (3) course aspects which were obstacles to learning.

3. Data analysis, results and discussion

3.1. Quantitative data

A key research issue was to investigate the merits and shortcomings of the MA course. Participants were asked to evaluate their engagement in the process (Table 1).

Table 1. Students' engagement

Engagement	LCE_510 n19	LCE_511 n19	LCE_512 n19	LCE_513 n19	LCE_514 n19	LCE_515 n19	LCE_516 n19	LCE_517 n19
Q1. Effort	n:10A n:9SA	n:1N n:6A n:12SA	n:1Nl n:5A n:13SA	n:6A n:13SA	n:10A n:9SA	n:1N n:6A n:12SA	n:1N n:8A n:11SA	n:1N n:8A n:11SA
Q2. Punctuality	n:2D n:5N n:3A n:9SA	n:1SD n:1D n:3N n:6A n:8SA	n:2D n:3N n:6A n:8SA	n:2D n:3N n:5A n:9SA	n:2D n:3N n:7A n:7SA	n:3D n:4N n:4A n:8SA	n:3D n:4N n:3A n:9SA	n:2D n:5N n:5A n:7SA
Q3. Participation consistency (webinars)	n: 3A n: 16SA	n: 5A n: 14SA	n: 5A n: 14SA	n: 5A n: 14SA	n: 3A n: 16SA	n:1D n: 3A n: 15SA	n:1D n: 3A n: 15SA	n: 5A n: 14SA

Time to evaluate: the students' perspective of an online MA in CALL programme

Q4. Consistency on weekly tasks	n:3D n:1N n:5A n:10SA	n:2D n:6A n:11SA	n:3D n:1N n:5A n:10SA	n:3D n:1N n:5A n:10SA	n:3D n:1N n:5A n:10SA	n:5D n:2N n:3A n:9SA	n:3D n:3N n:2A n:11SA	n:2D n:5N n:3A n:9SA

High numbers show that students believed to have put in a considerable amount of effort (Q1), and are highly consistent when it comes to attending webinars (Q3). However, numbers tend to drop in Q2 and Q4, regarding students' punctuality and consistency in completing their weekly tasks. While students feel they make great efforts to evolve as students and are present when there is immediate contact with their peers and instructors during online webinars, maintaining consistency and punctuality in their autonomous learning proved a challenge.

The study investigated structure and materials used in order to evaluate the quality of the course and its content. Table 2 displays data per module.

Table 2.   Course structure and material

Course structure and materials	LCE_510 n19	LCE_511 n19	LCE_512 n19	LCE_513 n19	LCE_514 n19	LCE_515 n19	LCE_516 n19	LCE_517 n19
Q1. Well organised	n:1N n:10A n:8SA	n:1N n:8A n:10SA	n:1N n:7A n:11SA	n:10A n:9SA	n:1N n:8A n:10SA	n:1N n:8A n:10SA	n:8A n:11SA	n:8A n:11SA
Q2. Webinars, readings, and assignments complemented each other	n:9A n:10SA	n:1N n:6A n:12SA	n:8A n:11SA	n:8A n:11SA	n:9A n:10SA	n:1N n:7A n:11SA	n:7A n:12SA	n:8A n:11SA
Q3. Materials were appropriate	n:1N n:8A n:10SA	n:1N n:8A n:10SA	n:8A n:11SA	n:8A n:11SA	n:1N n:7A n:11SA	n:9A n:10SA	n:9A n:10SA	n:9A n:10SA
Q4. Assignments contributed to my knowledge	n:2N n:10A n:7SA	n:2N n:7A n:10SA	n:5N n:4A n:10SA	n:3N n:8A n:8SA	n:8A n:11SA	n:10A n:9SA	n:9A n:10SA	n:8A n:11SA

The students' evaluations of the structure and material used throughout the MA programme offered insights on whether the planning and construction of the modules are well-presented, efficient, and beneficial to students' learning. The responses complement the previous segment of student engagement, as the structure and materials used in each module, to an extent, explain the positive outcomes of Table 1. In the current segment, the only section where students felt indifferent was in Q4, where they were asked about their assignments. This outcome was anticipated after the analysis of the first segment, as the students' greatest challenge was the consistency and punctuality of their assignments. This comes back to the nature of the online MA and the fact that students are encouraged to work autonomously and construct their learning. Their autonomous skills demand greater development, as students need further practice in self-training to reach the peak of their productivity.

3.2. Qualitative data

The qualitative component uncovered students' thoughts and opinions. The open-ended questions focussed on (1) strengths of the course, (2) parts that aided students' learning, and (3) parts that were obstacles to their learning of each module. Themes re-occurred for all modules and emerged from the data coding. The most common themes are described in Table 3 below.

Table 3. Students' thoughts and opinions

Course strength	Parts of the programme that aided students' learning	Parts that were obstacles to their learning
Flexibility	Guidance	No obstacles (6 students)
Clarity	Collaboration	Workload (4)
Constructivism	Computer-based tools	Meeting deadlines (3)
Reflection	Weekly activities	Continuous reflective journals (1)
Increased digital awareness	Reflections	Weekly reflection exhausted me sometimes (1)
Instant feedback	Resources	Sometimes feedback was not given promptly or it was given not long before submission deadlines (1)
Relatable to daily practice	Webinars	
CALL-focus		
Combination of theory and practice		

The students found the postgraduate programme materials, webinars, guidance, and content highly beneficial and they have advanced their CALL understanding and practice. Six stated they did not identify any parts of the programme hindering their learning. However, four found the workload heavy; three found meeting deadlines difficult. One found continuous reflective journal writing tiring; another found it sometimes exhausting. One also had an issue with feedback promptness.

One interesting outcome is that all modules have been similarly evaluated sharing the majority of the same positives and challenges.

4. Conclusions

There is a need to identify the extent to which programmes meet students' needs. The present paper reflects the effort to evaluate the MA in CALL from the students' perspective. The results were mostly positive, both in terms of student input and in terms of the programme evaluation. However, further investigation into the workload, weekly activities, and time limit issues are necessary.

References

Hauck, M., & Kurek, M. (2017). Digital literacies in teacher preparation. In S. Thorne & S. May (Eds), *Language, education and technology. Encyclopedia of language and education* (3rd ed.). Springer. https://doi.org/10.1007/978-3-319-02237-6_22

Hubbard, P., & Levy, M. (Eds). (2006). *Teacher education in CALL*. John Benjamins Publishing Company.

Jordano de la Torre, M. (2019). Training language professionals to be digitally proficient in an undergraduate and postgraduate context. In C. Goria, L. Guetta, N. Hughes, S. Reisenleutner & O. Speicher (Eds), *Professional competencies in language learning and teaching* (pp. 41-52). Research-publishing.net. https://doi.org/10.14705/rpnet.2019.34.913

Torsani S. (2016). *CALL teacher education: language teachers and technology integration*. Sense Publishers.

Tablets in second language learning: learners' and teachers' perceptions

Amira Shouma[1] and Walcir Cardoso[2]

Abstract. This study explores the perceptions of English as a Second Language (ESL) learners and teachers on using tablets in their language classrooms, focusing on the device's four inherent affordances: learnability, usability, motivation, and willingness to use the technology. Adopting a quantitative and qualitative approach for data collection and analysis, our findings revealed overall positive perceptions from both ESL learners and their teachers on all four measures adopted (all above 3.4/5); these results were also corroborated by our thematic analysis of the interviews.

Keywords: MALL, tablets, ESL learners, ESL teachers.

1. Introduction

The four themes that guided our study (i.e. learnability, usability, motivation, and willingness to use the technology) are commonly found in most Mobile Assisted Language Learning (MALL) perception studies. What is known about users' perceptions of MALL-based pedagogy (including tablet and non-tablet devices) is that students and their instructors view the use of these platforms positively. For instance, it has been acknowledged that the use of MALL-based pedagogy has the potential to enhance learning in the following ways: (1) it improves the overall learning experience, i.e. learnability (Diemer, Fernandez, & Streepey, 2013); (2) it increases learners' levels of comfort, i.e. usability (Itayem, 2014); (3) it boosts motivation (Cardoso, 2011; Huang, 2013); and (4) it increases students' willingness to use the technology (Cumming & Rodriguez, 2013).

---

1. Concordia University, Montreal, Canada; amshouma@yahoo.com; https://orcid.org/0000-0002-3895-6716
2. Concordia University, Montreal, Canada; walcir.cardoso@concordia.ca; https://orcid.org/0000-0001-6376-185X

How to cite this article: Shouma, A., & Cardoso, W. (2019). Tablets in second language learning: learners' and teachers' perceptions. In F. Meunier, J. Van de Vyver, L. Bradley & S. Thouësny (Eds), *CALL and complexity – short papers from EUROCALL 2019* (pp. 340-344). Research-publishing.net. https://doi.org/10.14705/rpnet.2019.38.1033

Although previous research has investigated the pedagogical use of tablets in the domain of higher education (e.g. Cidre, 2015), elementary and secondary education (e.g. Kirsch & Bes Izuel, 2016), students with disabilities (e.g. Cumming & Rodriguez, 2013), and teacher training (e.g. Hopkins & Burden, 2015), there is little research exploring the perceptions of ESL students and even less involving their teachers (Cifuentes, Maxwell, & Bulu, 2011).

2. Method

This study explores the perceptions of 45 young adult ESL learners and their 11 teachers on the use of tablets (predominantly Apple iPads) in their classrooms at an English language school in Montreal, Canada. A quantitative and qualitative approach was used to collect and analyze the data.

For the quantitative aspect of the study, participants were asked to anonymously fill-out a survey consisting of five-point Likert scale items (ranging from 'strongly disagree' to 'strongly agree' – learners' and teachers' surveys questions were adapted from Rossing, Miller, Cecil, & Stamper, 2012; and Young, 2016 respectively), which probed their perceptions of the four target themes: (1) learnability (n=14; e.g. using iPads helps me improve my listening skills in English), (2) usability (n=12; e.g. I find it is easy for my students to use iPads in reading activities), (3) motivation (n=11; e.g. using iPads motivates me to read English texts), and (4) willingness to use tablets (n=10; e.g. I will use the iPad for teaching my classes in the future). To verify the internal consistency of the items included under each perception marker, a Cronbach's alpha analysis was run on the survey data of all participants. All Cronbach's alpha coefficients were greater than .70, indicating high internal reliability within each theme adopted in the study.

Figure 1. General design of the study: themes and instruments

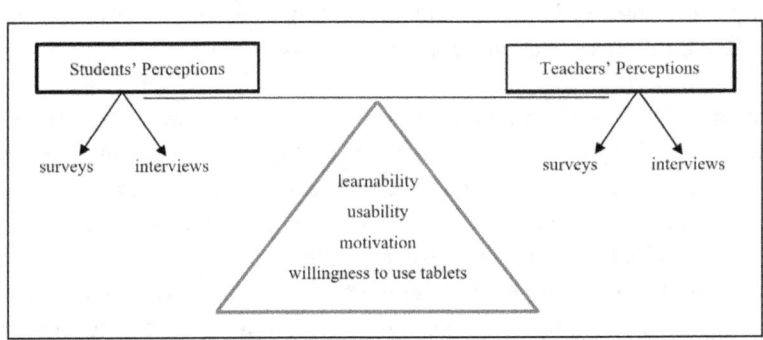

Finally, the qualitative data were obtained through face-to-face interviews (e.g. *What do you think are the benefits [or disadvantages] of using iPads for learning English?*), which were subjected to a thematic analysis. Figure 1 above displays the general design of the study.

3. Results and discussion

Our findings revealed positive perceptions from both ESL learners and teachers on all four measures adopted. As can be observed in Table 1, the participants rated their experience using tablets mostly above 3.4 (/5) on all four thematic measures adopted. Table 1 provides a detailed breakdown of the results.

Table 1. Learners' and teachers' perceptions on learnability, usability, motivation, and willingness to use tablets

	Learnability		Usability		Motivation		Willingness to use tablets	
	M/5	SD	M/5	SD	M/5	SD	M/5	SD
Learners	3.27	0.10	3.5	0.14	3.14	0.25	3.58	0.12
Teachers	3.42	0.21	3.57	0.17	3.16	0.17	3.46	0.24

Note. All mean values are out of 5.

These results were also corroborated by our thematic analysis of the interviews. Overall, users displayed positive attitudes toward using iPads pedagogically. From the learners' perspectives, for instance, participants believed that they: (1) improved their English ("I can increase my listening or practice my speaking") – learnability; (2) highlighted the convenience of using iPads in learning English ("we can take more notes in more details") – usability; (3) emphasized their motivation and interest in using the device ("I think it makes the education easier") – motivation; and (4) expressed their willingness to continue using tablets, particularly because of their professional needs ("I prefer to use iPads because our society is developing, so we need to use this in the future") – willingness to use.

Consistent with the literature, our results indicate that there was an overall positive attitude from both learners and teachers toward the use of iPads in L2 education. As such, our findings regarding users' perceptions on *learnability, usability, motivation*, and *willingness to use iPads* comply with previous studies on learners' and teachers' attitudes toward their use in L2 classrooms (e.g. Diemer et al., 2013; Young, 2016). In particular, our findings align with those reported in Itayem (2014), where a clear relationship was found between learners' perceived *learnability*, *usability*, and *willingness* to use iPads. As learners recognized the usability and learnability potentials of the device, they became more willing to use it in their future language learning endeavors.

4. Conclusions

To conclude, our findings revealed that, overall, both students and teachers view the pedagogical use of the target technology positively across the four themes. As such, the study's main contribution is to add more data and analysis to the investigation of users' perceptions of the pedagogical implementation of technology (tablets in our case), particularly including both learners and teachers. Another interesting contribution is that, contrary to most previous studies that acknowledged a potential 'novelty effect' in their findings (e.g. Cardoso, 2011, for whom the effect is claimed to positively affect performance in the initial stages of the pedagogical implementation of a new technology), most learners (n=31/45) and teachers (n=11/11) stated that they had been using iPads pedagogically for more than one year. This way, our findings can be said to provide a more accurate and reliable portrayal of users' perceptions of tablets, after the novelty effect has worn off.

Based on the results and the users' recommendations for implementing tablet-based L2 education, there are some implications that we would like to put forward, on the assumption that an ill implementation of any technology can considerably diminish its pedagogical impact (Rossing et al., 2012). Importantly, to ensure the proper and effective use of tablets in class, teachers need to build up their knowledge of technology through adequate training, in order to enhance their level of comfort with the device. Furthermore, providing teachers with devices and allowing them to have enough preparation time ensures a well-established pedagogical infrastructure (Young, 2016), which will foster higher comfort levels among its users (Diemer et al., 2013) and, consequently, increase the chances of the technology being effectively and efficiently integrated into the L2 classroom.

5. Acknowledgments

We would like to thank Dr Teresa Hernandez Gonzalez, Dr Denis Liakin, Dr Angelica Galante, and Ms. Jennifer Banton for their feedback and other assistance in the development of this study. Special thanks go to the students and teachers who participated in the study.

References

Cardoso, W. (2011). Learning a foreign language with a learner response system: the students' perspective. *Computer Assisted Language Learning, 24*(5), 393-417. https://doi.org/10.1080/09588221.2011.567354

Cidre, E. (2015). Using iPads as a dynamic learning tool to develop skills in graphic communication and enhance spatial awareness. In N. Souleles & C. Pillar (Eds), *iPads in higher education: proceedings of the 1st International Conference on the Use of IPads in Higher Education* (pp. 1-4). Cambridge Scholars Publishing.

Cifuentes, L., Maxwell, G., & Bulu, S. (2011). Technology integration through professional learning community. *Journal of Educational Computing Research, 44*(1), 59-82. https://doi.org/10.2190/ec.44.1.d

Cumming, T., & Rodriguez, C. (2013). Integrating the iPad into language arts instruction for students with disabilities: engagement and perspectives. *Journal of Special Education Technology, 28*(4), 43-52. https://doi.org/10.1177/016264341302800404

Diemer, T., Fernandez, E., & Streepey, J. (2013). Student perceptions of classroom engagement and learning using iPads. *Journal of Teaching and Learning with Technology, 1*(2), 13-25.

Hopkins, P., & Burden, K. (2015). iPadagogy: iPads as drivers of transforming practice in teaching education. In N. Souleles & C. Pillar (Eds), *iPads in higher education: proceedings of the 1st International Conference on the Use of IPads in Higher Education* (pp. 5-19). Cambridge Scholars Publishing.

Huang, H.-C. (2013). E-reading and e-discussion: EFL learner' perceptions of an e-book reading program. *Computer Assisted Language Learning, 26*(3), 258-281. https://doi.org/10.1080/09588221.2012.656313

Itayem, G. (2014). *Using the iPad in language learning: perceptions of college students*. Master's thesis. https://pdfs.semanticscholar.org/9bb0/e8c4cfb4b8f381765987052a900c076841b9.pdf

Kirsch, C., & Bes Izuel, A. (2016). Emergent multilinguals learning languages with the iPad app iTEO: a study in primary schools in Luxembourg. *The Language Learning Journal, 47*(2), 204-218. https://doi.org/10.1080/09571736.2016.1258721

Rossing, J. P., Miller, W. M., Cecil, A. K., & Stamper, S. E. (2012). iLearning: the future of higher education? Student perceptions on learning with mobile tablets. *Journal of the Scholarship of Teaching and Learning, 12*(2), 1-26.

Young, K. (2016). Teachers' attitudes to using iPads or tablet computers; Implications for developing new skills, pedagogies and school-provided support. *TechTrends, 60*(2), 183-189. https://doi.org/10.1007/s11528-016-0024-9

How EFL learners react to a learning framework integrating learning records on multiple systems

Hiroya Tanaka[1], Akio Ohnishi[2], Ken Urano[3], Shinya Ozawa[4], and Daisuke Nakanishi[5]

Abstract. This paper reports on the learning framework integrating a web e-portfolio and two mobile applications. It also reports on a preliminary study on how learners used different systems or materials to study for vocabulary tests in a particular general English course at a Japanese university, and how they recognized the usefulness of each system and material. Participants were 66 Japanese English as a Foreign Language (EFL) students from two intact classes who completed a questionnaire survey at the end of the course. The results of the survey revealed that, although the participants generally evaluated the usefulness of the different systems and materials in a similar way, one of the mobile applications was most often used to prepare for the in-class vocabulary tests followed by the e-portfolio and the wordlist.

Keywords: vocabulary learning, e-portfolio, mobile learning, EFL.

1. Introduction

Although vocabulary learning is of critical importance to language learners, it can also be a long and arduous process, especially in foreign language learning settings. Focusing on Japanese EFL learners, they typically study about 3,000 words through six years of junior and senior high school education (MEXT, 2009). If they choose

---

1. Hokkai-Gakuen University, Sapporo, Japan; tanaka-h@hgu.jp; https://orcid.org/0000-0002-3422-8914
2. VERSION2 Inc., Sapporo, Japan; a-ohnishi@ver2.jp
3. Hokkai-Gakuen University, Sapporo, Japan; urano@hgu.jp; https://orcid.org/0000-0003-2550-5227
4. Hiroshima Shudo University, Hiroshima, Japan; ozawa@shudo-u.ac.jp
5. Hiroshima Shudo University, Hiroshima, Japan; dnakanisi@gmail.com; https://orcid.org/0000-0002-5365-6957

How to cite this article: Tanaka, H., Ohnishi, A., Urano, K., Ozawa, S., & Nakanishi, D. (2019). How EFL learners react to a learning framework integrating learning records on multiple systems. In F. Meunier, J. Van de Vyver, L. Bradley & S. Thouësny (Eds), *CALL and complexity – short papers from EUROCALL 2019* (pp. 345-349). Research-publishing.net. https://doi.org/10.14705/rpnet.2019.38.1034

to study at a college level, they are required to learn more words depending on their needs and sometimes even to review or learn the words they should learn before they come to college, which involves both their independent and continuous efforts. In order to help such EFL learners and their instructors, this research project aims to build a learning framework by developing multiple e-learning systems according to both the learners' and instructors' needs and integrating the learning records on those systems so that the learners can metacognitively control their vocabulary learning over time. More specifically, we developed a web e-portfolio, Lexinote, a mobile application to implement a word rehearsal function of the e-portfolio, Lexinote Word Rehearsal (WR), and another mobile application for self-regulated vocabulary learning, DoraCAT. The learning framework using these three applications integrates the learning records of each system in the e-portfolio of each learner on Lexinote.

Lexinote can be used by an instructor as a tool to feed various forms of assignments and tasks and by learners as a self-study tool (Tanaka, Yonesaka, Ueno, & Ohnishi, 2015). Through in-class tasks, learners write essays, post comments to threads, search and record the words they want to learn, and rehearse them in step-by-step practice. Learners can use these recording and rehearsing functions in their self-study. In addition, they can also choose a text to study and compare it against their learning records to see the words they have learned or used and those designated by their instructor to study.

Using Lexinote WR on their mobile devices, learners can practice target words designated by their instructor as an assignment. DoraCAT is another mobile application for self-regulated vocabulary learning. Learners diagnose their vocabulary knowledge, choose the target words to learn, and rehearse them in a training mode. Whichever application they use, all the learning records are saved in the learner's own e-portfolio on Lexinote so that they can monitor and control their own vocabulary learning process and outcomes. In order to investigate how EFL learners actually study within this framework and other classroom materials, we conducted a small-scale empirical study with Japanese EFL learners.

The research questions in this study were:

(1) How do Japanese EFL learners use multiple systems and materials to prepare for in-class vocabulary tests?

(2) How do Japanese EFL learners evaluate the usefulness of multiple systems and materials for their vocabulary learning?

2. Method

Participants were 66 Japanese college students (30 females and 36 males) enrolled in a general English course from two intact classes. A 90-minute class was held once a week in a 15-week semester. The participants were required to study nine sets of 21 words, 189 words in total, as a vocabulary learning component of the course. They also took 12 in-class vocabulary tests based on these words. Besides these test, they engaged in various activities using Lexinote.

For the vocabulary tests, the participants were guided to use (1) a PDF wordlist, which they could also print out, (2) Lexinote, with which they could practice the target words on a PC using the word rehearsal function, and (3) Lexinote WR, on which they could do the same Lexinote practices using their own mobile devices. Some of the participants used notebooks or memos on their own to prepare for the tests. The participants were also introduced to DoraCAT and were encouraged to use it for their self-study. The instructor of the course ensured that the learning records on DoraCAT were counted as additional points in the course grading if they achieved the goal of studying 300 words during the semester.

The participants took a total of 12 vocabulary tests in 12 weeks, although some of them missed a few tests due to absences from class. After completing all the tests, they answered a questionnaire regarding their appraisals of vocabulary learning, their use of various systems and materials, and their evaluation of usefulness of those systems and materials in a six-point Likert scale. Although the questionnaire was not anonymous, the instructor, who was also one of the authors of this paper, carefully explained the purpose of the study and assured that their responses would not affect their course grades. This paper reports on the results of the participants' use (I used __ to prepare for the vocabulary tests) and their evaluation of the usefulness of the systems and materials for their study (I think __ is useful for my English study).

3. Results and discussion

The participants were first asked in the questionnaire how often they used each system and material in order to prepare for the in-class vocabulary tests. Table 1 shows the descriptive statistics of their use of systems and materials for the vocabulary tests (Research Question 1). The mobile application, Lexinote WR, was most commonly used by the participants, followed by the wordlist and Lexinote. The learner-made notebook and/or memo was least used. A repeated-measures analysis of variance (ANOVA) with a Greenhouse-Geisser correction showed a significant main effect [$F(2.61, 169.93)=10.2, p<.001, \eta^2=.105$]. Post hoc tests using the Bonferroni correction revealed that Lexinote WR was significantly more commonly used than the wordlist ($t=3.29, p=.007, d=0.34$), Lexinote on PC ($t=3.29, p=.007, d=0.34$), and the learner-made notebook ($t=5.49, p<.001, d=0.73$). Although it is impossible to identify the reason why Lexinote WR was most commonly used from the questionnaire results, it might be related to the environments the participants had. It can be fairly inferred that the participants always carried their mobile phone with them and Lexinote WR was the easiest choice when they had to prepare for the tests, especially just before them.

Table 2 shows the results of the items regarding the participants' evaluation of the usefulness of each system and material, including their self-study and in-class tasks using Lexinote (Research Question 2). Although DoraCAT was not related to the in-class vocabulary tests, the item regarding its usefulness was included for comparison. The numbers in the columns 'did not use' show the number of participants who answered they did not use the system or the material. Although the main effect was found to be non-significant with a repeated-measures ANOVA with a Greenhouse-Geisser correction [$F(4, 180)=1.85, p=0.122, \eta^2=.021$], the results here were somewhat different from those of their use because the participants evaluated the wordlist more positively than the other systems and tools, not Lexinote WR, which was most often used by the participants. The reasons for this will be further investigated with the other items in the questionnaire in the future.

Table 1. Descriptive statistics of learners' use of systems and materials (N=66)

	Wordlist	Lexinote (PC)	Lexinote WR	Notebook
M	3.85	3.85	4.89	3.15
Mdn	5.00	4.00	6.00	3.00
SD	2.05	1.81	1.59	1.83

Table 2. Descriptive statistics of learners' evaluations of the usefulness of systems, materials, and activities

	Wordlist	Lexinote Task	Lexinote Self-Study	Lexinote WR	DoraCAT
N	62	65	62	61	51
Did not use	4	1	4	5	15
M	4.77	4.58	4.42	4.57	4.25
Mdn	5.00	5.00	4.00	5.00	4.00
SD	0.98	0.97	1.11	1.01	1.20

4. Conclusions

This paper introduced an English learning framework that integrates the learning records of multiple applications and reported on Japanese EFL learners' behaviors and evaluations of those systems. The participants in this study used one of the mobile applications, Lexinote WR, most commonly to prepare for the vocabulary tests. However, their evaluation regarding the usefulness of the systems and materials did not vary substantially. We will further investigate and report on learners' behaviors and appraisals of vocabulary learning by analyzing their learning logs and the rest of the items in the same questionnaire in the future.

5. Acknowledgments

This work was supported by JSPS KAKENHI Grant Numbers JP16K02887 and JP19K00854.

References

MEXT. (2009). *Koutougakkou gakushu shidou yoryo gaikokugo eigoban kariyaku* [Study of course guideline for foreign languages in senior high school; provisional version]. http://www.mext.go.jp/a_menu/shotou/new-cs/youryou/eiyaku/1298353.htm

Tanaka, H., Yonesaka, S. M., Ueno, Y., & Ohnishi, A. (2015). An e-portfolio to enhance sustainable vocabulary learning in English. *The EuroCALL Review, 23*(1), 41-52. https://doi.org/10.4995/eurocall.2015.4663

Not a language course (!): teaching global leadership skills through a foreign language in a flipped, blended, and ubiquitous learning environment

Nobue Tanaka-Ellis[1] and Sachiyo Sekiguchi[2]

Abstract. This paper reports on the evidence learning found from a flipped, blended, ubiquitous learning Content and Language Integrated Learning (CLIL) course teaching global leadership skills using a Massive Open Online Course (MOOC) to Japanese undergraduates through English. The purposes of the current study are to see if (1) there was any evidence of learning found in the students' oral outputs, and (2) there were any changes in student perceptions about the course and their Target Language (TL) fluency over a 10-week period. The data were collected through two interview sessions conducted in Weeks 4 and 14. A similar set of questions were asked in both interviews to gauge student understanding of the course content, perceptual changes, and oral output skills. Three-semesters worth of interview data were transcribed and sorted into four categories; (1) *transfer of words*, (2) *transfer of phrases*, (3) *transfer of concepts*, and (4) *application of concepts*. The results indicated that the students' perceptions of the course shifted from an English as a foreign language course to a leadership course, and they produced more course relevant answers.

Keywords: CLIL, leadership education, student perception, MOOC.

---

1. Tokai University, Kanagawa, Japan; ellis@tsc.u-tokai.ac.jp; https://orcid.org/0000-0002-8867-6956
2. Meiji Gakuin University, Tokyo, Japan; sachiyos@ltr.meijigakuin.ac.jp; https://orcid.org/0000-0002-3820-5840

How to cite this article: Tanaka-Ellis, N., & Sekiguchi, S. (2019). Not a language course (!): teaching global leadership skills through a foreign language in a flipped, blended, and ubiquitous learning environment. In F. Meunier, J. Van de Vyver, L. Bradley & S. Thouësny (Eds), *CALL and complexity – short papers from EUROCALL 2019* (pp. 350-355). Research-publishing.net. https://doi.org/10.14705/rpnet.2019.38.1035

1. Introduction

This paper reports on Foreign Language (FL) development in Japanese undergraduates enrolled in a global leadership course created to meet the Japanese government's initiatives for cultivating young global leaders. The study was conducted at a mid-sized private university near Tokyo, which set up a new course to suffice the government's strategic plan (MEXT, 2012) for the tertiary education sector. The curriculum team, however, faced a challenge of needing to improve students' English skills without teaching the language itself. This was because there was a discrepancy in the perceived required skill sets for global leaders between the government and the university.

In order to make the TL learning invisible, a CLIL approach was employed as CLIL views learning of the TL should occur from *using* the TL, and unlike the traditional language education, fluency in the TL is regarded as more important than accuracy (Coyle, Hood, & Marsh, 2010). Also, materials from a MOOC course from FutureLearn (https://www.futurelearn.com/courses/cultural-intelligence) were used as the course content to provide authenticity and expose students to global-standard knowledge. The selected MOOC videos and articles were reorganised by using a mobile app, Handbook, to adjust the content level to suit the students' L2 levels – mainly Common European Framework of Reference (CEFR) levels B1, ranging from A2 to B2.

Handbook was used as the hub for accessing the course materials for self-study, which enabled flipped and ubiquitous learning. In the physical classroom, students had discussion and presentation tasks related to the flipped materials, with the help of Teaching Assistants (TAs) who were exchange students from the US. This complex environment was constructed to support student understanding of the materials, create opportunities to produce intelligible output in English, and provide a quasi-multicultural environment to exercise leadership skills learned in the course (see Tanaka-Ellis & Sekiguchi, 2019 for more details).

The purpose of this study was twofold: (1) to see if there was any evidence of learning in their oral output, and (2) to find out if there were any changes in their perceptions towards the course and their fluency in the TL over the course of ten weeks. For the first part of the investigation, two interviews, ten weeks apart (Weeks 4 and 14), were conducted asking them to describe the key concepts from the course. For the second part of the investigation, the first and the second interviews were compared to see if their answers regarding student perceptions of the course and their oral fluency had changed.

2. Method

In this paper, the audio- and video-recorded interviews of the students enrolled in the 2016 ($n=29$) and 2017 ($n=31$) courses were used due to the completeness of the data set. A total of 114 students participated in the study, however, only the data sets with both interviews were used ($n=95$).

For the student perception analysis, the 2018 data ($n=35$) were added because the data were available for that part. The interview sessions in Week 4 and 14 were conducted as one of the weekly in-class activities. The TAs acted as interviewers as the students were used to talking to them in their group discussions[3]:

- What is your name?

- Tell us why you decided to take this course.*

- What do you want to learn in this course?* / What did you learn in this course?**

- What is your understanding of cultural intelligence?

- What is your understanding of global leadership? Who is a global leader? Name one person and give some reasons.

- Previously we discussed what was in our core and flex. Having taken part in the past four weeks, is there anything you would add or change to your core and flex?**

Each interview lasted for two minutes and when students could not answer for ten seconds, the TAs were instructed to move on to the next question. The data were sorted into the following categories of learning evidence; (1) *transfer of words*, (2) *transfer of phrases*, (3) *transfer of concepts*, and (4) *application of concepts*.

The 2017 data set was used for testing interrater reliability for coding. The results of Cohen's kappa indicate (Transfer:.93; Perception:.85) a strong agreement between the two raters.

---

3. Questions with * indicates Interview 1 only, ** indicates Interview 2 only, no asterisk indicates asked in both interviews.

3. Results and discussion

3.1. Evidence of learning as transferred linguistic keywords and concepts

Table 1 below presents the transfer of words, phrases, concepts, and application of concepts found in Interview 2.

Table 1. Transfer and application of keywords and concepts

	2016	2017
1) Transfer of words	42	35
2) Transfer of phrases	3	0
3) Transfer of concepts	47	39
4) Application of concepts	42	46

As shown in the Table 1, the students were able to use the key concepts and applied the concepts by giving examples. As in the examples below, the students showed a better grasp of the key issues in Interview 2 compared to Interview 1.

Transfer of words (Q3): (Rumiko[4]: A2)

- Interview 1: The way to communicate with other people.

- Interview 2: I learned many important things, especially the biggest thing is *core* and *flex*, yeah.

Transfer of phrases (Q3): (Ikue: B1)

- Interview 1: I want to learn like things I haven't learned before.

- Interview 2: First of all, I learned about core to flex and flex to core.

Transfer of concepts (Q4): (Hotaru: A2)

- Interview 1: Cultural intelligence is to cooperate with ah, other culture's people or other background people, so we should cooperate with, how difference ah, from our own culture to other cultural people.

---
4. All first names are pseudonyms.

- Interview 2: I think cultural intelligence is to, *it's the ability to understand other cultural or other people.*

Application of concepts (Q5): (Mirai: B1)

- Interview 1: I think global person is maybe he or she has cultural intelligence like she can understand people and lead them.

- Interview 2: I think global leader is a person who is required to, required to think, think and understand other side of people. *Like, for example, Koike Yuriko who is a leader of Tokyo. She is the first leader who is woman and she has other, she has, ah, different point of view.*

3.2. Changes in student perceptions of the course and the TL fluency

Table 2 shows the change in perceiving the course after ten weeks. The numbers in brackets indicate the number of students who mentioned English related skills when they talked about academic skills.

Table 2. Change in perception of the course

	2016		2017		2018	
	Int. 1	Int. 2	Int. 1	Int. 2	Int. 1	Int. 2
Academic skills (English related skills)	26 (18)	3 (1)	30 (22)	3 (1)	27 (24)	3 (1)
Course content related	10	27	24	29	22	32
Others	9	1	9	1	8	0

Note: When one student had mixed opinions (e.g. academic skills and content related), one count for each category was added.

In Week 4, a large number of students viewed the course as an English course, however, their perceptions had changed to a leadership course ten weeks later. In terms of their English fluency, there was no notable difference between the two interviews (Table 3).

Table 3. Words produced in two minutes

	Interview 1			Interview 2		
	Maximum	Minimum	Average	Maximum	Minimum	Average
2016	197* (B1)	36 (B1)	106	189* (B1)	59 (A2)	107
2017	156 (B1)	40 (B1)	99	198 (B1)	45 (B1)	105

*The same student

The language proficiency did not seem to play a part in their performance or fluency. Despite the fluency results, other results and speech samples suggest that the students produced utterances more relevant to the course in Week 14.

4. Conclusion

From the results, the students' mindset shifted from perceiving the course as an English to a global leadership course. Although the fluency did not seem to improve between the first and second interviews, their answers to the interview questions were more succinct and were more relevant to the course content. The complex learning environment with CLIL seemed to be effective in delivering the authentic content through a FL and supported their content comprehension and the TL use. To examine the full effects of this learning environment and CLIL, complexity, fluency, and accuracy may be looked at in the future.

5. Acknowledgements

This work was supported by Meiji Gakuin University Education Reform Grants (2015-2018) and JSPS KAKENHI Grant Number JP16K45678 (2016-2019).

References

Coyle, D., Hood, P., & Marsh, D. (2010). *CLIL: content and language integrated learning.* Cambridge University Press.

MEXT. (2012). Project for promotion of global human resource development. http://www.mext.go.jp/en/policy/education/highered/title02/detail02/sdetail02/1373895.htm

Tanaka-Ellis, N., & Sekiguchi, S. (2019). Making global knowledge accessible to EFL speakers of an undergraduate leadership program through a flipped and ubiquitous learning environment. *Technology in Language Teaching & Learning, 1*(1), 3-20. https://doi.org/10.29140/tltl.v1n1.141

SimpleApprenant: a platform to improve French L2 learners' knowledge of multiword expressions

Amalia Todirascu[1] and Marion Cargill[2]

Abstract. We present SimpleApprenant, a platform aiming to improve French L2 learners' knowledge of Multi Word Expressions (MWEs). SimpleApprenant integrates an MWE database annotated with the Common European Framework of Reference for languages (CEFR) level and several Natural Language Processing (NLP) tools: a spelling checker, a parser, and a set of transformation rules. NLP tools and resources are used to build training and writing exercises to improve MWE knowledge and writing skills of French L2 learners. We present the user scenarios, the platform's architecture, as well as the preliminary evaluation of its NLP tools.

Keywords: NLP for L2 learners, MWE, interactive Web platform, CEFR.

1. Introduction

MWE knowledge improves proficiency in writing (Paquot, 2018). Given that language learners have difficulties using MWEs, characterized by strong lexical preferences, syntactic constraints and non-compositional sense (Baldwin & Kim, 2010), learners should use them in the right context and should apply the correct morphosyntactic constraints. For instance, *jeter l'éponge* 'to abandon', is the figurative sense and the determiner is singular, while *jeter les éponges* 'throw the sponges', is used with the real sense. Collocations have strong lexical preferences (*poser une question* 'put a question', but not **demander une question* 'ask a question'). Word-for-word MWE translation generally fails (*passer l'arme à gauche* 'to kick the bucket'*)*.

---

1. University of Strasbourg, Strasbourg, France; todiras@unistra.fr
2. University of Strasbourg, Strasbourg, France; cargillmarion@live.fr

How to cite this article: Todirascu, A., & Cargill, M. (2019). SimpleApprenant: a platform to improve French L2 learners' knowledge of multiword expressions. In F. Meunier, J. Van de Vyver, L. Bradley & S. Thouësny (Eds), *CALL and complexity – short papers from EUROCALL 2019* (pp. 356-361). Research-publishing.net. https://doi.org/10.14705/rpnet.2019.38.1036

Existing online platforms for L2 learners (Language Muse, WritingMentor) provide few lessons dealing with English MWEs. For French, projects such as Base Lexicale du Français (Verlinde, Binon, & Bertels, 2008) or DIRE Autrement (Hamel, 2010) represent MWEs' morphosyntactic and semantic features or collocation usage (Schneider & Graën, 2018). However, these resources do not propose graded CEFR exercises, except for a few websites (e.g. Bonjour de France, Le Point du FLE). To fill this gap, SimpleApprenant proposes graded exercises, annotated with CEFR levels, for MWE learning. The learner's level helps to select adequate content from the SimpleApprenant's database. Moreover, the platform provides immediate feedback by automatic error correction.

2. The SimpleApprenant platform and its scenarios

SimpleApprenant[3] is an open-source Web platform, aiming to improve French L2 learners' knowledge of MWEs and writing skills. For this purpose, the platform provides CEFR level-graded exercises for learning MWEs' definitions and usage. Additionally, the platform corrects and transforms learners' productions. SimpleApprenant integrates several NLP tools and resources: an MWE database, the spelling checker LanguageTool (Naber, 2003), and the parser Mind the Gap (Coavoux & Crabbé, 2017). We also developed a set of transformation rules, requiring parsed text as input, previously checked by LanguageTool.

SimpleApprenant proposes three scenarios for learners, who freely register on the platform by indicating their CEFR level. In the first scenario, the learner should match MWEs (compatible with learners' CEFR level) with the appropriate definition or gap-filling phrase. Thus, the learner learns MWEs' definition and usage, by repeating these exercises and with positive and negative feedback (Figure 1 below).

In the second scenario, the learner writes an essay, using at least one expression from a list of MWEs, labeled with the learner's CEFR level. The teacher evaluates the essays and gives a manual feedback about the MWE usage in context. These exercises might be repeated by the learner, with new MWEs.

---

3. https://simpleapprenant.huma-num.fr/SimplifyYourFrench/accueil

Figure 1. The learner matches MWEs and their definitions (first scenario). A green message is printed if the correct answer is selected, otherwise the right answer is printed in red

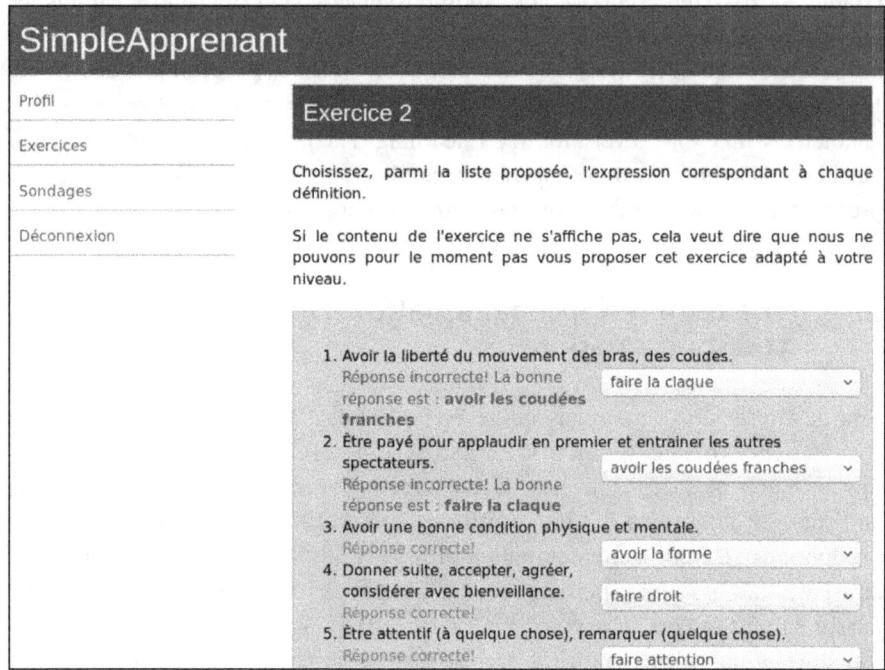

The last scenario aims to improve learners' writing skills. The learner feeds the texts to the platform, which are then processed by LanguageTool, the spelling checker integrated into SimpleApprenant. If necessary, the learner corrects the spelling errors identified by LanguageTool. Then, the corrected texts are parsed by Mind the Gap. If required, the learners apply one of the transformation rules on their parsed texts and receive the transformed text. This feedback should help the learners to avoid some grammar errors.

SimpleApprenant is currently used by French language learners and their teachers from Opole University (Poland) (A1-C1 levels) and the University of Cyprus (A1-A2 levels). We have several CEFR levels, comparable target publics (native speakers of Polish or of Greek), and the possibility to follow the same students for several years. The teachers and students use the platform during classes as an additional resource, but also at home, mainly for MWE learning or for collecting written essays. The platform is used gradually from the first (A1-A2) to the third scenario (B2-C1), according to learners' CEFR levels.

3. SimpleApprenant's architecture

For the three scenarios, SimpleApprenant uses a database of MWEs (partially annotated with the CEFR level), the spelling checker LanguageTool (Naber, 2003), Mind the Gap parser (Coavoux & Crabbé, 2017), and 21 manually defined transformation rules, requiring parsed texts as input.

We built the MWE database from Lexique-Grammaire (Gross, 1994) and from French vocabularies (Beacco, Bouquet, & Porquier, 2004). An MWE entry contains lemma, category (idiom, collocation), definition, gap-filling phrases (extracted from French Wiktionnaire), syntactic patterns, and CEFR level (Table 1). The CEFR level is automatically identified from a graded textbook corpus (Todirascu, Cargill, & François, 2019) or manually assigned from reference textbooks (Beacco et al., 2004; Gonzalez Rey, 2007).

Table 1. MWE examples

MWEs	Category	CEFR Level
Jeter l'éponge 'abandon'	idiom	B1
Faire la fête 'celebrate'	collocation	B2
Faire attention 'be careful'	collocation	A2

SimpleApprenant uses LanguageTool to detect spelling errors and Mind the Gap to create a dependency analysis of the corrected texts. The learner is asked to correct the spelling errors detected by LanguageTool. Then, the texts are parsed and the learner applies one of the transformation rules implemented in SimpleApprenant. Six deletion rules suppress adverbs and relative or participial clauses. Thirteen correction rules handle common mistakes such as verb agreement, determiner agreement, or negation errors. Complex transformation rules include passive to active voice or cleaved sentences transformed into a subject verb order structure. After the rule is applied, the learner consults the transformed text (Figure 2 below).

The transformation of learners' texts is a challenging task, due to erroneous input. Mind the Gap is a state-of-art French dependency parser: for unlabeled dependencies. For instance, the best F1 (harmonic mean of precision and recall measures) is 95.53% for reference data (Coavoux & Crabbé, 2017) but only 83.12% for learners' essays (obtained for 100 phrases of our corpus). We evaluated the transformation rules on 273 parsed sentences. Fifty-five (20.15%) were either not transformed or contained errors in the output. Out of those 55 sentences, 34 sentences (61.82%) did not show any change and 21 sentences (38.18%)

were transformed but contained errors. Deletion (82.71%) and correction rules (74.72%) are more effective than transformation rules. The rules failed because of parsing errors (due to erroneous learners' input) or syntactic patterns of the rule not matching the sentence. Even if some rules failed, agreement or negation errors are handled properly by the deletion and correction rules. As such, learners may still have feedback from these rules and see how their own text is transformed.

Figure 2. The learners apply the rule adding a second negation particle *pas* to the original dependency tree for *Je n' ai oublié de le demander* 'I do not forget to ask it', becoming *Je n' ai pas oublié de le mentionner dans mes messages*

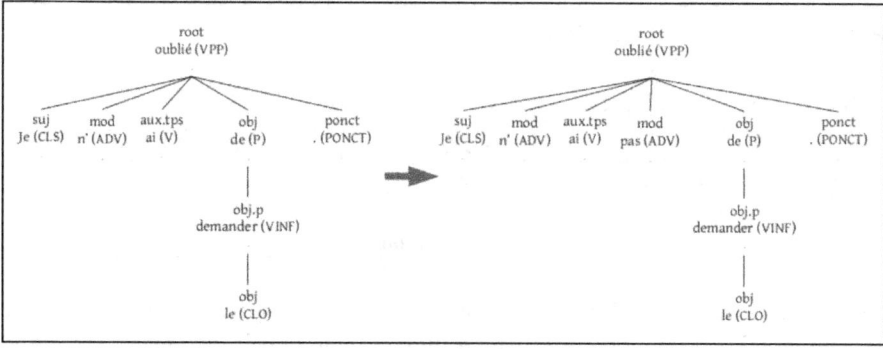

4. Conclusion and further work

We present an online platform for French L2 acquisition, SimpleApprenant, including NLP tools supporting reformulation strategies. A large MWE database, annotated with CEFR level, is used to create exercises focusing on MWEs. The exercises are selected according to learners' CEFR levels, generated with the help of preprocessing NLP tools: a spelling checker and a parser. The evaluation of transformation rules shows that some of them should be improved before being used by teachers and learners. We are currently revising the rules to improve the system's feedback. The evaluation of the platform via Web questionnaires started with beginner and intermediate learners (A1-A2) and by teachers. The questionnaires ask the learners to classify the exercises by their difficulties and usefulness. The evaluation is still in progress and will be extended to higher learners' levels (B2-C1).

5. Acknowledgments

This research is funded by the University of Strasbourg (June 2017 - February 2019). We thank Magda Dansko (University of Opole), Fabienne Baider, and Marina Christofi (University of Cyprus) and their students for testing the platform.

References

Baldwin, T., & Kim, S. N. (2010). Multiword expressions. In N. Indurkhya & F. J. Damerau (Eds), *Handbook of natural language processing* (pp. 267-292). CRC Press.

Beacco, J.-C., Bouquet, S., & Porquier, R. (2004). *Niveau B2 pour le français (utilisateur - apprenant indépendant) : un référentiel*. Didier.

Coavoux, M., & Crabbé, B. (2017). Incremental discontinuous phrase structure parsing with the GAP transition. In *Proceedings of the 15th Conference of the EACL: Volume 1* (pp. 1259-1270). Association for Computational Linguistics. https://doi.org/10.18653/v1/e17-1118

Gonzalez Rey, I. (2007). *La didactique du français idiomatique*. Editions Modulaires Européennes InterCommunication.

Gross, M. (1994). Constructing lexicon-grammars. In B. T. S. Atkins & A. Zampolli (Eds), *Computational approaches to the lexicon* (pp. 213-263). Oxford University Press.

Hamel, M.-J. (2010). Prototype d'un dictionnaire électronique pour apprenants avancés du français langue seconde. *Revue de l'APLIUT, 29*(1),73-82. https://doi.org/10.4000/apliut.937

Naber. D. (2003). *A rule-based style and grammar checker*. Ph.D. Thesis. University of Bielefeld, Germany.

Paquot, M. (2018). Phraseological competence: a missing component in university entrance language tests? Insights from a study of EFL learners' use of statistical collocations. *Language Assessment Quarterly, 15*(1), 29-43. https://doi.org/10.1080/15434303.2017.1405421

Schneider, G., & Graën, J. (2018). NLP corpus observatory – looking for constellations in parallel corpora to improve learners' collocational skills. In *Proceedings of the 7th Workshop on NLP for CALL at SLTC 2018*.

Todirascu, A., Cargill, M., & François, T. (2019). PolylexFLE : une base de données d'expressions polylexicales pour le FLE. *Actes de la conférence TALN 2019* (pp. 143-156).

Verlinde, S., Binon, J., & Bertels, A. (2008). La lexicographie au service de l'apprentissage / enseignement des combinaisons de mots. *Actes du Colloque international : lexicographie et informatique* (pp. 169-175).

CALL replication studies: getting to grips with complexity

Cornelia Tschichold[1]

Abstract. Calls for replication studies are becoming more frequent, and Computer Assisted Language Learning (CALL) has now reached sufficient maturity to offer numerous studies that lend themselves to replication. Realistic and successful replications rely on transparency in terms of data, results, and methodology. Two published studies in the area of vocabulary CALL will be discussed from the perspective of their suitability for replication: Franciosi, Yagi, Tomoshige, and Ye (2016) and Kim and Kim (2012). Alzahrani (2017) is a replication of Franciosi et al. (2016), confirming the findings with a markedly different learner group. The replication used the same methodology, a slightly modified list of target words, and Saudi participants. Kim and Kim (2012) compared vocabulary learning across three different screen sizes. The flashcard software is not specified any further, nor are the target words. While such an underspecified methodology is less likely to lead to a successful replication that can strengthen the validity and reliability of research results in our field, it can still provide a good training opportunity for students to learn about methodology in CALL.

Keywords: replication, vocabulary, teaching CALL.

1. Introduction

In Applied Linguistics, calls for replication studies are becoming more frequent (Marsden, Morgan-Short, Thompson, & Abugaber, 2018; Plonsky, 2015; Porte & McManus, 2018; Smith & Schulze, 2013). In the field of CALL, approximate replications crossing the boundary from 'traditional' (non-CALL) second language acquisition studies into CALL have been criticised as being problematic to some extent (Chun, 2012), but the field of CALL has now reached sufficient maturity to

---

1. Swansea University, Swansea, Wales, United Kingdom; c.tschichold@swansea.ac.uk; https://orcid.org/0000-0001-8487-2209

How to cite this article: Tschichold, C. (2019). CALL replication studies: getting to grips with complexity. In F. Meunier, J. Van de Vyver, L. Bradley & S. Thouësny (Eds), *CALL and complexity – short papers from EUROCALL 2019* (pp. 362-366). Research-publishing.net. https://doi.org/10.14705/rpnet.2019.38.1037

offer numerous studies that lend themselves to replication, even if the technology used for teaching languages continues to evolve.

Apart from the benefits to the research field in terms of increased reliability and generalizability of findings, replication studies also offer an excellent opportunity for students and young researchers to conduct their first independent piece of research. At Swansea University, the doctoral programme has included a replication study done by the student in their first year for some time now. Using replication studies in Master's and undergraduate programmes is a more recent development. For this level, smaller studies that do not require data collections lasting for more than a few weeks could be suitable for replication. Replicating such a study gives students the opportunity to learn about different research methods, how to critically review the literature in the field, what types of methodology and statistical analysis is appropriate for their study, and it will also clearly demonstrate the difficulty of drawing conclusions from the often limited amount of data. If we expect future language teachers to engage with the research findings in their field in order to improve their own teaching practice, having had the experience to conduct a small study themselves can prove very beneficial for their understanding of published research in CALL. Here, I compare two very different replication studies done by students as part of their Bachelor of Arts (BA) or Master of Arts (MA) studies.

2. Two examples of replications

Realistic and successful replications rely on transparency in terms of data, results, and methodology. While a clear description of results is usually assumed to be a prerequisite for publication, the methodology, and also the data can be somewhat underspecified, a fact that becomes very noticeable when a study is considered for replication. Two published studies in the area of vocabulary CALL will be discussed in this light: Franciosi et al. (2016) and Kim and Kim (2012).

2.1. A transparent study replicated

Alzahrani (2017) is a replication of Franciosi et al. (2016), confirming the findings with a markedly different learner group. Franciosi et al. (2016) compared the short- and long-term word gains after a session of playing the simulation game *Third World Farmer* (in addition to practising the 29 target words using *Quizlet*) to the gains after using only *Quizlet*, where the total time on task remained the same for both groups. The learners (n=162) were Japanese university students. The replication used the same methodology, a slightly modified list of target words, and younger, female, Saudi participants (n=196). A pre-test of the vocabulary level of the learners was added to the methodology. This study found much lower word gains than Franciosi et al. (2016), but a similar difference between the experimental and the control group. As mentioned in Tschichold and Alzahrani (2018), despite the lower "rate of vocabulary retention among the Saudi learners, we can [safely] conclude that the results broadly support the findings [of the original study, i.e. using games] in [English as a foreign language] classrooms is beneficial for vocabulary acquisition" (p. 339).

This year, two more MA students have replicated this study. In addition to keeping the pre-test as introduced by Alzahrani (2017), they have also introduced a third group. In addition to the original two groups (one group using Quizlet only, the other Quizlet for half the time, and the game *Third World Farmer* for the other half), the third group played the game for the entire time and did not spend any time using *Quizlet* vocabulary flashcards. All three groups thus represent CALL conditions, but one moves away from the intentional word learning into purely contextual, incidental vocabulary acquisition. Whether the data will still show significant levels of difference between the groups remains to be seen, especially as the group sizes are smaller than in the original study (results from these two studies were not available at the time of writing).

2.2. A less successful replication

The second study chosen for replication is Kim and Kim (2012). The authors compared vocabulary learning across three different screen sizes (iPod, smartphone, and Kindle size), using a sample of 135 Korean English as a second language students. The learners' task was to learn 30 words, with or without pictorial annotations. The "web-based self-instruction programme" (Kim & Kim, 2012, p. 65) used for this purpose is not specified any further, nor are the target words. This provides the opportunity for the students to choose the learning materials and the software for a (very approximate) replication. The group of undergraduate students tasked with this topic for their final assignment chose and piloted a list of academic words in order to be able to test both English native speakers and second language students as subjects. As screen sizes have evolved since Kim and Kim's (2012) study, the number of screen sizes to compare was reduced to just two, essentially a PC screen and a smartphone screen. In order to further reduce the complexity, the pictorial annotations were also dropped, as these would have been difficult to find for the relatively abstract words used in the replication. A total of 70 participants took part in the experiment, randomly divided between the two screen conditions. The trend in the results could be seen to confirm the superiority of the larger screen for vocabulary learning, but the differences did not reach significance. Given such an underspecified methodology in the original paper, the replication is unlikely to strengthen the validity and reliability of the findings. However, what this kind of very approximate replication can provide is a good awareness by the student researchers of the issues in the field.

3. Conclusions

Given our positive experiences with replications in the Ph.D. programme, we were interested in seeing how well replications would work in the MA and BA programmes. The aim of these replications by student researchers was not so much the strengthening of the validity of earlier findings, but the training in research methods this task would provide. With the publication of Porte and McManus (2018), this training task has now become more straightforward. A number of challenges do remain, not least a certain reluctance among students to do a replication for their thesis, as they are concerned about the originality of their work. With more replication studies being published, this particular point should become easier to address in the future.

4. Acknowledgements

The author would like to thank the students who conducted the replication studies mentioned here: Maha Alzahrani, Kira Davey, Jordan Dennison, Ieuan Thomas, Emma Trehane, Batoul Almahmoud, and Salma Al Shamrani.

References

Alzahrani, M. (2017). *Effect of using simulation game on vocabulary retention of Saudi secondary EFL learners*. Unpublished MA Dissertation, Swansea.

Chun, D. M. (2012). Replication studies in CALL research. *CALICO Journal, 29*(4), 591-600. https://doi.org/10.11139/cj.29.4.591-600

Franciosi, S. J., Yagi, J., Tomoshige, Y., & Ye, S. (2016). The Effect of a simple simulation game on long-term vocabulary retention. *CALICO Journal, 33*(3), 355-379. https://doi.org/10.1558/cj.v33i2.26063

Kim, D., & Kim, D. J. (2012). Effect of screen size on multimedia vocabulary learning. *British Journal of Educational Technology, 43*(1), 62-70. https://doi.org/10.1111/j.1467-8535.2010.01145.x

Marsden, E., Morgan-Short, K., Thompson, S., & Abugaber, D. (2018). Replication in second language research: narrative and systematic reviews and recommendations for the field. *Language Learning, 68*(2), 321-391. https://doi.org/10.1111/lang.12286

Plonsky, L. (2015). Quantitative considerations for improving replicability in CALL and applied linguistics. *CALICO Journal, 32*(2), 232-244.

Porte, G., & McManus, K. (2018). *Doing replication research in applied linguistics.* Routledge.

Smith, B., & Schulze, M. (2013). Thirty years of the CALICO Journal—Replicate, replicate, replicate. *CALICO Journal, 30*(1), i-iv. https://doi.org/10.11139/cj.30.1.i-iv

Tschichold, C., & Alzahrani, M. (2018). Replication? Open data? Yes, please! In *CALL your DATA Proceedings, Brugge, KULeuven & imec, 4 - 6 July 2018* (pp. 336-340). https://www.call2018.org/wp-content/uploads/2018/07/proceedings-CALL-2018.pdf?

Complexity and potential of synchronous computer mediated corrective feedback: a study from Sri Lanka

W. A. Piyumi Udeshinee[1], Ola Knutsson[2], and Sirkku Männikkö-Barbutiu[3]

Abstract. This paper discusses a qualitative study which examines the complexity and potential of using Synchronous Computer Mediated Corrective Feedback (SCMCF) for adult learners in English as a Second Language (ESL) classrooms in Sri Lanka. Chat conversation was assumed as the medium through which the teacher provides corrective feedback to the students. Five ESL teachers were interviewed for the study. The data gathered were analysed qualitatively using an affinity diagram which is discussed under an inductive thematic analysis. Findings of the study suggest that there is potential for provision of SCMCF through chat conversations, for teachers believe that SCMCF will improve language skills of the students; moreover, this approach needs only a limited use of technology. However, it was revealed that there could be some complexities, mainly due to teachers' existing workloads, some ethical aspects, and the low level of technology that is available in certain universities.

Keywords: SCMCF, ESL, affinity diagram, complexity, potential.

1. Introduction

Today, computer mediated communication has become reasonably promising because of its interactive, social nature (Leow, 2015; Satar & Ozdener, 2008). Further, when establishing the presence of 'noticing' in language learning which is comprehensively discussed by Schmidt (1990), the most productive platform for

---

1. Stockholm University, Stockholm, Sweden; piyumi@dsv.su.se; https://orcid.org/0000-0001-5427-4582
2. Stockholm University, Stockholm, Sweden; knutsson@dsv.su.se; https://orcid.org/0000-0003-1760-9130
3. Stockholm University, Stockholm, Sweden; sirkku@dsv.su.se; https://orcid.org/0000-0002-1016-3191

How to cite this article: Udeshinee, W. A. P., Knutsson, O., & Männikkö-Barbutiu, S. (2019). Complexity and potential of synchronous computer mediated corrective feedback: a study from Sri Lanka. In F. Meunier, J. Van de Vyver, L. Bradley & S. Thouësny (Eds), *CALL and complexity – short papers from EUROCALL 2019* (pp. 367-372). Research-publishing.net. https://doi.org/10.14705/rpnet.2019.38.1038

language learning is a synchronous process which helps the learner to be exposed to and engaged in processing L2 data (e.g. Leow, 2015). In such contexts, SCMCF can be "effective in providing a lower anxiety communicative environment for students who find oral production in [the] classroom stressful" (Beauvois, 1998, p. 213).

Although SCMCF has become a topic for many scholarly discussions, it is under-researched, especially in relation to L2 classroom contexts in developing countries where technology mediated classroom activities are hardly used. Besides, in Sri Lanka, most of the ESL students find oral production in the classroom stressful because they seem to have a 'love-hate relationship' with the English language (Goonetilleke, 1983). Thus, SCMCF in Sri Lankan L2 context warrants research. This study was designed to explore the following research questions.

(1) What are university teachers' perceptions on potential for SCMCF, and is there potential for SCMCF in terms of teachers' usage of technology?

(2) Do universities in Sri Lanka have the required learning conditions to provide SCMCF?

2. Method

2.1. Participants and data collection

Five teachers of English were asked about their perceptions on the potential for provision of SCMCF to students through chat conversations and on the complexities of this process in terms of fulfilling the learning goals. Interviews were semi-structured, and the teachers represented both private and state universities in Sri Lanka. Their experience in teaching English to undergraduates varied from 1.5 to 13 years while their age ranges from 27 to 40 years old.

2.2. Data analysis

Data collected from interviews was analysed thematically using an affinity diagram (Holtzblatt & Beyer, 2017). All transcripts were printed on paper and then cut into pieces containing just one point or issue. Then these were randomly selected, pasted on the wall, and were put into groups of four or five under several categories. Every category describes only one issue or a point. These categories were not pre-defined but emerged from data. Thus, 186 categories emerged (e.g. 'people have a love-hate relationship with English', 'students prefer technology-mediated activities', and 'we don't have enough facilities to cater to students'). These 186 categories were then put into groups which discuss the same point. For instance, all of the above categories were put into the following labels respectively: 'the socio-cultural background of the country', 'use of technology in the classroom is effective', and 'usage of technology in the classroom is not very effective'. When these groups were marshalled considering their relationship with each other, 11 main themes of analysis emerged (e.g. causes for students' negative attitudes towards learning English, potential of using technology in the language classroom, and challenges of using technology in the classroom).

3. Results and discussion

The affinity diagram helped 11 themes to emerge through data; however, this paper will present only two themes which are central to answer the research questions of the study.

3.1. Teachers' perspectives on potential for SCMCF in the ESL classroom

Teachers have positive attitudes towards the use of chat conversations for language education for they believe it will improve learners' language skills due to several reasons: (1) students prefer technology mediated activities, (2) though most of the students fear the language, they want to learn how to use it, (3) online chatting is popular and trendy among youngsters, (4) students like to chat with their teachers online, (5) chatting in computer game platforms has improved some students' language skills, (6) chat history could be later referred to for learning purposes, (7) the use of technology in language education should have human interaction, (8) technology is more attractive than a book, (9) chat conversations do not cause learner inhibitions, (10) it establishes learners' confidence, (11) almost all students own a mobile phone, and (12) they can even chat during the night.

Further, teachers believe that there should be some improvements in the provision of corrective feedback because the current generation is different:

> "There has to be some sort of change because... the kids nowadays are not really taking in the kind of feedback we give for the way we have

given it to them, so we have to find another way to get through to them" (Interviewee 2).

Thus, there is a potential for SCMCF since teachers are seeking new ways of providing Corrective Feedback (CF). Although most of the teachers believe the provision of CF could improve the language skills of students, they do not prefer correcting students' mistakes in front of the classroom, assuming it would cause learner inhibitions. Thus, they claim that the provision of CF through chat conversations could be effective and convenient.

The study also examined whether there is a potential for SCMCF in terms of teachers' use of technology. All teachers employed in the study use some sort of means of communicating via technology. Some teachers use social media, especially WhatsApp, to communicate with students – "it's easy for me to get in touch with them" (Interviewee 1) – and to share interesting subject related materials with the students. Some teachers allow their students to use mobile phones and laptops in the classroom.

"If I need to check something, I look at the phone, why shouldn't the student?" (Interviewee 5).

"I don't mind if they once in a while go to social media and relax and come back to the lesson" (Interviewee 3).

Thus, the findings of this study are in line with previous research findings that the provision of SCMCF is possible because it is flexible in terms of time and place, attracts students (Blake, 2013), and provides a comfort zone for the less vocal (Freiermuth, 2002).

3.2. Complexity in using SCMCF in the ESL classroom

The study also revealed several challenges in using SCMCF in the Sri Lankan context: (1) some teachers had limited knowledge in technology, (2) there was a lack of sufficient technology at some universities (e.g. strong WiFi connection), (3) the workload of the teachers, (4) some teachers' attitudes on ethical concerns: "if we are teaching, especially me, I'm 27 years old, I used to teach kids who are 26 years old. So when you're chatting with them, so, there's a bit of an ethical concern as well, I mean if you are a girl and if it's a boy, so that problem is there" (Interviewee 3), (5) teachers' negative attitudes on the efficacy of corrective feedback, and (6) teachers' perspective that student-teacher relationship should be distant.

Findings of the study reflect that the 'digital divide', i.e. an unequal access to digital technology and information (Tate & Warschauer, 2017), is a universal issue that can be seen in a computer assisted language learning context. Further, some other issues related to teachers' attitudes appear in the Sri Lankan context.

4. Conclusion

University teachers' perspectives are both positive and negative towards SCMCF. They believe SCMCF would be effective and convenient. They are negative about it mainly due to the issues related to facilities, workload, and ethics. Universities in Sri Lanka are not very sophisticated in terms of the usage of technology, but the study reveals that universities are equipped with the simple technology that is required for SCMCF: WiFi. The study also suggests that there can still be some difficulties because some universities do not have strong WiFi. Thus, it can be concluded that there is a potential for SCMCF in the Sri Lankan university context amidst its complexities. Further research is needed to examine learners' views on SCMCF.

5. Acknowledgements

We would like to thank all the teachers who were involved in the study and those who supported to get connected with those teachers.

References

Beauvois, M. H.(1998). Conversations in slow motion: computer mediated communication in the foreign language classroom. *The Canadian Modern Language Review, 54*(2), 198-217. https://doi.org/10.3138/cmlr.54.2.198

Blake, R. (2013). *Brave new digital classroom: technology and foreign language learning*. Georgetown University Press.

Freiermuth, M. R. (2002). Internet chat: collaborating and learning via e-conversations. *TESOL Journal, 11*(3), 36-40.

Goonetilleke, D. C. R. A. (1983). Language planning in Sri Lanka. *Navasilu, 5*, 13-18.

Holtzblatt, K., & Beyer H. (2017). The affinity diagram. *Contextual design: design for life,* 127-146. https://doi.org/10.1016/b978-0-12-800894-2.00006-5

Leow, R. P. (2015). The changing L2 classroom, and where do we go from here? In R. P. Leow (Ed.), *Explicit learning in the L2 classroom* (pp. 270-278). Routledge.

Satar H. M., & Ozdener, N. (2008). The effects of synchronous CMC on speaking proficiency and anxiety: text versus voice chat. *The Modern Language Journal, 92*(4), 595-613. https://doi.org/10.1111/j.1540-4781.2008.00789.x

Schmidt, R. (1990). The role of consciousness in second language learning. *Applied Linguistics, 11*(2), 129-158.

Tate, T., & Warschauer, M. (2017). The digital divide in language and literacy education. In S. L. Thorne & S. May (Eds), *Language, education and technology* pp. 45-56). Springer. https://doi.org/10.1007/978-3-319-02237-6_5

UCLouvain

Defining teachers' readiness for online language teaching: toward a unified framework

Koen Van Gorp[1], Luca Giupponi[2], Emily Heidrich Uebel[3], Ahmet Dursun[4], and Nicholas Swinehart[5]

Abstract. As part of a larger effort to support Less Commonly Taught Languages (LCTL) instruction in the United States, the LCTL Partnership at Michigan State University (MSU) and the LCTL Collaborative Partners initiative at the University of Chicago (UC) are supporting online LCTL courses to be offered to students across multiple institutions. As the initiatives were underway, it became clear that LCTL teachers' familiarity with online teaching ranged widely. This is not surprising, especially considering that many LCTL teachers have never participated in any kind of online learning experience – let alone taught online. This paper reports on the first phase of a collaborative project that aims to identify and define key competencies for Online Language Teaching (OLT) and conceptualize a set of OLT readiness can-do statements. In a next phase, this framework will be used to build an assessment that gauges teachers' readiness to teach language courses online and provide these teachers with formative feedback.

Keywords: online teaching readiness, key competencies, assessment, less commonly taught languages.

---

1. Michigan State University, East Lansing, Michigan, United States; vangorpk@msu.edu; https://orcid.org/0000-0002-2033-3852
2. Michigan State University, East Lansing, Michigan, United States; giupponi@msu.edu; https://orcid.org/0000-0002-8705-0523
3. Michigan State University, East Lansing, Michigan, United States; heidric6@msu.edu; https://orcid.org/0000-0002-8447-9703
4. University of Chicago, Chicago, Illinois, United States; adursun@uchicago.edu
5. University of Chicago, Chicago, Illinois, United States; nswinehart@uchicago.edu

How to cite this article: Van Gorp. K., Giupponi, L., Heidrich Uebel, E., Dursun, A., & Swinehart, N. (2019). Defining teachers' readiness for online language teaching: toward a unified framework. In F. Meunier, J. Van de Vyver, L. Bradley & S. Thouësny (Eds), *CALL and complexity – short papers from EUROCALL 2019* (pp. 373-378). Research-publishing.net. https://doi.org/10.14705/rpnet.2019.38.1039

1. Introduction

Online education continues to become more integral to the mission of post-secondary institutions in the United States, as demonstrated by the fact that one in three students is enrolled in at least one online course in a given semester (Seaman, Allen, & Seaman, 2018). Benefits of online education are numerous, including increased access, flexibility, just-in-time access to feedback, and affordability (Li & Irby, 2008).

In recent years, there has been a growing interest in online language education, both from a theoretical and practical perspective. Two of the initiatives currently underway in this area are the LCTL Partnership at MSU and the LCTL Collaborative Partners initiative at UC. While a full description of the projects falls outside the scope of this paper, both initiatives (as part of a larger effort to support LCTL instruction) are supporting online courses to be offered across multiple institutions within the Big Ten Academic Alliance, a consortium of universities in the United States. During our work, we discovered that teachers involved in the project possessed a wide range of familiarity with online pedagogy, probably due to the fact that a number of them did not have much experience with the medium.

2. Toward a useful framework for OLT skills

Current frameworks for OLT do not successfully address the current landscape of online education and there is no mechanism for translating these theoretical frameworks into practice. Our framework is based upon that of Compton (2009), who performed a review of key publications in computer assisted language learning, online (language) education, and teacher education published between 2000 and 2008. She concluded that there were very limited resources available to prepare language teachers for OLT. Furthermore, she provided a critique of existing skills frameworks for OLT and proposed her own framework breaking down OLT in three major skill domains:

> "The first set, *technological skills*, relate to knowledge and ability to handle hardware and software issues. Next, the *pedagogical skills* refer to knowledge and ability to conduct and facilitate teaching and learning activities. Lastly, the *evaluative skills* refer to the analytical ability to assess the tasks and overall course and make necessary modifications to ensure language learning objectives are met" (Compton, 2009, p. 81).

Each skill domain is further organized into three levels of expertise: novice, proficient, and expert. Compton (2009) includes a range of skills that should get primary focus in language teacher education programs, and acknowledges that other skills can (and, nowadays, should) be added to the framework.

In an effort to better prepare in-service and pre-service language teachers for OLT, the UC Language Center began developing an assessment instrument to evaluate their readiness for teaching in diverse online contexts (Dursun & Swinehart, 2017). The OLT Readiness Assessment is based on Compton's (2009) framework, with the addition of more-recent technological skills. What makes this instrument unique is that it not only asks teachers to self-assess their technological, pedagogical, and evaluation skills, but also measures their ability to put these skills into practice. Following a sequential design, the authors identified the key skills in each of Compton's (2009) skill domains, added relevant skills from reviewing recent literature, synthesized these skills into can-do statements, and wrote assessment tasks measuring knowledge and ability.

As the OLT Readiness Assessment was piloted at MSU, it became clear that the overall framework needed further definition before it could be operationalized. As a result, both partners collaborated to revise and update the framework, integrating aspects that have emerged in the practice of OLT since the development of Compton's (2009) framework, such as familiarity with accessibility guidelines, Instructional Design strategies, media production, and online presence strategies.

3. The updated framework

We kept the structure of Compton's (2009) framework largely intact. However, to account for teachers who may not be at all familiar with the principles and dynamics of online instruction, we added a base level that we identified as *limited*. We also redefined the four levels of expertise as follows:

- *Limited* teachers have rudimentary knowledge or awareness of the basic principles and dynamics of online instruction. They have limited to no ability and confidence to perform basic OLT tasks. Limited teachers are characterized by a tendency to directly transfer face-to-face practices and pedagogies to the online environment.

- *Novice* teachers have basic competence and can demonstrate a (marginally) acceptable performance. They are building up experience and confidence in OLT but are best suited at implementing courses designed by more experienced teachers and/or with guidance from more experienced teachers.

- *Proficient* teachers have effective and independent facility with all actions (competencies) required for successful OLT. They have a clear grasp of the affordances and constraints of OLT and can efficiently organize and implement OLT pedagogy.

- *Expert* teachers are highly proficient and have wide and varied experience in OLT. They can flexibly adapt OLT to meet new mandates and purposes, creatively offer novel solutions, and are capable of training less proficient teachers in the effective implementation of OLT.

Each level encompasses a distinct set of OLT competencies. A competency is more than just knowledge and skills; competency "is the ability to successfully meet complex demands in varied contexts through the mobilization of psychosocial resources, including knowledge and skills, motivation, attitudes, emotions, and other social and behavioral components" (Schleicher, 2007, p. 351). In the framework, we identified 11 OLT competency areas to be divided among three domains:

- Technology: (1) learning management system and educational applications, (2) course design, (3) accessibility, (4) learner support, and (5) educational media.

- Pedagogy: (6) presence strategies, (7) online language task design, (8) online assessment strategies, (9) dynamics of online instruction, and (10) online curriculum design principles.

- Evaluation: (11) conducting online task and course evaluations.

Next, the competencies needed to perform in each domain are operationalized in terms of can-do statements, as below:

- *Novice, Technology, Accessibility*: can identify and address 'low-hanging fruit' accessibility issues (e.g. text colors, HTML formatting, etc.).

- *Proficient, Pedagogy, Presence Strategies*: can utilize a variety of effective teaching, social, and cognitive presence strategies in an online course.

The competencies within each level can be developed individually or simultaneously, but they are necessary in order to proceed to the next level of readiness.

4. Conclusion

By conceptualizing an OLT readiness framework, we hope to stimulate discussion about what technological, pedagogical, and evaluation competencies present and future teachers need in order to be successful and effective online language teachers. By linking these competencies to four levels of expertise (limited, novice, proficient, and expert), we cater to the needs of both the teacher who has no real online teaching experiences but who transitions from a face-to-face classroom to a blended or fully online environment, and a more experienced teacher who is already teaching online but wants to improve their OLT skills. By identifying three different domains (technology, pedagogy, and evaluation), clusters of competencies (areas), and specific can-do statements, we hope to have designed a very practical framework that can serve as the basis of an assessment tool providing valid interpretation of teachers' readiness to teach online. In a next step, we will design and provide validation evidence for a performance assessment instrument based on the identified levels and competencies. Ultimately, we hope our framework will inform professional development initiatives and curricula of teacher education programs.

5. Acknowledgments

We would like to thank the Andrew W. Mellon Foundation for their generous support for both the LCTL Partnership at MSU and the LCTL Collaborative Partners at UC.

References

Compton, L. K. L. (2009). Preparing language teachers to teach language online: a look at skills, roles and responsibilities. *Computer Assisted Language Learning, 22*(1), 73-99. https://doi.org/10.1080/09588220802613831

Dursun, A., & Swinehart, N. (2017, May). *Ready or not: evaluating readiness for online language teaching*. Paper presented at the meeting of the Computer-Assisted Language Instruction Consortium (CALICO), Flagstaff Arizona.

Li, C.-S., & Irby, B. (2008). An overview of online education: attractiveness, benefits, challenges, concerns and recommendations. *College Student Journal, 42*(2), 449-459. https://link.galegroup.com/apps/doc/A179348426/AONE

Schleicher, A. (2007). Can competencies assessed by PISA be considered the fundamental school knowledge? *Journal of Educational Change, 8*, 349-367. https://doi.org/10.1007/s10833-007-9042-x

Seaman, J. E., Allen, I. E., & Seaman, J. (2018). *Grade increase: tracking distance education in the United States.* https://onlinelearningsurvey.com/reports/gradeincrease.pdf

Fostering cultural competence awareness by engaging in intercultural dialogue – a telecollaboration partnership

María Villalobos-Buehner[1]

Abstract. This study measured changes in cultural awareness levels between two groups of US students in their third semester of a Spanish class. One group (experimental group) collaborated via Skype with a group of English language learners from a Colombian university and the other group (control group) did not. The experimental group met seven times during the semester to discuss a variety of cultural topics such as health care and gastronomy. The control group addressed the same topics by examining them among members of the same class. Both groups answered a pre and post self-awareness questionnaire. Mixed factorial analysis of variance (ANOVA) results showed significant differences between the two groups. There was no change in scores from pretest to posttest for the control group, but scores in the trained group increased significantly. Students from the treatment group show substantial gains in skills, knowledge, and awareness of themselves in their interactions with others in one semester.

Keywords: telecollaboration, intercultural dialogue, cultural competence, cultural awareness.

1. Introduction

Cultural competence awareness is the process of being cognizant of different perspectives, value systems, and internal biases while being open and accepting of those differences (Western Center, 2017). One way to support the development of cultural competence awareness is by promoting cultural exchanges since

---

1. Rider University, Lawrenceville, New Jersey, United States; mvillalobos@rider.edu; https://orcid.org/0000-0002-5631-3706

How to cite this article: Villalobos-Buehner, M. (2019). Fostering cultural competence awareness by engaging in intercultural dialogue – a telecollaboration partnership. In F. Meunier, J. Van de Vyver, L. Bradley & S. Thouësny (Eds), *CALL and complexity – short papers from EUROCALL 2019* (pp. 379-384). Research-publishing.net. https://doi.org/10.14705/rpnet.2019.38.1040

they provide opportunities to develop the skills necessary to negotiate cultural differences (O'Rourke, 2007).

Thanks to the development of telecommunication platforms, telecollaboration partnerships have become widespread in language classrooms. Telecollaboration partnerships are "collaborative approaches to learning where knowledge and understanding are constructed through interaction and negotiation" (O'Dowd, 2016, p. 292). During the last two decades, through these partnerships, teachers have created a diverse portfolio of these experiences. These include practices from well-known e-pal programs established around 1996 to simpler forms of inviting a guest-speaker to connect with a group of language learners to explore societal aspects of a culture. In the last ten years, the field has also experienced growth in the amount of research in the effectiveness of these collaboration partnerships mainly in the area of language learning (Dugartsyrenova & Sardegna, 2018). O'Rourke (2007) divides telecollaboration partnerships into two models, e-tandem and intercultural collaboration.

This study used the intercultural collaboration model. This model emphasizes the integration of cultural and linguistic exchanges as part of the curriculum. The teachers are fully involved in the design of these experiences and create tasks that require their students to interact with their international partners to complete them. For instance, the e-pal partner became their first source of information when researching trends such as the use of social media. O'Dowd (2003) defines intercultural dialogue as "a process that comprises an open and respectful exchange of views between individuals and groups with different ethnic, cultural, religious and linguistic backgrounds and heritage" (p. 363).

Most of the studies in the area of intercultural awareness growth in classrooms are qualitative or are the result from other areas of focus such as students' L2 grammar development (Dugartsyrenova & Sardegna, 2018). This study offers a mixed method analysis to the growth of intercultural awareness through the use of intercultural dialogues with the use of a telecollaboration initiative. The main questions of this study are as below.

- Does the integration of an intercultural model of telecollaboration promote intercultural awareness?

- To what extent do students exhibit intercultural self-awareness during the telecollaboration and in their answers to the different tasks?

2. Method

2.1. Participants and context

The participants were 31 American college students in their third semester of a Spanish course. These students were mostly first and second year students. The control group had 15 participants and the experimental group had 16 participants. Their Spanish class met three times for 60 minutes each week. Both classes had the same textbook and covered the same number of units and topics. Both teachers embraced communicative approaches to language teaching and believe that language learning and cultural understanding go hand in hand.

The 16 participants from the experimental group met with another 18 college students from Colombia who were learning English. Both groups were at the B1 proficiency level of English and Spanish according to the Common European Framework of References for languages (CEFR). These groups met six times during class time for 30 minutes in English and 30 minutes in Spanish. After each meeting, the American students had to complete a task in Spanish with the information they gathered during each session. The main discussion topics were these: Personal relationships, Halloween celebration, college students' daily routine, digital stress, and tourism. Before each encounter, students had to prepare a series of five questions about the main themes. The researcher provided a start-up question for each topic. For instance, the start-up question for the topic about relationships was *How would you want to spend a day with friends?* After the encounter, each student had to submit a written report about what they found out, make a comparison, share it with the group using digital discussion boards, and react to three other member's reports by drawing a conclusion on what they all discovered.

2.2. Data collection and data analysis

The researcher collected data at different points in the semester. The 31 participants answered a demographic data gathering survey and a brief version of the cultural competence self-assessment checklist developed by the Greater Vancouver Island Multicultural Society (Western Center, 2017) at the beginning of the semester. The same students answered the cultural competence self-assessment at the end of the semester to measure cultural competence awareness growth. The researcher did a qualitative analysis of both the post-meeting reports the students had to submit and the notes taken from the videotaping of the six encounters. This study used inductive and deductive approaches to data analysis and used Byram's (1997) model as the framework to analyze their answers and interpret their interactions.

3. Results and discussion

The first question asked was whether the integration of an intercultural model of telecollaboration promoted intercultural awareness. According to the analyses performed using SPSS 26, the results show that the experimental group became more interculturally aware. For each question, a two (control group and experimental group) by two (pretest and posttest) mixed factorial ANOVA was performed with the use of the survey as a repeated-measure. Both the main effect of the test, $F(1,28)=10.74$, $p=.003$, $\eta=.53$, and the interaction were significant, $F(1,28)=6.66$, $p=.015$, $\eta=.44$. There was no change in scores from pretest to posttest for the control group, but scores in the experimental group increased significantly (see Figure 1).

Figure 1. Pretest and posttest: survey results – 1=Never, 2=Sometimes, 3=Fairly Often, and 4=Always

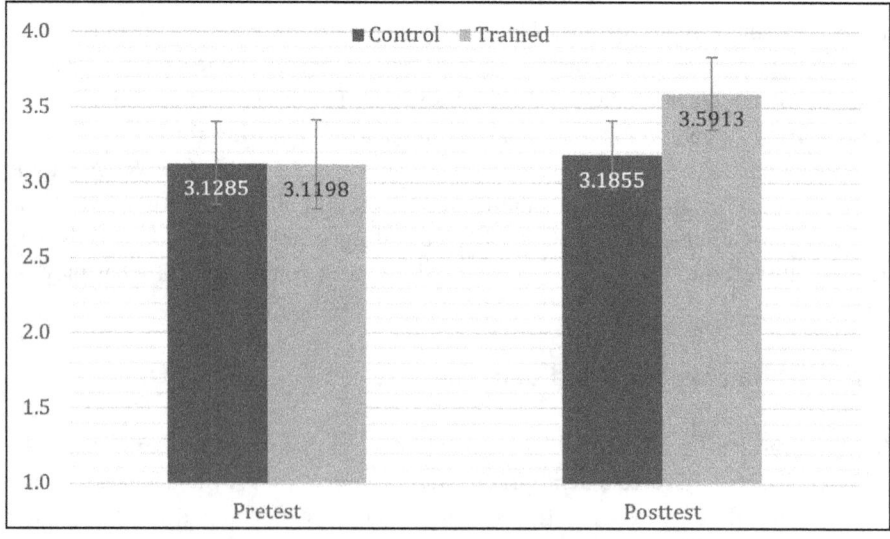

The statistical and practical scores of the experimental group in the areas of valuing diversity, how culture informs their judgment, willingness to share their culture, and openness significantly increased in the posttest in comparison with the control group. These are areas that demonstrate growth in cultural competence awareness.

The second question asked was to determine the extent to which students exhibited intercultural self-awareness during the telecollaboration and in their answers to the different tasks. After an inductive analysis of the qualitative data from the video observations and written reports, the researcher concluded that the emergent categories could be described using Byram's (1997) model of intercultural communicative competence. Some of the most common students' behaviors during the telecollaboration sessions were those of curiosity, openness, and a disposition to engage in the various conversations as equals. The experimental group largely remained conversing in Spanish during the time allocated for this task during the class. They demonstrated high interactivity and student engagement. These students demonstrated the ability to acquire new knowledge of Colombian culture and cultural practices in real-time communication and interaction by asking further questions beyond the ones they prepared in advance, and by smiling and maintaining eye contact. Alternatively, students were able to explain a significant amount of the social processes knowledge acquired during the interactions in the post meeting reports. One of the students' reactions to one of his peer's videos demonstrates this type of knowledge: "Great video! My partner, Santiago, also wakes up very early to attend classes at his college. It was surprising how early he woke up!" (Bob).

4.   Conclusion

This study supports the impact of telecollaboration initiatives in the development of cultural competence awareness. The results of the study show an increase in cultural competence awareness in the group that participated in the telecollaboration sessions. They also demonstrated intercultural communicative behaviors such as those of curiosity, openness, and a disposition to engage in the various conversations as equals. These exchanges also invite students to become responsible participants of a pluralistic society.

References

Byram, M. (1997). *Teaching and assessing intercultural communicative competence*. Multilingual Matters.

Dugartsyrenova, V. A., & Sardegna, V. G. (2018). Raising intercultural awareness through voice-based telecollaboration: perceptions, uses, and recommendations. *Innovation in Language Learning and Teaching, 13*(3), 205-220. https://doi.org/10.1080/17501229.2018.1533017

O'Dowd, R. (2003). Understanding the "other side": intercultural learning in a Spanish-English e-mail exchange. *Language Learning & Technology, 7*(2), 118-144. http://llt.msu.edu/vol7num2/odowd/

O'Dowd, R. (2016). Emerging trends and new directions in telecollaborative learning. *Calico Journal, 33*(3), 291-310. https://doi.org/10.1558/cj.v33i3.30747

O'Rourke, B. (2007). Models of telecollaboration (1): E(tandem). In R. O'Dowd (Ed.), *Online intercultural exchange: an introduction for foreign language teachers* (pp. 41-62). Multilingual Matters. https://doi.org/10.21832/9781847690104-005

Western Center. (2017). *Cultural competence self-assessment checklist*. Western Center for Research and Education on Violence Against Women and Children. http://rapworkers.com/wp-content/uploads/2017/08/cultural-competence-selfassessment-checklist-1.pdf

Towards the design of iCALL tools for beginner mandarin chinese learners in Ireland

Hongfei Wang[1] and Neasa Ní Chiaráin[2]

Abstract. The teaching of spoken Chinese in the context of post-primary education in Ireland faces several complexities. Learners of Mandarin Chinese as a Foreign Language (CFL), including both Irish and heritage learners, have demonstrated difficulty in learning spoken Chinese. This exploratory research is part of a larger project which aims to develop appropriate ad hoc intelligent Computer-Assisted Language Learning (iCALL) solutions by providing visualised instruction and a gamified feedback system for Mandarin tone acquisition, and using a spoken dialogue system to create a simulated virtual environment for practising spoken Chinese. This paper presents a qualitative needs analysis, in the form of semi-structured interviews, which has been conducted with 12 CFL teachers with various linguistic and sociocultural backgrounds. It aims to investigate learners' difficulty in learning spoken Chinese and teachers' willingness to implement technology in CFL curricula.

Keywords: iCALL, needs analysis, Chinese as a foreign language, spoken language acquisition.

1. Introduction

Chinese language education has been officially introduced to Irish post-primary education for seven years. The teaching of CFL faced several complexities, and the uptake of the subject has been relatively low (Zhang & Wang, 2018, p. 36). The first major obstacle is the shortage of suitably qualified teachers, as required by the Irish educational policy (Zhang & Wang, 2018, p. 41). A second major obstacle is that the majority of CFL learners have little or no exposure

---

1. Trinity College Dublin, Dublin, Ireland; wangh5@tcd.ie; https://orcid.org/0000-0001-7924-2683
2. Trinity College Dublin, Dublin, Ireland; neasa.nichiarain@tcd.ie; https://orcid.org/0000-0002-4669-5765

How to cite this article: Wang, H., & Ní Chiaráin, N. (2019). Towards the design of iCALL tools for beginner mandarin chinese learners in Ireland. In F. Meunier, J. Van de Vyver, L. Bradley & S. Thouësny (Eds), *CALL and complexity – short papers from EUROCALL 2019* (pp. 385-390). Research-publishing.net. https://doi.org/10.14705/rpnet.2019.38.1041

to a Chinese language environment and therefore lack any opportunity to communicate in Chinese outside designated class hours. It is within this context that we present exploratory research towards developing appropriate ad hoc iCALL solutions to address the issues regarding the teaching and learning of spoken Chinese at beginner level in Irish post-primary schools. This paper is the first step in ascertaining teachers' difficulties in teaching spoken Chinese as well as their opinions on the proposed iCALL tools and their willingness to use such technology.

2. Method

2.1. Instrument and data analysis

A semi-structured qualitative interview was adopted as the research instrument for needs analysis. Nine interview questions were prepared, three of which are presented here. The questions relate to the following issues:

- What are the main challenges in teaching spoken Chinese in an Irish context?

- To what extent is the technology currently incorporated into CFL teaching in Irish post-primary schools?

- Would CFL teachers be willing to use digital and iCALL tools in their classrooms?

The data from the question items was coded by the researchers (e.g. lack of language exposure, unfamiliar with Chinese phonology) and then content analysed for patterns.

2.2. Participants

A total of 12 individual interviews were conducted (see Table 1 below). Each interview lasted about 20 minutes.

Five interviews were conducted face-to-face in a place of the interviewees' choosing, while another seven interviews were conducted online. All interviews were audio recorded for later transcription.

Table 1. Demographic information of the teachers

Number of teachers	Number of teachers with > 3 years' experience	Teacher background	Learner background	Learner level/goal
4	2	Irish, teaching Irish students in secondary schools	Irish second level transition year (NCCA, 2012) students	Very basic, taster course
4	3	Chinese, teaching Irish students in secondary schools	Irish second level students in a school that has introduced Chinese – including both transition year and junior cycle Chinese courses (DES, 2017, p. 16)	CEFR A2 in both spoken and written proficiency
4	1	Chinese, teaching Chinese students in Chinese community schools	Irish students of Chinese parents who speak in various Chinese dialects but not Mandarin	Fluent in dialect but wish to acquire Mandarin pronunciation
Total: 12	Total: 6	Total: 4 Irish, 8 Chinese	All second level students	Varying from very basic to native speakers

3. Results

3.1. The main challenges currently faced by teachers in teaching spoken Chinese

The acquisition of Mandarin Chinese pronunciation. All three groups of interviewees cited learners' difficulty in perceiving and producing Mandarin Chinese tones as a significant challenge. For Irish CFL learners, the Chinese prosodic system is an entirely different system to be acquired. While for the Chinese heritage learners, they have already acquired models that are in many instances close to Mandarin, but due to language transfer, they had difficulty in incorporating these models in learning and using Mandarin Chinese.

Insufficient opportunity to practise spoken Chinese outside of designated class hours. Irish CFL learners generally do not have access to Chinese speakers.

Chinese speakers in Ireland typically have a high proficiency in English. Therefore, it was perceived that there was no 'need' for the Chinese to speak Mandarin to the Irish. For the Chinese heritage learners, they are immersed in a dialect environment at home while in public they are exposed to an English-speaking environment. Their other Chinese friends would speak either the same or a different dialect to themselves, and they tend to communicate either through dialect or through English, but not through Mandarin Chinese. Since they do not have exposure to the Chinese culture outside the home, culture embedded common expressions are often poorly grasped and as a consequence are used less and less.

3.2. The currently incorporated technologies in CFL teaching in Irish post-primary schools

Results show that some technology was adopted for language teaching and learning, but not much in the context of CFL classrooms. Eight of 12 interviewed teachers reported using online videos to demonstrate Chinese pronunciation. Irish CFL teachers often used these video demos as a model for their students as they were not confident in their ability to produce the correct pronunciation. Native Chinese teachers recommend their students use these videos as extra practice material. Duolingo, Pleco, and Memrise were also mentioned by three of the teachers. Three teachers reported never using technology, but this is due to practical reasons. Two native Chinese teachers reported that they never use technology in their CFL classroom because the necessary facilities are not available to them, while one Irish teacher commented that school policy on technology use was her reason for not pursuing technology use.

3.3. The willingness to use digital and iCALL tools in CFL classrooms

During the interviews, the interviewer briefly introduced the proposed iCALL tools to the teachers. Teachers demonstrated a very positive attitude towards the potential of using iCALL tools in the classroom. One of the Irish teachers bemoaned the lack of opportunity to practise and mentioned how she would find even a virtual Chinese interlocutor incredibly useful. Interaction is essential in language learning, and this was reflected in the results of the interviews; six of the 12 teachers emphasised the lack of interaction their learners had with Chinese speakers and commented on the need for tools to help with this. Optimising the language learning environment is crucial to enhance language learning (Young, 1991, p. 426). Three of the eight native Chinese teachers made this point strongly. They agreed that even a virtual world context could provide the necessary structures for their beginner learners.

All the teachers expressed a willingness to try new technology as it would come onstream and were very keen to be kept informed of any new developments in the field.

4. Discussion and future work

The results of the interviews indicated two distinct but interrelated issues in young learners' study of spoken Chinese in an Irish context. Based on these results, we propose a potential iCALL tool that could support the CFL learners. The first element of the iCALL tool would be a tone visualisation game, designed to address the issues in Mandarin tone acquisition. Learners would produce tones themselves in a game environment and see visualisations of their productions. Instant visual feedback would be incorporated insofar as the productions would be compared with the standard pronunciations. The gamification is proposed to increase enjoyment as well as to provide an immersive experience, which helps learners better perceive and more willingly produce Mandarin tones. The second part of the iCALL tool would be a spoken dialogue system as a virtual language partner (see Ní Chiaráin & Ní Chasaide, 2016). It would allow learners to practise communicating in Mandarin Chinese in a simulated, authentic Chinese environment in a virtual world.

5. Conclusions

The interviews provided insight into the main issues facing teachers, which formed the basis of the iCALL tool proposed and its evaluation in the future. More specific issues that emerged as part of the interview, such as the differences in Chinese and English phonological systems and the negative transfer of dialects in Mandarin tone acquisition, have further informed the content and the design of the tool. As teachers and learners indicated a willingness to use such a tool in the classroom, the next step of the research will be the design of this conceptualised iCALL tool.

References

DES. (2017). *Languages Connect: Ireland's strategy for foreign languages in education 2017-2026*. Department of Education and Skills. https://www.education.ie/en/Schools-Colleges/Information/Curriculum-and-Syllabus/Foreign-Languages-Strategy/fls_languages_connect_strategy.pdf

NCCA. (2012). *Transition unit: Chinese Culture and Language Studies*. https://www.ncca.ie/media/2514/chinese_culture_and_language_studies.pdf

Ní Chiaráin, N., & Ní Chasaide, A. (2016). Faking intelligent CALL: the Irish context and the road ahead. *Proceedings of the joint workshop on NLP for Computer Assisted Language Learning and NLP for Language Acquisition at SLTC 2016*. Linköping Electronic Conference Proceedings 130 (pp. 60-65).

Young, D. J. (1991). Creating a low-anxiety classroom environment: what does language anxiety research suggest? *The Modern Language Journal, 75*(4), 426-437. https://doi.org/10.1111/j.1540-4781.1991.tb05378.x

Zhang, C., & Wang, H. (2018). The development of Chinese language education in Ireland: issues and prospects. *TEANGA, the Journal of the Irish Association for Applied Linguistics, 25*, 34-51. https://doi.org/10.35903/teanga.v25i0.48

Computer-mediated communication in Chinese as a second language learning: needs analysis of adolescent learners of Chinese at beginner level in Ireland

Mengdi Wang[1], Ciaran Bauer[2], and Ann Devitt[3]

Abstract. Ireland's new strategy for foreign language education, *Languages Connect*, identifies the establishment of Mandarin Chinese as a curricular language as a key goal for the coming years. Within the curriculum specification for Mandarin at Junior Cycle (ages 12-15), "using digital technology is identified as a core component: the student uses technology and digital media to learn, communicate, work and think collaboratively and creatively" (NCCA, 2016, p. 6). While the introduction of Chinese courses in Ireland faces a number of challenges (e.g. a shortage of communication opportunities and appropriate learning resources), it also provides a unique opportunity to generate innovative solutions to these challenges through technology, specifically Computer-Mediated Communication (CMC). This paper outlines the overarching goal and Design-Based Research (DBR) methodology for this research project as well as the results of the initial learner needs analysis conducted at a post-primary school in Ireland. Participants in the needs analysis workshop consisted of 19 students aged 12-15 who are learning Chinese, and their teacher. The results of the needs analysis with students and their Chinese language teacher identified opportunities for meaningful communication, particularly with Chinese native speakers, and more learning about Chinese culture as the key needs to address within the broader research project, needs that could be addressed using CMC tools.

Keywords: CMC, DBR, needs analysis, Chinese as L2 learning/teaching.

---

1. Trinity College Dublin, Dublin, Ireland; wangm3@tcd.ie; https://orcid.org/0000-0002-1113-2821
2. Trinity College Dublin, Dublin, Ireland; ciaran@bridge21.ie
3. Trinity College Dublin, Dublin, Ireland; devittan@tcd.ie; https://orcid.org/0000-0003-4572-0362

How to cite this article: Wang, M., Bauer, C., & Devitt, A. (2019). Computer-mediated communication in Chinese as a second language learning: needs analysis of adolescent learners of Chinese at beginner level in Ireland. In F. Meunier, J. Van de Vyver, L. Bradley & S. Thouësny (Eds), *CALL and complexity – short papers from EUROCALL 2019* (pp. 391-396). Research-publishing.net. https://doi.org/10.14705/rpnet.2019.38.1042

1. Introduction

CMC is widely promoted in practice and has become one of the most important research subfields in computer assisted language learning since the 1990's. Herring (1996) defined CMC as "communication that take[s] place between human beings via the instrumentality of computers" (p. 1). There is a large body of research examining synchronous and asynchronous CMC in a range of language learning contexts (Blake, 2017; Goertler, 2009; Luo & Yang, 2018).

Through reviewing the current state of the art in CMC for Chinese as L2 language learning, the authors found that the number of previous research focused on post-primary contexts was limited compared with university level or primary level.

The launch of Languages Connect stresses that Chinese language learning has an important place at the national education level in Ireland. This project is the first of its kind in the Irish post-primary context for developing Chinese as a curricular language in Ireland today.

The overall objective of the broader research project is to draw on the most recent advances in CMC and task-based language teaching to design a collaborative task-based environment that optimises opportunities for adolescent learners of Chinese in Ireland to use their developing language resources meaningfully and to develop their intercultural awareness. To address this goal, the learning environment will be structured around communicative collaborative tasks that require Irish young learners at Chinese beginner level (12-15 years old) and Chinese native adolescents with the same age range to create Chinese language resources, such as videos, about a culturally relevant topic.

As a part of the first author's doctoral research, this short paper presents the methodology applied and the findings from adolescent learner needs analysis through focus group workshops.

2. Method

2.1. DBR approach

The project takes a DBR approach, an iterative, contextually grounded approach which emphasises collaboration between researchers and stakeholders in the educational context to solve real-classroom issues (Wang & Hannafin, 2005). DBR progresses in cycles of problem identification, solution design, implementation, and reflection to determine for re-design requirements, as in Figure 1. The overall project will include two DBR cycles with an initial Cycle 1 and a larger scale Cycle 2 where the implementation phase is designed as a quasi-experimental study. This paper presents the initial needs analysis phase of Cycle 1.

Figure 1.   DBR cycle structure

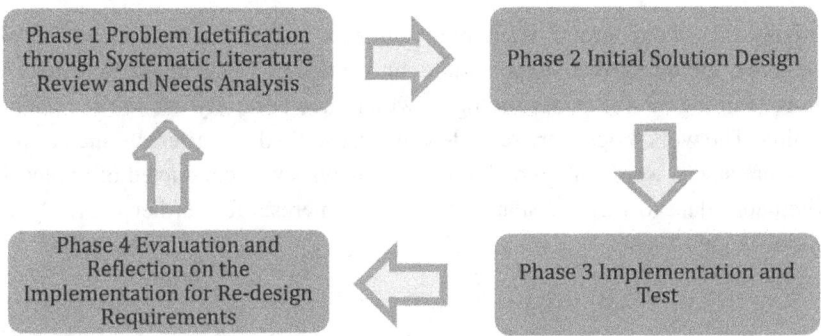

2.2.   DBR Cycle 1 Phase 1 student needs analysis workshop

The first phase of DBR research involves clearly identifying the problem space for the study in collaboration with stakeholders. In this study, Cycle 1 Phase 1 is composed of a systematic literature review of the literature on CMC for Chinese L2 learning and a needs analysis with adolescent learners and their teacher. The needs analysis was conducted in a post-primary school in Dublin where Mandarin Chinese is currently taught at Junior Cycle. The participants were an opportunistic sample of 19 students (Male 12, Female 7, age 12-15) and one Chinese teacher. The study was granted ethical approval and informed consent was obtained from all participants and the parents of the under 18 student participants prior to data collection.

The teacher needs analysis comprised a written teacher reflection and a semi-structured interview with open-ended questions which were structured around expectations for students, meaningful communication task design, and technology applied in the Chinese language class.

The student needs analysis was conducted in a workshop format to maximise discussion with three sections (see Figure 2): a think pair share activity on the most important and interesting aspects of learning Chinese, a three step interview on their experiences to date of learning Chinese and a focus group interview.

Figure 2.   Needs analysis workshop procedures

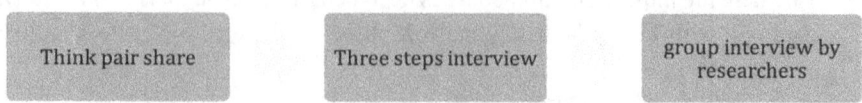

Through this focus group workshop, students shared their Chinese learning experience including their expectations and interests for Chinese language and culture learning as well as technologies which they currently use in their Chinese learning. The workshops were recorded and transcribed and artefacts such as think pair share sheets were gathered. A thematic analysis was conducted of the teacher and student data to identify shared needs and interests for further DBR Cycle 1 solution design phase.

3.   Preliminary results and discussion

The needs analysis with the students and their teacher identified opportunities for meaningful communication as the stakeholders' key need. In this Irish post-primary context, the learners start as pure beginner learners and for almost all of them the only opportunity to use Chinese is in the class with their classmates/teacher. There are limited authentic Chinese language contexts and communication opportunities. Students indicated they were highly motivated to learn Chinese and they wanted to 'use' this new language for communicative purposes. In particular, they noted that they would like to have more opportunities to communicate with Chinese native speakers, perhaps with the support of technology. Their interest in engaging with China, through native speaker contact, was also reflected in their interest in Chinese culture. All students wrote in group notes that the Chinese culture was the part they wanted to explore most, with cultural topics of interest shown in Figure 3.

As regards technology, the school regularly uses a range of technology and all students have a tablet as the main pedagogical resource. The students and teacher note they use MS Teams for school and class communication and sharing/ submission of files. In addition to this, the teacher uses a range of technologies in the classroom including MS OneNote, MS Sway, Whiteboard, Youtube videos, and Audacity for recordings and gamified learning websites such as Quizlet, Gimkit, and Kahoot.

Figure 3. Culture topics

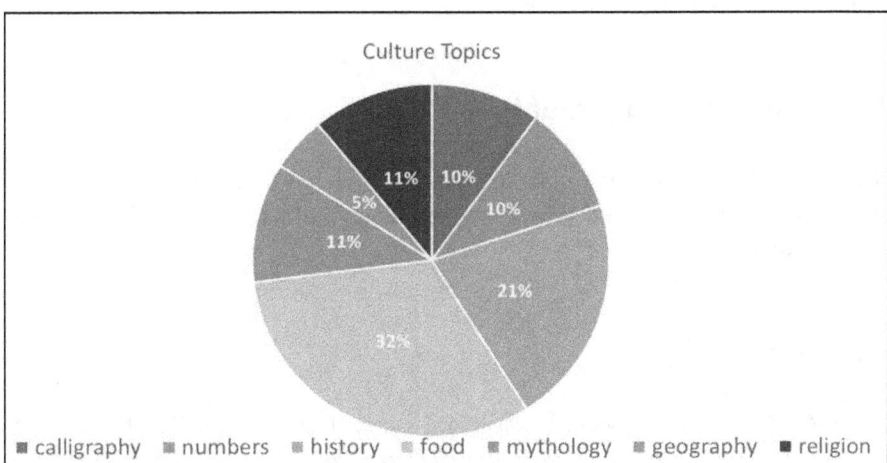

In the teacher interview, the teacher indicated that as regards language learning, technology is primarily used for developing student vocabulary and to model and showcase accurate and authentic oral language. However, the school context – where much of the school and classroom communication is mediated through technology with the use of MS Teams and OneNote – offers great potential to leverage this technology and offer opportunities for meaningful language use. As noted by Levy and Stockwell (2006), "any discussion of CMC needs to take into consideration the effects of the computer on the communication that occurs through it, as well as on the communication partners" (p. 84). In a context where CMC is the norm for school communication, CMC for language learning can build on the existing cross-linguistic digital communicative competence to support developing language competence.

4. Conclusions

CMC tools provide learners with an authentic communicative environment. Currently, there is a research gap as to how CMC tools facilitate post-primary learners to learn Chinese as an L2. In order to bridge this gap, it is proposed that researchers and Chinese language instructors should start from understanding young learners' needs. Moreover, the findings from the needs analysis indicate that: (1) meaningful communication with native speakers is the key need; and (2) exploring culture is a key interest. The upcoming phase of the study will involve the researchers and teacher co-designing a CMC implementation to address these needs within the post-primary school context.

5. Acknowledgements

We would like to thank the China Scholarship Council for granting this project. In the meantime, we also acknowledge the school and all participants who took part in this project.

References

Blake, R. J. (2017). Technologies for teaching and learning L2 speaking. In C. A. Chapelle & S. Sauro (Eds), *The handbook of technology and second language teaching and learning* (pp. 107-117). John Wiley & Sons. https://doi.org/10.1002/9781118914069.ch8

Goertler, S. (2009). Using computer-mediated communication (CMC) in language teaching. *Die Unterrichtspraxis/Teaching German, 42*(1), 74-84. https://doi.org/10.1111/j.1756-1221.2009.00038.x

Herring, S. C. (1996). *Computer-mediated communication: linguistic, social and cross-cultural perspectives*. Benjamins.

Levy, M., & Stockwell, G. (2006). *CALL dimensions: options and issues in computer-assisted language learning*. Lawrence Erlbaum Associates.

Luo, H., & Yang, C. (2018). Twenty years of telecollaborative practice: implications for teaching Chinese as a foreign language. *Computer Assisted Language Learning, 31*(5/6), 546-571. https://doi.org/10.1080/09588221.2017.1420083

NCCA. (2016, June). *Short course Chinese language and culture*. National Council for Curriculum and Assessment, Ireland.

Wang, F., & Hannafin, M. (2005). Design-based research and technology-enhanced learning systems. *Educational Technology Research & Development, 53*(4), 1042-1629. https://doi.org/10.1007/bf02504682

Joining the blocks together – an NLP pipeline for CALL development

Monica Ward[1]

Abstract. Intelligent Computer-Assisted Language Learning (ICALL) involves using tools and techniques from computational linguistics and Natural Language Processing (NLP) in the language learning process. It is an inherently complex endeavour and is multi-, inter-, and trans-disciplinary in nature. Often these tools and techniques are designed for tasks and purposes other than language learning, and this makes their adaptation and use in the CALL domain difficult. It can be even more challenging for Less-Resourced Languages (LRLs) for CALL researchers to adapt or incorporate NLP into CALL artefacts. This paper reports on how two existing NLP resources for Irish, a morphological analyser and a parser, were used to develop an app for Irish. The app, Irish Word Bricks (IWB), was adapted from an existing CALL app – Word Bricks (Mozgovoy & Efimov, 2013). Without this 'joining the blocks together' approach, the development of the IWB app would certainly have taken longer, may not have been as efficient or effective, and may not even have been accomplished at all.

Keywords: NLP, Irish, ICALL, Word Bricks, young learners.

1. Introduction

The development of CALL resources is challenging (Godwin-Jones, 2015) and it can be difficult to incorporate NLP technologies in CALL resources (Heift & Schulze, 2007). Technical challenges arise from the fact that the NLP tools may focus on language from a specified domain or linguistic standard. Cross-domain challenges relate to different foci and research aims between NLP and CALL researchers. Research that is focussed on building a robust NLP tool might be different to one that is suitable for foreign language learners. Another problem

---

1. Dublin City University, Dublin, Ireland; monica.ward@dcu.ie; https://orcid.org/0000-0001-7327-1395

How to cite this article: Ward, M. (2019). Joining the blocks together – an NLP pipeline for CALL development. In F. Meunier, J. Van de Vyver, L. Bradley & S. Thouësny (Eds), *CALL and complexity – short papers from EUROCALL 2019* (pp. 397-401). Research-publishing.net. https://doi.org/10.14705/rpnet.2019.38.1043

that can arise is that researchers from both domains may not really understand one another. NLP researchers may shy away from working with language learning and language teachers may be afraid of the complexities of NLP.

Natural languages are also complex, nuanced, and ambiguous, and this makes NLP challenging. NLP is a broad field and includes text to speech technology, grammar checkers, machine translation, and artificial intelligence chatbots, to name but a few. Some NLP tools are CALL ready. Text to speech technology is ready for use in L2 classrooms (Cardoso, Smith, & Garcia Fuentes, 2015), and automatic corrective feedback from grammar checkers have been shown to be beneficial (Ferris, Liu, Sinha, & Senna, 2013).

Often, ICALL artefacts will be built using already existing NLP tools. However, not all languages have the same level of resources. This makes developing new NLP tools for LRLs more challenging, and researchers have to be creative in how they work. This paper reports on how two NLP tools (a morphological analyser and a parser) were joined together to produce an NLP pipeline for an app designed for Irish, a LRL and a Less Commonly Taught Language (LCTL).

2. Context

2.1. Irish

Irish is a compulsory subject in schools in the Republic of Ireland. There are very few CALL resources for Irish and most of these are research-based and not widely used or are rather rudimentary in nature. It is not a major language, there is no commercial incentive to develop NLP resources for the language, and the pool of experts and researchers in the field is limited. These factors make it difficult to develop NLP resources for Irish.

2.2. Word Bricks

Word Bricks was originally developed for Japanese university students learning English (Mozgovoy & Efimov, 2013). It is based on a visual learning paradigm, facilitates an active learning (Prince, 2004), 'hands on' approach (Dewey, 1997), and channels the idea that perception precedes production (Flege, 1995). With Word Bricks, learners can experiment with the sentence structure of English. They can combine bricks (parts of speech) of different colours and shapes together to construct sentences and only grammatically correct sentences are possible. One of the motivations behind Word Bricks is to overcome the problem of students being limited to generic homework activities (Howard & Major, 2004) by enabling learners to play around with parts of speech. Word Bricks taps into the mobile learning 'game' idea which can increase learner motivation (Ducate & Lomicka, 2009).

2.3. IWB

The IWB app was derived from the original Word Bricks. The target learner group was primary school children in a classroom context. The initial phase (Phase 0) was an exploratory phase in which the feasibility of developing the IWB app was investigated. This phase was quite manual but demonstrated that the approach was feasible.

In Phase 1, the initial version of the IWB app was designed and developed with a team that included teachers, Irish CALL researchers and the original IWB team. A user-centred approach was used whereby the teachers were consulted before the development of content and throughout the process. Two existing Irish NLP resources – a morphological analyser (Uí Dhonnchadha, 2002) and a treebank and parser (Lynn, 2016) – were used manually as stand-alone resources to confirm the correctness of the information sent to the Word Bricks team. By adapting the existing Word Bricks app (with the original Word Bricks team) that had proved to be successful (Park, Purgina, & Mozgovoy, 2016), the authors were able to develop an interactive app for Irish that would otherwise have taken much longer to develop (if at all).

One limitation of the first version of the app was that learners could only use words from a pre-defined vocabulary list. In Phase 2 of the IWB app, the process was automated. The IWB team were able to integrate the NLP tools into the IWB app engine. This meant that the app can now process sentences with user-inputted words and gives the learners much more freedom and an improved platform for experimentation. Future research will focus on evaluating the new version of the IWB app.

3. Discussion

The IWB app has been used successfully by learners in two Irish primary schools (Ward, Mozgovoy, & Purgina, 2019). Students from the ages of seven to 12 have successfully used the app to revise five different sentence structures (possession, feelings, actions, locations, and questions). Students and teachers were surveyed after using the IWB app and the feedback was positive (Purgina, Mozgovoy, & Ward, 2017). A similar continuum to the mobile assisted language learning continuum (Barcomb, Grimshaw, & Cardoso, 2018) could be used in the ICALL context, with the observation that it is probably more challenging for teachers to move from adaptation through to creation in the ICALL domain. Without the collaboration between researchers with NLP expertise, CALL expertise, and teaching expertise combination, the non-NLP researcher would not have been able to develop the app alone, while the NLP experts would not have been able to envision how their NLP tools could be adapted for the primary school context. The development of the enhanced IWB app (Phase 2) indicates the success of the pipeline approach. The original NLP technologies were developed with machine translation in mind. However, with creative re-imaging of their purpose, they were able to be joined together to provide an NLP pipeline for the IWB app.

4. Conclusion

Just as technology should not be used for technology's sake, NLP should not be used 'just because it exists'. Pedagogical issues are primordial and this is why the user-centred approach was a key feature of the app development. The CALL community should learn from others and not reinvent the wheel (Gimeno-Sanz, Sevilla-Pavón, & Martínez-Sáez, 2018). This is especially important in the LCTL community where lessons can be learnt from 'bigger' languages. The IWB team learnt from the original Word Bricks team and were able to leverage their experience and expertise to develop the IWB app.

References

Barcomb, M., Grimshaw, J., & Cardoso, W. (2018). Instructors as MALL engineers: adapting, modifying, and creating mobile materials for listening practice. In P. Taalas, J. Jalkanen, L. Bradley & S. Thouësny (Eds), *Future-proof CALL: language learning as exploration and encounters – short papers from EUROCALL 2018* (pp. 11-15). Research-publishing.net. https://doi.org/10.14705/rpnet.2018.26.805

Cardoso, W., Smith, G., & Garcia Fuentes, C. (2015). Evaluating text-to-speech synthesizers. In F. Helm, L. Bradley, M. Guarda & S. Thouësny (Eds), *Critical CALL Proceedings of the 2015 EUROCALL Conference, Padova, Italy* (pp.108-113). Research-publishing.net. https://doi.org/10.14705/rpnet.2015.000318

Dewey, J. (1997). *Democracy and education: an introduction to the philosophy of education.* Free Press [First published 1916].

Ducate, L., & Lomicka, L. (2009). Podcasting: an effective tool for honing language students' pronunciation? *Language Learning & Technology, 13*(3), 66-86.

Ferris, D., Liu, H., Sinha, A., & Senna, M. (2013). Written corrective feedback for individual L2 writers. *Journal of Second Language Writing, 22*(3), 307-329. https://doi.org/10.1016/j.jslw.2012.09.009

Flege, J. (1995). Second language speech learning: theory, findings, and problems. In W. Strange (Ed.), *Speech perception and linguistic experience: issues in cross-language research* (pp. 233-272). York Press.

Gimeno-Sanz, A., Sevilla-Pavón, A., & Martínez-Sáez, A. (2018). From local to massive learning: unveiling the (re) design process of an English LMOOC based on InGenio materials. In P. Taalas, J. Jalkanen, L. Bradley & S. Thouësny (Eds), *Future-proof CALL: language learning as exploration and encounters – short papers from EUROCALL 2018* (pp. 77-82). Research-publishing.net. https://doi.org/10.14705/rpnet.2018.26.816

Godwin-Jones, R. (2015). Emerging technologies the evolving roles of language teachers: trained coders, local researchers, global citizens. *Learning and Technology, 19*(1), 10-22.

Heift, T., & Schulze, M. (2007). *Errors and intelligence in computer-assisted language learning: Parsers and pedagogues.* Routledge. https://doi.org/10.1017/s0958344009000044

Howard, J., & Major, J. (2004). Guidelines for designing effective English language teaching materials. *The TESOLANZ Journal, 12*(10), 50-58.

Lynn, T. (2016). *Irish dependency treebanking and parsing.* Doctoral dissertation, Dublin City University.

Mozgovoy, M., & Efimov, R. (2013). WordBricks: a virtual language lab inspired by Scratch environment and dependency grammars. *Humancentric Computing and Information Sciences, 3*(1), 1-9. https://doi.org/10.1186/2192-1962-3-5

Park, M., Purgina, M., & Mozgovoy, M. (2016). Learning English Grammar with WordBricks: classroom experience. In *Proceedings of the 2016 IEEE International Conference on Teaching and Learning in Education.*

Prince, M. (2004). Does active learning work? A review of the research. *Journal of Engineering Education, 93*(3), 223-231. https://doi.org/10.1002/j.2168-9830.2004.tb00809.x

Purgina, M., Mozgovoy, M., & Ward, M. (2017). MALL with WordBricks–building correct sentences brick by brick. In K. Borthwick, L. Bradley & S. Thouësny (Eds), *CALL in a climate of change: adapting to turbulent global conditions – short papers from EUROCALL 2017* (pp. 254-259). Research-publishing.net. https://doi.org/10.14705/rpnet.2017.eurocall2017.722

Uí Dhonnchadha, E. (2002). *An analyser and generator for Irish inflectional morphology using finite-state transducers.* Doctoral dissertation, Dublin City University.

Ward, M., Mozgovoy, M., & Purgina, M. (2019, forthcoming). A green Approach for an Irish app (refactor, reuse and keeping it real). *Celtic Language Technology Workshop, MT Summit XVII,* Dublin City University, August 2019.

UCLouvain

Digital stories: improving the process using smartphone technology

Jeremy White[1]

Abstract. With smartphone saturation at 100% among Japanese university students, educators are developing new and innovative ways to bring them to the forefront of learning, ensuring students are as engaged with their technology in their formal learning as they are with their informal learning. Smartphones of today are small, portable, have high spec cameras, microphones, and a large storage capacity. These devices also allow for videos to be edited within applications on the smartphone itself, without the need for a separate and expensive computer and editing software. Aspects such as these make using smartphones to make Digital Stories (DS) one possible way to effectively use this technology for formal learning purposes. This paper shows the results of a paper-based survey and discusses preliminary observations conducted with 38 Japanese university students undertaking a short-term study abroad experience in Australia and New Zealand.

Keywords: DS, smartphones, study abroad, Japanese university students.

1. Introduction

Educators are now implementing innovative ways to use smartphone technology, such as DS. DS help students present on a variety of topics in an innovative and engaging way. Reinders (2011) states that

> "[m]ost societies have culturally unique stories that have been passed down through the generations, in some cases going back thousands of years [and that] the power of stories is such that many anthropologists, psychologists, and other scientists see it as being at the core of what makes us human" (p. 1).

---

1. Ritsumeikan University, Shiga, Japan; jwhite@fc.ritsumei.ac.jp; https://orcid.org/0000-0002-5939-461X

How to cite this article: White, J. (2019). Digital stories: improving the process using smartphone technology. In F. Meunier, J. Van de Vyver, L. Bradley & S. Thouësny (Eds), *CALL and complexity – short papers from EUROCALL 2019* (pp. 402-406). Research-publishing.net. https://doi.org/10.14705/rpnet.2019.38.1044

This statement demonstrates the power of DS and the importance they can have on our lives. DS have been successfully used in elective classes in the Japanese university context "to conduct and video record interviews with non-Japanese speakers in preparation for the conversational demands of study abroad" (Brine et al., 2015, p. 92). In Japan, short-term study abroad programs are the most common means of studying in foreign countries (MEXT, 2015), and DS have gained a foothold as an important means for students studying abroad, specifically to prepare and overcome the cultural shock of daily life in their country of choice (White, 2018). Yet the finished products can sometimes be less than ideal due to (1) the students' inexperience in making DS, (2) inadequate instruction on what a DS is and how to make them, and (3) English language issues. This paper discusses the need for effective planning, basic training on how to take effective videos, and peer and teacher feedback and will conclude by providing a model of how DS should be administered to provide the most effective results.

2. Method

2.1. Population

The current research project was part of a three-year Japanese government funded grant into the use of DS for study abroad. The population for this study consisted of 38 18-22 year old ethnic Japanese undergraduate students from the College of Information Science and Engineering at a private university in western Japan. The students were all members of college organized study abroad programs to Australia and New Zealand which took place over five-weeks. Students had varying levels of overseas living and travel experience to English-speaking countries, and the Test of English for International Communication (TOEIC) level of the students ranged from 400, the minimum to take part in the program, to over 800.

2.2. Instrument

The instrument used included a post study abroad experience survey, asking if their expectations before they studied abroad were close to the reality experienced, and their opinion on the usefulness of DS. Questions for this survey were developed based on over ten years study abroad experience of two professors at the university. Questions and answers were written in Japanese, the native language of the students, and translated to English for the purpose of this paper. In addition, analysis of the DS making process from the researcher's perspective has been included.

2.3. DS

Students taking part in study abroad programs were required to make a three-minute DS in groups of three in relation to their classes, homestay life, most interesting and surprising experiences, and advice for future students. Students took photos and videos on their mobile phones during the five-week period and compiled them into a DS upon their return to Japan. The 24 students who studied in Australia were not given any DS training before their departure, whereas the 14 students who studied in New Zealand were given some basic training activities.

3. Results and discussion

Table 1 shows a selection of the results from the post study abroad survey indicating that students enjoyed making DS and felt watching DS before departure would have been beneficial to reduce the gap between their study abroad expectations and reality. This is in line with White's (2018) previous research. Even with the need for DS justified there are some issues when preparing students to make them. Firstly, it is difficult to find a format all students can agree on. Although this researcher suggested students use mobile devices to take photos and videos and then develop the DS, some preferred to use regular cameras and computers. It is impractical to insist on a certain format when students are using their own devices. Due to this, this researcher could not develop specific training videos, and lacked the experience to act as the expert with multiple software applications. Secondly, even though this researcher provided equipment including gimbles, microphones, as well as stock photos and drone images, feedback from the students suggest that this equipment was cumbersome and remained mostly unused.

Table 1. Selected questions post study abroad survey

Did you enjoy the process of making a digital story? Why/Why not?	New Zealand	Australia
Yes	11 (79%)	21 (88%)
No	3 (21%)	3 (12%)
Do you think watching a digital story of Christchurch/ Brisbane before your study would have been helpful?		
Yes	10 (71%)	18 (75%)
No	4 (29%)	6 (25%)

As it is impossible to control what equipment and software is used, this researcher will instead now focus efforts on developing effective DS training programs for the study abroad students. These could include basic camera and video training, how to frame shots appropriately, lighting, and the need for clear audio.

Furthermore, in this research, the Australian group produced videos of much lesser quality than the New Zealand group. This, as Reinders (2011) points out, is likely to be due to the training received before departure which did not give the students enough insight into the need for DS, how they would become part of their evaluation, and the quality expected of the students. In addition, from observations of both groups, it is clear that we cannot assume all students are in fact 'digital natives', even as is the case in this research if students come from a technical based faculty within the university.

This researcher, based on the results of this study, developed a preliminary DS implementation cycle (Figure 1), which is divided into four stages: planning, training, implementation, and evaluation. Future research will demonstrate whether the use of this model will help students build more effective and professional DS.

Figure 1. DS implementation cycle

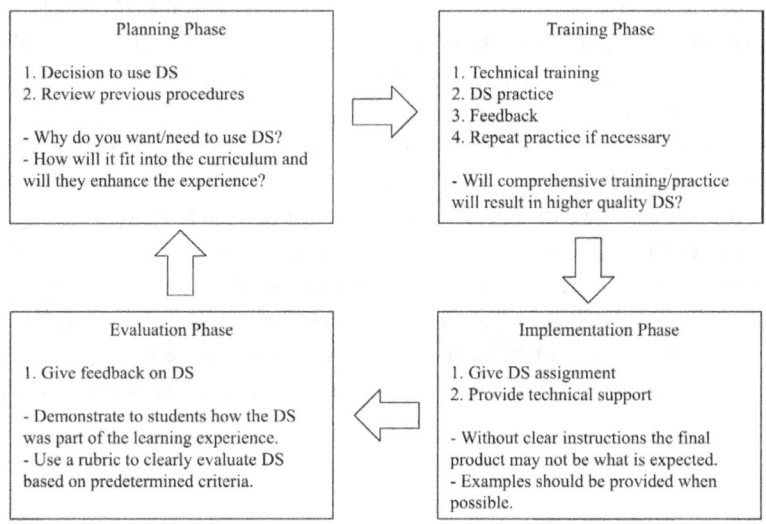

4. Conclusions

The use of DS is becoming an increasingly common way for students to have a voice. In the current paper, the author has shown that this voice does not occur without effort on the part of the student and the educator administering the task. Although the current generation has been provided with an abundance of technology possibilities, educators cannot assume students to be digital natives, and must provide training as they would with other non-technological activities. This paper has discussed the need for effective planning, training, implementation, and evaluation. It is hoped that by using the digital stories implementation cycle that more effective and professional DS can be developed.

5. Acknowledgments

This research project is partially conducted under support of the Kakenhi Grant-in-Aid for Young Scientists(B) #16K21482.

References

Brine, J., Kaneko, E., Heo, Y., Vazhenin, A., & Bateson, G. (2015). Language learning beyond Japanese university classrooms: video interviewing for study abroad. In F. Helm, L. Bradley, M. Guarda & S. Thouësny (Eds), *Critical CALL – Proceedings of the 2015 EUROCALL Conference, Padova, Italy* (pp. 91-96). Research-publishing.net. https://doi.org/10.14705/rpnet.2015.000315

MEXT. (2015). *The number of Japanese nationals studying overseas and the annual survey of international students in Japan.* Ministry of Education, Culture, Sports, Science and Technology. http://www.mext.go.jp/en/news/topics/detail/1372624.htm

Reinders, H. (2011). Digital story telling in the foreign language classroom. *ELTO Journal, 3*, 1-9. http://www.appstate.edu/~fountainca/5530/Reinders_2011.pdf

White, J. (2018). Digital stories to improve study abroad orientation. In D. Barr & A. Gimeno (Eds), 5th World CALL 2018 – Calling all the CALLers worldwide, Concepcion Chile (pp. 133-136). http://worldcall5.org/images/WorldCALL_2018_Proceedings_compressed.pdf

■ UCLouvain

Asynchronous online peer judgments of intelligibility: simple task, complex factors

Suzanne M. Yonesaka[1]

Abstract. Pronunciation learners can benefit from peer feedback in a Computer-mediated Communication (CMC) environment that allows them to notice segmentals and suprasegmentals. This paper explores the intelligibility judgments of same-L1 peers using P-Check (Version2, https://ver2.jp), a Learning Management System (LMS) plug-in that aggregates peer feedback on local intelligibility (Munro & Derwing, 2015). P-Check randomly delivers written prompts for learners to record. Recordings are randomly delivered to peers who choose from a drop-down menu which utterance was perceived. Aggregated judgments from peers and from the instructor are displayed to learners as feedback on intelligibility. This study used eight segmental contrasts: /b-v/, /s-θ/, /l-ɹ/, /l-ɹ/-clusters, /æ-ʌ/, /ɑ-ʌ/, /ɑ-oʊ/, and /i-ɪ/. Participants (N=38) made 3,451 intelligibility judgments on 1,203 recordings. The effects of rater listening discrimination proficiency and of utterance intelligibility were examined in six contrasts using Generalized Estimating Equations (GEE). Results showed that intelligibility was generally a significant predictor of judgment accuracy, but rater listening discrimination proficiency was not.

Keywords: pronunciation, intelligibility, peer feedback.

1. Background

In pronunciation learning, the effectiveness of same-L1 peer feedback in English as a foreign language environments has yet to be fully explored. There is some evidence that same-L1 learners can benefit from peer pronunciation feedback, especially in asynchronous CMC environments that allow repeated listening to recorded speech, giving learners time to notice pronunciation features (Correa & Grim, 2014; Gilakjani, Ahmadi, & Ahmadi, 2011). However, feedback

---

1. Hokkai-Gakuen University, Sapporo, Japan; suzanne@hgu.jp; https://orcid.org/0000-0002-2534-1632

How to cite this article: Yonesaka, S. M. (2019). Asynchronous online peer judgments of intelligibility: simple task, complex factors. In F. Meunier, J. Van de Vyver, L. Bradley & S. Thouësny (Eds), *CALL and complexity – short papers from EUROCALL 2019* (pp. 407-412). Research-publishing.net. https://doi.org/10.14705/rpnet.2019.38.1045

from same-L1 learners may be problematic in task-based communication due to learners converging on a shared non-standard pronunciation. Walker (2005) recommends preventing convergence through highly-controlled activities. Thus, the present study directs participants' feedback to selected features by having them make a forced-choice judgment of local intelligibility (Munro & Derwing, 2015).

Pronunciation instruction would benefit from a better understanding of what factors underlie the accuracy of these same-L1 peer judgments of intelligibility. This exploratory study focuses on two aspects: the stimulus and the learner. The research questions are: (1) to what extent does the accuracy of local intelligibility judgments by same-L1 peers vary depending on the targeted phoneme and utterance accuracy, and (2) to what extent does it depend on rater listening discrimination ability?

2. Method

2.1. Participants

The 38 participants (M=17, F=21) in this convenience sample were Japanese university students enrolled in an elective first-year practical English phonetics course who provided their informed consent following Teaching English as a Second Language (TESOL) standards.

2.2. Classroom environment

The language targets were eight segmental contrasts that are difficult for this learner population: /b-v/, /s-θ/, /l-ɹ/, /l-ɹ/-clusters, /æ-ʌ/, /ɑ-ʌ/, /ɑ-oʊ/, and /i-ɪ/. Materials consisted of 47 pairs of two-line contrastive conversations with L1 glosses. The first line of each conversation differed in one phoneme, such as:

> Conversation 1. A: *He is a good leader.* B: *Everyone trusts him.*

> Conversation 2. A: *He is a good reader.* B: *He loves books.*

After receiving focused instruction on the targeted phoneme, participants did individual online listening discrimination and pronunciation practice. Due to time constraints, this practice was not completed for the /s-θ/ or /ɑ-oʊ/ contrast.

The learning sequence included a listening discrimination pre-test, shadowing, listening discrimination practice, visual input, pronunciation practice, and choral repetition of the contrastive conversations to familiarize participants with their meaning and pronunciation. Finally, participants engaged in online peer judgments of intelligibility for approximately 15 minutes per contrast.

2.3. Software

The peer judgments were conducted using P-Check, a plug-in for Glexa, a proprietary LMS that has been used by more than 100,000 students in over 1,000 university courses throughout Japan. P-Check randomly presented the first line of one of the two conversations onscreen for the learner to record. Recordings were randomly delivered to peers who selected the appropriate second line of the conversation from a drop-down menu. After recordings received four judgments, they were taken out of circulation. A Native-Speaker (NS) rater also used P-Check to judge the intelligibility of all recordings. Peer and NS rater feedback for each recording was displayed to individual participants.

2.4. Data collection and analysis

Data were gathered from the P-Check database. Data consisted of participants' intelligibility judgments ($n=3,451$) which were compared to the NS rater's judgments of the 1,215 recordings produced by participants.

In further analysis, the relative effects of utterance intelligibility and rater listening discrimination proficiency were modeled for the six contrasts listed in Table 3. GEE, which produces a population-average model, was used because it can accommodate repeated categorical outcomes while accounting for a different number of outcomes per participant.

The model included one centered covariate, listening discrimination proficiency, and one factor, intelligibility of the utterance. The events-in-trials outcome variable was accurate/inaccurate judgment of intelligibility. The models used binomial distribution with a logit-link function, exchangeable structures, and robust standard errors (Heck, Thomas, & Tabata, 2012). Models were run separately for each contrast and those with the lowest QICC[2], a criterion used in model selection, were chosen. An alpha level of .05 was used for all statistical tests.

---

[2]. Quasi likelihood under independence model criterion

3. Initial results and discussion

Research Question 1 asks to what extent the accuracy of local intelligibility judgments vary depending on the targeted phoneme and utterance accuracy. Table 1 suggests that participants were more likely to make accurate judgments when the utterance was intelligible (to the NS rater) than when it was not.

Table 1. Accuracy of peer judgments by perceived intelligibility

Peer judgment	Accurate (%)	Inaccurate (%)	Total (%)
Intelligible	1,819 (52.7)	437 (12.7)	2,256 (65.4)
Unintelligible	460 (13.3)	735 (21.3)	1,195 (34.6)
Total	2,279 (66.0)	1,172 (34.0)	3,451 (100)

Of all judgments, 21.3% occurred when peers were unable to recognize an intelligible phoneme; these may be related to low listening discrimination ability. Only 12.7% of judgments involved participants judging an unintelligible phoneme to be intelligible; these judgments may involve using knowledge of the L1 phonology.

Table 2 indicates substantial variation in mean intelligibility among the contrasts. The least intelligible contrasts were /s-θ/ and /ɑ-oʊ/, which had been taught but not fully practiced, and /l-ɹ/ clusters. The /æ-ʌ/ and /ɑ-ʌ/ contrasts were most intelligible and were judged most accurately.

Table 2. Accuracy of peer intelligibility judgments by contrast

Contrast	Intelligibility (NS)		Peer Judgments	Peer Accuracy	
	M	SD	n	M	SD
/b-v/	.80	.401	334	.65	.479
/s-θ/	.72	.452	426	.66	.473
/l-ɹ/	.73	.445	342	.64	.480
/l-ɹ/ clusters	.68	.466	395	.59	.493
/i-ɪ/	.73	.444	480	.71	.453
/ɑ-oʊ/	.65	.476	627	.63	.484
/ɑ-ʌ/	.80	.403	429	.70	.457
/æ-ʌ/	.86	.346	418	.69	.463
Total			3,451		

Reseach Question 2 asks to what extent the accuracy of judgments depends on rater listening discrimination ability. This was measured for six contrasts by the listening discrimination pre-test at the beginning of the teaching sequence. Participants heard 20 pairs of words, half minimal pairs (e.g. *lake, rake*) and half tokens of the same word (e.g. *lake*1, *lake*2), and they marked each pair same or different. Table 3 indicates that participants discriminated /æ-ʌ/ the best and /l-ɹ/-clusters the least well.

Table 3. Listening discrimination scores by contrast

	n	Min.	Max.	M	SD
/b-v/	30	11	18	14.33	1.77
/l-ɹ/	37	10	19	14.05	2.25
/l-ɹ/ clusters	32	6	17	11.44	2.41
/i-ɪ/	31	15	20	18.29	1.53
/ɑ-ʌ/	32	14	20	17.25	1.83
/æ-ʌ/	31	15	20	18.97	1.25

Results of the GEE analysis were as follows. For the /b-v/ and /l-ɹ/-clusters contrast, neither intelligibility nor listening discrimination were significant predictors of judgment accuracy. For the remaining contrasts, parameter estimates showed that unintelligible utterances received accurate intelligibility judgments at a significantly lower rate than intelligible utterances (/l-ɹ/: Wald $\chi2(1)=6.054$, $p=.014$, $\beta=-.584$); /i-ɪ/: Wald $\chi2(1)=12.388$, $p<.001$, $\beta=-.949$; /æ-ʌ/: Wald $\chi2(1)=11.158$, $p=.001$, $\beta=-.928$; /ɑ-ʌ/: Wald $\chi2(1)=69.707$, $p<.001$, $\beta=-2.979$). For /ɑ-ʌ/, listening discrimination was also a predictor of judgment accuracy (Wald $\chi2(1)=5.888$, $p=.015$, $\beta=.141$).

4. Conclusion

Intelligibility was a significant predictor of judgment accuracy, except for /b-v/ and /l-ɹ/-clusters. Closer examination reveals further variation even within some contrasts. For example, /b/ had 75% judgment accuracy while /v/, a phoneme not in the participants' L1 inventory, had only 56% accuracy. A different pattern was seen for /l/ and /ɹ/, both of which were judged with 61% mean accuracy. However, the /l-ɹ/ contrast showed strong variation at the item level, with accuracy ranging from 25% (*long*) to 91% (*lamp*).

Although a detailed analysis is beyond the scope of this paper, it is clear that intelligibility judgments were highly sensitive to target variability. Unexpectedly, listening discrimination ability was found to predict judgment accuracy only for one contrast, possibly indicating that a more robust measure of this covariate is needed.

References

Correa, M., & Grim, F. (2014). Audio recordings as a self-awareness tool for improving second language pronunciation in the phonetics and phonology classroom: sample activities. *Currents in Teaching & Learning, 6*(2), 55-63. https://www.worcester.edu/Currents-Archives/

Gilakjani, A., Ahmadi, S., & Ahmadi, M. (2011). Why is pronunciation so difficult to learn? *English Language Teaching, 4*(3), 74-83. https://doi.org/10.5539/elt.v4n3p74

Heck, R. H., Thomas, S., & Tabata, L. (2012). *Multilevel modeling of categorical outcomes using IBM SPSS*. Routledge. https://doi.org/10.4324/9780203808986

Munro, M. J., & Derwing, T. M. (2015). Intelligibility in research and practice: Teaching priorities. In M. Reed and J. M. Levis (Eds.), *The handbook of English pronunciation*, (pp. 377–396). Malden, MA: Wiley Blackwell. https://doi.org/10.1002/9781118346952.ch21

Walker, R. (2005). Using student-produced recordings with monolingual groups to provide effective, individualized pronunciation practice. *TESOL Quarterly, 39*(3), 550-558. https://doi.org/10.2307/3588495

■ UCLouvain

Author index

A
Albasha, Ali 57
Alhudaithy, Hana 1
Allen, Christopher 7
Alm, Antonie 13
Arnett, Carlee 169
Artieda, Gemma 19
Avgousti, Maria Iosifina 157

B
Bacher, Sonja 26
Bahous, Rima 57
Bauer, Ciaran 391
Bédi, Branislav 33
Bercuci, Loredana 75
Berns, Anke 39
Blake, John 45
Boulton, Alex 51
Bradley, Linda 57
Butcher, Peter 144

C
Canals, Laia 63
Cardoso, Walcir 69, 340
Cargill, Marion 356
Castro, Edson 39
Cheng, Li 118, 124
Chitez, Mădălina 75
Christoforou, Maria 82
Chua, Cathy 33
Clayton, John 199
Clements, Bindi 19
Clifford, Elisabeth 88
Cotter, Matthew 94, 163

D
Delforge, Carole 100, 252
Devitt, Ann 321, 391
Dizon, Gilbert 107
Dodero, Juan Manuel 39
Domanchin, Morgane 113
Dong, Liu 118, 124
Dong, Shixin 118, 124
Dunn, James D. 130
Dursun, Ahmet 373

F
Forti, Luciana 137
Foucher, Anne-Laure 263
Frankenberg-Garcia, Ana 144

G
Gettings, Robert 252
Giannikas, Christina Nicole 334
Giupponi, Luca 373
Godwin-Jones, Robert 151
Gutiérrez-Colón, Mar 270

H
Habibi, Hanieh 33
Hadjistassou, Stella 157
Hagley, Eric 163
Hansen, Dirk 169
Harrold, Peter 174
Heidrich Uebel, Emily 373
Hendry, Clinton 180
Henin, Véronique 285
Hinkelman, Don 94

I
Iino, Atsushi 186
Irwin, Bradley 193

Author index

Iwata, Jun 199

J
Jauregi Ondarra, Kristi 206
Jolley, Kym 212

K
Kanareva-Dimitrovska, Ana 218
Kassim, Samar 223
Kiforo, Enos 69
Knight, Tim 252
Knutsson, Ola 367
Koenraad, Ton 229
Korkealehto, Kirsi 236, 241
Kramer, Brandon 257
Kyppö, Anna 247

L
Lambacher, Stephen 327
Lander, Bruce 252
Leier, Vera 241
Lew, Robert 144
Louca, Petros 157
Lyddon, Paul A. 257

M
Madden, Oneil N. 263
Manegre, Marni 270
Männikkö-Barbutiu, Sirkku 367
Martinez-Lopez, Ruth 33
Martins, Claudia Beatriz 275
Matthews, Blair 280
Meshgi, Kourosh 291, 297
Meunier, Fanny vii
Meurice, Alice 100, 285
Mirzaei, Maryam Sadat 291, 297
Montaner-Villalba, Salvador 304
Morgana, Valentina 252
Mošaťová, Michaela 310
Mota, José Miguel 39

N
Nakanishi, Daisuke 345
Ní Chasaide, Ailbhe 314
Ní Chiaráin, Neasa 314, 385
Nic Réamoinn, Susan 321
Nishida, Toyoaki 297

O
Obari, Hiroyuki 327
Ohnishi, Akio 345
Ozawa, Shinya 345

P
Papadima-Sophocleous, Salomi 82, 334
Pleines, Christine 88

R
Rayner, Manny 33
Rees, Geraint 144
Richardson, David 7
Roberts, Jonathan 144
Ruivivar, June 180
Ruiz-Rube, Iván 39
Ryynanen, Oona 39

S
Sekiguchi, Sachiyo 350
Selwood, Jaime 252
Sénécal, Anne-Marie 69
Sharma, Nirwan 144
Shouma, Amira 340
Stone, Adam 223
Suñer, Ferran 169
Swinehart, Nicholas 373

T
Tanaka-Ellis, Nobue 350
Tanaka, Hiroya 345
Tang, Daniel 107
Thomas, Hilary 88

Todirascu, Amalia 356
Tschichold, Cornelia 362

U
Udeshinee, W. A. Piyumi 367
Urano, Ken 345

V
Van de Vyver, Julie vii, 100, 252
Van Gorp, Koen 373
Van Reet, Marie 285
Villalobos-Buehner, María 379
Výškrabková, Jana 310

W
Waddington, David 69
Wang, Hongfei 385
Wang, Mengdi 391
Wang, Shudong 199
Ward, Monica 397
Werner, Lissy 39
Werner, Maristela 275
White, Jeremy 402
Winchester, Susanne 88
Witkin, Neil 223
Wu, Guanzhen 118, 124

X
Xerou, Eftychia 82

Y
Yamauchi, Mari 252
Yonesaka, Suzanne M. 407

Z
Zhang, Qiang 297

www.ingramcontent.com/pod-product-compliance
Lightning Source LLC
Chambersburg PA
CBHW071435300426
44114CB00013B/1449